Maritime Casualties
Causes and Consequences

Capt. Tuuli Messer-Bookman
Foreword by Capt. Robert J. Meurn

CORNELL MARITIME PRESS
A Division of Schiffer Publishing, Ltd.

For Barry

Other Schiffer Books by the Author:
Master's Handbook on Ship's Business, 3rd Ed.
ISBN 978-0-87033-531-0

Close Quarters: A Woman's Guide to Living and Working in Masculine Environments
ISBN 978-0-7643-3631-7

Other Schiffer Books on Related Subjects:
Maritime Error Management. Geoffrey W. Gill,
ISBN 978-0-87033-626-3

Dictionary of Maritime and Transportation Terms.
Gerald H. Ullman, ISBN 978-0-87033-569-3

U.S. Regulation of Ocean Transportation Under the Shipping Act of 1984. Gerald H. Ullman,
ISBN 978-0-87033-470-2

Cover image and images on pp. 63, 64, 74, 105, 123, 131, 141, 143 © The Associated Press.

Front cover image: The tanker MV *Erika*, her hull broken, sinks off the coast of northwestern France, releasing thousands of tons of fuel oil into the ocean. *(AP-Photo / French Navy / The New York Times)*

Designed by John P. Cheek
Cover design by Matt Goodman
Type set in Garamond Premier Pro

ISBN: 978-0-87033-641-6
Printed in China

Published by Schiffer Publishing, Ltd.
4880 Lower Valley Road
Atglen, PA 19310
Phone: (610) 593-1777; Fax: (610) 593-2002
E-mail: Info@schifferbooks.com

For our complete selection of fine books on this and related subjects, please visit our website at www.schifferbooks.com. You may also write for a free catalog.

This book may be purchased from the publisher. Please try your bookstore first.

We are always looking for people to write books on new and related subjects. If you have an idea for a book, please contact us at proposals@schifferbooks.com.

Schiffer Publishing's titles are available at special discounts for bulk purchases for sales promotions or premiums. Special editions, including personalized covers, corporate imprints, and excerpts can be created in large quantities for special needs. For more information, contact the publisher.

Contents

Foreword

Maritime casualties continue to occur and have ramifications throughout the world. Many of these vessels are outfitted with the latest navigational and anti-collision technologies. The causes are often shrouded in mystery and controversy.

Captain Messer-Bookman's account of these casualties illustrates both how the causes are often not due to equipment malfunctions but increasingly to human error, and the need to plan ahead. Also demonstrated are failures to cross-check vessel positioning information with independent systems and overreliance on electronic information. It is noted that a major contributing factor is often the apathy derived from hours of uneventful watchstanding.

One of the most fundamental aspects of this honorable profession is the necessity of keeping a safe navigational watch. The requirements of appraisal, planning, monitoring, and execution of a navigational passage are paramount. The examination of maritime casualties expands the ability to recognize a potential scenario that may result in a collision or grounding. It is easy through hindsight to say as a watchstander, "That would never happen to me," but until you are placed in an identical situation you cannot say whether or not you would commit the same error.

The critical need for watch officers and masters to be familiar with all bridge equipment and procedures in order to navigate safely as a team is illustrated in this book. Correct actions that are intuitive and instinctive in the event of a potential grounding or collision are best accomplished through hands-on and simulator training, and the perusal of previous maritime casualties. This book should be required reading for any watchkeeper, and in the library of anyone who has an interest in safety at sea.

Capt. Robert J. Meurn

Preface

A few years ago, in the minutes before class started, I was standing behind the lectern discussing the *Titanic* tragedy and the resulting SOLAS Convention, when a young cadet in the front row raised his hand and asked, "You mean that really happened? I thought the *Titanic* was just a movie!" It was then I realized how startlingly little is known about the casualties that shape the maritime industry.

This book was born out of my desire to offer a casualty seminar to senior deck cadets of the California Maritime Academy. Finding no up-to-date, comprehensive texts on maritime casualties, and, more specifically, their consequences, I set out to write one myself. In so doing, I realized how little I too understood the events that gave rise to the major international conventions under which I had worked as a merchant marine officer. The research to write this book was primarily conducted to educate myself.

The book presents major maritime casualties and their consequences, and will set forth details of the three most important international maritime conventions:

- SOLAS, The International Convention for the Safety of Life at Sea
- MARPOL, The International Convention for the Prevention of Pollution from Ships
- STCW, The International Convention on Standards of Training, Certification, and Watchkeeping for Seafarers

When determining which casualties to include, I chose to include only major commercial casualties that either prompted operational changes within the industry, national legislation, or international conventions and treaties, or that were noteworthy in some other regard. I did not include casualties of war (except for two), or pleasure craft, or crimes such as piracy, or casualties that, though perhaps horrible, resulted in no appreciable changes within the industry.

I also do not offer extensive critique of the behavior or decisions of the involved individuals beyond what was obvious or included in an investigative report. One thing I learned in researching this book was how much geography and demographics determine the flavor and fervor (or lack of fervor) of the international reaction to any given casualty. I discovered early on that it didn't seem to matter so much how many died in an incident, but who.

Information sources often differed on specifics, such as the quantity of oil spilled, the exact times of events, the spelling of names, and even the numbers of dead or injured, thus many values are necessarily approximate. Tonnages and sizes of vessels are approximate. Those types of specifics are not the focus of this work and are not necessary for understanding the connections between events and consequences. This book presents a bird's-eye view, spanning decades so the reader can better grasp trends and changes.

There are some tales of suspected arson, murder, and other sorts of intrigue. Teasing out verifiable facts about events in distant lands or in countries with relatively unsophisticated legal systems was often difficult or even impossible. In order to include the event, I was sometimes forced to relate the story as gleaned from local news sources and websites, many of which are neither official nor confirmed. The reader is advised to read those incidents for the larger story, and not to take every detail as fact.

I chose to begin with 1912 and the loss of the RMS *Titanic*, because it was the first maritime casualty that prompted the major maritime powers to come together to standardize minimum safety equipment and practices aboard merchant vessels.

In the decades prior to the *Titanic*, there were of course casualties, some very significant, but they were not sufficient to overcome the inertia, and perhaps the complacency, of the maritime nations and prompt them to address safety standards in harmony with each other.

To date, two disasters, both wartime casualties, represent the greatest documented loss of life at sea. The *Lancastria* had losses estimated at between 4,000 to over 6,000 people, and the German hospital ship *Wilhelm Gustloff*, sunk by a Russian sub during World War II, had a similar staggering number of casualties, with some estimates at approximately 9,400 lost. Though this work focuses on commercial casualties, the losses from these two events were so great that I felt compelled to include their stories, briefly, in this book.

Exact numbers of persons lost in dynamic, large-scale wartime disasters are often difficult to calculate. Also distressingly imprecise are loss statistics for ferry casualties in developing nations, where passenger headcounts and other statistics are often, at best, estimates.

When tallying casualties, as with any statistics, units are important. Different sources categorized casualties based on varying criteria, such as deadweight ton, sea miles, or numbers of vessels flying a given flag, so direct comparisons were difficult. Since this book is meant to inform broadly, rather than drill down into minutia, I have endeavored to capture the scope and scale of noteworthy casualties without too much emphasis on exact values, as often there were multiple, sometimes conflicting, sources of information about the casualties and subjects I covered.

My father used to say, "Only a fool learns from his own mistakes." In that spirit, I hope the reader will learn from others' mistakes, better understand the legal and international framework of the conventions that control the maritime industry, gain a healthy appreciation for the personal and professional liability that now comes with going to sea, and share that knowledge with his or her contacts in the maritime world. It is also my fervent wish that the more powerful maritime nations (and their media) would take a keener interest in preventing casualties in developing nations, which seem to go largely unnoticed.

Acknowledgments

I would like to thank my faculty colleagues and the academic administrators at the California Maritime Academy who supported my sabbatical application, which in turn allowed me the time off to focus on writing this book. I also want to acknowledge California's taxpayers, who (unknowingly) support the California State University System, of which the Academy is a part, and who have ultimately funded this project. Thank you taxpayers!

Academy librarians Mark Stackpole and Michelle Van Hoeck were instrumental in getting me the books and papers I needed and Cadet Marcos Alemendras helped me research ships at the Academy library. Attorney Jeremy Korzenik at the U.S. Department of Justice was most forthcoming and helpful in explaining certain procedural aspects of U.S. law and public welfare statutes.

Kandace Korth of Korth's Pirates Lair Marina of Isleton, California, (and Tom, and the rest of the gang there) were most gracious in allowing me unfettered use of their lounge and internet connection, which enabled me to work well into the evenings while "on vacation." It was a lovely, quiet setting and I am most grateful for their accommodation. The place is heaven on earth.

I would like to acknowledge Captain Wolfgang Shröder, and all other mariners who have endured injustice at the hands of the law. Know that there are people watching and fighting to make the system more rational and equitable.

And finally, I'd like to thank my husband Barry for his unwavering support, consistently cheerful disposition, eagle-eyed editing, and for once again putting up with my late nights and sporadic absences. This one is for you, my love.

List of Abbreviations and Glossary

AB Able-bodied seaman; an unlicensed sailor ranking above an "ordinary seaman" and who has lookout, steering, seamanship, and maintenance skills and duties. The normal ranking of unlicensed deck crew is from ordinary seaman (an entry-level position) to AB, and then a senior AB is often hired as a Boatswain, who runs the unlicensed deck crew under the guidance of the chief mate.

ABS American Bureau of Shipping, a classification society

AFRAMAX Size of a crude oil tanker that uses Average Freight Rate Assessment (AFRA) to calculate cost of transportation (70,000–120,000 DWT)

AIS Automatic identification system, a radar-based system that displays the name and other information of vessels on a radar

AMVER Automated Mutual-Assistance Vessel Rescue System

ANS Alaskan North Slope (crude oil)

APA Administrative Procedures Act (5 USC §500 et seq.)

ARPA Automatic radar plotting aid

AWO American Waterways Operators

Barrel U.S. barrel (of oil) is 42 gallons

BBC British Broadcasting Company

BBL A U.S. or Canadian barrel of oil, 42 gallons (Outside of the United States and Canada, most countries measure volume in cubic meters.)

BCH code Code for the Construction and Equipment of Ships Carrying Dangerous Chemicals in Bulk

Bell book A booklet to record the vessel's engine status and the passing of major navigational aids, and other events, such as arrival, departure, or first or last line, which will ultimately be transcribed into the smooth deck log

Bell log (electronic) A computer program that records the various engine commands from the bridge

BIMCO Baltic and International Maritime Council Organization

Boatswain (or Bosun) An unlicensed member of the deck department aboard a merchant vessel, usually the senior most unlicensed person in the deck department, responsible for running the unlicensed deck gang, reports directly to the vessel's chief mate

BRM Bridge resource management, usually refers to management of the equipment found on the bridge

BTM Bridge team management, usually refers to the management of the people comprising the bridge watch

Calving The breaking off of ice from a glacier

CEDRE (French) Centre of Documentation, Research, and Experimentation on Accidental Water Pollution

CFR Code of Federal Regulations

CHIRP Confidential Hazardous Incident Reporting Program, based in the United Kingdom

CLC The International Convention on Civil Liability for Oil Pollution Damage, 1969

CLIA Cruise Lines International Association

CNN Cable News Network

Cofferdam A void space, often between an engine room or pump room and cargo spaces, also a void space between inner and outer hulls, a space between two usually watertight spaces

COFR Certificate of Financial Responsibility; this program is run by the U.S. Coast Guard's National Pollution Funds Center. The amount of liability coverage required is determined by the size and hull construction of the vessel or type of facility (33 CFR §138).

COLREG The Convention on the International Regulations for Preventing Collisions at Sea, also called the International Rules of the Road

Conn A nautical term meaning to steer or control the movements of a vessel

COSPAS-SARSAT Satellite search and rescue system, a joint system between France, Russia, Canada, and the United States

CPA Closest point of approach, the nearest one vessel will get to another, usually displayed by an ARPA that is tracking acquired vessels

CRISTAL Contract Regarding an Interim Supplement to Tanker Liability for Oil Pollution, a voluntary industry agreement in response to the *Torrey Canyon*

CWA The Clean Water Act (33 USC §1251 et seq.)

Danger signal Five or more short blasts on a ship's whistle, signifies the sounding vessel is unsure of the other vessel's intentions and is concerned

DECCA A hyperbolic electronic navigation system, discontinued completely in 2001, largely replaced by GPS

Dead reckoning Estimating the location of a vessel based solely on its course and speed, without regard to wind, current or other factors influencing the vessel's position

Displacement The weight of the ship, cargo, fuel, stores, and everything else aboard. The total weight of the vessel and everything aboard her; the weight of water she displaces when floating.

DR Dead reckoning

Draft The depth of a ship in the water, the distance from the waterline to the bottom of the keel; sometimes used when referring to the depth of water alongside a dock or anchorage

DWT Deadweight tons, the total weight-bearing capacity of a vessel, including the weight of cargo, fuel, people, stores, water, etc. It does not include the weight of the ship itself. Usually now expressed in units of metric tons (or tonnes) of 2,204.6 pounds but can also be in the traditional long tons of 2,240 pounds. It is the total displacement weight of the vessel (including cargo, stores, fuel, etc.) less the light-ship weight of the vessel itself.

ECDIS Electronic Chart Display and Information System

EEZ Exclusive Economic Zone (usually extends 200 miles from the coast for most nations)

EMSA European Maritime Safety Agency; founded in the wake of the *Erika* and *Prestige* incidents, the EMSA provides accident investigation, ship tracking, pollution preparedness with contracted vessels, and "inspects the inspectors" of classification societies and assesses port state control officers.

EPA U.S. Environmental Protection Agency

ETA Estimated time of arrival

EPIRB Emergency position-indicating radio beacon

FAA U.S. Federal Aviation Administration

FBI U.S. Federal Bureau of Investigation

FEMA U.S. Federal Emergency Management Agency

Fidley The space or deck surrounding a vessel's smoke stack

Flag of convenience A ship's flag of registry from an open-registry nation, meaning the owner and crew need not be citizens of the flag nation

Flag state The nation whose flag a vessel is flying

FR Federal Register, published daily by the U.S. federal government, the official journal of the U.S government

Freeboard The distance from a vessel's waterline to the uppermost continuous watertight deck, a measure of reserve buoyancy, usually determined by a loadline painted on the vessel's sides, which require typically higher freeboard for non-protected waters or winter seasons

Fund Convention The International Oil Pollution Compensation Fund

FUND International Convention on the Establishment of an International Fund for Compensation for Oil Pollution Damage

FWPCA The Federal Water Pollution Control Act (also called the Clean Water Act, 33 USC §1251 et seq., and codified in other sections as well)

GISIS Global Integrated Shipping Information System

GLA General Lighthouse Authority

GLONASS Global Navigation Satellite System (Russian)

GMDSS Global Maritime Distress and Safety System

GPS Global Positioning System

GRT Gross registered tonnage (now just "gross tonnage") is the total internal volume of a ship in units of 100 cubic feet, not all of which can be used to carry cargo. See *NRT*.

HAR Harbor Advisory Radar System

Heave-to To stop the vessel in the seaway, usually referred to when stopping in a storm or rough weather

Heel The lean to port or starboard a vessel takes on due to an external force, like wind (as opposed to list, which is caused by an internal off-center weight)

HMS Her majesty's ship

HNS Hazardous and noxious substances

IACS International Association of Classification Societies

ICCL International Council of Cruise Lines

ICLL International Convention on Load Lines

ICS International Chamber of Shipping, represents ship owners at IMO, established 1921

IHSA Intervention on the High Seas Act (33 USC §1471-1481)

ILO International Labor Organization

IMCO Inter-Governmental Maritime Consultative Organization, changed name in 1982 to the International Maritime Organization (IMO)

IMDG International Maritime Dangerous Goods Code

IMO International Maritime Organization (ex-IMCO)

INTERTANKO The International Association of Independent Tanker Owners

IOPCF International Oil Pollution Compensation Fund

IOPP International Oil Pollution Prevention Certificate

IOTPF International Tanker Owners' Pollution Federation

ISM International Management Code for the Safe Operation of Ships and for Pollution Prevention (part of SOLAS)

ISPS International Ship and Port Facility Security Code

ITCP International Technical Cooperation Program

IUMI International Union of Marine Insurers

Lighter To discharge some cargo to lighten the vessel, usually done between ships, to achieve a desired draft, to allow a vessel to proceed to a shallower location to finish its cargo discharge

List The lean to port or starboard due to some internal uneven weight distribution (as compared to heel, which is a lean due to external causes, like wind)

LNG Liquefied Natural Gas

LOF Lloyd's Open Form, a type of salvage agreement, and the one most frequently used because it is considered fairest to both ship owner and salvor

LORAN Long-range navigation system; a passive, hyperbolic, electronic navigation system used in the United States and Japan that used time differences between the arrival of signals that had been sent simultaneously to triangulate a vessel's position. Charts were overlaid with time difference lines, and navigators used to plot the actual time difference lines of position before the system receivers were upgraded to display latitude and longitude. The system was developed by the United States during World War II and discontinued in 2010, being effectively replaced by GPS. European nations are reinstating the system in response to GPS jamming and spoofing concerns.

LRIT Long range identification and tracking (of ships)

LUA Liverpool Underwriters Association of the United Kingdom

MAIB Marine Accident Investigation Branch (United Kingdom)

MARAD U.S. Maritime Administration

MARPOL The International Convention for the Prevention of Pollution from Ships

MARS Mariners' alerting and reporting scheme, a confidential reporting system based in the United Kingdom

Master The person in command of a vessel. (The term "captain" is a military rank or commercial mariner's title, and not technically the term for a person in command of a merchant vessel. Captains of merchant ships carry licenses as "masters.")

Mbbl One thousand U.S. barrels

MEPC Marine Environment Protection Committee (of the IMO)

MMbbl One million U.S. barrels

MMC Merchant mariner's credential, issued by the U.S. Coast Guard

MS Motor ship

MSC Maritime Safety Committee (of the IMO)

MSO U.S. Coast Guard Marine Safety Office

MT Motor tanker

MTSA Maritime Transportation Security Act of 2002 (33 CFR §101-017), the U.S. implementation of the ISPS Code

MV Motor vessel

NMC U.S. Coast Guard's National Maritime Center

NMEA National Marine Electronics Association

NOAA U.S. National Ocean and Atmospheric Administration

NPFC U.S. Coast Guard's National Pollution Funds Center

NPRM Notice of Proposed Rule Making, an announcement by a government agency

NRT Net registered tonnage (now "net tonnage") is the gross tonnage (GRT) minus spaces that cannot be used to carry cargo, such as living quarters, engine spaces, etc. In units of 100 cubic feet, it is a volumetric measure of the cargo-carrying capacity of a vessel.

NTSB U.S. National Transportation Safety Board

NVIC Navigation Vessel Inspection Circular, issued by the U.S. Coast Guard to explain regulations and to offer guidance on compliance

OBO Oil/Bulk/Ore ship

OCIMF Oil Companies International Marine Forum

OILPOL The Oil Pollution Convention of 1954

OOD Officer of the Deck, usually the officer having the bridge watch on a military vessel

OOW Officer of the Watch, more commonly used in the military

OPA 90 The Oil Pollution Act of 1990 (33 USC §2701 et seq.)

OPRC International Convention on Oil Pollution Preparedness, Response and Cooperation 1990

OSHA U.S. Occupational Safety and Health Administration

OSLTF The Oil Spill Liability Trust Fund

PANAMAX Largest sized ship which can transit the Panama Canal, 965 feet long, 106 feet wide, 39.5-foot draft. The new Panamax size as of 2009 is 1,400 feet long, 180 feet wide, and 60-foot draft. New Panamax–sized ships must use the new third lane of locks opened in 2014.

P&I Protection and indemnity insurance or insurers

PLB Personal locator beacon

POLMAR French oil pollution response plan

PSC Port State Control, the right of a signatory nation to inspect vessels coming into its ports to ensure compliance with IMO conventions and national laws

PWSA Ports and Waterways Safety Act of 1972 (33 USC §1221)

RACON A radar signal sent from a navigational aid to facilitate locating it on radar, especially used to mark the center span passage under bridges and major navigational buoys

Radar Radio detection and ranging

RDF Radio direction finder, a navigational aid carried aboard ships to take bearings of radio stations; the United States has discontinued support for shoreside marine radio stations used for this purpose

REC U.S. Coast Guard Regional Exam Center

RMS Royal Mail Steamer or Royal Motor Ship

RO Recognized organization; an organization recognized and trusted by a nation state to conduct flag state regulatory inspections

Ro/Ro A roll-on/roll-off vessel

Sailing Directions A U.S. government publication offering pertinent information to navigators about foreign ports of the world, including information on safety hazards, navigation regulations, communications, pilotage, weather, and the availability of repairs, food, water, and fuel

SAR Search and rescue

SART Search and rescue transponder

Scantlings The dimensions for the construction of a vessel, the thickness of its steel or timbers, sometimes used generally to refer to the sturdiness of its construction

SCOPIC Special Compensation Protection and Indemnity Clause on a Lloyd's Open Form salvage agreement

Seaman's Manslaughter Statute 18 USC §1115 of the U.S. Criminal Code, passed in its current form in 1852, creates criminal liability for ship owners, operators, officers, and crew, and related corporate officials for simple negligence that results in a death related to a U.S. flag vessel. Simple negligence, which requires neither intent nor willfulness, is a much lower threshold than is normally required to characterize an event as a crime. From 1848 to roughly 1990, mariners were charged under the statute on only eight major accidents. In the last fifteen years, prosecutors seem to charge mariners under the statute almost automatically if an accident resulted in a death. Many feel the frequency and zeal of its application has resulted in overly draconian punishments for accidents.

Set and drift The direction toward which a current flows and the speed of a current, also the effects of the current on a vessel, as a ship needs to overcome the set and drift of a current to make good a desired course

SIRE Ship Inspection Report Program (of the OCIMF)

SMS Safety Management System

SOLAS The International Convention for the Safety of Life at Sea

SOPEP Shipboard oil pollution emergency plan required by OPRC '90

Soundings The depth of the water; also used to refer to the depth markings on a chart; also used to mean a measurement of fluid in a tank

SRI Seafarers' Rights International

SS Steam ship

STCW The International Convention on Standards of Training, Certification and Watchkeeping for Seafarers

SUEZMAX The maximum size of a vessel which can transit the Suez Canal when loaded. Since the Suez Canal has no locks, draft and air draft are the primary limiting factors. Ships are limited to 66 feet of draft with a maximum allowable deadweight of 240,000 tons. Airdraft is also limited to pass under the Suez Canal Bridge, and must be below 223 feet.

TAPS Trans-Alaska pipeline system

TEL Turbo-electric liner (the *Morro Castle* was such a vessel)

TEU Twenty-foot equivalent unit; a typical twenty-foot-long shipping container, usually used as a measure of carrying capacity of container ships

TOAR Towing Officers' Assessment Record

Tonne Metric ton or tonne equals 2,204.6 lbs.

TOVALOP Tanker Owners Voluntary Agreement concerning Liability for Oil Pollution, a voluntary industry agreement in response to the *Torrey Canyon*, administered by the IOTPF

TSAC U.S. Coast Guard Towing Safety Advisory Committee

TSS Traffic separation scheme

ULCC Ultra large crude carrier (320,000–550,000 DWT)

UN United Nations

UNCLOS United Nations Convention on the Law of the Sea

UNCTAD United Nations Conference on Trade and Development

UNEP United Nations Environment Program

USC United States Code

USCG United States Coast Guard

VDR Voyage data recorder, similar to the black boxes aboard aircraft, records critical vessel data, some including voice. The NTSB can retrieve information off a VDR post-incident.

VHF Very high frequency; a radio usually used aboard ships to communicate with other ships and shoreside installation, which has a line-of-sight range of roughly 20–25 miles)

VLCC Very large crude carrier (180,000–320,000 DWT)

VLOC Very large ore carrier

VTS Vessel traffic service, similar to air traffic control for aircraft

WIDAR Wireless detection and ranging, a precursor to radar

WMU World Maritime University in Malmo, Sweden

Introduction

Absent a few major incidents, casualty statistics have improved steadily over the past one hundred years. Seafaring used to be one of the most dangerous professions, with roughly one sailor in five dying at sea, but thanks to diligent lawmakers, advances in construction and machinery, and enhanced training of mariners, going to sea has become exponentially safer in recent decades.

One of the most reliable and broad sources of casualty information is Lloyd's World Casualty Statistics, which records not lives lost at sea, but total losses of merchant ships that are over 100 gross registered tons (GRT). Lloyd's has statistical tables going as far back as 1878.

At the 2011 International Maritime Statistics Forum in Hong Kong, Lloyd's List Intelligence presented marine casualty profiles.[1] At the time, Lloyd's had determined the world's fleet of commercial vessels of over 100 GRT to be approximately 85,000 vessels.

In researching this book, I consulted numerous sources, many of which differed on loss rates and casualty statistics. Rather than bog the reader down in statistical minutia, I have generalized somewhat, so citations for specific values would be inappropriate.

Safety-Related Loss Rates of Ships

The average loss rate for all ship types over 100 GRT is about 1.4 per 1,000 vessels, with about ninety ships of over 500 GRT lost each year, not counting acts of piracy and other security-related casualties. The primary casualty type is still overwhelmingly loss by foundering and/or sinking either because the vessel broke apart or leaked catastrophically. The next most frequent losses are caused almost equally by stranding, fire, and explosion. Hull and machinery failure only cause about 2 percent of all maritime casualties. The reader must understand that one massive ferry casualty will dramatically skew these statistics, but even so, these are pretty good odds.

Security Related Losses

Since 2002, the loss rates for security issues like piracy and terrorism have been fairly constant, with 250 to 400 hostile acts per year. During most reported security incidents, crew members are usually hijacked, held hostage, and eventually released. Roughly twelve mariners are recorded as being killed annually, some just go missing, and many are wounded but not killed. An average of twenty-three ships are hijacked each year, and rates are increasing. For the years 2002–2009, security-related incidents were reported by roughly 0.3 percent of vessels.

Casualties by Ship Type

As to which type of ship has more casualties, general cargo, dry bulk, passenger ships, and container ships all share roughly the same rate, with liquid tankers and gas tankers having the lowest, but, some argue, the most devastating types of casualties. Certain types of casualties seem to plague certain types of vessels. Ro/Ro ferries, for example, seem to have problems with bow doors and a catastrophic loss of stability when large, continuous decks flood. Tankers, on the other hand, are more prone to loss by explosion.

Dangerous Sea Areas

Due to ships following historical and efficient routes, casualty rates are higher in certain areas. Casualty hot spots are predictably clustered in congested waters like the South China Sea and crowded areas around India, China, Indonesia, and the Philippines. The Baltic and Eastern Mediterranean, Japanese, and Korean sea areas also experience a seemingly disproportionate number of casualties because of their heavily-used shipping routes. Interestingly, the Eastern Mediterranean has a lower level of shipping activity than North Europe or Asia, and yet has a higher casualty rate. Lloyd's attributed this to an older fleet sailing in the region (the average vessel in the area is over twenty years old, as opposed to Europe and Asia's average vessel age of twelve years) and the higher percentage of "dubious" flag registries plying the Eastern Mediterranean. In 2010, the areas with the most numerous serious casualties were, in order, the Eastern Mediterranean and Black Sea, Northern Europe, and the South China Sea.

Classification Societies

When ranking casualties by classification society, relative to fleet size, by far the worst safety record was held by the Hellenic Register (Greek), followed by the Bulgarski Koraben Register (Bulgarian), and Turk Loydu Vafki (Turkish). The American Bureau of Shipping came in with a very respectable ranking, but just barely better than the China Registry.

Deaths at Sea

The IMO (International Maritime Organization) and IHS (International Handling Services) Fairplay estimate the total number of seafarers worldwide to be approximately 1.2 million mariners, and the total number of ferry passengers at roughly 1.5 billion per year.[2] In another statistic, for the years 2002–2009, 0.18 to 1.14 lives were lost per million lives at sea per year. When compared to the total number of lives lost, the odds of a mariner losing his or her life at sea is on the order of 1:0.000000333. Going to sea, while certainly posing varying degrees of hazard based on location, season, and vessel type, is relatively safe—at least statistically.

Since 2006, the average number of lives lost aboard ships ranged from about 100 to over 400 per year. The greatest percentage of deaths (approximately 39 percent) occurs on ships classified by the IMO as "other"—these include dredges, high-speed craft, offshore supply boats, non-self-propelled vessels, research vessels, and other unclassified types of vessels. The next highest percentage of deaths (17 percent) occurs on cargo ships. Bulkers and tankers account for 12 percent and 11 percent, respectively. Less than 10 percent of deaths occur aboard container ships, passenger ships, and towing and pushing vessels.

Oil Spills

Between 2002 and 2009 an average of three spills (of over 700 tons) per year occurred from ships subject to IMO conventions. When one looks at the trend of oil spilled versus the tons of oil shipped, the ratio is consistently declining, absent an occasional massive spill. The general trend is improving. On average, less than 30 tons of oil was discharged per million ton-miles, per year, during the years 2002–2009.

Per the Cable News Network (CNN), this is a list of the top ten worst oil spills, not all of them from ships:[3]

1. January 23, 1991: During the Gulf War, the Iraqi Army intentionally released 240 million gallons of oil into the Persian Gulf. (Spill estimates of this event vary widely by source at 25–460 million gallons. The Oil Spill Intelligence Report reported 240 million gallons.)
2. April 20, 2010: An explosion occured aboard the British Petroleum–contracted Transocean Ltd. *Deepwater Horizon* oil rig, spilling approximately 210 million gallons of oil into the Gulf of Mexico.
3. June 3, 1979: Ixtoc 1, an exploratory well, blew out, spilling 140 million gallons of oil into the Bay of Campeche off the coast of Mexico.
4. March 2, 1992: A Fergana Valley oil well in Uzbekistan blew out, spilling 88 million gallons of oil.

5. February 4, 1983: An oil well in the Nowruz Oil Field in Iran blew out, spilling oil into the Persian Gulf. One month later an Iraqi air attack increased the amount of oil spilled to 80 million gallons of oil.
6. August 6, 1983: The *Castillo de Bellver*, a Spanish tanker, caught fire near Cape Town, South Africa, spilling 78.5 million gallons of oil.
7. March 16, 1978: The tanker *Amoco Cadiz* ran aground near Portsall, France, spilling 68.7 million gallons of oil.
8. November 10, 1988: The British-owned tanker the *Odyssey* broke apart during a storm, spilling 43.1 million gallons of oil approximately 700 miles east-northeast of Newfoundland, Canada.
9. July 19, 1979: The tankers *Atlantic Empress* and the *Aegean Captain* collided near Trinidad and Tobago. The *Atlantic Empress* spilled 42.7 million gallons of oil. On August 2, 1979, the *Atlantic Empress* spilled an additional 41.5 million gallons near Barbados while being towed away.
10. August 1, 1980: Production well D-103 blew out, spilling 42 million gallons of oil southeast of Tripoli, Libya.

Other groups, citing different data, list other spills as being in the top ten, including:

- May 28, 1991: The ABT *Summer* exploded off of Angola, spilling 51–80 million gallons
- March 16, 1978: The *Amoco Cadiz* spilled 68 million gallons when she grounded off France
- April 11, 1991: The *Haven* spilled 42 million gallons when she exploded during tank cleaning in the Mediterranean
- March 18, 1967: The *Torrey Canyon* spilled 32–37 million gallons when she went aground off the UK
- December 19, 1972: The Korean tanker *Sea Star*'s collision with a Brazilian tanker caused a 35-million-gallon spill
- November 13, 2002: The tanker *Prestige* lost her cargo of 20 million gallons when she broke apart in bad weather off Spain

You may have noticed that many famous oil spills, such as the *Exxon Valdez* and *Torrey Canyon*, are not on this list. As devastating as they were, those spills do not rank in the top ten worst oil spills.

Even given the statistics above, the overall rate of maritime casualties of every sort has declined (by almost any measure) thanks to improvements in construction materials and design, enhanced training of mariners, and better shoreside and onboard management practices.[4]

While the number and frequency of casualties has declined over the past decades, new concerns are emerging, promising different kinds of casualties, and perhaps increasing frequency. These concerns include:

- Over the last thirty years, the number of commercial vessels has roughly tripled, and is now approximately 104,000 hulls. Cargo too, measured in tons loaded, has almost tripled over the last thirty years.[5]
- The size (both tonnage and length) of ships has increased steadily, especially during the late 1950s through the 1970s with the introduction of supertankers. In the days of the *Titanic*, the average ship was around 1,300 gross tons. Now the average ship is over 9,000 gross tons.[6] The largest tanker ever afloat was the *Knock Nevis* (ex–*Jahre Viking*), an ultra-large crude carrier (ULCC) at 1,504 feet long and 565,000 DWT. She was too big for the English

Channel, let alone the Suez or Panama Canals. She was scrapped in 2010. The largest container ship currently afloat is the 2013 *Mærsk McKinney-Møller*, a Mærsk Triple-E Class ship, which carries 18,000 twenty-foot equivalent units (TEU). At 1,306 feet long, she is the largest cargo vessel of any sort afloat. She has a crew of twenty-two.[7]

- The complexity of ships has increased steadily over the past eighty years, especially with regards to bridge electronics. Though electronics are considered a tool, they are an "additional" tool and require new levels of multitasking and proficiency to integrate them into the watchstanding workload. Modern bridge equipment looks more like the controls of a space shuttle than a traditional ship. While information is useful, too much information and too many choices can be overwhelming and have already contributed to a loss of situational awareness in many casualties.

  In past decades a ship's deck officer could board any ship and could, within a few minutes, comfortably operate the equipment. Modern electronic charting systems are exponentially more complex than the radars and chart plotters of past decades. A modern ECDIS requires literally hundreds of decisions and choices that must be made, including such mundane selections as which icon the mariner wants to use for "own ship" or what color he wants for the trackline display. In addition, given the vast differences in symbology, vocabulary, step-sequencing, and "knobology" between brands, mariners need manufacturer-based "type-specific" training on a given brand of electronic charting system just to understand it. Gone are the days of "have license, will travel." Mariners will no longer be able to shift easily from one vessel to another with a common set of core skills, and modern licensing requirements are lagging behind this reality.

- The number of passengers carried on cruise ships and the size and complexity of those vessels has increased exponentially, making speedy evacuation almost impossible. The largest passenger ship currently in operation, Royal Caribbean's *Allure of the Seas*, stretching 1,181 feet, carries over 6,000 passengers. It is doubtful she could be evacuated quickly.

- The workloads of merchant mariners have increased and diversified as crew sizes and turnaround times have shrunk. In order to remain competitive in a period of increasing globalization, shipping companies have increased economic efficiency by broadening the job descriptions of mariners. Ships' bridge watchstanding officers now routinely perform duties once performed by pursers, radio officers, cargo mates, and even cooks and messmen.

- Increasing numbers of vessels now carry increasingly diverse multinational crews, exacerbating language and cultural barriers.

- Cultural barriers also affect relations between vessels. Despite English being the official language of the seas, and in spite of advancements in ship-to-ship communication, language barriers between ships have increased.

- As local or national fleets age, casualty hot spots are found, currently most notably in the Eastern Mediterranean and Black Sea area. In addition to its being a crowded area, many of the vessels sailing those waters are registered in nations with less than robust records of regulatory compliance. Enforcement of international treaties, especially in developing countries, remains less than vigorous. Part of the problem is the complexity of handling people, cargoes, and vessels from multiple nations. The countries with the most tonnage flying their flags are Panama and Liberia, neither of which has a record of strong enforcement. When comparing tonnage values, the United States, with a strong history of enforcement, doesn't even rank in the top twenty maritime nations.[8]

Despite all the advances in vessel construction and design, routing, communications, training and health screening, navigation, and search and rescue, human error remains the single most intractable cause of the vast majority of casualties. Human elements include the behavior of shoreside management as well as shipboard crews, and shoreside managers are increasingly being charged with crimes, under the responsible corporate officer doctrine, when ships under their control have pollution incidents or other serious casualties.

Shipboard crews are frequently overworked and fatigued, often while enduring pressure from shoreside managers to beat the competition (see the *Torrey Canyon* and *Herald of Free Enterprise* disasters). The inability of technology to eclipse human failures is no better highlighted than by the recent grounding of the Italian cruise ship *Costa Concordia,* a senseless disaster that left thirty-two dead—a thoroughly modern vessel carrying a full complement of experienced bridge officers and the most advanced navigational tools available, and nothing had malfunctioned or broken. Though fatigue may or may not have been a factor, it is an illustration of the critical role the human element plays in casualties.

No doubt additional regulations will be promulgated trying to address this issue, but human behavior is, and probably will always be, the weakest link in any operation.

Given the information above, I hope I have piqued your curiosity and that the information that follows will lead, ultimately, to safer seas.

Notes

1. Information on casualty statistics was drawn from: Lloyd's List Intelligence, Marine Casualty Profiles, presentation at International Maritime Statistics Forum, Hong Kong, May 31, 2011, www.lloydslistintelligence.com; Casualty Statistics and Investigations 2006 to 2011, IMO Subcommittee on Flag State Implementation FSI20/INF.17, http://www.imo.org/KnowledgeCentre/ShipsAndShippingFactsAndFigures/Statisticalresources/Casualties/Documents/FSI%2020%20INF-17%20%20Casualty%20statistics%20-%20loss%20of%20life%20from%202006%20to%20date.pdf; Review of Data Measured Against Performance Indicators, IMO Council 105th Session C 105/3/(a)/1, September 30, 2010; Lloyd's Register Fairplay, World Fleet Statistics 1900–2010; IHS Fairplay, World Fleet Statistics 2010.

2. IMO International Shipping Facts and Figures from *Information Resources on Trade, Safety, Security, Environment,* http://www.imo.org/KnowledgeCentre/ShipsAndShippingFactsAndFigures/TheRoleandImportanceofInternationalShipping/Documents/International%20Shipping%20-%20Facts%20and%20Figures.pdf. IHS Fairplay is a global information company, with offices in thirty-one countries. Many organizations, including the IMO, rely on their statistics. Casualty statistics can be found at IMO Document CWGSP 12/3 based on IHS Fairplay for loss of lives, Shippax for number of passengers, BIMCO/ISF Manpower 2010 update for numbers of seafarers.

3. Spill estimates vary slightly by source. From CNN: http://www.cnn.com/2013/07/13/world/oil-spills-fast-facts.

4. Lloyd's Register *World Casualty Statistics 1900–2010.*

5. Lloyd's Register Fairplay *World Fleet Statistics 1900–2010; UNCTAD Review of Maritime Transport,* 2011.

6. Ibid.

7. The Mærsk website, http://www.worldslargestship.com.

8. Lloyd's List Intelligence, Marine Casualty Profiles, presentation at International Maritime Statistics Forum, Hong Kong, May 31, 2011, www.lloydslistintelligence.com.

Chapter 1
Foundational Information

Laws and Treaties

To better understand the regulatory reaction to maritime casualties, it is necessary to have a fundamental grasp of law, enforcement, and general legal structure. What follows is a summary of how laws and regulations are made in the United States, how treaties are proposed and passed, and how they become binding.

Laws either require something (a behavior or action) or prohibit something. Laws are often written in response to something bad happening, like a major accident or catastrophic environmental damage. Laws are also written because they are politically expedient. The term "law" can be generally defined as a set of rules that are enforceable by governments.

So, what is a law, a statute, a regulation, a code, and a treaty? What is a "protocol?" Is an international treaty a law here in the United States?

Most people are justifiably confused by "the law." To begin our discussion of how laws are made in the United States, a brief refresher on civics would prove helpful. The founding fathers created three branches of government:

- The legislative branch of elected officials (Congress) is tasked with creating laws
- The executive branch is tasked with enforcing laws
- The judicial branch interprets the law when questions or conflicts arise

There are two main types of law: black letter, or positive, law and case, or common, law. Positive (black letter) law is the body of written codes, statutes, and regulations that are enforced by a governmental agency. Common (or case) law is a body of law resulting from cases adjudicated by the courts, often interpreting existing black letter law.

How Congress Makes Law

When Congress makes a law, it is called a statute. Regardless of which branch of Congress proposes a new law, the proposal must be passed by both the House of Representatives and the Senate, and ultimately be signed by the President before it can become law.

The idea for a new law may originate from an elected politician (this is after all, what they are paid to do), or an individual citizen or group may petition their respective legislators to pass a law. There are several ways to propose a new law, with bills being by far the most common. On average, over 10,000 bills are introduced each year. (There is no sign of this letting up any time soon.) Bills proposed by members of the House of Representatives are prefaced with "H.R." and bills originating from the Senate are prefaced with "S."

Once a bill is proposed, it gets sent to the appropriate Congressional Standing Committee for consideration. During this time the public usually has an opportunity to comment on the proposed law. To inform their consideration of the proposed law, Congressional committees will often seek input from relevant executive branch agencies, such as the Environmental Protection Agency or U.S.

Coast Guard, and may even solicit input from the public, including interested civilian groups such as, for example, the U.S. Power Squadron. If, after thorough review, the committee likes the proposal, it then submits a report to the legislature and explains why the proposed law should be approved.

Congress Passes Statutes

If a law is passed by the legislature, it is called a "statute." Since politicians are usually not subject-matter experts in any practical disciplines (other than perhaps fundraising) the language of their statutes is often broad and vague. Let's consider an overly simplified example and say that Congress passed a statute that stated, "Vessels shall not spill oil into the water." That statute would then be codified into the U.S. Code (USC) and organized with other statutes of a similar topic. It is then up to an executive branch agency (or agencies) to define and clarify the terms and specifics of the new law.

So now we know that the legislature passes broadly worded statutes, which are then codified into various sections of the U.S. Code, which is organized by subject matter. The U.S. Code, which records the general laws of the country, was created in 1926 to consolidate all the statutes, which by then were a confusing, unorganized morass. The U.S. Code is updated annually, with a new edition published every six years. The U.S. Code does not contain federal or state regulations, local laws or ordinances, or courtroom decisions by judges or juries. So then, what exactly is a regulation and how does it differ from a statute?

Executive Branch Agencies Make Regulations

In our statutory example, "Vessels shall not spill oil into the water," several questions arise. Does the term "vessel" mean the rule only applies to ships but not rowboats? Does the term "spill" mean it must be an accidental discharge or have to run off of something into the water (as opposed to burble up from below)? Does "oil" include fish oil, coconut oil, or other natural, animal-based substances? How much oil must be spilled before the law is triggered? Would this law regulate the slick formed when an oily sunbather jumps in the water? Does the term "water" include an inland lake? What are the penalties for violating this law? Could a child be sent to prison?

The details of statutes and the specifics of fines and penalties are set forth in "regulations" which are generated by executive branch agencies—the U.S. Coast Guard, the Environmental Protection Agency, the Federal Aviation Administration, and the Federal Communications Commission, etc.—since they usually have more subject-matter expertise than members of Congress.[1]

Despite the founding fathers' creation of three branches of government in order to balance power, executive branch (enforcement) agencies actually do make laws...and they make a lot of them! Many feel the sheer volume of these executive branch agency regulations make the system almost unworkable.[2]

Regulatory History

In the 1930s, as part of the New Deal, President Roosevelt created new executive branch agencies that promptly started promulgating regulations—that was, after all, their job. In short order there were so many regulations that no one could keep things straight, and no one knew what the other branches of government were doing. Things were so confused that there was even an instance of one federal agency trying to enforce a regulation that had been revoked by an executive order. The situation today may not be much better.

To put an end to this chaos, Congress passed the Federal Register Act. The Federal Register is a booklet printed on thin newsprint published every business day by the National Archives and Records Administration, which lists all executive orders and proclamations, all documents that could impose a fine or penalty, and any document that has legal effect. When an agency wants to enact a new regulation, it is announced in the Federal Register.

In 1937 Congress created the Code of Federal Regulations to organize and publish regulations promulgated by federal agencies. Compared to statutes, regulations are excruciatingly detailed.

In 1946, to further clarify and streamline the prolific lawmaking activities of federal agencies, Congress passed the Administrative Procedure Act (APA) which details how federal agencies are to generate the regulations necessary to implement and enforce statutes passed by the legislature.[3]

The APA requires that when a regulation is proposed, the issuing agency must first publish a Notice of Proposed Rulemaking (NPRM) in the Federal Register. This gives the public notice of and a chance to comment on the proposed legislation. The NPRM will explain the rationale for the new regulation, the proposed new rule, and the proposed date it should become effective.

Regulations affecting the maritime industry are primarily promulgated by the U.S. Coast Guard and are found in Title 46 CFR and Title 33 CFR. Title 46 CFR covers shipping and outlines the rules for the training, licensing, and certification of seamen, as well as regulations concerning vessel design, construction and outfitting of machinery and safety devices, and other subjects related to the shipping industry. Title 33 CFR deals with aids to navigation, collision avoidance rules, maritime security, bridges, pollution, and recreational boating safety.

So far we have confined our discussion to federal, national laws. There are also state and local laws that must be followed as one crosses into a state's territorial sea and other local jurisdictions.

International Conventions and The International Maritime Organization

A treaty, sometimes called a convention, is an agreement between two or more nations that becomes binding law in all signatory countries.[4] Treaties are used to describe the rules of wars and end them (like the Treaty of Versailles), to facilitate international rights and obligations with activities such as mail, telecommunications, or the use of natural resources, or even to address concerns about the use of space or Antarctica.

A protocol is a document that amends, adds to, or changes an existing treaty or convention. A self-executing treaty means that if a nation is a member of the body passing the treaty, the treaty automatically becomes law in that nation. A non-self-executing treaty is one for which a nation must create domestic laws specifically codifying the treaty's provisions into the domestic laws of the nation.

In the United States, an international treaty must have two-thirds of the Senate's consent in order to become U.S. law. A document called an "executive agreement" is like a treaty, except the President can approve it without any congressional support. Although 90 percent of international agreements are "executive agreements," most U.S. presidents will choose to follow a formal treaty process to ensure congressional support and the subsequent enacting legislation and funding that will make the document binding under U.S. law.

The industrial revolution of the eighteenth and nineteenth centuries and the resulting increase in international commerce led to the adoption of a number of international treaties related to shipping. The subjects covered included provisions detailing how ships were to be measured for tonnage certificates, rules for preventing collisions at sea, signalling and communications standards, and other details aimed at facilitating international maritime trade. By the end of the nineteenth century there was an obvious need for a permanent international maritime organization, but it took decades, and the formation of the United Nations in 1945, for such a group to be created. Meanwhile, international agreements and treaties continued to be drafted and adopted by seafaring nations.

In 1948, three years after its formation, the United Nations created the Inter-Governmental Maritime Consultative Organization (IMCO) to address international maritime issues. After IMCO's formation, a convention was drafted giving IMCO a mission to "provide machinery for cooperation among Governments in the field of governmental regulation and practices relating to technical matters of all kinds affecting shipping engaged in international trade..." During its first ten years, the nations which chose to have representation on IMCO adopted several important international conventions, including the International Convention for the Safety of Life at Sea of 1948, the International Convention for the Prevention of Pollution of the Sea by Oil of 1954, and treaties dealing with load lines and the prevention of collisions at sea.

Ten years after its creation IMCO changed its title to its current name, the International Maritime Organization (IMO). The IMO is now responsible for over thirty-five international conventions and agreements, and numerous protocols and amendments.

Making an International Convention
The IMO has two main arms, the Assembly and the Council, as well as multiple committees. Each nation that belongs to the IMO sends delegates to partake in IMO proceedings, and these delegates populate the committees. Some non-governmental agencies, having specific subject matter expertise, also partake in committee meetings and often make valuable contributions.

Proposing a New Convention or Amendment to an Existing Convention
Normally a suggestion to amend or add a provision to a convention is first made in one of the committees. If agreement is reached in the committee, the proposal goes to the Council and, as necessary, to the Assembly. Once authorization to proceed is given, the committee writes a detailed draft. Once the draft is approved, a recommendation is made to convene a convention to consider the draft proposal. Member states are then invited to attend a conference where the new document will be considered. The draft document is sent out ahead of time to all interested parties and plenty of time is allowed for comments and suggestions. At the conference, the draft document, and all comments and suggestions, are carefully considered. The document is revised until the majority of the member nations present consider it acceptable.

Ratification of the Convention
Once the proposal draft is finalized, it is "opened for signature" by the member nations, usually for twelve months. Signatories can ratify the convention (accede). A signatory need not agree to the entire treaty. If there are specific provisions with which a nation does not agree, it can add a "reservation" at the time of its signing.

Adoption of the Convention and Entry into Force
Once the convention has been ratified, each nation must then formally "accept" it before it can be binding on them individually. Each convention will have different threshold requirements that must be met before a convention enters into force. For example, for the Safety of Life at Sea Convention (SOLAS) 1974 to take effect, twenty-five nations whose merchant fleets comprised not less than 50 percent of the world's gross tonnage had to accept it. Once the specified approval threshold has been met, the convention will enter into force for the nations that accepted it. There is usually a phase-in period to allow nations to get the convention codified into their domestic laws and to secure and designate the funds required to comply with the new provisions.

The period from drafting a convention to its final adoption can take years (though in emergency situations the process can, and has, been significantly accelerated). Currently, the average time from draft to entry into force is roughly five years.

Enforcement and Jurisdiction
While the UN can enforce a registered treaty in the UN's International Court of Justice, the UN has no army and really no means of dragging a violator into court. Likewise, the IMO has no means to enforce a convention. The agencies of the UN, including the IMO, depend upon member nations to enforce conventions. Member nations that have ratified a convention codify the provisions into

their own domestic laws, thus member nations effectively enforce international conventions on their own flag ships by enforcing their own domestic law. This is a source of endless frustration to environmentalists and other activists who see minimal enforcement of established international conventions, such as the banning of killing whales, setting fishing or air pollution standards, and other conventions that impact all the earth's people, but to which not all nations have agreed. If a signatory nation breaches a treaty or convention, it usually relieves the other signatories of their obligations under the treaty, but usually non-breaching nations will elect to remain in compliance, the treaty being in their own best interest.

A nation is responsible for enforcing convention provisions on its vessels no matter where their ships are. If a flag ship of another signatory nation is within the territorial waters of a fellow signatory nation, a concept called "port state control" allows the host nation to board and check documents required by the various conventions, and even check the condition of the vessel. SOLAS '74 gives host nations the right to detain unseaworthy vessels visiting their ports. Host nations can either enforce the provisions of a convention on the visiting vessel, or ask the guest vessel's flag state to take appropriate action.

The right of a nation state to enforce international conventions on the ships of other nations while they are on the high seas can be problematic. It's one thing if a vessel is in a host nation's port. It's another issue entirely when the suspect vessel is on the high seas, but is threatening a pollution incident on a different nation's shores. This jurisdictional problem was highlighted when tankers of one nation state experienced casualties on the high seas that threatened the coastlines of other nations. No one had jurisdiction to intervene in situations like this until the 1969 Convention Relating to Intervention on the High Seas gave contracting nations the power to act against ships of other countries on the high seas if there is a grave risk of oil pollution.

Absent some threat to a coastal state, if a vessel is on the high seas, only its flag state has enforcement authority against it.

Flags and Registries

Ships have nationalities just like people do. For hundreds of years ships have flown the flags of their nations.[5] By doing so, a vessel claims her nation's nationality, and is bound by the laws and customs of her flag state. The Geneva Convention requires that the flag state control its vessels, and govern them under the jurisdiction of the flag nation. Generally the laws of the flag state will apply to a vessel's internal workings (such as labor and wage rules), no matter where she is. When a ship enters a port of a different nation, her external activities, such as vessel movements and rules regarding her crew's behavior while ashore, are governed by the host nation. If the internal workings of a vessel threaten the host nation's peace and order, the host nation may exert its jurisdiction aboard the visiting vessel (for example if a murder was committed while the vessel was in a host port). Traditionally, vessels flying a nation's flag meant the ship was built in, and owned and operated by citizens of that nation. This is no longer the case. Now, vessels can be built anywhere, and manned and operated by anyone.

There are two types of flag registries, "closed" and "open."

The United States (and most other first-world maritime nations) is a "closed registry" nation, meaning only U.S. citizens can own and operate a ship flying the flag of the United States.

In contrast, open registry nations, typically not powerful maritime states themselves, are nations that, for a fee, will allow vessels to register in their open registry and fly their flag. These are often called "flags of convenience" ships because the ship has no real ties to the nation whose flag it's flying. For some countries, the flagging of ships is a major, sometimes sole source of legitimate revenue.

Many open registry nations have no coastline, no ports, no history of seafaring, and are not economically or commercially sophisticated countries. They often have lower regulatory standards than closed registry nations, little ability or desire to enforce the regulations they do subscribe to, have low (or no) taxes on the vessel's profits, and allow non-citizens to own and operate the vessels flying their flags. One can now register and flag a vessel over the internet, using a credit card to pay the fee.

There are many nations offering flags of convenience, such as Greece and Bermuda, but none as prolific as Panama. Panama was the first, and is currently the largest open registry in the world, with Liberia a close second.

So why Panama? Even weirder—why Liberia? Both are relatively small, developing nations lacking robust traditions of maritime commerce. Liberia, created in the 1840s, had no seafaring history at all. It didn't even have a viable port until World War II.

So, why Panama? Easy. World War I, costly regulations, and Prohibition.

In 1903, with the backing of the United States, Panama seceded from Columbia. In return, the United States was given a 500-square-mile zone, called the Canal Zone, over which the United States had sovereignty. Within the Canal Zone, English was spoken and the American dollar was used. The U.S. Postal Service operated there. During the period from 1904 to 1914, the United States built the Panama Canal.

Recall, that from 1914 to 1918, World War I was raging. (The United States joined the war in 1917.) During the first half of the war, when the United States was not yet officially involved, American manufacturers were looking for ways to ship war supplies, while still allowing the United States to remain neutral.

The Panama Canal had recently opened, and there was a strong American presence in the area, and though Panama was a sovereign nation, many felt America really ran the show. This fertile combination of war and the control of the region by the United States gave birth to the façade known as an "open registry."

In 1917, Panama opened the world's first flag of convenience, an open registry under which anyone could flag a ship. Everyone knew that Americans owned and operated most of the ships flying the Panamanian flag, but it allowed American shippers to move war supplies under a foreign flag, in ships the Americans effectively controlled. It was a perfect solution to a sticky problem.

In 1915 the United States passed the Seaman's Act, which gave enhanced rights and protections to seamen, but which economically disadvantaged U.S. shipping companies. In 1920 the United States passed the Prohibition Act, making alcohol illegal to manufacture or transport. These two events prompted increasing numbers of American ship owners to re-flag their vessels under the Panamanian flag, thus bypassing American laws while keeping ownership and complete control of their vessels. After all, it wasn't illegal to ship rum on a Panamanian flagged vessel.

By the 1940s, the United States corporate tax rates had risen to over 30 percent, and another wave of ship owners flocked to Panama to escape the new and oppressive taxes. Panama's flagging business was bustling. After World War II, Panama became politically unstable, and ship owners, now used to the idea of open registries, were looking for another place to register their vessels. Enter Liberia.

A bit of background on Liberia, a tiny nation on the west coast of Africa, would be helpful here—as would an introduction to Edward Stettinius.

During World War I, Edward Stettinius's father had worked for J. P. Morgan, financing weapons sales to France and Great Britain. Edward Stettinius grew up wealthy on Staten Island and worked for General Motors, rising to the level of Vice President in Charge of Industrial Relations by the age of thirty-one, right in the middle of the Great Depression. He started an unemployment relief program and met Franklin D. Roosevelt as a result. He worked both in the private and public sectors, and, in 1934, he joined U.S. Steel, becoming its Chairman in 1938. In the late 1930s the United States granted the right to U.S. Steel (with Edward Stettinius at the helm) to explore the

Bomi Hills area of Liberia for iron ore, but discovering there was no port to facilitate the shipping of the ore, U.S. Steel lost interest.

Then, in 1939, World War II broke out. By 1939, bouncing comfortably between public service and private enterprise, Edward Stettinius was running the War Resources Board. Towards the end of the war, the Liberian President went to Washington to revisit the idea of a geological survey of Liberia's iron ore resources.

In December of 1943, agreement was reached to build a port in Monrovia using U.S. Lend-Lease funds. During the years from 1941 to 1943, Edward Stettinius was, conveniently, the administrator in charge of the Lend-Lease funds. The new port would provide a naval base for U.S. warships in Africa and the eastern Atlantic, but also would be of tremendous, if coincidental, benefit to shippers of iron ore and rubber.

Once that post ended, President Roosevelt appointed Edward Stettinius to be Secretary of State, and he served in that post from 1944 to 1945. During this period, the United States, seeking to increase its iron production, helped Liberia to increase its ore production. It was a win-win arrangement.

Towards the end of the war, Edward Stettinius was pivotal in the creation of the United Nations, and then, not surprisingly, he was appointed to be the U.S. Ambassador to the new organization. He became close with William Tubman, the (American) Liberian President. In 1947, Stettinius helped form the Liberia Company, a group focused on convincing American businessmen to invest in Liberia.

Edward Stettinius Jr.
U.S. Department of State.

In the 1940s, Edward Stettinius called a meeting of powerful lawyers and lawmakers to rewrite Liberian law (corporate tax codes, maritime laws, etc.) which resulted in tangible benefits to the (American-owned) Liberian companies that mined iron ore, the ships that carried it, and Liberia itself. Also not coincidentally, Liberia had become a major exporter of iron ore. The new corporate codes and tax structures made conditions in Liberia so favorable that by the late 1940s ship owners (of all types) were flocking there to register their ships. The Liberian government charged a flat fee per ton to register a ship, and then a flat fee each year afterwards. For corporations that registered there, but which operated outside of Liberian territory, Liberia had a corporate tax rate of zero—in stark contrast to the 48 percent corporate tax rate the United States was charging.

Registering a vessel in Liberia allowed ship owners to avoid not only taxes, but also the more stringent safety and maintenance requirements of the United States, and the requirement that American ships be built by (expensive) American yards and be manned by (expensive and litigious) American crews. All of this could be avoided by simply "flagging out."

In those days, it was common knowledge that anyone could easily obtain Liberian seamen's papers or licenses. All one had to do, it was rumored, was copy a license, write in a new name, mail it to Liberia, and voila! A new Liberian document was mailed back.

Getting a ship flagged out of Liberia was facilitated by the fact that Liberian Corporate Services was located in New York, conveniently in the same building as the Liberian Bureau of Maritime Affairs. Financing for the ship could be had through the International Bank of Washington, which also owned the International Trust of Liberia (also created by Edward Stettinius). Basically, all of Liberia's maritime affairs, from documents, to flag registry, to financing, was run by Americans and started or organized by Edward Stettinius. The revenue from ship registry fees ultimately amounted to about 8 percent of Liberia's gross national product.

In 1948, the SS *World Peace* became the first ship to fly the Liberian flag. Twenty years later, Liberia had surpassed the United Kingdom as the nation with the most tonnage under its flag. By 1970, Liberia, having the most ships, was the largest flag registry in the world. In 1990, Liberia partnered with the Marshall Islands and created a mega-registry called the "International Registries."

The Liberian civil war, which raged from 1989 to 1996, precipitated Liberia's decline as the world's leading flag state. During the war years, warlord Charles Taylor took over the country's "Liberian International Ship and Corporate Registry" and used its proceeds to fund the war. Some say it was his only source of legitimate revenue. Uncomfortable with the instability in Liberia, owners returned their attentions to Panama, and by 1999 Panama was once again the world's largest registry. A second Liberian civil war from 1999 to 2006 rendered Panama's flag even more attractive.

Ships flying flags of convenience are often manned by inexpensive labor, sometimes having crews hailing from over twenty different countries. This is especially true aboard cruise ships, as you will discover when you read about the MV *Costa Concordia* disaster. Language and cultural difficulties have contributed to many maritime casualties, especially aboard ships flying flags of convenience.

Marine Insurance

There are several types of marine insurance. Vessel owners certainly want to insure their vessels, but ship operators and charterers also need to protect their unique interests.[6]

Insurance of the ship itself is usually referred to as hull and machinery insurance. This insurance covers losses due to causes such as fires, collisions, or groundings. The cargo is typically insured separately. Because the value of a ship or cargo is measureable, businesses offering this type of insurance can reasonably rely on statistical information to inform their decisions on the rates or premiums appropriate for various types of coverage. Marine insurers covering hull, machinery, and cargo losses are typically for-profit corporations that charge premiums. Claims are paid from the proceeds of these premiums.

Insurance for liability to third parties is called protection and indemnity insurance (P&I) coverage. P&I coverage is not offered by traditional marine insurers (probably because losses are less predictable), but are instead covered by nonprofit P&I Clubs, consortiums of members who pool their resources to spread the risk of loss. Losses in this area can be substantial. Losses covered by P&I insurance include coverage for deaths and injuries, specific coverage for war risks, coverage for the cleanup, remediation, and restitution costs of pollution incidents (added after the SS *Torrey Canyon* disaster in 1967), and coverage to a cargo owner for cargo loss or damage if the ship is ultimately found to be at fault.

You might be wondering why cargo is insured twice, both by traditional coverage and P&I insurance. If a cargo is lost or damaged, the primary cargo insurance carrier pays the claim, but then will pursue the ship owner for reimbursement. If it turns out the cargo was lost or damaged through the fault of the vessel, then P&I coverage would ultimately cover the claim and reimburse the primary cargo insurer. If the ship is found faultless, or successfully claims an exemption from liability, then the primary cargo insurer would be stuck paying the claim with no right to reimbursement from the P&I insurer.

P&I clubs spread the risk of loss amongst their members, typically ship operators themselves, who each put money in a pool. Every member contributes money based on the number of ships (or tonnage) they themselves have at risk. Claims from any of the members are then paid from that pool of money. If there's a big loss and there isn't enough money in the pool, then members are expected to pitch in more to cover the loss. If there is a surplus, club members may get a refund from the pool.

Classification Societies

In the seventeenth century, men began meeting at Edward Lloyd's Coffee House in London to discuss shipping. Other coffee shops existed and attracted people involved with other ventures, but Lloyd's specialized in shipping. By 1730 Lloyd's coffee shop specialized in providing marine information and a place to secure marine insurance. Today, Lloyd's of London is one of the world's premier insurers of marine risks. Lloyd's also insures other unique endeavors and assets, including, reportedly, the 44-inch legs of a Victoria's Secret model.

To be profitable, the risks insurers take must be educated risks. To insure their financial interests wisely, Lloyd's needed a way to inspect and rank the seaworthiness of the vessels it was insuring. In 1760 Lloyd's started a classification society to inspect the hulls and machinery of ships seeking insurance.[7]

By the second half of the eighteenth century, Lloyd's had developed a letter grading system (or "class") for the ships it insured, and generated a document called Lloyd's Register Book listing the ships' particulars and their "class." Ship hulls were classed annually and earned grades of A (the best), E, I, O, or U, and machinery was graded G, M, or B (for good, middling, or bad) which were eventually replaced with 1, 2, or 3. This may be the origin of the English term "A-1" meaning "the best."

By 1830, Lloyd's classification society became Lloyd's Register of British and Foreign Shipping, a true classification society, independent of the insurance side of the house, and it began to promulgate "rules" for the construction and inspection of vessels.

The new "rules" were actually recommendations. They did not require that a ship be built a certain way, have a specific freeboard, or even be in good condition. However, a ship owner couldn't obtain insurance if his vessel didn't comply with the demands of the insurers. Without insurance, it would be nearly impossible for a ship owner to find a shipper willing to trust his cargo with the vessel. Thus, insurance requirements proved just as effective, if not more so, than the existing laws.

Gradually, other insurance markets saw the wisdom of promulgating construction standards, classing ships, and recording their grades. Eventually, classification societies sprang up in other countries and became businesses in their own rights.

Modern classification societies are for-profit companies (as are insurers) that inspect ships, promulgate design and construction standards, and issue certificates to vessels that meet these standards indicating that the vessel is "in class." Classification societies are hired by a ship owner to survey his vessel and issue the class certificate, proving the vessel's condition to shippers who are deciding whether to ship cargo on it.

If a vessel has a valid certificate indicating she is "in class," all it means is that at the time of the inspection, the ship met the requirements of that class. It does not mean she is seaworthy or safe. Once classed, a ship will be issued a classification certificate, with notations indicating her class, her service, her construction, any geographical limits to her service, and so on. There are several types of surveys conducted throughout the life of the vessel. As the ship ages, the inspections get more rigorous. Typically, a classification society will inspect a ship at least annually.

In 1930, one of the provisions of the new Load Line Convention was that classification societies collaborated to generate uniform requirements for freeboard. This provision resulted in several classification societies meeting to forge agreements on load lines and other issues. Eventually, in 1968, the International Association of Classification Societies (IACS) was born and classification societies could share their technical expertise and experiences. Most maritime nations now have at least one classification society. To be a member of the IACS, a classification society must agree to abide by its Quality System Certification Scheme. Although over fifty groups call themselves "classification societies," only thirteen belong to IACS and it is these thirteen which class over 90 percent of the world's commercial tonnage.

Recognizing the value of such concentrated maritime knowledge, the IACS became a consultative body to the IMO in 1969. The IACS's role is to promulgate rules in support of IMO conventions and resolutions.

The United Nations Convention on the Law of the Sea (UNCLOS) sets forth the duties of signatory nations to keep their fleets in good repair and to ensure safety at sea. In response to UNCLOS, IMO member nations have agreed to a set of basic standards for all merchant ships so that ships can travel the waterways freely and be admitted to foreign ports. These standards, called "statutory requirements," cover the ship's basic design and structural integrity, shipboard operations as regards pollution control, accident and fire prevention, and post-accident capabilities like escape routes, escape mechanisms, and spill containment. A classification society that is a member of IACS would ensure these "statutory requirements" are reflected in their classification rules.

So much trust is placed in classification societies that IMO's Safety of Life at Sea Convention (SOLAS) has provisions for a flag state to authorize recognized organizations (RO), such as classification societies, to conduct statutory inspections on behalf of the flag state. This would be similar to the Department of Motor Vehicles allowing a private, for-profit automobile business to inspect cars on the government's behalf, with the owners of the cars paying the auto business for the cost of inspection.

Flag states, especially open registry nations offering flags of convenience, which either don't have the expertise or the manpower to conduct statutory inspections, can certify a classification society which has been approved as an RO, to perform the statutory inspections for them. All IACS member societies have been approved as ROs by the SOLAS signatory nations. This means that in the United States, for example, private American Bureau of Shipping (ABS) inspectors can conduct statutory inspections of ships and those inspections will satisfy U.S. Coast Guard requirements. IACS surveyors will not generally perform a statutory inspection for ships they don't already class.

If a ship fails its classification survey, it falls "out of class" and the society will notify the flag state. The flag state will usually, as a result of the ship falling out of class, revoke her statutory certificates. The classification society will post the ship's status on their website, so all insurers and shippers can easily check the status of a vessel's class.

This all sounds very convenient, but because it is the ship owner who pays the costs of inspection and certification, a classification society's allegiance is rightfully questioned, as conflicts of interest are unavoidable. As you will read in some of the casualties where hull condition was at issue, this was a factor recognized by the investigating bodies. It is unclear whether classification societies can be held legally responsible for casualties caused by deficiencies a survey should have caught. (See especially the *Kirki* incident of 1991.)

Notes

1. For a very detailed explanation of U.S. Coast Guard rulemaking, see *Proceedings of the Marine Safety and Security Council: The Coast Guard Journal of Safety and Security at Sea.* Spring 2010.

2. As of 2008 the Federal Register and CFRs are available online at www.federalregister.gov and http://ecfr.gpoaccess.gov.

3. 5 USC §551 et seq.

4. For information on IMO treaties, see www.imo.org.

5. Sources for information on ship's registries: Elizabeth R DeSombre, *Flagging Standards: Globalization and Environmental, Safety, and Labor Regulations at Sea* (Cambridge, MA: MIT Press, 2006); Clifford B. Donn, *Flag of Convenience Registry and Industrial Relations; The Internationalization of National Flag Fleets* (Syracuse: Le Moyne College, Institute of Industrial Relations, 1988); David Charles Moerschel, *Flags of Convenience: The Mercenary Merchant Marine* (master's thesis, American University, 1966), reproduced by University Microfilms International, Ann Arbor, MI:1982.

6. For information on marine insurance, see www.lloyds.com.

7. For information on classification societies, see www.iacs.org; www.lloyds.com; www.eagle.org; and Tormod Rafgård, *"Classification Societies: Accountable or Not?"*, article on the liability of classification societies when they don't find deficiencies that later cause a major casualty, found on his blog *Tankers, Big Oil and Pollution Liability,* http://www.oilpollutionliability.com/classification-societies-accountable-or-not.

Chapter 2
1912 to 1929

1912: RMS *Titanic* sinking and the Safety of Life at Sea (SOLAS) Convention
1915: RMS *Lusitania*, wartime sinking and devastating loss of life
1915: The formation of U.S. Coast Guard and the Posse Comitatus Act
1915: The SS *Eastland,* capsizing at the dock; loss of over 830 lives
1920: The U.S. Merchant Marine Act (also known as the Jones Act, 46 USC §861 et seq.)

The RMS *Titanic*

Even in the twenty-first century, when people are asked to name a maritime disaster, most will cite the sinking of the "unsinkable" British-flagged Royal Mail Steamer (RMS) *Titanic* on April 15, 1912. As most everyone knows, she hit an iceberg and sank, causing the death of over 1,500 people. Of the 2,228 people aboard (sources differ on head count), only 706 survived.[1]

She departed Queenstown, England, at 1400 on April 11, 1912 under the command of Captain Edward J. Smith, the senior master of the White Star Line who was on his final voyage before retirement. The weather was ideal, visibility was clear, and the ship was making excellent speed. Ice reports had come in before departure, but the reports indicated the ice was north of the ship's track line and was of little concern.

The *Titanic* departing Southampton on April 10, 1912. *"RMS* Titanic *3" by F.G.O. Stuart (1843–1923).*

Many of the ship's features, or lack of features, contributed to the great loss of life. The vessel was magnificent and was outfitted with the most modern navigational equipment available. She was the first merchant ship to be fitted with WIDAR (wireless detection and ranging), a precursor to modern radar, and she was assumed to be unsinkable due to her "watertight" bulkheads and electrically operated watertight doors. The *Titanic's* innovative design allowed any two adjacent compartments to be flooded and still have the ship remain afloat and upright. It was this compartmentalization that rendered the vessel "unsinkable" in the eyes of her designers. Breaching two compartments would normally only happen if the ship hit another vessel, which was unlikely. But even if she did collide with something, it was considered almost impossible to compromise more than two adjacent spaces.

As a result of this assumption, it wasn't felt necessary that she be fitted with lifeboats for all persons aboard; the chances of all of the passengers and crew needing to abandon the vessel were just too remote to contemplate. The *Titanic's* twenty lifeboats could only hold 1,178 people of the 2,228 aboard, and not even half of the 2,566 passengers she was designed to carry, not counting the crew.

The lifeboats were nested, one tucked snugly inside the other, which ultimately delayed and complicated the deployment of the few boats she did carry. Given the opulence of the ship's outfitting, it surely was not economic concerns that motivated her designers to skimp on lifeboats. She did, after all, comply with existing regulations, which based the number of required lifeboats on the ship's tonnage, not the number of souls aboard.

Eager to show off the ship's capabilities, especially given the fine weather and sea conditions, J. Bruce Ismay, the managing director of the White Star Line, pushed for full speed, hoping for an early arrival in New York.

For unknown reasons, on Sunday April 12, Captain Smith decided to forgo the usual abandon ship drill. He did, however, conduct his usual religious ceremonies and ship's inspection. As the ship neared the Grand Banks, where ice had been reported, extra boilers were brought to pressure and her speed was increased, in an effort to arrive on Tuesday night, rather than the scheduled Wednesday morning arrival of April 15. During the day, no fewer than five ships had reported ice in the vicinity of the *Titanic's* track and Captain Smith must have known that ice lay in his path, however, these ice reports were never communicated to the watchstanders on the *Titanic's* bridge.

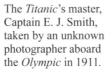

The *Titanic*'s master, Captain E. J. Smith, taken by an unknown photographer aboard the *Olympic* in 1911.

No one seemed too concerned, as the ship's speed was slowly increasing as boiler pressure built, and no efforts were made to slow her down as everyone was hoping for a showy, early arrival Tuesday night. No warnings to keep the engines on standby for immediate maneuvering were issued. No extra lookouts were posted as evening fell. The weather and visibility were fine.

This did not seem imprudent by the standards of the day. For the years preceding the *Titanic*, ships only reached modest speeds of ten knots or so, allowing time to sight and avoid ice, or effectively slow or even stop the ship if necessary to avoid hitting a berg. But speed was the hallmark of the trans-Atlantic liners of the day, and as ships' speeds increased no thought was given to the resultant decreased maneuverability and reaction time. Captain Smith probably acted as most other ship masters would have, given the prevailing conditions, the abilities of his ship, and the acceptable practices of the time.

The radio officers aboard did not work directly for the White Star Line, but instead for the radio firm Marconi Marine Company. Their job was primarily to generate revenue for the Marconi

Company by sending messages for passengers. They also handled operational traffic for the ship. On that fateful night, the ship *Californian* was trying to send the *Titanic* an ice report, but the *Titanic*'s radio officer, who already knew there was ice, was more concerned about getting the revenue-generating passenger traffic broadcast, and abruptly dismissed the *Californian*'s radioman. The master of the *Californian* had wisely decided to stop his ship that night due to the ice, but he was north of the *Titanic*'s track. Though it is doubtful the *Californian*'s ice warnings would have made any difference, the final ice report was never taken by the *Titanic*, and thus never made it to her watchstanders on the bridge.

When ice was reported by the *Titanic*'s lookout at 2340 on the dark, moonless evening of April 14, the watch officer put the wheel hard over and reversed the engines. The *Titanic* had triple screws, but only the two outboard shafts could provide astern propulsion with the center screw providing wash to a single rudder. Some feel this lack of 100 percent astern capability materially contributed to the inability to slow the ship. Also, because the engines were put into reverse upon sighting the berg, too late to be of any practical use, the center screw was stopped, which stopped the flow of water over the ship's single rudder, which meant when the rudder was thrown hard over, it had much less turning effect than it would have if the center engine had been left turning ahead. All attempts to maneuver the great ship, frankly, were in vain, as the berg was sighted too late.

The *Titanic* was steaming at over twenty-two knots when she struck ice, ripping open five of her watertight compartments.

Once it was determined the ship was doomed to sink, the *Titanic* sent out distress calls. In those days both "CQD" and "SOS" were used as distress signals. The closest ship, the *Californian*, most likely about nineteen miles from the *Titanic* (or less, as some reports indicate they sighted each other), had a radiotelegraph set, but it was not being monitored and had no auto-alarm, so the *Californian* did not hear nor respond to the *Titanic*'s distress calls.

The 1912 post-incident findings, relying in part on statements from the *Californian*'s boilerman Ernest Gill and other ship's officers, determined that Captain Lord of the *Californian* was only five to eight miles from the *Titanic* and was aware of the distress, but didn't respond. This conflicts with Captain Lord's position, and volumes of hard evidence, that he was actually stopped much farther north, roughly nineteen miles from the *Titanic*. Ernest Gill had reportedly been paid a year's salary for his statements to the newspaper, and after telling his story and being paid he promptly departed the ship and disappeared. The other ship's officers testifying against Captain Lord had major inconsistencies in their stories. Most of the witness testimony against Captain Lord was later proved unreliable.

The *Titanic* started firing distress rockets at around 0045 April 15. There are some reports the crew of the *Californian* saw white flares in the distance, but possibly assumed they were flares celebrating the *Titanic*'s maiden voyage, and thought nothing more of them. Additionally, the crew of the *Californian* reported seeing the flares low on the horizon, equal to or even lower than the height of a ship's masthead light. Some reports indicate other vessels saw flares as well, but also did not respond. The confusion may have been caused by the existing regulations, which at the time allowed distress flares to be of any color. Additionally, at the time, flares were used as a means of routine communication, not just distress. Sadly, it wasn't until forty-six years later that signal flare colors were standardized and distress flares were required to be red and used only for distress.

The fact that observers aboard the *Californian* reported a smallish to medium-sized ship and flares low on the horizon supports Captain Lord's position that he was indeed nineteen miles away, and not five to eight miles as many have surmised. In their 1992 article appearing in the magazine *Naval History*, NOAA Lieutenant Commander Craig McLean and David L. Eno, a U.S. government investigator, provide a compelling argument that any evidence that the *Californian* was aware of the *Titanic*'s distress but failed to act is unsupported and completely discredited. The fact that both vessels' crew testified they flashed a bright signaling light, but neither vessel received a response, may indicate that other vessels were in the vicinity. Some think it may have been the Norwegian sealing vessel *Samson*, but this is still in question.

The crew of the *Californian* may have seen a ship, but it was probably not the *Titanic*.

The *Carpathia*, roughly sixty miles from the scene, learned of the *Titanic*'s fate and rushed to her aid. At 0150 April 15 the *Titanic*'s radio went silent. The *Titanic* was not designed to withstand the flooding of five adjacent compartments, and as water topped the watertight bulkheads, she flooded progressively, eventually losing all her reserve buoyancy. It took the mighty ship over two hours to sink. She finally slipped below the icy Atlantic waters at 0220 on April 15, 1912.

The *Carpathia*, arriving after the *Titanic* had disappeared beneath the surface, proceeded to pick up survivors. Other vessels also rushed to the area to render aid. Captain Smith and Thomas Andrews, the ship's designer, were lost with the ship. Ismay survived, along with 705 others.

Many scholars argue that were it not for the lack of lifeboats, confusion with distress signaling, and lax radio regulations, many more lives could have been saved. Yet others disagree.

Aftermath

In response to the *Titanic* disaster, the government of the United Kingdom organized a conference, attended by representatives of thirteen major maritime nations, in order to generate international agreements on the safety of merchant ships at sea.[2] This conference was the International Convention for the Safety of Life at Sea, now known as the SOLAS Convention.

The International Convention for the Safety of Life at Sea (SOLAS)

The SOLAS treaty was passed in 1914.[3] The 130-page document was signed in London on January 20, 1914. Each of the thirteen nations in attendance had several representatives, for a total of fifty-six people in attendance, eleven representing the United States and twelve representing the United Kingdom and its territories. Despite the large number of delegates, the convention was passed less than two years after the loss of the *Titanic,* demonstrating record efficiency for passage of an international treaty.

Prior to this convention, laws concerning merchant vessels tended to be specific to a given nation or region, and mostly involved regionally specific trade and commerce issues, not safety. Neighboring nations and trading partners usually had bilateral agreements concerning seafaring trade between them, but they pertained to monetary issues and usually did not extend beyond the commercial interests of the two trading partners. International agreements on safety standards were largely nonexistent prior to SOLAS. The loss of the *Titanic* sent shudders through the maritime world and prompted maritime nation states to address industry-wide operational practices and equipment safety standards.

The original SOLAS treaty had eight chapters concerning the safety of life at sea, including: the ships to which the convention applied, safety of navigation, vessel construction, radiotelegraphy, lifesaving appliances and fire protection, safety certificates, and a general chapter, in addition to a section promulgating associated regulations.

SOLAS applied to all mechanically propelled merchant vessels, and vessels carrying twelve or more passengers for hire, but it only applied to voyages that ran beyond the signatory states' domestic waters, thus domestic voyages were exempt from the convention's regulations.[4] The provisions of SOLAS applied to vessels voyaging beyond 200 miles from shore.

In Article 6 of the original convention, in direct response to the loss of the *Titanic*, we find the birth of the International Ice Patrol. Article 6 called for the "High Contracting parties to undertake all steps to ensure the destruction of derelicts" in the northern Atlantic, as well as a service for the study and observation of North Atlantic ice conditions, and a service of ice patrol. The convention called for three vessels to perform these services, and stipulated that for the entirety of the ice season, all three vessels shall be employed in ice patrol. The United States was invited to manage the ice patrol, with signatory nations bearing percentages of the costs in proportions suitable for their interests along the North Atlantic trade routes. The ice and weather reporting codes and meanings assigned to Morse code signals that were articulated in SOLAS 1914 are similar to the ones still used on modern ships today.

Article 12 dealt with the problem of flares not being of defined color, type, or capability, and the practice of flares being used for both routine communications as well as distress. This article in SOLAS '14 required that distress flares not be confused with any other sort of flares. Since no standard color was yet prescribed, this effectively meant no ship should fire off a flare of any sort, unless it was in distress, but SOLAS did not specify a color.

Other articles required things we now take for granted, such as:

- A compulsory stern light and second masthead light
- Disallowing any signals that could be confused for distress signals
- An international radiotelegraph distress signal and requirements to carry a radiotelegraph set if there are fifty or more persons aboard
- Requirements to maintain a continuous radiotelegraph listening watch
- Requirements concerning emergency radiotelegraph installations
- The requirement to respond to a distress signal
- The requirement for lifeboat capacity and life jackets for everyone aboard
- Independently powered emergency lighting
- Muster lists detailing the emergency duties of crew members and where passengers are supposed to assemble
- Appropriate construction subdivision requirements to enhance stability
- Fireproof bulkheads
- Escape hatches in watertight compartments
- Recording of opening and closing of watertight doors in the official logbook

The above list may seem like common sense, but it was the first international agreement to articulate such details. There was thoughtful, if politically incorrect, dissent on the requirement to have lifeboat or liferaft capacity for every person aboard.

Some of the arguments against carrying "lifeboats for all" included the position that on an average 600-foot vessel, only 400 feet of flat rail space was available for launching lifeboats. This would limit the number of boats that could be launched simultaneously. It was argued by some that even under ideal circumstances, in perfect weather and with a trained crew, people could only be offloaded at a rate of about 1,000 per hour. It was also pointed out that in a casualty severe enough to sink the ship, many passengers would most likely be killed, and thus not need lifeboat evacuation. Most disasters also took place in the vicinity of other vessels, so the use of their lifeboats could be contemplated, as could the repeated use of the stricken vessel's own lifeboats to shuttle survivors to nearby vessels. And lastly, the odds of a large passenger vessel sinking quickly were, and still are, astronomically low.

The SOLAS Convention has been amended over the years to respond to changes in seafaring technology and evolving environmental and humanitarian concerns. As you will read in future chapters, the original SOLAS Convention is like a regulatory tree trunk, constantly growing, changing and branching to address myriad maritime concerns not contemplated by the original drafters.

During the period immediately after the adoption of SOLAS, signatory nations were busy amending their nation's laws to incorporate the provisions of SOLAS and start enforcing them. During this period, the United States was reorganizing the regulation of its maritime industry and resources, and generating legislation to protect its maritime commerce.

As a result of the *Titanic*, the United States enacted the Act to Promote the Welfare of American Seamen in the Merchant Marine of the United States, also called the La Follette Seaman's Act, which, among other provisions, mandated "boats for all." The Act was later amended by the U.S. Merchant Marine Act of 1920.

The Automated Mutual-Assistance Vessel Rescue System (AMVER)

AMVER was another safety system organized in the wake of the *Titanic* disaster. AMVER was designed as a worldwide system to notify and direct nearby vessels to the scene of a distress. On the night the *Titanic* sank, passing vessels had noticed her flares but assumed they were celebratory pyrotechnics, not distress flares. Unless they specifically heard a distress call, vessels of the day had no way of learning about nearby vessels in distress, as, prior to AMVER, there was no central, international alerting system. Unfortunately, the manual charting methods, personnel requirements, and radio systems available at the time were insufficient to run an effective international reporting system. AMVER didn't become fully operational until 1958. AMVER, as we know it today, relies on modern computer technology and is highly effective. Read more about AMVER in Chapter 5.[5]

The RMS *Lusitania*

The wartime sinking of the *Lusitania* is such a noteworthy casualty, and led to such a staggering loss of civilian life, that I felt compelled to include it in this book, though it was not, technically, a commercial vessel at the time of her sinking.

Prior to the war, the *Lusitania* was a Cunard Line ocean liner in the trans-Atlantic trade, similar to the *Titanic*. She was a finely outfitted vessel, equipped with the latest in turbine propulsion technology. She boasted a speed of twenty-five knots, which earned her the Blue Riband, an award for the fastest Atlantic crossing. The vessel had elevators for passengers, electric lights, and radio communications. At the time, she could carry more passengers than any other liner.

With the outbreak of hostilities in World War I, the British Admiralty intended to use her as a troop ship, but allowed her to remain a passenger liner with the proviso that she carried government cargoes.

She set sail from New York, eastbound for Liverpool, on May 1, 1915. The Germans had declared the waters around the United Kingdom to be a war zone, and, with ominous prescience, had even warned their citizens not to sail on the *Lusitania*, perhaps knowing she was a favored target.

On May 7, 1915, the *Lusitania* was torpedoed without warning off the coast of Ireland. The "Cruise Rules" of the war required a warning before a warship could attack a non-military vessel but because the *Lusitania* was listed as a "naval auxiliary cruiser" and because she was carrying wartime munitions components, the German submarines considered her a military target.

The initial torpedo damage was bad, but it was a second, internal explosion that truly devastated her. She sank in eighteen minutes, taking approximately 1,198 lives with her.[6]

Formation of the U.S. Coast Guard

During this period, the U.S. Revenue Cutter Service (previously called "Revenue-Marine" when it was formed in the 1790s) was a federal maritime law enforcement branch serving under the Department of the Treasury. It was, as its name implied, a service tasked with protecting the revenue stream generated by trade tariffs. Specifically, the Revenue Cutter Service existed to thwart smugglers.

The Revenue Cutter Service enforced trade embargoes and blockades, intercepted ships carrying slaves, and pursued pirates. Eventually, since they were the only federal agency on the seas, they began rendering aid to vessels in distress. In 1830, Congress officially tasked the Revenue Cutter Service with the duty to render aid at sea, which in 1915 facilitated its efficient merger with the Lifesaving Service, ultimately creating the U.S. Coast Guard we know today.

The relatively new Coast Guard soon became a sort of maritime catchall for maritime-related tasks the federal government needed done, but which were inappropriate for the U.S. Navy. For example, the task of maintaining the nation's lighthouses fell to the Coast Guard in 1939 when it absorbed the Lighthouse Service. In 1942, when it took on the duties of the Steamboat Inspection Service, the Coast Guard began inspecting ships.

By 1942, the United States Coast Guard was responsible for myriad and often unrelated (sometimes moderately conflicting) maritime interests. Their mission has continued to grow and diversify over the decades, some would argue to the point of inefficiency.

The U.S. Coast Guard currently operates under the Department of Homeland Security, a federal executive branch agency. Currently, the Coast Guard's responsibilities include, among others:

- Enforcing federal drug laws, environmental laws, immigration law, and fishing laws at sea
- Coordinating public and private resources in response to accidents and environmental incidents
- Generating regulations for the construction, operation, and inspection of vessels
- Inspecting commercial vessels for compliance with construction, maintenance, and outfitting regulations
- Examining commercial mariners for fitness and competence and issuing mariners' credentials
- Acting as prosecutors during fault-finding administrative proceedings against mariners' credentials
- Acting as the primary post-incident investigator for marine crimes being prosecuted by other federal agencies, most usually the FBI or EPA, against defendant mariners
- Rescuing mariners in peril and arranging for commercial salvage of maritime equipment
- Maintaining aids to navigation (lighthouses and buoys)
- Running the nation's Vessel Traffic Service programs
- Operating the Global Positioning System (GPS) and other electronic navigation systems, which are used, free of charge, by the entire world

To get a better feel for the current all-encompassing scope of the U.S. Coast Guard's mission, and how truly conflicted this author thinks their mission has become, consider this analogy.

The current situation, if applied to aviation, would have the U.S. Air Force specifying construction standards for commercial planes, inspecting commercial planes, maintaining airports and towers, running the radars for air traffic control, licensing air traffic controllers, examining and issuing licenses to commercial airplane pilots, holding the hearings to give tickets or apply penalties, or even to take pilots' licenses away, and lastly, rescuing planes in peril and rendering aid and comfort.

But the U.S. Air Force does not regulate commercial airlines—the Federal Aviation Administration does. Why? Because under posse comitatus it would be against the law to have the military involved in regulating a commercial activity. In addition, the Air Force is not exactly a subject-matter expert when it comes to commercial aviation.

Posse comitatus, Latin for "the power of the country," is a federal law passed in 1878 prohibiting the United States military from enforcing federal domestic law. (There have since been several exceptions.) In other words, under posse comitatus, the military can only act against foreign aggressors, not our own people, and technically not on our soil. So how is it the U.S. Coast Guard not only writes federal regulations but also enforces those same regulations against civilians?

The U.S. Coast Guard was exempted from posse comitatus because it has, as its primary mission, enforcement of federal law. It also has a regulatory job. But why isn't the Maritime Administration (MARAD, the maritime version of the FAA) servicing the U.S. merchant marine the way the FAA services the commercial airline industry? Some mariners feel it inappropriate to task a military agency like the Coast Guard with writing domestic regulations and then enforcing those laws against citizen mariners and commercial companies. Since it is the Coast Guard that is called to rescue lives and lead remediation efforts in casualty situations, some think its investigation and law enforcement roles are riddled with potential conflicts of interest.

Currently, both the National Transportation Safety Board (NTSB) and the U.S. Coast Guard have jurisdiction over maritime accidents. A memorandum of understanding between the two agencies (revised on December 19, 2008) sets forth which agency will be the lead agency for a given incident, and calls for cooperation between the agencies where joint jurisdiction exists. The NTSB derives its authority from 49 USC §1131 to investigate incidents defined as "major marine casualties" as described in 49 CFR §850 and 46 CFR §4.40. Normally, the NTSB would investigate casualties involving the loss of three or more lives on a passenger ship, the loss of life or serious injury to twelve or more persons, the loss of a commercial power vessel over 1,600 GRT, any marine casualty with loss of life involving a highway, bridge, railroad, or shoreside structure, serious threats to life, property, or the environment by hazardous materials, and significant safety issues relating to Coast Guard safety functions. It is the NTSB that would recover the information off a voyage data recorder, and then offer the information to the Coast Guard. Under 46 CFR §6301 the U.S. Coast Guard investigates any casualty involving death, serious injury, material loss of property or damage to vessels, and serious harm to the environment.

An excellent example of the sometimes rocky relationship between the (civilian) NTSB and the (military) Coast Guard was the investigation of the horrific collision between the USCG Cutter *Blackthorn* and the tanker *Capricorn* in Tampa Bay, Florida, on a clear, still, moonlit night in January 1980. Essentially, the USCG *Blackthorn* cut across the bow of the *Capricorn*, and got impaled by the tanker's anchor, which resulted in the *Blackthorn* being dragged bodily along the *Capricorn*'s hull, until the cutter finally flipped and sank.

The *Blackthorn* had just completed an extended yard period, and the fifty-man crew was inexperienced by commercial maritime standards. The *Blackthorn*'s commanding officer had just come off of five years shore duty. Both the navigator and the Officer of the Deck (OOD) that fateful night were on their first day of sea duty. Not one of the deck officers in the wheelhouse had ever navigated Tampa Bay before their arrival into the Gulf Tampa Drydock in October 1979. The Coast Guard allowed their vessels to hire local pilots, but the commanding officer testified after the incident that he didn't know how to actually go about hiring a pilot, thus no pilot was aboard.

To say the bridge watch of the *Blackthorn* was inexperienced and unprepared is an understatement. In contrast, the civilian mariners sailing the 600-foot-long *Capricorn* had decades of seagoing experience, and had navigated Tampa Bay many times. The *Capricorn* also had a local pilot aboard who had navigated Tampa Bay over 1,000 times on vessels of a similar size.

Both vessels were approaching an area called "the combat zone" where a nineteen-degree turn is located dangerously close to the bridge. The combined approach speed was about twenty-five knots, with three minutes before impact, and neither vessel had yet seen the other. The *Blackthorn* got underway and adjusted her course to the edge of the shipping channel to allow a large, brightly lit passenger vessel to pass. The commanding officer ambled out to the bridge wing. After the passenger ship passed, the cutter passed under the Skyway Bridge and the commanding officer re-entered the wheelhouse. When he noticed the *Capricorn* about a half-mile away he reportedly said, "Where the **** did he come from?"

The *Blackthorn* continued on her track until she had crossed the mid-channel line and was solidly on the *Capricorn*'s side of the channel when the *Capricorn*'s master said to the pilot, "What's that guy trying to prove?" The pilot was convinced that if the *Blackthorn* just kept her course and speed, she would pass clear ahead. After unsuccessful attempts to reach the *Blackthorn* by radio, the *Capricorn* blew maneuvering signals and came left to effect a starboard to starboard passing. She then sounded the danger signal just as the *Blackthorn* began to come right. Seconds later, the *Capricorn* and *Blackthorn* collided almost head on.

The *Capricorn*'s port anchor, held only by a friction brake and ready for letting go as is the custom on arrival into port, was driven into the *Blackthorn*'s berthing areas as the cutter scraped down the tanker's side. As a result, the *Blackthorn* was dragged backwards, listing dangerously and taking on water.

The scene on the *Blackthorn* was understandably chaotic, but lax conditions aboard the Coast Guard vessel made the situation even worse. Most of the crew did not know their emergency stations and they were unfamiliar with the ship. Lifejackets were stowed in lockers topside; orders to "abandon ship" went largely unheard; the emergency lighting failed; attempts to free an inflated liferaft failed, (two liferafts were over twenty-five years old and of an obsolete model, one was missing the inflation canister); a newer raft had "BAD" marked on it and was also missing a canister.

As the ship continued to roll sideways, some crew who had gathered at the messdeck mistakenly ran to the engine room, thinking that would be a safer route out.

Amid the darkness and chaos, the *Blackthorn* eventually rolled belly up and sank, taking twenty-three lives with her.

After arguing over jurisdiction, both the National Transportation Safety Board and the U.S. Coast Guard investigated the tragedy, with stunningly different conclusions. The U.S. Coast Guard investigation rightly put the blame on their own cutter for careless navigation and poor leadership, but also on the tanker for failure to sound whistle signals and for not hugging the right side of the channel. (There was some confusion on the Coast Guard's part as to the exact channel limits.)

The NTSB saw things differently and placed almost no blame on the tanker, which due to her size and draft, was restricted to the channel. Not only did the NTSB blame the *Blackthorn* for failing to keep to her side of the channel, it noted that the Coast Guard requires more objective and comprehensive qualifications for civilian seafarers and commercial vessels, than it does for its own. Additionally, had the cutter *Blackthorn* been a commercial vessel, it and its crew would have catastrophically failed a Coast Guard safety inspection. The NTSB noted with concern the lack of a local pilot aboard the cutter, as well as a long list of operational shortcomings.

There are other noteworthy casualties involving U.S. Coast Guard vessels. On October 20, 1978, just two years before the *Blackthorn* incident, the USCG *Cuyahoga* turned in front of a loaded coal freighter in Chesapeake Bay. The USCG *Cuyahoga* sank less than five minutes after impact and eleven of her crew died. As a result of these and other incidents, the Coast Guard has worked to continually improve its training and vessel inspection procedures.

In a November 27, 2012 memo, the NTSB listed a long list of casualties involving Coast Guard personnel in which none were tested post-incident for drugs or alcohol and none were investigated the way a commercial mariner in the same situation would have been. The NTSB recommended in the strongest of terms that Coast Guard personnel be subject to the same strict drug and alcohol regulations as the commercial mariners against whom it enforces its regulations.

When a Coast Guard vessel causes a collision, or has vessels that could not pass routine commercial-level inspections, or allows personnel who are less qualified than their civilian counterparts to operate Coast Guard vessels, or requires examinations of civilian mariners that its own seagoing officers could not pass, it damages the Coast Guard's credibility in these areas. Coast Guard regulations hold the commercial maritime world to standards the Coast Guard itself does not meet. If there is lingering mistrust for the Coast Guard in its capacity to regulate the commercial maritime industry, it is born of this history.[7]

The SS *Eastland*

In the wake of the *Titanic*, despite credible, thoughtful arguments *against* requiring lifeboats and/ or rafts for everyone aboard, regulations were changed to require lifeboat capacity for every soul aboard. This requirement, while sounding reasonable at first blush, carried with it profound impact on some of the vessels subject to the new requirements.

To understand the *Eastland* tragedy, a short lesson on ship stability would be helpful. A ship's transverse stability, her tendency to right herself if inclined, is measured in part by a value called "metacentric height." Metacentric height is the vertical distance between a vessel's center of gravity and a spot called the "metacenter."

A ship's metacenter is located where a vertical line from the center of buoyancy while the ship is floating at equilibrium crosses a vertical from the new center of buoyancy when she is listed. As long as the vessel's center of gravity remains lower than the metacenter, the vessel will have positive stability and will tend to right itself. The farther apart the vertical center of gravity and the metacenter, the more robust a vessel's righting tendency will be.

The distance between vertical center of gravity and the metacenter is called metacentric height, and is a measure of a vessel's initial stability. Metacentric height is routinely calculated on merchant vessels. If one thinks of a child's inflatable clown toy, weighted at the bottom and light at the top, which constantly rights itself when punched, one can grasp the general idea. Basically, ships need to keep weight low in order to be stable.

A "tender" vessel has low metacentric height, and tends to be slow to right herself if inclined. A tender vessel is often comfortable in a seaway, offering a long, easy roll to her passengers. If a vessel is too tender, she can be subject to capsize. This condition is caused when there is too much weight high on a vessel, or not enough weight low, and the ship's center of gravity rises too near her metacenter.

Conversely, a "cranky" or "stiff" vessel has large metacentric height and tends to rapidly right herself. If a vessel is too stiff, it can be uncomfortable for the crew and can even damage cargo and strain cargo-securing gear and other shipboard equipment. A vessel with zero, or close to zero, metacentric height will flop from side to side, sometimes flopping to one side and resting there. This angle of flop is called an "angle of loll" and is an indication of an extremely dangerous stability condition. Contrary to a layman's intuition, simply moving weight from the low side to the high side is the worst thing one can do if a list or "flop" is due to zero or negative metacentric height. If weight is simply shifted from low to high, the usual effect is for the vessel to flop to the other side, and to flop farther over. If the list is so severe it immerses open side ports or other hull openings that allow free communication with the sea, the flooding will rapidly compromise the vessel's stability further.

Another stability concept one must understand is free surface. When a fluid is allowed to slosh freely in a tank or compartment, it has the effect of virtually decreasing metacentric height, which negatively impacts stability. Thus, an empty tank, or a completely full tank, will not cause the free surface effect, but partially full tanks will.

Both conditions, a low metacentric height and free surface effects, plagued the *Eastland*.

The *Eastland* was built in 1903 as a Great Lakes passenger steamer. The ship was 275 feet in length, had four decks, and five gangways, and was originally certified to carry 2,800 people. She drew ten to twelve feet of water. One unique (and unfortunate) design feature, which left her particularly vulnerable, was large openings in her hull, and near the waterline, through which to pass the gangways. When empty, the gangway openings were about four feet above the water, but when loaded this distance decreased to about two feet. This was to prove a pivotal element in her eventual capsizing. She also had a ballast system configuration that contributed to her vulnerability.

Her original design stability calculations contemplated her carrying cargo as well as passengers, and her metacentric height was designed to be about eighteen inches, not unusual for this type of small cargo vessel on the Great Lakes. But the *Eastland* was used primarily as a passenger vessel, with "cargo" weights (people) that varied widely and moved around. According to George Hilton, in his book "Eastland: *Legacy of the* Titanic," a more appropriate stability requirement would have been two to four feet of metacentric height. There is no evidence that the ship's stability was ever actually measured (by an inclining experiment) during her entire working life.

Over the course of her lifetime, the *Eastland*'s carrying capacity varied from a high of 3,300 persons to a low of 1,950, depending on her configuration, number of cabins, and the condition and capacity of her lifesaving equipment. On July 22, 1915, just twenty-two days before the disaster, the *Eastland* was issued a certificate allowing her to carry 2,570 passengers.

The crew considered the *Eastland* a "cranky" ship, though the more correct term would be "tender," as the ship had historically unreliable stability. She was known to list easily as passengers boarded, especially if they crowded the upper decks, and the engineers would ballast her tanks in an effort to keep her reasonably upright and on an even keel. Due to several modifications to her structure and equipment, including adding a layer of cement to an upper deck floor, and continuous changes to her passenger allowance, over the years her stability became less and less reliable. The passage of the La Follette Seaman's Act of 1915, requiring "boats for all" in the wake of the *Titanic* disaster, resulted in the *Eastland* adding lifeboats, liferafts, and the requisite launching gear to her upper decks, further raising her center of gravity and further eroding what little positive stability she had. The addition of boats also allowed her to carry more paying passengers.

There were reports that, in combination with structural and equipment changes effected to reduce her draft and increase her speed, and the addition of an air conditioning system in 1904, her metacentric height had been reduced to roughly four inches.

With such a top-heavy vessel, and passengers allowed to board and flock to the upper decks (common on hot days), and considering the practice of the engineers to add small amounts of water ballast to the ship's tanks to keep her even while loading, it is a wonder the disaster didn't happen sooner. It didn't happen sooner probably because the ship had been sailing well below capacity for years.

On Saturday July 24, 1915, the *Eastland* was docked at Clark and South Water Street in Chicago. She was one of several modest passenger steamers chartered to carry employees of the Western Electric Company to a company picnic in Michigan City, Indiana, a short trip across the lake. Passengers purchased tickets sold through an employee club, and there is evidence that some felt compelled to buy tickets or face losing their jobs. Of the five steamers available, the *Eastland* was the most popular ship not only because was she the fastest of the five available ships, but she also had the earliest departure time, which would afford her passengers the most time at the picnic. Regardless of the reason, by 0700 the *Eastland* was packed with over 2,000 eager people.

Though never of reliable stability, her stability problems had been most dramatically experienced eleven years earlier when over 2,000 terrified passengers had to be forced (some accounts say they were forced with powerful streams from fire hoses) to shift from one side of the lolling ship to the other in order to correct her list. There were other accounts of the ship's instability.

The problem was the *Eastland* had a low value for metacentric height. She was tender in that she had a lazy, but comfortable, roll in a seaway, but would adopt lists, sometimes dangerous lists, with the slightest provocation.

On the morning of July 24, hundreds of merry passengers, oblivious to the unseaworthy condition of the ship, streamed across her gangway and filled the upper decks. The ship began to take an odd list almost right away. As passengers continued to board she would lazily flop to the other side and come to a tentative rest. But no one seemed to notice or care.

Just before 0700, the *Eastland*'s chief engineer noticed the list to port and decided to fill a starboard ballast tank to counteract it. As he filled the starboard tank, no doubt decreasing the vessel's stability due to free surface effect, the vessel flopped to starboard. Over the next fifteen minutes, the ship continued to flop back and forth, listing to port, then starboard, then back again. Passengers continued to press aboard.

At 0723 the ship listed sharply to port and the chief engineer sent men to the crowded decks to tell the passengers to go to the starboard side, but only a few complied. The master became concerned and ordered the inside doors opened and that passengers be sent back ashore, but it was too late and the *Eastland* rolled further to port, this time flooding the lower decks with water.

The flooding was so extensive and rapid that almost no one aboard could escape before she rolled completely to port and sank at the dock, with only eight feet of her starboard side left exposed above the water.

The attending tug cut her line and positioned herself so survivors could traverse from the bow of the *Eastland* across the tug's decks and get back to the main pier. People swarmed to help and those ashore who found something buoyant threw the items to the victims in the water. A few hundred managed to climb over the starboard side to safety. Welders arrived with cutting torches to cut holes in the hull to extricate survivors who were pounding in the inside of the hull in a panic to get out. Several holes were cut—one such hole became an escape route for forty survivors.

Not a single crew member was lost, but over 830 (accounts vary) passengers lost their lives that day.

Twenty years later an official determination was made that the fault for the accident lay solely with the ship's engineers for not having the vessel properly ballasted. However, the real cause of the accident was probably a combination of a possible defect in the vessel's design regarding her stability, the lack of ballast in her tanks, which would have added weight low in the vessel, lowering her center of gravity and increasing her righting arm when she was loading thousands of passengers topsides, and the fact that her U.S. Coast Guard certificate of inspection had been frequently changed to allow increasing numbers of passengers, despite requiring no changes to the vessel, nor any tests of her stability.

Though arguably not the sole cause of the disaster, the unintended result of adding lifeboat and liferaft capacity for all, which added weight aloft, and not determining the effect on the *Eastland*'s stability, was an unintended consequence of the Le Follett Seaman's Act, which, in an effort to save lives, required "lifeboats for all."[8]

The U.S. Merchant Marine Act

The U.S. Merchant Marine Act of 1920 (commonly known as the Jones Act) primarily dealt with maritime trade.[9] It was drafted, in part, to protect the maritime commercial interests of the United States, but it also mandated minimal protections for seamen, effectively ending truly horrific practices and conditions aboard many merchant ships. One feature of this act relevant to our exploration of casualties was the creation of a construction fund to stimulate construction of new American bottoms (sailor talk for hulls). Private shipbuilding money had virtually dried up.

In his paper, *The Peculiar Fate of the Morro Castle,*[10] William McFee points out that:

> In spite of a closely protected coastal service, in spite of the denial of American registry to foreign-built ships, in spite of high wages (100 percent higher than Great Britain), in spite of long term building loans at small interest and generous operational subsidies, in spite of mail contracts which could hardly be distinguished from charitable requests, there was no Merchant Marine and almost no shipbuilding. Capitalists were no longer interested in risking their capital in American ships.

Congress reacted by passing a new Merchant Marine Act, the Jones-White Bill of 1928, which authorized a $250 million fund to construct American ships. The federal government offered twenty-year loans to American shipping companies (at the very favorable rates governments can afford to offer) for up to 75 percent of a ship's construction costs. The new subsidies for mail ships were based on speed and tonnage, which theoretically motivated ship operators toward greater efficiency.

The New York and Cuba Mail Steam Ship Company (also called the Ward Line) was one of the companies which availed itself of this new construction loan program to build the ill-fated TEL *Morro Castle*, which was to suffer a catastrophic fire in 1934, a mere four years after her launch.

Currently, the Jones Act has a broad mission as set forth in 46 USC §50101, which states:

(a) It is necessary for the national defense and the development of the domestic and foreign commerce of the United States that the United States have a merchant marine—

    (1) Sufficient to carry the waterborne domestic commerce and a substantial part of the waterborne export and import foreign commerce of the United States and to provide shipping service essential for maintaining the flow of the waterborne domestic and foreign commerce at all times;

    (2) Capable of serving as a naval and military auxiliary in time of war or national emergency;

    (3) Owned and operated as vessels of the United States by citizens of the United States;

    (4) Composed of the best-equipped, safest, and most suitable types of vessels constructed in the United States and manned with a trained and efficient citizen personnel; and

    (5) Supplemented by efficient facilities for building and repairing vessels.

Notes

1. Sources for RMS *Titanic* information: Richard A. Cahill, *Disasters at Sea:* Titanic *to* Exxon Valdez (San Antonio: Burke Publishing, 1990); United States Coast Guard, *International Ice Patrol*, last modified January 26, 2012, http://ww.uscg-iip.org/cms/index.php?; Department of Transport Marine Accident Investigation Branch, *RMS* Titanic: *Reappraisal of Evidence Relation to SS* Californian (London: HMSO), last modified March 12, 1992, http://www.maib.gov.uk/cms_resources.cfm?file=/titanic.pdf; Lieutenant Commander Craig McLean, NOAA, and David L. Eno, "The Case for Captain Lord," *Naval History,* Spring 1992, 26–29; Titanic *Judgment and the Advisory Committee's Report, Marine Engineer and Naval Architect* 35 (1912–13).

2. The thirteen nations in attendance were: Germany/Prussia, Austria/Hungary, Belgium, Denmark, Spain, the United States, France, Great Britain (which at the time included Ireland, the British dominions beyond the seas, and India), Italy, Norway, the Netherlands, Russia, and Sweden.

3. Source for SOLAS information: www.imo.org.

4. Article 2 of the original convention is found in the IMO archives, http://www.imo.org/Knowledge-Centre/ReferencesAndArchives/HistoryofSOLAS/Documents/SOLAS%201914.pdf.

5. Source for AMVER information: www.amver.com.

6. Sources for RMS *Lusitania* information: Thomas A. Bailey, *The* Lusitania *Disaster: An Episode in Modern Warfare and Diplomacy* (New York: Free Press, 1975); Robert D. Ballard, *Exploring the* Lusitania: *Probing the Mysteries of the Sinking That Changed History* (New York: Warner Books, 1995); Patrick O'Sullivan, *The* Lusitania: *Unraveling the Mysteries* (Cork: Collins Press, 1998); Diana Preston, Lusitania: *An Epic Tragedy* (New York: Walker and Co., 2002); Library of Congress digitized newspapers from 1886–1922 at: http://chroniclingamerica.loc.gov/ and http://www.loc.gov/search/?q=Lusitania.

7. For information on the U.S. Coast Guard, see http://www.uscg.mil/history. For an interesting article on Coast Guard mistakes, see G. W. Shultz, "Coast Guard's deadly accidents highlight lapses in safety,

leadership," *San Francisco Chronicle*, June 28, 2014, by the Center for Investigative Reporting, http://www.cironline.org/reports/coast-guard%E2%80%99s-deadly-accidents-highlight-lapses-safety-leadership-6486. For information on the *Blackthorn/Capricorn* collision, see USCG Marine Casualty Report No. USCG 16732/01279, *Marine Casualty Report USCGC* Blackthorn*, SS* Capricorn*; Collision in Tampa Bay on 28 January 1980 with Loss of Life*; National Transportation Safety Board Press Release SB 80-69/3013; NTSB Hearings, Marine Accident Report NTSB-MAR-80-14; NTSB Summaries M-99-23; Judy K. Nunez, *28 January 1980* Blackthorn *and* Capricorn*: Collision with History in Tampa Bay*, master's thesis (Florida State University, November 10, 2003).

8. Sources for *Eastland* information: George Hilton, Eastland: *Legacy of the* Titanic (Stanford, CA: Stanford University Press, 1995); Edward Snow, *Sea Disasters and Inland Catastrophes* (New York: Dodd, Mead and Co., 1980).

9. The U.S. Merchant Marine Act, 46 USC §50101 et seq.; ABS Consulting, *Maritime Laws of the United States* (Rockville, MD, 2001).

10. William McFee, "The Peculiar Fate of the *Morro Castle*," in *The Aspirin Age, 1919–1941,* Samuel Hopkins Adams and Isabel Leighton, eds. (New York: Penguin, 1949), 320.

Chapter 3
1930 to 1939

1930: The International Load Line Convention of 1930 and Samuel Plimsoll
1934: The TEL *Morro Castle,* a case of arson and 135 tragic deaths
1936: The Merchant Marine Act of 1936

The International Load Line Convention of 1930

It has long been recognized that buoyancy, and specifically freeboard, bears a direct relationship to a ship's longevity and many maritime nations imposed some limits on the overloading of ships, but it was not a universal practice. Lloyd's of London, a maritime insurer, had a pecuniary interest in the safety of ships at sea and a keen interest that they not be overloaded. To protect their interests, Lloyd's required a certain minimum freeboard for all ships it insured and in 1835 generated loading recommendations for vessels. Lloyd's recommended freeboards as a function of the depth of the hold (three inches per foot of depth). These recommendations, used extensively until 1880, became known as "Lloyd's Rule."

To protect themselves against devastating losses, insurers pooled their resources and spread the risk between many members, rendering no one insurer in any real danger of being financially devastated by any single loss. This had the unintended consequence of making the fate of any one ship rather inconsequential to an individual insurer. Additionally, some ships and cargoes could be insured for more than they were worth. The moral hazard and disastrous motivations encouraged by such a practice is obvious.

In the 1870s Mr. Samuel Plimsoll, a member of the British Parliament, was concerned with the suffering and deaths caused by losses of vessels due to overloading, and he argued for mandated minimum freeboard and legislation limiting the loading of ships. In the 1800s, an average of one in five mariners died at sea, a mortality rate higher than any other industry.

Plimsoll supported his arguments for shipping regulations to his parliamentary colleagues by showing them completed insurance forms that listed cargo details such as cargo weights and quantities, and the insurance premiums paid. The documents proved that ship owners of the day had no rational or compelling financial interest in the welfare of the ships or the men who sailed them, and that indeed, ship owners could actually profit if their ships went down. Because of the amount and type of insurance coverage, these vessels would generate a profit for their owners whether or not they (or their crews) survived to deliver their cargos.

Samuel Plimsoll, affectionately called the "sailor's friend," focused his efforts on remedying the plight of sailors who sailed the "coffin ships"—the overloaded, overinsured, and dangerously unseaworthy ships Plimsoll sought to regulate.

Contrary to modern sensibilities, given the large numbers of ship owners sitting as members of Parliament, Plimsoll's efforts were not well received. In his final plea to lawmakers and other influential people, and with barely a nod to conventional punctuation, Plimsoll wrote:

> Whoever you are who read this, help the poor sailors, for the love of God. If you are a man of influence, call a meeting and confer on this appeal; if you are not, and will write to me, I will try to show you how to help. If you refuse—but this I cannot think—but if you refuse or neglect to use your influence. Before another year has run its course at least five hundred—five

hundred men!—now in life will strew the bottom of the sea with their dead, unburied, unresting bodies, and desolation and woe will have entered many and many a now happy home; but if you do render your help, we can secure such life-preserving activity in precautionary measures that the sailor will have no fear; and then the storms of winter may come, but with good tight ships under them, and sound gear to their hands, their own strong arms and stout hearts can do the rest, and as after a night of storm and tempest, which but for your fraternal care would have overwhelmed them in death and sent bereavement and anguish into their humble homes, they reach their desired haven, weary and worn it may be, but still safe—chilled to the marrow, but still alive—the blessings of those who are ready to perish will be yours: nor shall there be lacking to you those richer blessings promised by the Great Father of us all, to those who visit the widow and fatherless, for that to the high and the noble and the sacred duty of visiting them in their affliction, you have preferred the higher, the nobler, and the yet more sacred duty of saving women and children from so sad a fate.

Samuel Plimsoll
111, Victoria Street, London, S.W.
December, 1872[1]

Despite heated outbursts and a reprimand, Plimsoll eventually got his bill passed. Ultimately, the financial success of British maritime commerce, rather than concern for human life, was probably the primary motivating factor for the 1872 establishment of the Royal Commission on Unseaworthy Ships.

By 1876 the United Kingdom Merchant Shipping Act required vessels to have a loadline mark, now known as a "Plimsoll Mark," indicating her maximum draft. In a characteristic display of modesty and dedication to his cause, despite re-election, Plimsoll gave up his seat in Parliament to a man he thought could better advance the cause of maritime safety. Despite Plimsoll's success, loading limits were not universally recognized internationally, and the United Kingdom Merchant Shipping Act could not extend its reach beyond British ships and those ships plying British waters.

The first international limits on loading of ships didn't come into effect until over fifty years later, when loading limits were set forth in the International Load Line Convention of 1930, which was ratified by fifty-four nations.[2] Finally, in 1966, the IMO prescribed freeboard requirements that were determined mathematically, based on a vessel's construction and stability, her location, and the season of her travels.

Current loadline treaties have been ratified by nations representing 99 percent of the world's tonnage. Foreign vessels in U.S. waters must carry an International Load Line Certificate indicating their compliance with the International Convention on Load Lines (ICLL), an IMO treaty.

International efforts to unify loadline requirements, and the uncounted numbers of lives and vessels saved can be traced directly back to the efforts of one impassioned man, Samuel Plimsoll. Even today, Plimsoll's legacy survives on the feet of British school children, because the rubber-soled sneakers they wear are called "plimsolls"—if water gets above the rubber trim of the shoes, they're sunk.

The TEL *Morro Castle*

The *Morro Castle* was a U.S flagged luxury ocean liner of the Ward Line that ran between New York and Havana, Cuba. She was named after the Morro (which means "rock" in Spanish) Castle fortress, built in 1589 by the Spaniards, which rests on the north tip of the entrance to Havana Bay. At a cost of approximately $10 million, the *Morro Castle* was constructed largely with monies borrowed from the federal government made available through the newly enacted Merchant Marine Act. She was christened in January 1930.

She was a lovely, modern liner, with a graceful 508-foot hull. Interestingly, she was powered by twin turbo-electric steam-driven engines that drove twin screws, and this is the origin of her designation of TEL, for turbo electric liner. She carried just short of 500 passengers in splendor, served by 240 officers, staff, and crew. In addition to being lovely, at eighteen-plus knots, she was fast and by 1934 had made over a hundred passages to Havana without incident. Though called a "millionaire's yacht" she carried primarily tourists and businessmen.

The Ward Line wisely kept the passenger rate for the week-long run between Cuba and New York affordable. A round trip cost only $75.00, which included meals and a two-night stay in Havana—inexpensive even by Depression standards! Despite the Depression, the *Morro Castle* was profitable in the passenger trade due in no small part to the fact that people could enjoy alcoholic beverages once the ship sailed outside the territorial sea, since the Prohibition didn't apply on the high seas. The trip was called a "whoopee cruise" for obvious reasons. The boozing didn't necessarily stop in Cuba, where liquor was plentiful, legal, and cheap. Alcohol purchased in Cuba for the trip home had to be consumed before the ship reached her dock in New York, so the last night at sea was often the most rambunctious party of all.

In short, the *Morro Castle* was busy, profitable, and lively. Her turnaround time in New York was literally just a few hours. She would disgorge her passengers every Saturday morning and leave that night with a fresh batch of eager revelers. This pace proved to be a heavy strain on the crew, and there was often a 50 percent turnover in personnel each trip. This would prove to be catastrophic in times of emergency, as it meant half the crew was unfamiliar with this ship and each other.

The *Morro Castle* set sail from Havana on her return leg bound for New York on September 5, 1934, under the command of Captain Robert Wilmott, a senior master with over twenty-five years experience with the Ward Line. Aboard were 318 passengers and a crew of 231. There were reports that Captain Wilmott had been acting strangely, becoming less gregarious and even becoming paranoid that someone was trying to kill him. As the ship made her way northward, weather conditions were worsening and, with winds shifting to the east, a nor'easter was developing.

On the evening of September 7, the last night at sea before landfall the next morning, the most extravagant dinner of the cruise, the captain's dinner, was being held. Captain Wilmott wasn't feeling well and had taken dinner in his cabin. It was highly unusual for the outgoing Captain Wilmott to miss this dinner, but he had spent the day battling stomach cramps. The passengers missed him, but were unaware as to the real reason for his absence. Wilmott had died in his cabin,

apparently of a heart attack, and, while the partiers danced and drank in the dining halls, command of the *Morro Castle* fell to the unassuming chief mate, William Warms.

The *Morro Castle* on fire off the coast of New Jersey.
International News Photos, Inc.

Warms' sudden command was even more daunting because Captain Wilmott had retained control over many of the responsibilities usually performed by a chief officer, making Warms' leap to command even wider.

In the dark morning hours of September 8, at around 0250, smoke was detected on B-Deck in the First Class Writing Room, which was roughly in the middle of the ship next to the passenger lounge. A crewman reported the smoke to the bridge, and an officer was sent to investigate. The officer confirmed there was indeed a fire and the fire alarm was sounded. Smoke was also seen in the stokehole fidley, but the engine room reported that there was no fire down there.

Local weather conditions had deteriorated, and the winds were at near gale force. Due to the late hour and weather conditions, most passengers and crew were in their cabins. Radioman George Alanga smelled the smoke and woke chief radio officer George Rogers, who sent Alanga to the bridge to see if the (new) master wanted to send a distress call. Radioman Alanga never really liked Rogers, but being a good seaman, Alanga complied with the instruction.

The bridge was in chaos. Captain Warms, only in command a few hours, was yelling at the chief engineer. Alanga could not get the master's attention in all the chaos, so he left and returned to the radio room. He told Rogers, "they're all crazy up there," but Rogers sent him back to the bridge, and this time Captain Warms recognized him but didn't give the OK to send a distress call.

By now the fire had been burning for over twenty-five minutes. The radio room bulkheads were hot, and the room was full of smoke, but by 0315 still no distress call had been sent.

Rogers could hear other radios calling the Coast Guard asking if a ship was on fire because there was a glow on the horizon. Finally at 0318, almost thirty minutes after the fire had started (sources differ, some indicate the call went out eighteen minutes after the onboard fire alarm was sounded), Radioman Alanga got the OK from the master to send a distress call. Other ships, seeing the glow of flames on the horizon, had already sent out distress calls on behalf of the stricken vessel.

Shortly after Alanga returned from the bridge, the batteries in the radio room exploded, blasting acid all over the decks of the radio shack. Despite blistering his hands trying to reattach wires to the emergency radio, Rogers finally got the distress call off at 0323. (There is some speculation that Rogers, tired of waiting for the master to issue the order, had sent the distress signal on his own.) Meanwhile, Captain Warms recklessly proceeded ahead at full speed of nineteen knots, into pouring rain and pounding seas under the assumption that the crew was getting the fire under control.

Within five minutes of the broadcast (it was to be the only distress call the ship got off) the fire had compromised the emergency generator, rendering further radio communication impossible. In under thirty minutes, the fire had burned through the vessel's electrical wiring so completely that the entire ship went dark. Next to fail was the ship's steering, as the hydraulic lines were melted by the fire. Within an hour, the vessel was engulfed in flames, unable to steer and helplessly in the dark in near gale conditions.

Captain Warms, no doubt recognizing attempts to quench the fire were in vain, ordered the engines stopped and he dropped anchor off the New Jersey shore.

Passengers were awakened by the sounds of alarms, crowds running down the passageways, and screams. Other reports indicate that when the fire alarm eventually did sound, their sounds were too muffled to be clearly heard.

Regardless, it was absolute chaos. No doubt many passengers were still intoxicated from the evening's parties. As the fire in the center of the ship raged, passengers were beginning to congregate on the stern, while many crew, shirking their responsibility for the passengers' well-being, moved forward toward safety. Many bulkheads were hot to the touch, breathing was difficult due to the smoke, and the deck was so hot it melted the soles of some people's shoes.

Shrapnel from exploding windows posed an additional danger. Passengers began weighing their alternatives: jump into the rough, confused, black sea or burn to death. Some wriggled out of portholes to the water below. Some of the passengers who survived were burned so badly they could never work again.

By the time Captain Warms had ordered abandon ship, most people had already jumped into the water.

Some diligent crew members attempted to launch lifeboats but in the end, only six of the ship's twelve lifeboats were successfully launched. Ultimately, only eighty-five people made it to the lifeboats, most of them crew who had abandoned their posts.

Since the winds were from the northeast, the starboard side was to windward and experienced the roughest seas, but it was likely somewhat free of smoke. This probably was the reason that five of the six successful lifeboat launches were on the starboard side. Only one lifeboat was launched to port, which was in the lee, but probably too smoky and hot to be accessible.

Of all the poor seamanship displayed that morning, chief engineer Ebon Abbott's behavior was, by some accounts, the most reprehensible. He did not go to the engine room as required when the fire alarm sounded. Instead, he wasted valuable time cowering on the bridge, unable or unwilling to follow orders. He finally jumped in a lifeboat and ordered it lowered, contrary to Captain Warms' yelling for it *not* to be lowered. It ultimately was lowered with Ebon Abbot, twenty-six crew, and three passengers, fewer than half the sixty-three people it was able to carry. Not all of the crew members abandoned their posts—there were exceptions and several crew members displayed great compassion and bravery.

Many of the passengers had no idea how to don their lifejackets. Some passengers, who did not know how to enter the water safely, jumped from very high decks and were knocked unconscious by the impact and drowned, or were killed by the buoyant force of the lifejacket snapping their necks when they hit the water. Passengers who stayed aboard to help flung anything that floated over the rails for swimmers to grab.

Captain Warms and thirteen crew members, including radiomen Alanga and Rogers, stayed aboard the burning vessel.

Eventually, four merchant ships arrived at the scene, but the sea and swell were so rough it was dangerous to get too close and difficult to see survivors in the water. The U.S. Coast Guard dispatched two vessels, but they too stood off and rendered little aid. Once local media started reporting that dead bodies were washing up on the New Jersey shore, the Coast Guard finally sent float planes to look for survivors. The most effective aid came from small boats arriving at the scene, and from the Governor of New Jersey, Harry Moore, who flew his plane over the scene. He directed nearby boats by flying over the area and dipping his wings or dropping markers where survivors or dead bodies were seen.

As the wounded and dead washed up on New Jersey's beaches, locals came to the waterfront to help the wounded, reassemble families that had been scattered by the disaster, and drag the dead further ashore. In the end, of the 549 passengers and crew aboard the *Morro Castle*, 86 passengers and 49 crew members were lost.

By mid-morning, the vessel had been completely abandoned, her anchor was dragging and she was drifting slowly with the current. Attempts to tow her into port failed when the towline broke. By late afternoon, her smoldering hulk drifted aground at Asbury Park, New Jersey, less than 300 feet from broadcast station WCAP and announcer Tom Burley, who had been broadcasting the story. She was a total loss. Her charred remains languished there, near the Asbury Park Boardwalk and Convention Hall, where she became a macabre attraction, with tourists paying for souvenirs and postcards of the once glorious liner. After enduring this indignity for seven months, she was ultimately towed away in March of 1935.[3]

What Went Wrong?

The fire aboard the *Morro Castle* was so devastating due to a combination of operational practices (or lack thereof) and construction materials and techniques. This incident is a noteworthy example of an error chain.

Construction Problems

The *Morro Castle* had installed the best available technology in safety features. She had forty-two fire stations, fire detectors in many spaces, and automatic fire doors designed to close when a certain temperature had been reached. In short, her systems were state of the art. But there were problems—not all of them with the ship.

Though the ship had automatic fire doors, many of them failed to activate and the crew did not think to close the doors manually. Closing the fire doors may have been a futile exercise anyway, as the ship's steel ceilings had wood-lined chase ways between the steel and the wood overheads that ran above the tops of the fire doors, allowing the fire to easily jump between zones whether or not the fire doors had been closed.

As a luxury liner, the *Morro Castle*'s passageways were beautifully paneled with highly flammable wood, glued veneers, and plywood. Rules requiring fire-retardant construction materials had not been written yet. Additionally, the vessel, though only four years old, was constantly being painted, in order to maintain her spiffy appearance. The buildup of oil-based paints, coupled with the lavish use of wood, contributed to the ferocity of the fire.

The fire detectors were located in staterooms, the engine room, and other working spaces, but none were located in lounges, dining halls, or in the writing room where the fire began. In fact, none of the public spaces had fire detection systems. It was probably assumed that these places were so frequently inhabited that alarms were unnecessary. Cargo spaces, in contrast, had sniffer lines that ran to the bridge so the watch officer could tell what compartment smoke was coming from should there be a fire.

The writing room held blankets in its lockers—blankets that had been dry-cleaned using highly combustible fluids, though it is doubtful significant amounts of dry-cleaning residues would have remained. Also stowed in the writing room, since it was close to the bridge, was the vessel's line-throwing gun, which is used to pass a line to another vessel in order to transfer passengers or equipment in an emergency. The heat from the fire ultimately caused the gun's propellant charge to explode, which blew out windows and allowed the blustery winds to blow throughout the space and spread the fire even more effectively. (Modern vessels carry explosive items in a pyrotechnic locker.)

Operational Problems—The Human Element

Though vessel layout and construction techniques and materials can be instrumental in preventing or mitigating fire, a vessel's operations and people are usually more critical to the prevention of incidents. It is the human element that is often the difference between safety and disaster. Such was the case with the *Morro Castle*.

It was a party ship. Andrew Furuseth, then president of the Seaman's Union, said that sailors didn't need to get wages on this run, because they made so much money smuggling dope.[4] The night of the fire, despite a crew of over two hundred, only seven crew members were on duty.

When the crew learned of the fire, having no meaningful firefighting training, they opened most of the forty-two fire hydrants, dropping the water pressure below any useable level, because when the fire main system was designed it was assumed that no more than six hydrants would ever be in use at one time. In addition, many of the hydrants on the Promenade Deck had been disconnected after a passenger had reportedly slipped on a wet deck due to a leaky hydrant, and sued the shipping line. (Another source said the passenger had slipped during a drill, and that Captain Wilmott had ceased holding fire drills as a result.[5])

In their efforts to reach passengers, some well-intentioned but ignorant crewmen broke portholes and windows, which breached any fire segregation the glass had afforded.

Regulations in place at the time required fire drills be held each voyage and attended by the crew (but not the passengers). Despite the drills, inquiries after the disaster found that the crew did not report to their assigned fire stations, made no organized attempt to fight the fire or even to close the fire doors, were largely not helpful in assisting passengers to safety, and that after the six lifeboats had been launched (and they carried mostly crew) the boats did not return to the stern of the vessel to assist people in the water.

The new master was ultimately criticized for not authorizing the distress call sooner, for not leaving the bridge to assess the damage himself (though staying on the bridge would probably be considered prudent by modern standards), for maintaining course and excessive speed for too long after the fire was reported, and for making no attempt to use emergency steering or lighting systems after the primary systems failed.

Surely exacerbating the situation was the fact that the vessel had high crew turnover, and with the death of Captain Wilmott, each deck officer had advanced one rank into a position requiring duties with which he was not familiar.

Ultimately, Captain Warms, Chief Engineer Abbott, and the Vice President of Ward Lines were indicted for willful negligence and sent to jail. The convictions were overturned on appeal and the blame oddly was attributed to Captain Wilmott, who died the night before the fire. Speculation about the true cause of the fire abounds.

Originally made out a hero for sending the distress call (possibly without the master's approval), chief radio officer George Rogers is sometimes attributed with starting the fire. Though his past was checkered, his motives for setting the fire, if he indeed did, are hard to fathom. Rogers, whose parents died when he was young, was a teenage thug who was expelled from school. He spent some time at a reform school and was eventually accused of everything from arson to sodomy. He had a propensity to use fire. He was also a thief. He was usually intensely disliked by those around him and he had the ability to stir the pot wherever he went, often pitting coworkers against each other.

He managed to get himself trained as a radio operator and later joined the Navy, from which he was eventually discharged after an accident involving a battery that landed him in a Naval Hospital. He bounced around, working both at sea and ashore as a radioman. In 1929, his employer, Wireless Egert Company, accused him of setting a fire, but it was never proven.

In 1936, two years after the fire, Rogers got a job with the New Jersey Police Department installing radios in police cars. He at one point confided things about the *Morro Castle* fire to his supervisor, Vincent "Bud" Doyle, that only the person who set the fire could have known, and Doyle became suspicious.

Worried he was about to be exposed, Rogers attempted to murder Doyle, allegedly by using an electric fish tank heater. Doyle was crippled in the attempt and spent the rest of his life trying to prove Rogers had set the *Morro Castle* fire. Rogers eventually died in prison in 1958, having been convicted in 1954 of murdering a neighbor couple for money. He is also suspected of poisoning Captain Wilmott. Rogers, during his thirty-year marriage to Edith Rogers, even reportedly killed her dog.

The ultimate cause of the fire has never been officially determined. It could have been arson by a crew member, though any motive for this seems elusive; it could have been caused by faulty wiring, spontaneous combustion of the blankets in the writing room, or heat generated by the ship's funnel, which was just aft of the writing room. There have even been allegations the ship was smuggling arms to the Cuban dictatorship, and had thus become an attractive target to Cuban Communist insurgents.

Aftermath

As a result of the *Morro Castle* disaster, international safety practices were improved in the 1948 SOLAS Convention, including the requirement to use fire-retardant materials in the construction of passenger ships, more rigorous drills, which must include passengers, and firefighting training for officers. In the 1948 SOLAS Convention, three new parts (D, E, and F) were added to Chapter II, which dealt specifically with fire safety, largely in response to the *Morro Castle*.

In an effort to recover their reputation after the *Morro Castle* disaster, Ward Line adopted new company colors and changed its name to the Cuba Mail Line. In the early 1950s, socialist-leaning Cuban rebels led by Fidel Castro were attempting to oust the existing government led by Cuban President Fulgencio Batista. The armed conflict had escalated to the point that in 1958 the United States imposed an arms embargo on Cuba. Obviously, this had a devastating effect on the Ward Line and their "whoopee cruises." The company survived until 1959 when declining demand for travel to the embattled island put them out of business.

The Merchant Marine Act of 1936

Largely in reaction to the fire and tragedy aboard the *Morro Castle*, Congress passed the Merchant Marine Act of 1936, which, among other things, created the U.S. Maritime Commission, and addressed the qualifications and welfare of sailors.[6] A whole chapter was dedicated to maritime education and training, which planted the seed for the U.S. Merchant Marine Academy, which formed the nation's first U.S. Merchant Marine Corps of Cadets two years later. The Act also had chapters addressing directed studies, reportage of marine safety issues, as well as other non-safety-related sections.

Notes

1. Samuel Plimsoll, *Our Seaman: An Appeal* (rep. by Kenneth Mason, Hampshire, UK, 1979, from the original edition printed by Virtue and Co. London, 1873), 128.

2. Sources for International Load Line Convention and Plimsoll marks information: IMO conventions at:http://www.imo.org/about/conventions/listofconventions/pages/international-convention-on-load-lines. aspx; U.S. Coast Guard information at: http://www.uscg.mil/hq/cg5/cg5212/loadlines.asp; Nicolette Jones, *The Plimsoll Sensation* (London: Little Brown, 2006).

3. Sources for *Morro Castle* information: Hal Burton, *The* Morro Castle (New York: Viking Press, 1973); Richard A. Cahill, *Disasters at Sea*; Gretchen Coyle and Deborah Whitcraft, *Inferno at Sea: Stories of Death and Survival Aboard the* Morro Castle (West Creek, NJ: Down the Shore Publishing, 2012); Thomas Galla-gher, *Fire at Sea: The Mysterious Tragedy of the* Morro Castle (Guilford, CT: The Lyons Press, 2003); Thomas Gordan and Max Morgan Witts, *Shipwreck: The Strange Fate of the* Morro Castle (New York: Stein and Day Publishers, 1972); William McFee, *The Peculiar Fate of the Morro Castle*; Lloyds's Register 1933–34, http://www.plimsollshipdata.org/pdffile.php?name=33b0616.pdf; The Sea Girt Lighthouse Citizens Committee, http://www.seagirtlighthouse.com/page/The-Morro-Castle.aspx; The U.S. Coast Guard National Maritime Center, www.uscg.mil/nmc/about_us/pdfs/history_nmc.pdf; the Ward Line website, www.wardline.com.

4. McFee, *The Peculiar Fate of the Morro Castle,* 322.

5. *The Strange Tragedy of the Morro Castle*, New Jersey History's Mysteries, http://www.mjhm.com/mor-rocastle.htm.

6. The Merchant Marine Act of 1936 (46 USC §1101 et seq.), http://www.usmm.org/mmact1936.html; http://www.usmaritimelaw.org/us-laws-codes/morro-castle-merchant-marine-act/.

Chapter 4
1940 to 1949

1940: HMS *Lancastria,* wartime casualty resulting in a massive loss of life
1945: MV *Wilhelm Gustloff,* the deadliest maritime disaster to date
1945: Formation of the United Nations in the wake of World War II
1946: Licensing of civilian mariners by U.S. Coast Guard
1948: Formation of the Inter-Governmental Maritime Consultative Organization (IMCO)
1949: The first vessel traffic service (VTS) established in Liverpool

Although these were the "war years" of World War II when most casualties were caused by wartime hostilities, I have chosen to detail some of the most noteworthy casualties involving civilians.

The HMS *Lancastria*

Most nations have provisions allowing them, in times of war, to commandeer commercial ships, usually passenger liners, for use as troop carriers. Such was the case with the *Lancastria*, a splendid Cunard liner in the trans-Atlantic passenger trade. The *Lancastria* was made a troop ship in 1940 and was redesignated HMS *Lancastria*, for "Her Majesty's Ship," her new prefix reflecting her new vocation.

After the Dunkirk evacuation, the *Lancastria* was enlisted to partake in "Operation Ariel," to evacuate remaining British civilians and military troops from France. In the summer of 1940, there were roughly 67,000 people needing to get out of France and they had gathered at St. Nazaire hoping to board a flotilla of waiting ships.

Evacuations began on June 17, 1940, and people were shuttled out to the *Lancastria*, which was anchored about ten miles off the coast of St. Nazaire, by small boats running between ship and shore. Her capacity, under normal circumstances, was roughly 2,100 people, but due to the exigencies of war, these limits were suspended and the British Navy ordered the *Lancastria*'s master to take as many people aboard as he possibly could. Some estimates put the number aboard the day she sank at over 6,000 souls. The highest estimates report she had over 9,000 people aboard.

That afternoon, the Nazis started bombing the area, first striking a nearby ship. After the first air raid, the British Navy urged the *Lancastria* to depart, but the master refused to do so without naval protection against German U-boats, so he stayed anchored where he was. A second German air raid later that afternoon rained bombs onto the deck of the *Lancastria*, landing three (some sources say four) direct hits. The Nazi planes continued to relentlessly assault the ship throughout the day. She started to sink by the bow, but her forepart touched the river bed and stopped her descent. The once proud liner, her stability compromised, then lurched suddenly to port, flinging people into bulkheads and over the side.

Some people jumped overboard, choosing to take their chances in the sea. Some, improperly jumping from too high a deck, reportedly had their necks broken by the sudden buoyant force of their lifejackets. No one had been taught the modern practice of entering the water with legs crossed, while holding the lifejacket down with one hand, and one's nose with the other. The scene in the water was so gruesome that one sighting originally reported coconuts floating in the water, but as the observers drew closer, they realized to their horror that the "coconuts" they had reported were human heads. Others who had survived and were floating in the bay couldn't effectively hang on to anything, as their hands were too slippery with the thick oil that had spilled into the sea.

As the *Lancastria* began to settle onto her side, less-panicked survivors were able to walk down the starboard side of the hull and lower themselves into the water. As they inched their way down the slippery hull, some peered through the portholes in the side of the ship, taking in the grisly sight of their shipmates trapped below, while German warplanes ruthlessly continued to attack survivors who were floundering in the floating wreckage.

The ship finally rolled over and sank twenty minutes later, spilling her fuel, which Nazi planes ignited with their strafing machine-gun fire, incinerating swimmers trapped in the oily waters.

Of the people who died, most died from drowning, or burns, or were killed when German planes strafed the water for survivors. Of everyone aboard, only 2,477 survived. The loss of life was so horrific that the British government ensured that the media and vessels that had been involved in the rescue efforts suppressed details of the attack.

The sinking of the *Lancastria* is included here because it was a horrific wartime casualty in which it is estimated 4,000 to 9,000 lives were lost, more than the *Titanic* and the *Lusitania* combined.[1]

The MV *Wilhelm Gustloff*

The German hospital ship *Wilhelm Gustloff* set sail on its final voyage from Gdynia, Poland, to Kiel, Germany, where she was to evacuate German refugees during the final days of World War II. The official passenger manifest listed 6,050 people on board, but many civilians had boarded without being recorded. Some reports estimate as many as 10,582 passengers and crew were aboard the doomed ship.

On January 30, 1945, a Soviet sub spotted the *Wilhelm Gustloff* and fired four torpedoes into the ship. The passengers scattered and due to overcrowding and panic many were trampled in the rush for lifeboats. It was a cold winter night and immersion in the icy Baltic Sea was fatal within minutes. Most estimates put the number of dead at around 9,400, making the *Wilhelm Gustloff* disaster the deadliest in maritime history to this day.[2]

Formation of the United Nations (UN) in 1945

Prior to the formation of the UN in 1945, a similar international body called the League of Nations had been formed in 1919 under the Treaty of Versailles, as a reaction to World War I. The League of Nations was formed to promote international cooperation and to achieve peace and security, but it was dissolved after it failed to prevent World War II.

By the end of World War II most civilized nations yearned for an end to the chaos, loss, and devastation of war. The name "United Nations" was coined by U.S. President Franklin D. Roosevelt at a meeting where representatives of twenty-six nations pledged to keep fighting together against the Axis Powers. The United Nations was officially founded in 1945 at the end of World War II when fifty-one nations signed the United Nations Charter in San Francisco and pledged their commitment to maintaining open lines of communication between nations to facilitate international peace and friendly international relations. The nations of the UN also committed themselves to promoting basic human rights and improved living standards.

Through its various councils, the UN has four main purposes:

1. To keep peace throughout the world.
2. To develop friendly relations among nations.
3. To help nations work together to improve the lives of poor people, to conquer hunger, disease and illiteracy, and to encourage respect for each other's rights and freedoms.
4. To be a center for harmonizing the actions of nations to achieve these goals.

Currently, 193 countries belong to the United Nations. Before the UN was formed, nations still had to cooperate on various issues of international importance, such as telecommunications standards, international mail, railroad tracks between countries, time zones, and even motion pictures. Prior to the UN, industry-specific agencies had been created to handle these issues. Now, nations routinely cooperate on myriad issues most of us take for granted, such as standardization of credit cards, paper sizes, CDs, DVDs and computer protocols. Many of these issues are now more efficiently addressed by specialized standardization agencies within the United Nations.[3]

International maritime concerns, such as standardized buoyage systems, chart symbols, radio frequencies, and collision regulations warrant a separate agency within the UN—an agency now known as the International Maritime Organization (IMO).

The Licensing of Civilian Mariners by the U.S. Coast Guard

The first federal licensing of mariners was required by the Steamboat Act of 1852, which authorized the Steamboat Inspection Service to issue licenses to pilots and engineers of steam-powered vessels carrying passengers. The Steamboat Inspection Service was absorbed by the newly created U.S. Department of Commerce and Labor in 1903. Ten years later, that department split and the Steamboat Inspection Service answered to the Department of Commerce, now separate from the Department of Labor.

In 1937, in response to the Merchant Marine Act of 1936, passed in the wake of the tragedy aboard the *Morro Castle*, the Steamboat Inspection Service was renamed the Bureau of Marine Inspection and Navigation, and its responsibilities were expanded to include approval of construction plans for passenger vessels. The Motorboat Act of 1940 further expanded the authority of the Bureau of Marine Inspection and Navigation to include examination of and issuing licenses to operators of smaller, power-driven vessels carrying passengers for hire. On July 16, 1946, the U.S. Coast Guard inherited the Bureau of Marine Inspection and Navigation, which put the licensing of mariners and vessel safety under the purview of the U.S. Coast Guard, and for the first time in U.S. history placed all responsibility for maritime safety under the auspices of one federal agency. In 1982, the Coast Guard established regional exam centers (RECs) to administer exams and process mariners' documents. Currently there are seventeen regional exam centers in the United States.

There were, however, discrepancies between RECs in different parts of the country and how they handled mariners. As a result, mariners would "forum shop" for an REC most likely to handle their affairs favorably. For example, some RECs would allow mariners to take exam modules in any order, while others followed more strict guidelines. During these years, mariners submitted their applications and sat for their exams at their local REC (or their favorite REC).

In 1997, possibly partly motivated to standardize procedures as well as streamline them, the U.S. Coast Guard opened the National Maritime Center (NMC) in Arlington, Virginia, as a centralized processing house for the licensing and credentialing of merchant mariners. In 2008, the NMC moved to Martinsburg, West Virginia, and centralized its mariner license document program, changing its name to the U.S. Coast Guard Merchant Mariner Credentialing Program and changing the role of the RECs into that of clearing houses and advisory centers for mariners.

Now, a mariner submits his application to a local REC, where Coast Guard personnel scrutinize the application packet to ensure it is complete, and then the REC forwards a completed, perfected packet to the NMC on behalf of the mariner. The mariner never deals directly with the NMC, but if there's a problem, he instead deals with an advocate from his local REC. With modern computing technology, mariners can now easily track the progress of their applications through the NMC pipeline. Though skeptical at first, I have been pleased with the procedural upgrades and increased efficiency of the new system.

In 2009, the Coast Guard issued its first new Merchant Mariner Credential (MMC), which looks like a red passport booklet. In past years, mariners carried a merchant mariner's document (which was called a "Z-card"), a small laminated card that listed all the unlicensed ratings a mariner could perform. In addition, licensed mariners carried an 8" × 11" paper license, which looked like a diploma, that listed the highest license the mariner held and detailed endorsements, such as radar observer or pilotage routes, on the back.

Aboard ship, federal regulations require the posting of the ship's officers' licenses in a public place. Most ships post the licenses under glass on a board called a license rack. Now, all mariners are issued a passport-style MMC, and all licenses, endorsements, and credentials are detailed in the MMC booklet. Although it is certainly more efficient and neater, and perhaps less of a hassle than carrying multiple documents, many mariners, including me, miss the stately engraved beauty of the traditional paper licenses. Fortunately, mariners can still order them for a fee, but they are no longer required to be carried or posted.[4]

Formation of the Inter-Governmental Maritime Consultative Organization (IMCO) in 1948

In 1948 the United Nations created the Inter-Governmental Maritime Consultative Organization (IMCO) to address maritime issues of international importance. After IMCO's formation, a convention was drafted, stating IMCO's mission as being to "provide machinery for cooperation among Governments in the field of governmental regulation and practices relating to technical matters of all kinds affecting shipping engaged in international trade..."

IMCO's primary task was to generate international agreements, called conventions, which, by signing, UN member states would agree to follow. It was (and is) not required that every member state sign every convention. Conventions are not law and neither IMCO (now called the International Maritime Organization, IMO) nor the United Nations has the ability to enforce a convention. To make the terms of a convention enforceable, each member must codify the terms of the convention into their own legal system. This is why the terms of many conventions are left rather broad. In the United States, provisions of international conventions we have signed are codified into the U.S. Code, and ultimately into the Code of Federal Regulations, which offers specific guidance.

The original SOLAS Convention of 1914 focused on maritime safety in the wake of the *Titanic* disaster. SOLAS '14 was amended in 1929. When the IMCO met for the first time in 1959, it was for the purpose of adopting a new version of the SOLAS Convention, this time within the structure of an organized international group under the United Nations.

Though maritime pollution was becoming a concern, IMCO's primary focus remained maritime safety until the disastrous *Torrey Canyon* oil spill in 1967 added maritime pollution to the organization's purview. As international maritime issues multiplied and diversified, the mission of IMCO necessarily increased in scope to tackle these concerns.

In May of 1982, IMCO changed its name to its current title, the International Maritime Organization (IMO). Currently, the IMO is a specialized agency of the United Nations responsible for international maritime concerns including:

- Maritime safety
- Maritime security
- The marine environment
- Maritime legal issues, specifically liability and compensation schemes
- Maritime human element concerns
- Facilitation of the ship/port interface, especially standardization and security issues
- Technical support to nations lacking maritime expertise
- Holding international maritime conferences, which are offered in six languages

The official mission of the IMO is to:

Promote safe, secure, environmentally sound, efficient, and sustainable shipping through cooperation. This will be accomplished by adopting the highest practicable standards of maritime safety and security, efficiency of navigation and prevention and control of pollution from ships, as well as through consideration of the related legal matters and effective implementation of IMO's instruments with a view to their universal and uniform application.

The IMO boasts 173 member nations, including the United States, which joined in 1950, and three associate members, the Faroe Islands, Macao, and Hong Kong. The newest member is Palau, which joined in 2011.

The workhorses of the IMO are its agencies (both governmental and non-governmental), which specialize in discrete areas of concern. Currently, the IMO has sixty-three inter-governmental agencies (such as the International COSPAS-SARSAT Program that handles search and rescue satellites), and seventy-eight consultative non-governmental agencies (such as Greenpeace International), which are also members.[5]

The First Vessel Traffic Service (VTS)

A vessel traffic service (VTS) functions for ships much like air traffic control functions for airplanes. It is a system of traffic lanes and monitoring systems designed to minimize the frequency of collisions and organize ship traffic in busy, congested areas. VTS systems also enhance port security by monitoring port areas. The first organized VTS system was a radar-based ship observing system in Liverpool in 1949. Seven years later, the port of Rotterdam in the Netherlands had a similar shore-based radar system for observing ship traffic. The idea quickly spread through Europe.[6]

A Vessel Traffic Service workstation at Staten Island, New York.
U.S. Coast Guard photo by PA2 Mike Hvozda.

The United States was slower to embrace radar-based port management of ship traffic, and a VTS-like system wasn't in place until 1968 when the port of San Francisco installed a Harbor Advisory Radar. As the name implies, the system was completely voluntary.

It took the collision of two Standard Oil (now Chevron Oil) ships, the *Arizona Standard* and the *Oregon Standard* in San Francisco Bay to finally nudge the United States to impose mandatory compliance with VTS. For more information on this collision, please refer to Chapter 7.

Notes

1. Sources for *Lancastria* information: Jonathan Carroll, *The Sinking of the* Lancastria*: The Twentieth Century's Deadliest Naval Disaster and How Churchill Made It Disappear* (New York: Graf Publishers, 2005); Brian Crabb, *The Forgotten Tragedy: The Story of the Sinking of the* HMT Lancastria (Donington: Shaun Tyas, 2002); Jonathan Ferby, *The Sinking of the* Lancastria*: Britain's Greatest Maritime Disaster and Churchill's Cover-Up* (New York: Simon and Schuster, 2005); Hugh Sebag-Montiefiore, *Dunkirk: Fight to the Last Man* (London: Viking Press, 2006), 487–495; The *Lancastria* Archive, http://www.lancastria.org.uk/.

2. Sources for *Wilhelm Gustloff information*: Christopher Dobson, et al., *The Cruelest Night* (Boston: Little, Brown, 1979); Irwin J. Kappes, "*Wilhelm Gustloff*—The Greatest Marine Disaster in History...and why you probably never heard of it," *Military History Online*, 2003, http://www.militaryhistoryonline.com/wwii/articles/wilhelmgustloff.aspx; The *Wilhelm Gustloff* Museum, http://www.wilhelmgustloffmuseum.com/.

3. Source for United Nations information: www.un.org.

4. Sources for information on U.S. Coast Guard and licensing of mariners: U.S. Coast Guard National Maritime Center, http://www.uscg.mil/nmc/; U.S. Coast Guard history, http://www.uscg.mil/history/articles/Steamboat_Inspection_Service.asp.

5. Source for IMCO (now the IMO International Maritime Organization) information: www.imo.org.

6. Sources for Vessel Traffic Services information: World VTS Guide, http://www.worldvtsguide.org/; U.S. Coast Guard Navigation Center, http://www.navcen.uscg.gov/?pageName=vtsHistory.

Chapter 5
1950 to 1959

1954: International Convention for the Prevention of Pollution of the Sea by Oil (OILPOL '54)
1956: SS *Andrea Doria* and the MS *Stockholm,* a "radar-assisted" collision
1958: Atlantic Merchant Vessel Emergency Reporting System (AMVER)

The International Convention for the Prevention of Pollution of the Sea by Oil (OILPOL) 1954

Prior to World War II, the demand for fuel and petrochemicals were modest by today's standards, and most ships still carried kerosene for lighting. With the invention of the gas-powered automobile, and the post-war prosperity that allowed middle class families to own one, demand for petroleum products of all sorts increased. The oil tankers of the time were predominately T2 tankers of just over 16,000 DWT, quite small by today's standards.

After the war, as car ownership, industrialization, and the commensurate demand for petroleum increased, so did the number and size of the oil tankers supplying the western world. The first tanker of 100,000 DWT (almost five times the carrying capacity of a T2 tanker) was delivered in 1959. The ship was built to carry oil from the Middle East to Europe, bypassing the Suez Canal, which had been closed just three years earlier due to political unrest and was considered an unreliable route. This new ship was too large to fit through the Suez Canal anyway. Ship sizes continued to grow throughout the late 1950s and into the 1960s when Very Large Crude Carriers (VLCCs) of over 180,000 DWT were being built to take advantage of the economies of scale offered by such massive vessels.

The international maritime experts at the newly formed IMCO understood that most oil pollution came from routine operations, like pumping oily bilge water over the side, washing tanks and then pumping the oily wash-water overboard, and discharging dirty ballast into the sea. All these practices were legal and common at the time.

The International Convention for the Prevention of Pollution of the Sea by Oil (OILPOL) 1954 was the first convention adopted by the newly formed IMCO.[1]

OILPOL '54 prohibited discharging of oil, or oily mixtures, near land or in "sensitive areas" that were so environmentally sensitive they could not withstand the same level of pollution as other, supposedly more robust, areas could. It also specified oil discharge concentrations of no more than 100 parts-per-million. What it didn't do was give states the right to enforce anything beyond their territorial seas, three miles off their coasts.

The United Nations Conference on the Law of the Sea, also taking place during this period, extended a nation's right to enforce limited "sanitation regulations" out to twelve miles from their coast.

In addition to a lack of jurisdictional teeth, OILPOL '54 had other shortcomings, which caused some Mediterranean nations like France and Italy to decline ratification of the original convention. One problem was that OILPOL '54 made the Atlantic Ocean a "special area," which meant ships had to dispose of their oily slops in the Mediterranean, before entering the Atlantic.

The *Torrey Canyon* spill of 1967 showed that the provisions of OILPOL '54 were inadequate to address all the issues brought to light by a massive oil spill off a sensitive, economically important coastline. New pollution-prevention conventions were eventually drafted that dealt specifically with the legal aspects of who should pay for cleanup efforts, and how victims of pollution should be compensated. But the new conventions took years to take effect, so to address immediate concerns, amendments had to be made to OILPOL '54, even prior to its effective date.

Despite infrequent but spectacular spills like the *Torrey Canyon*, most oil pollution still came from tank washing. Addressing this operational source of pollution was a 1969 amendment to OILPOL '54 that required tankers to handle dirty tank washing water in a new way. Instead of washing a tank with sea water, and then just pumping the wash-water over the side, the wash-water was to be kept aboard and sent to a decanting tank. While in the decanting tank, as the vessel made her way in ballast to the next load port, the water and oil would separate. On arrival at the load port, the now relatively clean water on the bottom of the decanting tank could be pumped overboard, leaving the oil in the tank. Special water-indicating paste was applied to the metal tank sounding tapes so ship's personnel knew exactly where the cut was between water and oil, and how much water they could pump out. The new cargo of oil could then be loaded right on top. This was called the "load on top" method.

Another amendment took effect in 1971 limiting the size of cargo tanks, presumably to limit the amount of oil spilled should a tank become compromised.

Most of the amendments to OILPOL '54 were passed without much fuss, probably because it was quietly recognized that most nation states, even the most powerful nations at the time, could not really enforce the provisions much beyond their shores. Understanding these limitations, it is not surprising that even the major oil companies supported most of the new provisions.

Plagued with gaps and omissions though it was, OILPOL '54 was, at least, a start.

Recognizing the inadequacy of OILPOL '54, even with all its amendments, to address issues surfacing with the new supertankers, a new convention was drafted to address pollution of the oceans, and not just by oil.

In 1973, a new conference was held to draft a more inclusive pollution control convention, the International Convention for the Prevention of Pollution from Ships 1973 (MARPOL' 73). For details on MARPOL '73 see Appendix A.

The SS *Andrea Doria* and the MS *Stockholm*

There is a common misconception amongst people who don't have a solid grasp of the collision regulations, that one vessel can be entirely at fault for a collision between two moving vessels. Nothing could be farther from the truth. The collision of the sumptuous Italian passenger liner *Andrea Doria* and the Swedish American Lines' *Stockholm* on July 25, 1956, just off the coast of New York will illustrate why, in any collision, both vessels are often, to some degree, at fault. The collision resulted in one of the greatest rescues in history, with 1,644 people plucked from the sea.

The *Andrea Doria*, carrying an almost full complement of passengers, was westbound from Europe, just a day from her New York destination. On the afternoon of July 24, while about 150 miles east of the Nantucket Lightship, she encountered fog, which is not uncommon during summers along the northeast coast below Nantucket, where the Labrador current carries icy waters southward, toward the warm waters of the northbound Gulf Stream.

The *Andrea Doria* was equipped with two radars, and all the usual navigational equipment of the day, and everything was in good working order. The magnificent ship, in accordance with the new safety and construction requirements of SOLAS '48, had two-compartment subdivision, which meant any two compartments could be flooded and the vessel would remain afloat. She also had double bottoms and cofferdams around the engine room. She had aluminum lifeboats with capacity for 200 more people than the *Andrea Doria* could carry. Neither she nor the *Stockholm* had a bridge-to-bridge VHF radio, which is now required communication equipment.

People felt safe on the trans-Atlantic liners, and rightly so. Since World War 1 not a single person, of the over 26 million people that had traveled the routes, had died due to a shipwreck or collision on the Europe-to-U.S. run.

When the fog set in, Captain Piero Calamai started sounding the *Andrea Doria*'s fog signal and put the engines on standby, but he maintained the ship's speed at around twenty-one knots, probably in an effort to maintain his scheduled arrival time at New York. To have been in complete accord with the collision regulations of the day, Captain Calamai would have had to slow his vessel to the point that he could stop her in half the prevailing visibility, which in a thick fog would, essentially, require she be stopped, and few if any ship's masters of the day complied with such an unrealistic mandate.

The *Stockholm* was proceeding outbound from New York, eastbound for Gothenburg, Sweden, under the command of Captain Harry Nordenson. As a result of a collision between an American steamer and a French ship in the fog off Nantucket in the 1850s which killed over 300 people, recommended shipping routes had been established off the east coast (under the North Atlantic Tracking Agreement) to keep ships going in opposite directions apart. The SOLAS '48 Convention recommended (but did not require) that eastbound ships follow a track twenty miles south of the Nantucket lightship.

For the *Stockholm*, such a route would have added 40 miles to the eastbound Atlantic crossing, so, the safer route not being required, Captain Nordenson opted for a more northerly course that would take him just one mile south of the Nantucket lightship, rather than the recommended twenty miles. He had done this many times before without incident. This decision meant the *Stockholm* and the *Andrea Doria* were bound for almost the same spot off Nantucket, and were following almost reciprocal paths from and to New York's harbor.

The *Stockholm*'s third mate assumed the watch at 2000 on July 24, and, though the weather was clear at the time, he was instructed to keep a sharp lookout for traffic and fog. The Nantucket lightship was about forty-three miles off, fine on the port bow. He checked his radar and saw no contacts.

Captain Nordenson went to his cabin at about 2200, leaving instructions to call him when the ship approached the Nantucket lightship. At around 2200 the *Stockholm*'s third mate took a fix using radio direction finding (RDF) beacons and discovered the ship was experiencing a northerly set, but he chose not to adjust his course. At about 2230 he took another fix and this time, discovering he was almost three miles to the north of the track line, he ordered the helmsman to steer a course two degrees to the right to compensate for the current and keep the lightship to port.

Later in his watch, around 2250, he ordered another two-degree course alteration to starboard. At the same time he also noticed a new radar contact. The third mate began a radar plot of the contact when it was about ten miles off, but did not notify Captain Nordenson of the new contact.

The third mate testified that the contact's bearing was opening, so he had assumed the vessel would pass well clear at about three-quarters of a mile to port, which was less than Captain Nordenson's prescribed minimum passing distance of one mile. The third mate stated that he had planned to turn right a bit more to get the one-mile passing distance, but was waiting for a visual sighting before coming right any further. When the contact was four miles away, the *Stockholm*'s third mate said that he decreased the radar range from fifteen to five miles, but, puzzlingly, he still couldn't see the approaching vessel visually. (There is strong evidence that the radar was not actually on the fifteen-mile scale as the third mate testified, but was instead on a five-mile range. There is also solid reconstruction evidence the contact could not have been where he said it was.)

The *Stockholm* was in clear visibility, but the third mate said he couldn't see the lights of the nearby approaching vessel in the darkness. It probably didn't occur to the unseasoned third mate that the other vessel, the *Andrea Doria,* was shrouded in fog, which would have masked the glow of her navigation lights.

The *Stockholm*'s third mate testified he was also concerned that if his vessel kept setting to the north, he could pass too close to, or even north of the Nantucket lightship, which would put him dangerously near Nantucket Shoals, which lay just north of the lightship.

Despite his doubts, the third mate never called the master, nor did he slow the vessel down.

Given conflicting testimony, and multiple reliable reconstructions of the incident, there is every indication the *Stockholm*'s third mate did not correctly relate the times and circumstances surrounding the incident, so the exact times of some events and activities aboard the *Stockholm* are unknown.

Meanwhile, the westbound *Andrea Doria* passed the Nantucket lightship at 2220 and altered course slightly northward, almost due west, while steaming in thick fog at twenty-one knots.

In contrast with the manning of the *Stockholm*'s bridge by a lone, unseasoned third mate, the *Andrea Doria*'s Captain Calamai was in the wheelhouse, as is prudent in such circumstances, along with two other deck officers. At around 2245 the *Andrea Doria*'s second mate picked up a radar contact at seventeen miles, about four degrees on the starboard bow, and, due to its relative motion, he correctly determined the contact was eastbound and would probably pass about a mile to starboard. Despite the *Andrea Doria* being equipped with a modern Marconi Locator Graph, which allowed rapid-plot solutions for radar contacts, no one made any effort to plot the contact, so maneuvering decisions were not based on any calculations or disciplined observations. No one was concerned as it appeared the eastbound ship would pass clear to starboard, as long as neither vessel changed course.

The *Stockholm*'s radar indicated the contact was getting closer, and the third mate was weighing his options. The *Stockholm* was headed easterly at about nineteen knots. Despite all evidence indicating the *Andrea Doria* was indeed to *Stockholm*'s starboard, the *Stockholm*'s third mate elected to come starboard, right toward the *Andrea Doria*.

Back aboard the *Andrea Doria*, Captain Calamai was on the bridge and was concerned about the approaching contact, and when the *Stockholm* was about three-and-a-half miles off, he ordered a slight course change of four degrees to port to open the passing distance. Because changes in a contact vessel's course can take minutes to become apparent on radar, the *Stockholm*'s course alteration to starboard was not yet apparent.

The *Andrea Doria* emerged from the fog when the *Stockholm* was only about two miles away. The *Andrea Doria*'s Captain Calamai was shocked to see the aspect of the *Stockholm* on the starboard bow, since she was previously steaming eastward and would have passed comfortably starboard-to-starboard, but was now crossing from starboard to port! Captain Calamai ordered hard left rudder, but it was too late, and, at 2311, the *Stockholm*'s bow rammed into the starboard side of the *Andrea Doria*, just forward of the wheelhouse, at full sea speed.

The collision tore open the hull of the *Andrea Doria* and water began flooding the ship. The *Stockholm* penetrated nearly forty feet into the *Andrea Doria,* and crashed through five of her decks, penetrated at and below the waterline, and crashed seven feet into her double bottoms. It being near the end of her voyage, most of the *Andrea Doria*'s fuel tanks were empty or nearly so. Several of *Andrea Doria*'s starboard fuel tanks were ruptured and flooded with

The MS *Stockholm* after her collision with the SS *Andrea Doria*. *Digitized by the State Library of Queensland.*

seawater. The five empty fuel tanks on her port side remained intact but the flooding of the starboard tanks and resulting imbalance caused a dangerous starboard list that could not be remedied.

The ships were locked together for about thirty seconds, but as they began to separate the *Andrea Doria* still had some way on, and she dragged herself along the crumpled bow of the *Stockholm* until they finally separated and the *Andrea Doria* slipped away into the fog.

The *Stockholm* experienced flooding forward and was dangerously down by the head, but was able to empty her forward tanks such that she was floating and stable. Five of the *Stockholm*'s crew died in the collision.

Aboard the *Stockholm*, right after the collision, crew members heard a young girl's voice speaking Spanish. To their amazement they found a girl lying behind a bulwark. The girl, Linda Morgan, had been sharing a cabin aboard the *Andrea Doria* with her half-sister. The impact had thrown Linda onto the crushed bow of the *Stockholm*, where, but for a broken arm, she landed safely and with full consciousness. Her half-sister perished in the crash but Linda survived and became known as the "miracle girl."

At about 2320, roughly ten minutes after the collision, the *Andrea Doria* transmitted a signal on her radiotelegraph that would automatically activate radio alarms on nearby ships. Roughly thirty minutes after the collision, the *Andrea Doria* had taken on a devastating, uncorrectable starboard list of about twenty degrees. Captain Calamai elected to abandon ship but decided not to sound the general alarm as he didn't want to panic passengers. The significant list probably panicked them enough. Captain Calamai instead gave the order for passengers to go to their muster stations.

Passengers gathered on the high (port) side of the vessel, not realizing that lifeboats couldn't be launched from that side. Many had carried their luggage with them to the muster stations, assuming they could bring all their belongings with them in the lifeboats. All the baggage clogged the decks.

Though the *Andrea Doria* carried enough lifeboats, half of them were unusable due to the list. The eight lifeboats on the starboard side that could be launched only had capacity for 1,008 people, not the 1,706 aboard, and launching those boats was extremely hazardous. Crew struggled to free the eight boats on the starboard side, even if it meant having to load passengers while the lifeboats were in the water. Fortunately, this happened in a busy shipping lane, and several vessels responded to render aid. Since the incident occurred relatively near land, television crews also arrived.

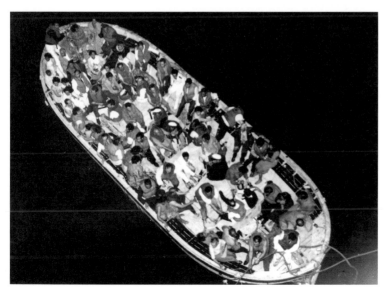

Survivors from the SS *Andrea Doria* crowded into a lifeboat. *Associated Press.*

The *Île de France*, a large French liner which was eastbound, turned around and arrived at the scene three hours later, using ten of her lifeboats as shuttle craft. She was instrumental in rescuing the majority of the *Andrea Doria*'s passengers. The *Stockholm* had taken many survivors aboard, as had other vessels which had come to the scene. Sadly, some of the *Andrea Doria*'s crew had abandoned the ship before helping passengers. By daybreak, all surviving passengers had been taken off the *Andrea Doria*. The list continually worsened, and at 1009 July 26, 1956, the *Andrea Doria* sank, thankfully with no souls aboard but forty-six of the *Andrea Doria*'s passengers and five crewmen of the *Stockholm* died as a result of the collision. She had remained afloat for eleven hours after initial impact.

Hours after the MS *Stockholm* hit her, the sumptuous Italian liner SS *Andrea Doria* finally rolls over and sinks. *Associated Press / Harry Trask.*

Aftermath

Over a thousand lawsuits were filed in New York, and the unwieldy cases were eventually consolidated into one massive suit. Due to a speedy financial settlement, a public court case was avoided and fact-finding efforts, rendered moot, were abruptly stopped, no doubt to the relief of both sides.

Though there are competing versions of the events leading up to the casualty, reliable eyewitness testimony and detailed analysis of the collision indicates that both versions of the radar sightings could not be simultaneously correct. Captain Calamai of the *Andrea Doria* insisted the two ships were passing starboard-to-starboard, the third mate of the *Stockholm* insisted they were passing port to port. One version obviously had to be mistaken, or worse, a lie.

Captain Robert J. Meurn of the United States Merchant Marine Academy (an instructor of mine when I was a cadet) has, with his colleague John C. Carrothers, spent decades researching the collision.

Their findings are detailed in Captain Meurn's book *Anatomy of a Collision: Are the Passengers Safe?* By using data from both vessels' course recorders, credible eyewitness testimony, and other evidence collected over many years, Captain Meurn was able to reconstruct the track of both vessels and conclusively prove that the *Stockholm*'s version of the incident is physically impossible.

Physical evidence based on courses, speeds, and distances indicate the *Stockholm*, for whatever reason, turned to starboard, directly in the path of the westbound *Andrea Doria*. Capt. Meurn believes that the third mate of the *Stockholm* probably misinterpreted the radar information he was getting and drastically overestimated the distance between the ships, and then lied about the circumstances surrounding the incident. Capt. Meurn opines that poor design and poor lighting of the range settings on the radar, and operating at night in a dimly lit bridge may have contributed to this error and led to a casualty that a simple low wattage light bulb may have prevented.

As a result of this collision, the necessity for reliable communications between vessels on the high seas was brought to the forefront. At the time of the collision, vessels on inland waters of the United States were already using radios to communicate when negotiating passing arrangements, but radio communication was not required. It wasn't until 1972 that the United States required vessels of over 300 gross tons on inland waters to carry a VHF radio. This applied to any vessel calling at a U.S. port, thus the natural result was that many ocean-going vessels equipped themselves with VHF radios specifically for the U.S. trade, and just left them in place. Even having the radios aboard, however, was not enough to convince mariners of the merits of their use, and it was years before radio communications between vessels became commonplace.

The need for better training on the use of radar to prevent collisions was another weakness exposed by this incident. The collision rules (COLREGS) were, largely in response to this incident, amended to encourage the use of radar plotting, not just observation, and radar courses and certifications were soon required for deck officers. Radars are now better designed, with less ambiguity and more understandable user interfaces.

Other changes included the modern requirement to carry 100 percent lifeboat capacity on each side of a vessel (in case a severe list, fire, or other problem precluded launching from one side), not just 50 percent per side, as was the case on the *Andrea Doria* and other ships of that era.

Regulations now require officers to take classes in bridge team management. Modern requirements dictate that companies maintain policies setting forth how many officers must be on the bridge in restricted visibility and other critical circumstances. Cruise ships, for example, now require at least two officers on the bridge at all times, and more in congested waters, restricted visibility, and during arrival and departure.

The dramatic public sinking of the *Andrea Doria* marked the end of the trans-Atlantic liner trade, as trans-Atlantic jet travel became the travel mode of choice.[2]

The Atlantic Merchant Vessel Emergency Reporting System (AMVER)

AMVER is probably the most delayed consequence of the *Titanic* disaster of 1912. Though the idea of an international ship tracking and distress reporting system isn't new, it required modern computers and communications to bring it to reality. AMVER is still the only worldwide system of its kind. The system, which benefits all nations, is paid for by American taxpayers, just as is GPS and other navigational aids.

AMVER became operational in 1958 as an experimental and voluntary program housed at the New York Customs House. Though AMVER was an American program, ships of over 1,000 GRT of all nations were encouraged to participate if their voyages lasted over twenty-four hours. During the initial phase, the system only covered the North Atlantic.

Participating vessels communicate their position, course, and speed once daily to AMVER. Ships also report their departure and arrival ports and dates, and their anticipated routes and speeds.

Participating ships complete vessel profiles ahead of time, detailing the ship's complement, if any medical personnel are carried aboard, if the vessel has any special firefighting or salvage capabilities, or other equipment that might prove useful in an emergency.

The original computer system, crude by today's standards, was an IBM RAMAC (Random Access Method Accounting Control) that could predict a vessel's future position using dead reckoning formulae. The computer would generate a picture of all participating ships in a given area of the ocean.

By 1960 over 5,000 vessels had agreed to participate. During a typical twenty-four-hour day, an average of over 700 vessels would be tracked and plotted. Two years later, search and rescue centers could access AMVER information and use it to locate a vessel in distress and then to route nearby ships to the stricken vessel.

The system was so successful that by 1963 AMVER was tracking ships worldwide. The "A" in the acronym AMVER, initially meaning Atlantic, was no longer appropriate for a worldwide system, so AMVER was changed to mean Automated Merchant VEssel Reporting program, but its function remains unchanged.

As AMVER's success became more widely known, increasing numbers of coastal radio stations volunteered to participate, their frequencies being published in the *AMVER Bulletin* magazine.

In 1971, the system's name (but not the acronym) was again changed, this time to mean Automated Mutual-assistance VEssel Rescue, but the world still simply referred to it as AMVER.

In the 1980s, AMVER embraced satellite technology and began cooperating with the joint U.S. and Russian COSPAS-SARSAT satellite search and rescue system. Also in the 1980s, the United States made participation in AMVER mandatory for U.S. flag ships. AMVER had finally replaced the U.S.MER service that tracked only U.S. flag ships.

As search and rescue technology evolved to include the Global Maritime Distress and Safety System (GMDSS), Emergency Position Indicating Radio Beacons (EPIRBs) that uplink distress location to satellites, and satellite communications became commonplace, AMVER redefined its role to assisting with diverting vessels to investigate possible casualties and marshalling nearby ships and rescue resources if the distress call turns out to be legitimate.

Over 22,000 ships from hundreds of nations currently participate in AMVER. AMVER handles an average of 4,000 ships and 14,000 messages per day, and the numbers continue to grow as more nations and companies recognize the benefits of participation.[3]

Notes

1. Sources for OILPOL 1954 information: Alan Khee-Jin Tan, *Vessel-Source Marine Pollution: The Law and Politics of International Regulation* (New York: Cambridge University Press, 2006); www.imo.org.

2. Sources for *Andrea Doria/Stockholm* information: Craig Allen, *Farwell's Rules of the Road* (Annapolis, MD: Naval Institute Press, 2004); Richard A. Cahill, *Collisions and Their Causes, 3rd ed.* (London: The Nautical Institute, 2002); Richard A. Cahill, *Disasters at Sea*; Richard Goldstein, *Desperate Hours: The Epic Rescue of the* Andrea Doria (New York: John Wiley and Sons, 2003); Capt. Robert J. Meurn, *Anatomy of a Collision: Are the Passengers Safe?* (Mustang, OK: Tate Publishing, 2013); *The Sinking of the Andrea Doria,* Secrets of the Dead Series on Public Broadcast Service, http://www.pbs.org/wnet/secrets/the-sinking-of-the-andrea-doria/142/.

3. Source for AMVER information: http://www.amver.com/.

Chapter 6
1960 to 1969

The Suez Canal

The closing of the Suez Canal briefly in 1956 and again from 1967 to 1975 was more than an expensive inconvenience for ship owners and operators. The political turmoil of the Middle East, and resultant interference with this vital trade route between Asia and Europe, impacted shipping and influenced the type and scale of new shipbuilding far into the next decades. It is important to appreciate the historical context of the region in order to understand the shipbuilding trend of the 1960s and '70s of building increasingly massive ships, and the catastrophic casualties that befell these behemoths.

The Suez Canal, long contemplated by myriad rulers and visionaries, was meaningfully conceived in 1858 when French diplomat and engineer Vicomte Ferdinand Marie de Lesseps finally convinced Egyptian Viceroy Said Pasha to take on the project. La Compagnie Universelle du Canal Maritime de Suez was formed—with shares being owned by French and Egyptian concerns—and given the authority to dig the canal and operate it for ninety-nine years, after which control of the canal would return to Egypt.

On November 17, 1869, after ten years of construction that went massively over budget, the 101-mile-long canal opened, linking the Gulf of Suez at the northern end of the Red Sea with the Mediterranean Sea, and efficiently linking Asia and Europe for the first time.

In 1875, debt forced Egyptian interests to sell their shares in the Canal Authority. The British, despite initially opposing the building of the canal, were a major sea power and trading nation and viewed the new canal as now vital to their interests, so the British bought the Egyptian shares.

The 1888 Convention of Constantinople, an international convention signed by most European nations, ensured the canal would remain open to ships of all nations and assigned Britain the duty to keep the canal open and neutral, even during periods of war. Even so, control of the canal remained contentious.

Roughly fifty years later, the Anglo-Egyptian Treaty of 1936 made Egypt fundamentally independent, but gave Britain the right to maintain military control of the entry points to the canal. This never sat well with Egyptian nationalists—especially after World War II—and they remained resolved that the canal should be entirely under Egyptian control.

Despite British military control (and despite the 1888 Constantinople Convention), when Israel was formed by the United Nations in 1948, the Egyptian government responded by prohibiting vessels coming from, or headed to, Israel from using the canal. By 1951 Egypt was demanding Britain withdraw from the Canal Zone and repudiate the 1936 Treaty.

In 1954, the British and Egyptians signed a seven-year agreement repealing the provisions of the Anglo-Egyptian Treaty, providing for the withdrawal of British troops from the Canal Zone, and allowing Egypt to take over the British posts. It is important to note that by 1955, approximately two-thirds of Europe's oil was shipped through the Suez Canal. The British had completely withdrawn their troops from the Canal Zone by June of 1956.

In the 1950s, with financial support from the United States and Britain, Egypt was building the Aswan Dam, but by 1956 both western nations had withdrawn their support. In response, on July 26, 1956, Egypt's President Gamal Abdel Nasser announced he was nationalizing the canal (presumably in order to collect canal fees to help pay for the Aswan Dam project) and transferring ownership and control to a newly formed, and entirely Egyptian-run, Egyptian Suez Canal Authority. Nasser summarily expelled all British oil workers and embassy officials.

On October 29, 1956, Israel, joined almost immediately by France and Britain, invaded Egypt to regain control of the canal and ensure it remained open to all vessels. Two days after the invasion, on October 31, the British began bombing raids on Cairo and Cairo International Airport. In response, Egypt blocked the canal and sank forty ships. The Arab world still characterizes the attack as "the Tripartite Aggression," while the western world refers to these events as the "Suez Crisis."

By November 7, 1956, the western forces claimed to have control over the Canal Zone. Demonstrating record efficiency, within a month of the Israeli invasion the United Nations had negotiated a truce between Egypt, Israel, Britain, and France. Canadian Lester Pearson, then serving as Canada's Secretary of State for External Affairs, proposed the creation of the first UN Peacekeeping Force, to be stationed at the Sinai to keep the canal free and open for everyone to use, and who could only be removed if both Israel and Egypt agreed. The UN, fulfilling Pearson's vision, formed the United Nations Emergency Force and posted armed peacekeepers to keep the canal open. On November 21, 1956, UN troops landed at Port Said, Egypt. All British, French, and Israeli troops were cleared from the Canal Zone by midnight, December 22, 1956. As a result of the truce, the sunken ships were cleared away, and the Suez Canal reopened in March 1957. Lester Pearson was later awarded the Nobel Peace Prize for his innovative solution to the conflict.

By 1962 Egypt had finally paid off its debt to La Compagnie Universelle du Canal Maritime de Suez and took complete control of the canal, but conflict in the area continued.

A mere five years later, on June 5, 1967, at the beginning of the Six-Day Arab-Israeli War, Egypt again closed the Suez Canal—this time for exactly eight years. The Suez Canal didn't reopen until June 5, 1975, at the end of the Yom Kippur War, with the signing of a disengagement accord. The shock to international trade was without measure. The closure was so unexpected that fifteen ships, called "the yellow fleet," got trapped inside.[1]

The Age of the Supertankers

The first tanker of 100,000 DWT was delivered in 1959 (two years after the Suez Canal had been reopened) and was designed to carry oil from the Middle East to the oil-thirsty markets in Europe and the West, by way of the Cape of Good Hope, avoiding the political instability of the Suez Canal. Trading nations, rightfully concerned about reliable accessibility of the Suez Canal, began ordering ships, especially tankers, of increasingly larger size to retain some economies of scale despite having to bypass the Suez Canal and thus travel farther to reach Europe.

In 1966, the first tanker over 200,000 DWT was launched, double the size of the average large tanker of just five years earlier. Tanker growth was not a slow process, but a sudden surge in deadweight, and a commensurate increase in length, beam, draft, as well as all dimensions associated with cargo piping systems and pumps. By the mid-1960s, Very Large Crude Carriers (VLCCs) of 180,000 DWT and larger were being ordered routinely. The first VLCC entered service in 1968.

By the 1970s, supertankers were the primary class of vessel carrying oil from the Middle East. These are not the modest 532-foot, 16,500 DWT T2 tankers of World War II, but are massive, lumbering behemoths of over 1,000 feet in length, carrying millions of gallons of oil. The largest ships, the Ultra Large Crude Carriers (ULCCs) have carrying capacities upwards of 500,000 DWT, over thirty times the carrying capacity of T2 tankers. The *Knock Nevis*, a ULCC and the largest tanker ever built, carried 564,763 DWT and was over 1,500 feet long. At her load draft of eighty feet, she was too deep even for the English Channel. Only a few ULCCs are still in service, their size and operational demands being too restrictive to be practical.

For perspective, a deadweight ton (metric tonne) is 2,204.6 pounds, which would average about 315 gallons, depending on the density of the product. Not all of a vessel's deadweight capacity can be used to carry cargo. Thus a "small" VLCC of 180,000 DWT could carry about 80 million gallons of cargo, and a "large" ULCC of 400,000 DWT could carry roughly 126 million gallons.

Tankers have always been more susceptible to fire and explosion than dry cargo vessels, but the increasing size of the tank vessels being built during this period made the consequences of tanker casualties truly staggering. The ships were complex and massive. When they exploded, grounded, or collided, which they were doing with discomforting regularity, the scale of the incidents was devastating. If the casualty happened far at sea, or near a third-world or developing nation, the industrialized world took little notice. But as you will read, when a casualty or pollution incident occurred near a populated, first-world nation's coast, the industrialized world reacted.

During this period, ships were blowing up with increasing frequency, often during tank cleaning operations when the cargo tanks were empty.

During a horrible three weeks in December of 1969, three VLCCs exploded—all were cleaning tanks at the time. Two of the ships, the *Marpessa* and the *Mactra*, both ships of over 200,000 DWT, were Shell Oil tankers. The *Marpessa* was just two months old, and her loss held the record for the largest vessel ever lost at the time. She exploded off Dakar, Senegal, while tank cleaning on December 12, 1969. Two crew members were killed and the ship sank three days later, her back broken by the explosion and resulting flooding stresses.

Seventeen days later, on December 29, 1969, another Shell tanker, the *Mactra*, blew up while cleaning tanks in the Mozambique Channel in Africa. Two people died. She remained afloat and was towed to Durban, where she was repaired and eventually returned to service. The next day, December 30, 1969, a third ship, the Norwegian *Kong Haakon* VII, owned by H. Reksten, was, at 219,000 DWT, the largest ship in the Norwegian fleet at the time. She exploded while cleaning tanks off the coast of Monrovia. She was just seven months old. Fortunately, no one was killed and the ship was repaired and returned to service.

When fluids are passed through a small orifice under pressure, as happens during tank cleaning, static electricity is generated. Shell Oil deduced that the high-pressure jets of oil and water used to clean cargo tanks were at such a high velocity that they were creating static electricity inside the tank. As the size of the ships (and thus their tanks) grew, and high-pressure automatic tank-washing machines were increasingly being used to clean the sticky residue off the surfaces of cargo tanks, tanker explosions started happening with almost predictable regularity.

During tank washing, it was discovered, there were literally lightning bolts arcing across the tanks, which, having just carried oil, now had an explosive mixture of air and petroleum vapors inside. If the ratios of fuel and oxygen were right, all it took was a single spark of static electricity to ignite the mixture.

As a result of these explosions, Shell started "inerting" all cargo tanks on its tankers. Inerting a tank is the process of flooding a space that has an explosive mixture of fuel and air with an oxygen-deficient gas, which deprives the fire triangle of oxygen so nothing can burn, thus, theoretically, nothing can explode. Some tankers carrying clean cargos (like gasoline or naphtha) used nitrogen as the inert gas, so as not to contaminate the delicate cargo. Crude oil ships used engine exhaust gas which had been cooled and cleaned of sulfur and other corrosive contaminants. A properly inerted atmosphere will have an oxygen content at or below 5 percent, which is far below the 16 percent needed to sustain combustion.

Tankers have been exploding since they were first built, and Socal Oil Company (now Chevron) had experimented with inerting cargo tanks as early as the 1920s, but not for safety reasons. Inert gas, being low in oxygen (the oxidizer necessary for rust to form) was thought to offer enhanced corrosion resistance to the tank's steel. After trying inert gas as a corrosion inhibitor, the oil companies found no appreciable benefit and abandoned the practice.

Tanker explosions were nothing new. In 1932, a Sun Oil tanker, the *Bidwell*, exploded while she was cleaning tanks—she exploded four separate times, as adjoining tanks blew up. Sun Oil's experts knew that shoreside refineries were already inerting their tanks, so Sun Oil fitted inert gas systems on all its tankers. Contrary to others' experience with inerting, Sun Oil discovered significantly reduced corrosion rates in tanks that were inerted.

Despite Sun Oil's positive experience with inerting tanks, during World War II tankers were generally not inerted and continued to either blow up on their own, or explode, rather than just burn, when they were struck by bombs or torpedoes. Tanker explosions continued with fairly predictable regularity into the 1950s and '60s.

The U.S. Navy, Esso, and other companies flirted with inert gas systems during the 1960s. In 1963, British Petroleum was the next company to inert its tankers, though their implementation was, again, primarily for corrosion resistance. By the mid-1960s, as discussed above, tanker size began to grow exponentially, so when they exploded, the results were truly spectacular.

Despite explorations into tank inerting as far back as the 1930s, and the implementation of inerting by some enlightened tanker operators, it was not mandated in the United States until 1974, but even then, only for new crude oil tankers over 100,000 DWT, which were trading in the United States.

By the 1980s, maritime insurers were experiencing increased financial losses due to tanker casualties, and they began to recognize a relatively new and increasingly costly and unpredictable source of financial exposure—the environmental impact of ship disasters. As mentioned in Chapter 1, sometimes an insurance requirement can be more effective than legislation at prompting, or even forcing, change. Such was the case with tank inerting.

In response to the escalation in tanker explosions, the IMO generated requirements for inert gas in 1978, but the requirements were slow to phase in. Lloyd's of London started charging an extra surcharge to VLCCs that didn't have inert gas systems. Not surprisingly, in response to both regulatory and insurance pressures, by 1983 most VLCCs had inert gas systems.

Some maritime experts feel, as does this author, that the IMO, being a body of nations sensitive to the economic impact of regulation, labors under an inherent conflict between promulgating conventions that enhance safety and environmental protections and the member states' desires to maintain a robust, economically competitive commercial maritime sector. In light of this natural tension within the IMO, insurance requirements for inert gas systems may have accelerated their implementation faster than anything the IMO did.

Another reason often cited for the increased severity of marine casualties during this decade was the increasing use of "open registry" nations to register ships, especially tankers, and the commensurate decrease in regulatory compliance that often came with flying a flag of convenience.

It is not to say that all ships flagged under open registries should be automatically suspect. Some of the best equipped and best run ships in the fleet today are operated by major oil companies under flags of convenience, but during this decade open registry states were typically developing nations offering the prospect of weak or nonexistent enforcement to ship owners.

The group most motivated to see stricter regulation was, understandably, the insurance lobby. Open registry states, typically poor nations eager for the revenue stream generated by ship owners paying to flag their ships, are often not enthusiastic about enforcing regulations their customers don't also embrace. Classification societies, which are paid by the ship owner, were also not natural supporters of regulations perceived as too demanding or too expensive by their customers. Ship owners, whose business is to make a profit, do not historically lead the charge for more regulation unless doing so ultimately enhances their profitability. Thus, it is the insurers, the entities which really feel the economic consequences of a loss, that often spearhead change.

These dynamics, especially the logical aversion to regulation harbored by most businesses, may account for some of the seemingly unforgivable delays in safety regulations during this period.[2]

The SS *Torrey Canyon*

Though a major international oil pollution convention existed (OILPOL '54 was in force in most major maritime nations) oil pollution was still not a major consideration for most countries, in fact, it was barely on the legislative radar during the first half of this decade. But the world was beginning to wake up to the environmental costs of highly industrialized oil-based economies and the cumulative effects of pollution from oil and refinery byproducts. In 1965, the IMO established a Sub-Committee on Oil Pollution specifically to handle oil pollution issues.

The grounding of the *Torrey Canyon* in 1967 changed everything. The disaster was the largest spill to date and it polluted the popular Cornish and Devonian beaches, which are environmentally delicate, highly visible areas of a powerful maritime nation. The grounding highlighted not only the shortcomings of OILPOL '54, but also the ineffective measures then in place to compensate for economic losses flowing from pollution incidents. The grounding of the *Torrey Canyon* ultimately inspired amendments to MARPOL and other conventions, which were designed to provide mechanisms to compensate for economic losses.

The grounding of the *Torrey Canyon* was an example of an almost perfectly forged error chain, the disaster being the result of multiple errors in judgment, multiple examples of poor navigational practice by multiple officers, and communication difficulties due to a personality conflict between officers. Because this casualty directly and indirectly impacted so many lives, it has been heavily researched and modern mariners should learn from its timeless lessons.

Any one of the modern bridge team management (BTM) dictates, such as proper communications between the watch team and the master, cross-checking of all navigational equipment, or the charge to cross-check a vessel's position using all available tools, could have broken the error chain that doomed the *Torrey Canyon*. As you read her story, consider how differently a properly run bridge team employing bridge team management and bridge resource management (BRM) skills would have handled a similar situation.

The *Torrey Canyon* was built by Newport News Shipbuilding and Drydock Company of Virginia in 1959 and flew, as was becoming the custom for tankers of her sort during this period, the Liberian flag. The *Torrey Canyon* was owned by the Barracuda Tanker Company of Bermuda, a subsidiary of Union Oil of California, and she was named after a California oil field that had been discovered by (and named after) one of the founders of Union Oil. In 1965 she was jumboized by Sasebo Heavy Industries of Japan, which cut her in half and added a longer midsection, thus increasing her length from 810 to 974 feet, almost doubling her cargo capacity. After her jumboizing, she was one of the largest vessels afloat at the time.

The *Torrey Canyon,* with a deadweight capacity of 120,000 tons, though perhaps average by today's standards, was a massive crude oil tanker for her time and multiple times larger than previous decade's modest T2-class tankers.

The *Torrey Canyon*'s final voyage began with her departure on February 19, 1967, from Kuwait's refinery at Amina al-Ahmadi, laden with a full belly of Kuwaiti crude oil (approximately 32–37 million gallons) bound for the refinery in the ancient port of Milford Haven, Wales, under a single voyage charter for British Petroleum. Too large for the Suez Canal, she made her way westward around the southern tip of Africa and the Cape of Good Hope and headed north along the western coast of Africa, to the Canary Islands. She passed between Tenerife and the Grand Canary Island on her way to Bishop Rock off the Isles of Scilly, in Cornwall, just to the southwest of the tip of the United Kingdom.

The thirty-six-man crew was entirely Italian. The master, Captain Pastrengo Rugiati, had fifteen years in command of ships. His chief mate also had significant seafaring experience and had been aboard the *Torrey Canyon* for over a year. Unfortunately, the relationship between the master and his chief mate was chilly.

According to Captain Cahill, who has made extensive study of the stranding, the vessel was appropriately outfitted for her mission and the times, except she was lacking a DECCA Navigation system, which he felt could have averted the grounding. DECCA (primarily used in Europe) was similar to LORAN (which was used in the United States and some ports in the Far East), in that it was a hyperbolic radio navigation system and very accurate for the day. The ship was outfitted with the usual complement of navigational equipment, including a gyro compass, an auto pilot (with a backup), a depth sounder, and a radar. Satellite navigation had not yet been invented, so the vessel relied primarily on celestial navigation for position fixing when not steaming within radar range of land or electronic navigation systems.

Bishop Rock, a destination point for the *Torrey Canyon*, is an intimidating jab of stone, with nothing on it but a solitary lighthouse. Conditions there are so rough that the original iron lighthouse was washed away by the violent action of the seas. Bishop Rock is the termination of the eastbound trans-Atlantic shipping routes and stands as a warning for the cluster of rocks known as the Scilly Islands that lay to the northeast. Five of the Scillys are inhabited, but most of the archipelago is barren, windswept rock. Roughly seven miles to the northeast of the Scillys lies a cluster of reefs named The Seven Stones. The Seven Stones have been a graveyard for over 200 ships. The entire area carries a grave warning in the Sailing Directions.

It was for these waters the *Torrey Canyon* was bound after she turned the corner at the Cape of Good Hope, and headed northward toward Wales. Fortunately, Bishop Rock and the Scilly Islands offer excellent radar returns.

As the vessel steamed northward, she fixed her location by way of celestial navigation. On March 17, 1967, a noon celestial fix placed the vessel about 300 miles south of the Scillys. Between celestial fixes the bridge watch was dead reckoning and waiting for land to appear on the radar scope. The winds were from the northwest, forward of the port beam, at roughly Beaufort Force 5, a fresh breeze of seventeen to twenty-five knots. No allowances had been made for set and drift and, since the noon fix, no fixes had been made for eighteen hours. (Having no positive position fix for hours was not unusual in those days.)

For the anticipated arrival at Bishop Rock on March 18, the master had left night orders to be woken either at 0600 or when the Scilly Islands appeared on radar, whichever came first. By 0600 the islands were not yet on the radar, so the chief mate woke the master at 0600 as instructed.

The Scilly Islands and Bishop Rock began to appear on radar by 0630 and their location on the port bow indicated the vessel had been set to the east, as would be expected since the vessel was on a northerly course with northwesterly winds. The chief mate determined Bishop Rock lay twelve degrees off the port bow at twenty-four miles and he adjusted course to the left to bring Bishop Rock (or what he *thought* was Bishop Rock) dead ahead. When he told the master of his course change, the master told the mate to bring the ship back to her original heading, as long as she would still clear the Scilly Islands to the east, which the master was informed, she would.

These are the same Scilly Islands upon which well over 1,400 sailors perished in a single day in October 1707, when four British warships ran aground during stormy weather, largely because, it was presumed, they could not determine their position. The Scilly Islands disaster, the most dramatic of a long history of gruesome shipwrecks there, is what prompted the British Government to pass the Longitude Act in 1714, which promised a reward to anyone who could invent a clock reliable enough to facilitate determining longitude at sea.[3]

After issuing his brusque orders, the master left the bridge, and the mate swung the ship back to starboard, and resumed the original heading. The mate took the vessel off the autopilot and into hand steering during this time—not an unusual practice when making a course change, especially when near land. No one made any attempt to determine the vessel's actual position, and no one compared the current radar information to the previous day's fix to ascertain set and drift.

Despite his assurance to the master, the mate had not positively determined if the vessel would indeed clear the Scillys to the east if she remained on her original course. In fact, the vessel's original course would have taken them right through the Scillys, if the mate had correctly identified Bishop Rock. But it was St. Mary's, a major island in the Scillys, that the mate had mistaken for Bishop Rock, and putting the ship to her original course was now taking her directly into the graveyard known as the Seven Stones.

The master arrived back on the bridge around 0700 while the ship was still roughly two hours away from the Seven Stones—she was steaming directly for them. There is no explanation as to why neither the master nor mate on watch double-checked the vessel's position. The master relied entirely on the (flawed) information given to him by a mate, who was likely disinclined to be helpful to a master who had rubbed him raw with public scolding.

The vessel plowed onward at sea speed, with no one making use of available navigational equipment, such as the ship's depth sounder or radio direction finder, to verify and cross-check the radar information. Post incident, investigators found no indication a thorough voyage plan had ever been drafted, nor had any contingency plans for set and drift been made. Captain Rugiati's night orders offered no instructions for handling a deviation from the intended track. Indeed, there was no copy of the area's Sailing Directions aboard, which admonished in no uncertain terms that large vessels should not pass between the Scilly Islands and Seven Stones and that vessels should pass east of the Seven Stones lightship. (There is in fact room for vessels to pass between the Scillys and the Seven Stones, but there is no real benefit in doing so.)

The *Torrey Canyon* was scheduled to dock at 2300 on March 18, 1967, which was the time of high water at the dock. The vessel's draft and her sag amidships necessitated that she go to anchorage upon arrival and shift cargo between cargo tanks in order to adjust her draft to accommodate the soundings at the berth. The cargo shifting was expected to take approximately five hours. If Captain Rugiati didn't make the high tide at the dock on March 18, he would have to wait for the next high tide on March 24, a delay which would be a considerable expense, which no doubt was a motivating factor in his decision to press onward, on his original course.

By 0800 on March 18, when the ship's third mate assumed the watch, fishing vessels were pestering Captain Rugiati and impeding his ability to change course to port in order to pass between the Scillys and the Seven Stones. His plan was to round the Scillys to port, and pass between the Scillys and the Seven Stones, leaving the deadly reef to his east. In reality, taking a route safely to the west of Bishop Rock would have only cost him an extra thirty minutes.

When he finally was able to change course, the master put the vessel in hand steering, but then put her back on the "iron mike" (the auto pilot) after the course changes were completed, even when surrounded by fishing vessels. (Many mariners view this as imprudent, as a vessel is most safely steered by hand when close to land or other vessels.)

The third mate, a relatively unseasoned mariner, was taking radar positions using only a single range and bearing. Not only was the third mate unwise to rely solely on a single range and bearing, the absolute minimum information required for a fix, but the fixes he ultimately generated were unreliable.

By 0840 the vessel was steaming to the east of the Scilly Islands, in autopilot, at full sea speed of seventeen knots, being pestered by fishing boats and looking to make a turn to port—but meanwhile steering directly for the Seven Stones Reef. With a shudder and crunch, the vessel ran aground at full speed at 0850 March 18, 1967, on Pollard's Rock of the Seven Stones Reef.

The SS *Torrey Canyon,* broken in two on Pollard's Rock of Seven Stones Reef off the English coast. *Associated Press.*

The spill was massive and devastating. Though dwarfed by some modern spills, at the time the *Torrey Canyon* disaster was the worst spill in history. It remains the worst spill in the history of the United Kingdom. It is estimated that 32 million to 37 million gallons of crude oil was spilled and the subsequent handling of this environmental disaster, was, by all accounts, itself a disaster.

The slick was roughly thirty-five miles long and twenty miles wide, and acres of the local beaches were covered in sludge. Over 120 miles of coastland was contaminated and over 15,000 seabirds died as a result of the oiling. Countless marine creatures were killed, injured, or sickened by the spill. Barrier booms were unsuccessful due to high seas.

Cleanup crews began spraying detergents immediately, to try and emulsify and disperse the spill. Over 10,000 tons of dispersants (ironically, also manufactured by British Petroleum) were sprayed. Experts have determined that the harmful effects of oil on living creatures are often exacerbated by the use of powerful detergents. Detergents not only break up the oil into smaller particles that are easier to ingest and absorb, they also disperse it more vertically in the water column, making it more easily absorbed by fish, which normally swim below a floating slick. Fortunately, partly as a result of this spill, the environmentalists learned about the toxicity of detergents and the same mistake was not repeated for the *Amoco Cadiz* spill in 1978.

The day of the spill, salvors from Bureau Wijsmuller, a Dutch salvage team, boarded the *Torrey Canyon* to assess the damage and explore options to salvage the ship, but rough seas made the transfer of equipment impossible. The next day, thirty-two of the thirty-six crew members were taken off the stricken vessel, leaving the master and three crew members to work with the salvage team.

On March 21 salvors opened the ship's engine room to inspect for gas they suspected was accumulating from oil leaking from the pump room. When the salvor opened the engine room door, a massive explosion blew off the vessel's engine room hatches three decks above. The blast sent several salvors into the sea, resulting in the death of one salvage engineer, and injuries to eight others. By March 23 the weather was worsening—by March 25 the winds had reached gale force.

The next day, while four salvage tugs tried to pull her off the rocks, the *Torrey Canyon* broke her back, sending even more oil into the sea. Her two sections eventually broke into three, and settled onto the reef. By March 28, ten days after the grounding, there was nothing left that could be done for the *Torrey Canyon* and Bureau Wijsmullers closed their salvage contract.

That same day the British military started dropping bombs to get the ship to sink, and flammables to set the spilled cargo oil ablaze and keep it from damaging any more shoreline. They were also hoping to burn off the remaining 40,000 tons, roughly 12 million gallons, of oil that were suspected to still be aboard. Within a day, the British authorities had dropped over 60,000 pounds of bombs (apparently, only 75 percent hit the intended target). They also dropped over 5,000 gallons of gasoline, eleven rockets, and lots of napalm (or perhaps it was liquefied petroleum jelly). Despite the onslaught, the ship just wouldn't sink, and high tides had squelched the flames. The military onslaught continued until March 30.

According to the BBC, on March 29, the oil pollution stretched from the area of Hartland Point in North Devon, to Start Point, southwest of Dartmouth. Oil was expected to reach the Solent, the strait separating the Isle of Wight from the coast of England, by April 8. Another slick was heading toward the French coast of Normandy.

The post-incident Liberian Board of Inquiry placed the blame squarely on the *Torrey Canyon*'s master, due to his unnecessary and ill-fated decision to pass between the Scilly Islands and the Seven Stones Reef. Nothing broke. None of the navigation equipment was faulty. This was an entirely man-made disaster rooted solely in one man's poor decision. As a result of the incident, Captain Rugiati had his (Liberian) master's license revoked and he never sailed again. Ironically, the bow section of the *Torrey Canyon* was eventually salvaged, with her name still visible on the bow. She was converted to a storage barge in Malta, and was renamed *Ifrikia*. The bow of the *Torrey Canyon* served as a storage barge until 1985, when it was sold to scrappers.[4]

Aftermath

ITOPF, TOVALOP, and CRISTAL

The maritime industry's immediate response to the *Torrey Canyon* disaster was the creation of the non-profit International Tanker Owners Pollution Federation (ITOPF) in 1968, which was created to indemnify victims of oil pollution. The original purpose of the ITOPF was to administer the Tanker Owners Voluntary Agreement concerning Liability for Oil Pollution (TOVALOP), a voluntary oil spill compensation scheme developed by the oil industry in the wake of the *Torrey Canyon* disaster, but this was not a regulatory scheme. Another industry agreement was the Contract Regarding an Interim Supplement to Tanker Liability for Oil Pollution (CRISTAL). Both TOVALOP and CRISTAL were voluntary schemes, created by the oil industry, and both were set to expire in 1997.

Currently, the ITOPF acts as a resource to maritime organizations and businesses, offering technical expertise on incident response, cleanup techniques, damage assessment, contingency planning, maritime training, and providing information regarding marine environmental incidents.

The *Torrey Canyon* disaster brought to light two major shortcomings in the regulatory scheme that existed at the time:

- There was no international program to compensate victims of pollution incidents
- A coastal state whose shores were threatened by a pollution incident beyond their territorial seas had no jurisdiction to intervene

In direct response to the *Torrey Canyon* disaster, the IMO set about drafting documents to address these concerns: The International Convention on Civil Liability for Oil Pollution Damage (CLC) 1969, and The International Convention Relating to Intervention on the High Seas in Cases of Oil Pollution Casualties (INTERVENTION) in 1969.

Compensation for Victims of Oil Pollution

Though the CLC was adopted in 1969, it didn't enter into force until 1975. Its aim was to ensure that adequate financial compensation was available from the owner of the offending ship to victims (people or countries) suffering losses due to oil pollution from that ship. The convention applied to all seagoing vessels carrying oil in bulk. Other than a few exemptions, the liability is "strict," meaning the owner of the spilling vessel will be liable for damages, regardless of fault. This sounds harsh, but if the incident happened through no fault of the owner, then the ship owner's liability was limited, and manageable. The convention does not apply to warships or other vessels owned or operated by a nation and used in government service.

In 1971, the IMO adopted the International Convention on the Establishment of an International Fund for Compensation for Oil Pollution Damage (FUND), which, as its name implies, established a pool of money from which to compensate victims. The FUND, drawing money from cargo interests, relieved ship owners of bearing the entire financial burden of a pollution incident. It also afforded victims financial relief if the ship owner either could not cover the loss, or could not cover the loss adequately.

In 1992, both the CLC and the FUND were amended, and effectively superseded, with two new instruments, the 1992 Civil Liability Convention and the 1992 Fund Convention, which increased the scope and liability limits of previous documents. Both instruments came into force in 1996.

With the ratification by most maritime nations of the 1992 Civil Liability Convention and the 1992 Fund Convention, and their entry into force in 1996, TOVALOP and CRISTAL became redundant, and both were simply allowed to expire in 1997.

After two more incidents, specifically the *Erika* (which broke in two during a storm off the coast of France in 1999) and the *Prestige* (which broke apart during a storm off Spain in 2002), the IMO drafted the Protocol to the 1992 Fund Convention (Supplementary Fund Protocol), which was adopted in 2003, to allow compensation in addition to that available under the 1992 Fund Convention. This fund is supported by contributions from signatory countries receiving oil by sea, and is a pool of money meant to compensate victims when the ship owner's liability has been exceeded.[5]

The International Convention Relating to Intervention on the High Seas in Cases of Oil Pollution Casualties (INTERVENTION) 1969

The *Torrey Canyon* disaster exposed the tangled web of international laws addressing jurisdiction, liability, and compensation issues. The incident revealed the impotence of a coastal state in controlling incidents beyond its territorial seas, even if its shores were directly threatened, if the action would affect foreign ships, cargo owners, and perhaps even other nations. Existing sources of jurisdiction were convoluted, overlapping, and confusing.

To address this issue, the IMO created an ad hoc Legal Committee to deal specifically with the jurisdictional issues presented by the *Torrey Canyon*. This was timely, because, as mentioned earlier, three super tankers, including Shell Oil's *Marpessa*, whose spill was even larger than the *Torrey Canyon*'s, exploded in December 1969.

The INTERVENTION Convention of 1969 entered into force on May 6, 1975, and clarified the right of a nation to take action to protect itself from pollution threatening its shores caused by an incident beyond its territorial waters. The INTERVENTION Convention allows the threatened state to act, but only so far as is necessary to protect itself, and only after consultation with all involved parties and nations. The INTERVENTION Convention applies to all seagoing vessels except warships or other state-owned vessels. In the United States, the Clean Water Act (CWA) and later the Federal Water Pollution Control Act (FWPCA) allow the government to take action to address pollution (and threats of pollution) within the three-mile territorial sea.[6] Beyond the territorial sea, authority to act or intervene against threatened pollution from incidents on the high seas is given under enabling legislation from 1975 that codified the IMO INTERVENTION Convention into U.S. law, as the Intervention on the High Seas Act (IHSA).[7]

The United States, as well as other nations that incorporated the provisions of the INTERVENTION Convention into domestic legislation, could now act to intervene on waters beyond their territorial seas should their coasts be threatened with an actual or potential discharge of oil, or any other hazardous substance, including (now) airborne pollutants. This legislation allowed the Secretary (of the department under which the U.S. Coast Guard is operating, currently the Department of Homeland Security) to act to prevent, mitigate, or eliminate the danger of pollution caused by incidents beyond the territorial seas if the threat is imminent. That being said, in 1990 the FWPCA was amended to extend its coverage to the limits of the Exclusive Economic Zone (EEZ), which extends 200 miles offshore. The 1990 amendment extending jurisdiction under the FWPCA to 200 miles may lessen the need for jurisdictional authority under the IHSA.

The Oil Companies International Marine Forum (OCIMF)

In 1970, largely in response to the *Torrey Canyon* disaster and other oil tanker incidents, the major oil companies of the world joined together in forming the Oil Companies International Marine Forum (OCIMF). The OCIMF has consultative status with the IMO and provides a vehicle for unified industry input and technical advice to the IMO and other rulemaking agencies.

1973 International Convention for the Prevention of Pollution from Ships (MARPOL '73)

After the *Torrey Canyon* grounding, the IMO called an Extraordinary Meeting of its Council to address the technical and legal aspects of the disaster and oil pollution in general. Though the *Torrey Canyon* spill was horrific, in terms of volume of oil in the sea, it was understood that routine operations, such as discharging wash-water from dirty oil tanks, was still the most significant source of vessel-source marine pollution, even when compared to an occasional (if monstrous) spill.

Despite the previous amendments to OILPOL '54, the Convention was increasingly recognized as largely inadequate to address the issues posed by the exponential growth of the international oil trade, and the unprecedented threats posed by the increased size and number of tankers plying the environmentally sensitive waters of the world.

The *Torrey Canyon* incident gave rise to the 1973 International Convention for the Prevention of Pollution from Ships (MARPOL '73), later modified by the Protocol of 1978, which supplanted OILPOL '54. Through numerous enhancements and amendments, MARPOL now covers not only oil pollution from ships (whether accidental or operational) but also sewage, garbage, chemical pollution, pollution by packaged goods, and even vessel-sourced air pollution. MARPOL is now the predominate convention addressing pollution of the sea.

Notes

1. Sources for Suez Canal information: D. A. Farnie, *East and West of Suez: The Suez Canal in History 1854–1956* (Oxford: Clarendon Press, 1969); Patrick B. Kinross, *Between Two Seas: The Creation of the Suez Canal* (New York: Morrow, 1969); website of the Suez Canal Authority, www.suezcanal.gov.eg; "The Suez Crisis Key Maps," *BBC News*, last updated July 21, 2006, http://news.bbc.co.uk/2/hi/middle_east/5195068. stm.

2. Sources for supertankers and tanker casualties information: Jack Devanney, *The Strange History of Tank Inerting,* Abstract (Center for Tankship Excellence), http://www.c4tx.org/ctx/pub/igs.pdf; Noel Mostert, *Supership* (New York: Warner Books, 1975); Roger A. Peterson, *Maritime Oil Tanker Casualties 1964–1977: An Analysis of Safety and Policy Issues* (PhD diss., University of Tennessee, 1980).

3. For more on the invention of an accurate timepiece for ships at sea, see Dava Sobel. *Longitude* (New York: Walker, 1998).

4. Sources for *Torrey Canyon* information: Richard A. Cahill, *Disasters at Sea*; Norman Hooke, *Maritime Casualties:1963–1996, 2nd ed.* (London: Lloyd's Maritime Information Services, 1997); Roger A. Peterson, *Maritime Oil Tanker Casualties*; Richard Petrow, *Black Tide: In the Wake of the* Torrey Canyon (London: Hodder and Staughton, 1968); Anita M. Rothblum, *Human Error and Marine Safety*, U.S. Coast Guard Research and Development Center, http://www.bowles-langley.com/wp-content/files_mf/humanerrorand-marinesafety26.pdf; Laura Moss, "The 13 Largest Oil Spills in History," *Mother Nature Network*, July 16, 2010, http://www.mnn.com/earth-matters/wilderness-resources/stories/the-13-largest-oil-spills-in-history; "March 29, 1967 Bombs Rain Down on Torrey Canyon," *BBC On This Day*, http://news.bbc.co.uk/onthisday/hi/dates/stories/march/29/newsid_2819000/2819369.stm; www.imo.org.

5. Sources for information on the International Convention on Civil Liability for Oil Pollution Damage (CLC) 1969 and the International Convention Relating to Intervention on the High Seas in Cases of Oil Pollution Casualties (IHSA): The IMO website, http://www.imo.org/About/Conventions/ListOfConventions/Pages/Default.aspx; The U.S. Coast Guard website, http://www.uscg.mil/international/affairs/publications/mmscode/english/AppendC.htm.

6. FWPCA also called CWA (33 USC §1251 et seq.).

7. 33 USC §1471-1487.

Chapter 7
1970 to 1979

1971: SS *Arizona Standard* and the SS *Oregon Standard*, collision; mandatory participation in VTS

1973: SS *Sea Witch* and the SS *Esso Brussels*, collision leading to changes in SOLAS

1975: SS *Edmund Fitzgerald* sinking on Lake Superior during a fierce winter storm

1976: MV *Argo Merchant*, spill off Nantucket, leading to changes in MARPOL

1978: MV *Amoco Cadiz,* grounding and spill, leading to changes in MARPOL

1978: The Standards of Training, Certification, and Watchkeeping (STCW) 1978

1979: SS *Atlantic Empress* and the SS *Aegean Captain*, little known fourth-largest spill

This decade witnessed the most numerous, and some of the world's worst, casualties. Tanker accidents, explosions, and related deaths and oil spills peaked in the 1970s. The largest tanker loss was the 1979 explosion of the Liberian-flagged *Energy Determination* (320,000 DWT) while transiting the Strait of Hormuz in ballast, but that incident did not result in any reaction from industry or international maritime bodies, nor did many other noteworthy and record-setting losses of this decade. Tanker casualties had become rather expected, it seemed, with an average of twenty-six tankers lost per year during this decade. Because many of the incidents occurred off the coasts and to crews of third-world nations, many first-world nations remained relatively unconcerned. It took the 1976 grounding of the *Argo Merchant* off the coast of Massachusetts to finally nudge the U.S. legislature into action.

The SS *Arizona Standard* and the SS *Oregon Standard*

In the early 1970s, San Francisco Bay had an experimental, voluntary Harbor Advisory Radar (HAR) system that advised vessels of the positions of other vessels in and around San Francisco Bay, using VHF radio channel 18A as a working channel. HAR did not interpret radar information, and did not offer information on a vessel's course, speed, or proximity to other vessels. Participating vessels would report their position, course, speed, and other pertinent information when they entered or exited the system. The U.S. Coast Guard had no authority to require vessels to participate, but it was the policy of Standard Oil and Chevron that their vessels participate in San Francisco's HAR. It didn't help them much on a foggy evening in January 1971.

At 0140 on January 18, 1971, in thick fog, two Standard Oil T2 class tankers, the *Arizona Standard* and the *Oregon Standard*, both operated by Chevron, collided just a few hundred yards west of the Golden Gate Bridge. Both tankers were 504 feet long, and had 6,000 horsepower steam turbo-electric power. Both vessels had two radar sets, and both were in operation on each vessel at the time of the collision. The masters and chief mates of both vessels were very senior mariners, with extensive time at sea. Both vessels had working VHF radios. Both vessels were fully laden. The *Arizona Standard* was inbound from sea, while the *Oregon Standard* was outbound from Richmond's Long Wharf facility, with a full load of bunker fuel in her cargo tanks.

On arrival at 0100 at the main ship channel into San Francisco Bay, and in dense fog, the *Arizona Standard* reduced her speed to about thirteen knots. The master was conning, the chief mate was manning the radar, and the second mate was handling the engine order telegraph. The bridge wing lookout was sent to the bow.

At approximately 0120, HAR notified the *Arizona Standard* that the tanker *Oregon Standard* was just north of Alcatraz Island, outbound for sea. At 0127 the chief mate of the *Arizona Standard* noted a radar contact, the *Oregon Standard*, at a range of six miles and about a half-mile south of Angel Island's Pt. Blunt. The chief mate continued to monitor the contact, but made no further plots.

When the *Oregon Standard* was about a mile northeast of the center of the Golden Gate Bridge, it disappeared from the *Arizona Standard*'s radar. (It was determined later that the *Oregon Standard*'s radar return may have blended with that of the bridge, but no expert testimony was provided.) At 0130 HAR notified the *Arizona Standard* that the *Oregon Standard* was one mile east of the Golden Gate Bridge and the *Arizona Standard* was approaching Mile Rock abeam. That was the last report from the Harbor Advisory Radar system.

The *Arizona Standard* made several attempts to hail the *Oregon Standard* on the VHF radio, to no avail. As it turns out, after her initial check-in with HAR on VHF channel 18A, the *Oregon Standard* had switched her radios to channels 10 and 16. The visibility had dropped to 200–300 yards and the *Arizona Standard* dropped her speed to roughly eleven knots, but her helmsman reported difficulty maintaining course at the reduced speed. At 0134, the *Arizona Standard* again tried to hail the *Oregon Standard*. At 0136 the master heard the fog signal of the center span of the Golden Gate Bridge, and ordered a new course of 058°, a two-degree course change to the right. Two minutes later, at 0138, the HAR advised the *Arizona Standard* that it had been unable to reach the *Oregon Standard* by radio. The *Arizona Standard* replied back that she was about to pass under the Golden Gate Bridge.

The *Oregon Standard* had her radar set to the 1.5-mile scale. The first radar identification the *Oregon Standard* made of the *Arizona Standard* came at 0139, when the *Oregon Standard* was just one-tenth of a mile east of the bridge. The *Oregon Standard* saw the *Arizona Standard*'s radar return at eight-tenths of a mile bearing twenty-five degrees on their port bow. It was later determined that the *Oregon Standard* failed to see the *Arizona Standard* on radar because the *Oregon Standard*'s radars were set at too low a scale, and that the bridge officers were distracted doing other things, and were not consistently monitoring their radar scopes.

At 0139, the master of the *Arizona Standard* noticed the red sidelight of the *Oregon Standard* fine on his starboard bow, at about 200 yards. He ordered hard left rudder and stop engines. The *Oregon Standard*, which was making approximately four knots, ordered full astern at the same time.

The bow of the *Arizona Standard* penetrated the port side of the *Oregon Standard* at about a forty-five degree angle.

The two vessels, now locked together, drifted into San Francisco Bay with the flood tide, and eventually anchored off Pt. Knox, Angel Island. The collision resulted in a spill of over 800,000 gallons of bunker fuel from the cargo tanks of the *Oregon Standard*. No lives were lost, but both vessels were extensively damaged.

The investigation determined four major factors contributed to the collision, any one of which, had it been addressed, would have prevented the accident. Both vessels were found to have violated the Inland Rules of the Road by not keeping to their respective starboard sides of the channel; both vessels were found to have inadequately used their radars to determine the risk of collision (not checking their scopes frequently enough, and/or having them on the wrong scales); and both vessels were found to have been using an "immoderate speed" for the prevailing visibility conditions.

The issue of "immoderate speed," of which both vessels were found guilty, is interesting because at the time, safe speed was determined to be the speed at which a vessel could stop in half the visibility distance. It is doubtful a modern board of inquiry would consider four knots in fog to be immoderate; however, that speed, combined with pea-soup fog and an inability to use or interpret radar information supported the board's conclusions. The fourth factor was the inability of either vessel to ascertain the center of the main ship channel under the Golden Gate Bridge.

Neither vessel clearly heard the fog signals of the other, due in part to the high noise level caused by the diaphones and fog horns of the bridge itself. The Harbor Advisory System, which lacked the authority to regulate vessel movements or offer interpretive advice, had radars monitoring vessel traffic in the area, but the *Oregon Standard* wasn't monitoring the Harbor Advisory radio channel, so the Harbor Advisory Radar oversight offered no advantage. Additionally, the *Arizona Standard* couldn't raise the *Oregon Standard* on any radio channel, so it was determined the *Oregon Standard* either had the volume too low to hear the calls, or her bridge team wasn't paying attention.

It was the largest spill the sensitive San Francisco Bay had ever experienced. The ensuing ebb tide then carried the spilled oil out to sea. The spill affected the coastline as far south as Half Moon Bay (twenty-five miles south of San Francisco Bay) and as far as twenty miles north to Kellam Beach. Hundreds of sea birds perished, despite a massive public outpouring of volunteers to help with the cleanup. With the limited technology of the time, it was impossible to determine the extent of the environmental damage.

Aftermath

As a result of the spill, the Bridge to Bridge Radiotelephone Act (Title 33 CFR §26 et seq.) was enacted, requiring vessels to monitor certain VHF channels. Also as a result of this incident, the Ports and Waterways Safety Act (PWSA) of 1972 (33 USC §1221 et seq.) was enacted. Under the authority of the Ports and Waterways Safety Act, the U.S. Coast Guard began to establish mandatory Vessel Traffic Services (VTS) in critical, congested ports. VTS are similar to the air traffic control systems run by the FAA to control airplane traffic patterns. In 1972 San Francisco and Seattle acquired the first Vessel Traffic Service operated and manned by the U.S. Coast Guard.

After the *Exxon Valdez* grounding and spill in 1989, the newly enacted Oil Pollution Act of 1990 mandated that the U.S. Coast Guard generate regulations requiring participation in Vessel Traffic Services.[1]

Given that there were so many senior, competent mariners on the bridges of both the *Arizona Standard* and the *Oregon Standard*, the final report highlighted the need for research into bridge layout and design, watch workload, and task organization. They didn't call it "Bridge Team Management" or "Bridge Resource Management" at the time, but that is exactly what the board of inquiry felt was missing on the bridges of the *Arizona Standard* and the *Oregon Standard*. They even mentioned the 1969 "Human Factors in Ship Control" study by General Dynamics, conducted for MARAD, where these topics were explored.

In a similar vein, and no doubt with similar motivations, in the early 1970s the IMO assembly passed a resolution requiring mandatory traffic lanes, or traffic separation schemes (TSS).[2]

The SS *Sea Witch* and the SS *Esso Brussels*

Just before 0100 on June 2, 1973, the fully loaded American Export Lines container ship *Sea Witch* lost steering and allided with the anchored Belgian tanker *Esso Brussels*. The *Esso Brussels*, loaded with Nigerian crude oil, was peacefully anchored in the southeast corner of federal quarantine anchorage #24 in Stapleton, Staten Island, New York. Most of the crew of the *Esso Brussels* was asleep, her anchor and deck lights brightly burning in the wee hours of the morning. Here is the story.

Late in the evening of June 1, 1973, after taking on a full load of containers at Howland Hook Container Terminal on Staten Island, the *Sea Witch* proceeded outbound for sea by way of the Kill Van Kull on the northern end of Staten Island under the guidance of a docking pilot and two tugs. At New Brighton she slowed to debark her docking pilot, and the Sandy Hook harbor pilot commenced conning the vessel. Once the tug was away and clear, at 0025 June 2, the harbor pilot brought the ship's engines to half-ahead, as the *Sea Witch* made her way out of the Kill Van Kull. Four minutes later, at 0029, her speed was brought up to full-ahead maneuvering (about thirteen knots) as she made her way toward the Verrazano-Narrows Bridge, with the federal anchorages #23 and #24 laying off to starboard. The chief mate, the boatswain, and a seaman were on anchor detail on the bow. The anchor pawls were down, and the stoppers were on, but loose. (Normally, to be ready for immediate deployment, only the anchor pawls will be down, or sometimes the anchors will be just riding on the brake.) The tide was ebbing and the weather was fine.

The harbor pilot ordered various courses as the vessel made her way to sea, but at 0037 the helmsman reported that the vessel was not steering properly. The ship was drifting slightly to starboard. The pilot ordered hard left rudder as the master took control of the helm. When the helm didn't respond properly, the master reportedly said, "...that damn steering gear again..." The master tried switching steering systems from the starboard hydraulic system to port, to no avail. No steering gear alarms had sounded on the bridge and the rudder was stuck at roughly twelve degrees to starboard.

The vessel was still at full harbor speed as her swing to starboard accelerated. The *Sea Witch*, now swinging fast to starboard, narrowly missed the tug *Barbara Moran* and her barge. The harbor pilot sounded the danger signal on the ship's whistle and then locked it so it would sound a continuous blast. As the *Sea Witch*'s bow lined up dangerously toward the stern of the anchored *Esso Brussels*, the pilot rang full astern and ordered the port anchor dropped and the general alarm sounded, but the ship kept swinging to starboard until she was aimed directly at the midships section of the resting tanker.

The *Sea Witch*'s chief mate and the boatswain, both on the foredeck, tried in vain to free the riding pawl from the port anchor, but they couldn't get it free and the anchor could not drop with the riding pawl down. They then tried to free the starboard anchor. They were able to release the pawl, release the chain stopper, and loosen the windlass brake, but the starboard anchor did not drop either. Moments before impact, the harbor pilot ordered the bridge cleared and ordered the chief mate and boatswain off the bow. (After the incident, the *Sea Witch*'s starboard anchor was found lying on the deck of the *Esso Brussels*.) Aboard the *Esso Brussels*, the watch mate, seeing that a collision was imminent, sounded the general alarm.

Aboard the *Sea Witch*, the chief engineer was retiring to his stateroom when he heard the general alarm bell sounding. He immediately returned to the engine room to answer the engine orders from the bridge. The collision happened moments after the chief engineer had reported back to the engine room.

The allision was so forceful that *Sea Witch*'s bow punched forty feet into the *Esso Brussels*, locking the two ships together and rupturing three of the *Esso Brussels*' cargo tanks. Both vessels burst into flames almost immediately. The ships were hopelessly locked together, engulfed in a raging fire fed by the contents of the *Esso Brussels*' ruptured tanks, and both now hanging tentatively solely on the *Esso Brussels*' anchor, which was not holding well against the ebb current.

Aboard the *Sea Witch* smoke was drawn into the engine room by the negative air pressure created by the boilers, making it difficult to breathe or see. When the engine crew finally had to abandon the engine room due to smoke, the engines were at full astern. The engine lasted about eight or nine minutes before giving out. Once the main plant died, the emergency generator kicked in and provided power for the emergency fire pump and lighting, though the smoke was too dense for emergency lighting to be effective. The emergency generator ran for two days after the incident.

The crew of the *Esso Brussels* tried to lower lifeboats, but their efforts were hampered by flames on the water and difficulty releasing the falls. Also, once they got a lifeboat launched, due to crowding of the frightened crew around the lifeboat engine, there wasn't enough room to hand-crank the engine and get it started. They then tried to use oars to push the lifeboat away from the burning ship, but the wind was enough to pin the lifeboat alongside. Some of the crew jumped into the burning waters to escape the flames on the surface.

The crew of the *Sea Witch* ran down the port side of her decks, trying to avoid the heat, flames, smoke, and debris being blown by the fire-driven winds. Containers that had wooden floors or plastic-laminated sides burned fast and hot, exposing their contents, which also then burned. Some crew tried to fight the fire, but the exterior fire hoses were all inaccessible due to the flames, so they were forced to use the smaller interior hoses, which proved ineffective. All the fire hose nozzles were of the "straight stream" type, which, shooting water in a powerful, straight stream, proved less than effective for cooling hot surfaces. Most of the crew of the *Sea Witch*, despite efforts to fight the fire, ultimately had to take refuge in the aft house. Some jumped overboard.

The fire on the *Esso Brussels* was so hot it ruptured pipelines, melted brass components of the steam smothering lines and vent lines, and burned tank gaskets which allowed the cargo's flammable vapors to escape, exacerbating the fire.

The collision caused 1.3 million gallons of crude oil to spill from the *Esso Brussels'* cargo tanks. The ebb tide and the wash from the *Sea Witch's* propellers circulated the spilled oil and the flames on the water quickly spread. The burning oil drifted under the Verrazano-Narrows Bridge, burning the bridge's paint, damaging light fixtures, and forcing closure of the bridge to vehicular traffic, but no one on the bridge was hurt.

At some point, the *Esso Brussels'* anchor broke free, and both vessels began to drift.

Once the alarm went out, help swarmed in. The police sent boats, the U.S. Coast Guard sent boats and helicopters, commercial tugs responded, even the Army Corps of Engineers responded to the fire. Communications were chaotic, as no one was in charge of the rescue efforts. It wasn't until 0140 that the U.S. Coast Guard finally assumed on-scene command. At 0215 the main ship channel was finally closed to maritime traffic. By 0400 the U.S. Coast Guard had a cargo manifest for the *Sea Witch*, which showed she had considerable quantities of flammable cargo aboard, but nothing particularly hazardous.

The vessels were left stuck together until 0630, when they were finally able to be separated. As they pulled apart, the *Sea Witch's* starboard anchor slipped off the deck of the *Esso Brussels* and dragged along the seabed until the chain went taut as she approached Gravesend Bay.

Authorities were eventually able to extinguish the fire in the *Esso Brussels'* cargo tanks, but her above-deck houses continued to burn.

As the *Sea Witch's* anchor chain became taut, it was cut and the *Sea Witch* was intentionally beached. The *Esso Brussels'* anchor chain was then attached to the stub of the *Sea Witch's* anchor chain, effectively mooring her to the beached *Sea Witch*.

The fire continued to burn aboard the *Sea Witch*, as firefighting efforts were hampered by stability concerns; officials didn't want her to lose stability due to too much fire fighting water in her hull. Her fires burned for two more weeks. Ultimately, most of the 1.3 million gallons of oil that had been spilled were consumed by the fire, but the shores of Manhattan, Jones Beach, Staten Island, Sandy Hook, Norton's Point, and Coney Island all saw residue from the spill.

Both masters were killed, along with two crew members from the *Sea Witch* and twelve crew from the *Esso Brussels*. The harbor pilot died of a heart attack not long after the incident.

In the five years before this fatal casualty, the *Sea Witch* had experienced no fewer than twelve steering gear failures, not at all normal for any type of vessel. Regulations only required notification to the Coast Guard if repairs exceeded $1,500, so it is doubtful her history of steering gear failures was known to the authorities, but the master clearly knew of the steering system's unreliability.

The steering loss aboard the *Sea Witch* was due to the failure of a tiny, $3/16$-inch square key in the steering gear. Regulations in place at the time required two independent steering systems, but the Coast Guard had approved the *Sea Witch's* steering system even though it was only redundant up to the point of the hydraulic steering gear pumps. After the pumps, it was a single system, and it was in that part of the system that the failure occurred.

Findings Concerning the *Sea Witch*

Although the primary cause of the incident was a steering casualty, the master of the *Sea Witch* was faulted for not slowing or stopping the ship immediately upon learning of the steering casualty. It is opined that had the master of the *Sea Witch* slowed his ship immediately upon notification of the steering problem, rather than just moments before impact, the impact would have been lessened, possibly averting a fire. Had there been no fire, no lives would have been lost. The chief mate of the *Sea Witch* was faulted for not ensuring both anchors could be let go effectively. The *Sea Witch* had a manually-operated emergency wheel (called a "trick wheel") in the steering gear room which could have been used to steer the vessel, but no one aboard was instructed on it, and its use was never contemplated.

The crew of the *Sea Witch* had no formal fire-fighting training. Thinking they could pressurize all the ships fire stations, they left all the fire stations open, which reduced the fire main pressure to well below what was necessary to be effective. Also, the *Sea Witch* didn't have breathing apparatuses in strategic places which would have allowed the engineers to remain in the engine room longer, and keep critical systems running. The way the cargo was stored also contributed to the severity of the fire aboard the *Sea Witch*: the on-deck containers were stored in a massive 320-foot by 30-foot block on which the fire could feed unfettered.

Findings Concerning the *Esso Brussels*

The loss of life on the *Esso Brussels* could have been avoided or lessened had the lifeboats been deployable, and had the crew been able to start the lifeboat engine. Had the lifeboats been fitted with a stored hydraulic pressure starting system, or some other system that didn't require so much room to swing a crank, it likely would have allowed the crew to escape the burning oil that was surrounding the ship and their lifeboat.

The brass and bronze fittings of the *Esso Brussels'* cargo systems melted in the heat, releasing flammable vapors and worsening the fire. Many of the *Esso Brussels'* house fixtures were also flammable, which helped fuel the fire. A new IMCO rule A.213 (AII), passed just before this incident, prohibited the use of flammable fittings in above-deck houses for just such a reason. In contrast, the fire-retardant paneling aboard the *Sea Witch* helped slow the spread of her fire.

Aftermath

While the fitting of whistles on lifejackets was of some assistance in locating survivors, had there been retro-reflective tape and lights on the lifejackets the survivors would have been much more visible in the dark, oily waters. The bright international orange color of the cotton-covered lifejackets was of no aid, as they were stained dark with crude oil. The inquiry's conclusions recommended some sort of oil-resistant finish for lifejackets to preserve their visibility. Modern life jackets are covered with oil-resistant international orange cloth, as well as retro-reflective tape, lights, and whistles. Some are even fitted with personal locator beacons (PLBs).

Other recommendations included:

- Changing the fire regulations to require combination, rather than straight stream nozzles, at all fire stations
- Exploring various methods of starting lifeboat engines
- Considering fire-retardant materials for the construction of shipping containers
- Setting speed limits in New York Harbor
- Changing anchorage locations
- Updating regulations involving ventilation system closures and shipboard spaces that should be kept at positive pressure
- Adding a requirement that lifejackets have battery-operated lights

As a result of this accident and the difficulty rescuers had in locating oil-soaked survivors in the dark, oily waters, IMCO's Maritime Safety Committee proposed that vessels voluntarily fit retro-reflective material to lifesaving appliances.

The findings also included recommendations about emergency communications and coordinated search and rescue efforts, escort tugs, speed zones in congested waters, and required better recordkeeping concerning steering gear units. The National Transportation Safety Board also recommended to the Coast Guard that vessels be fitted with an automatic recording device to "preserve vital navigational information."[3]

At the time, SOLAS was being revised, and as a result of this incident, the U.S. Coast Guard asked that a means of releasing both lifeboat falls simultaneously, and under tension, be explored. Another law that came about as a result of this incident is the requirement for a steering gear failure alarm. The fifth SOLAS convention of 1974 was largely prompted by the *Sea Witch / Esso Brussels* collision.[4]

At the time, it was one of the worst maritime disasters New York had ever witnessed.

(In a bizarre coincidence, five years earlier, on July 7, 1968, the *Esso Brussels* had herself hit an anchored ship, the *Aldebaran*, which was anchored in thick fog. The *Esso Brussels* had just let go her anchor, and was backing down and holding 135 feet of chain on her port anchor, when she hit the stern of the *Aldebaran*.)

The SS *Edmund Fitzgerald*

Ships sinking in heavy weather on the Great Lakes is nothing new. In fact, more Great Lakes mariners were lost during the three-day storm in November of 1913 known as the "Deadly White Hurricane" than in any Great Lakes storm since. During that deadly storm, the winds howled to fifty knots or more and temperatures dropped to the single digits. Nineteen ships were lost, an equal number were stranded, and over 250 people lost their lives. At the height of the storm, wind gusts were clocked at eighty miles per hour and the pressure on the barometer had menacingly dropped below twenty-nine inches.

Despite the tragedy of 1913, it was Gordon Lightfoot's haunting song about the sinking of the *Edmund Fitzgerald* that drove that particular disaster into the American psyche, and raised national awareness about the perils of the Great Lakes.

The 729-foot ship, her keel being laid in 1957, was to be the largest bulker on the Great Lakes. She was built to just fit the soon-to-be constructed St. Lawrence Seaway and she could carry 26,000 tons of cargo in three holds, accessed by 21 hatches. In short, she was huge. Just over a year later, her record size was bested by the SS *Murray Bay*, which was just a foot longer.

She was christened in June of 1958 as the *Edmund Fitzgerald*, after the Chair of the Board of Directors of the Northwestern Mutual Life Insurance Company, the company that commissioned her construction. Northwestern Mutual Life Insurance Company invested heavily in the mineral industry and commissioning the building of an ore ship was a novel investment for the firm, but not beyond the scope of their financial interests. But they were not ship operators, and they hired Oglebay Norton Corporation to operate the vessel.

The christening of a ship, to bless her and ask the gods of the seas to protect her, dates back to ancient Greek, Roman, and Egyptian practices, when slaves were expected to lay across the ways and anoint the ship with their blood as she rolled over them on her trip down the rails. As civilization progressed, this practice was abandoned for a more acceptable fluid, and wine (and modernly, champagne) became the christening sacrifice of choice.

Despite christening's rather gruesome origins, if a ship isn't properly christened, it is considered bad luck. If the christening bottle didn't break on the first blow, well, that would portend particularly bad luck. If you believe, as this author does, that ships have souls, then the *Fitz* must have known a violent end awaited her, and she almost refused to be born.

It took Mrs. Elizabeth Fitzgerald three tries just to get the champagne bottle to break during her christening (which must have sent a chill down every sailor's spine). Then the launch crew couldn't get the keel blocks released, and then, as she finally slid sideways down the ways into the water, she crashed into a pier.

But she launched and she floated. She carried a record-breaking load through the Soo Locks on September 28, 1959, and continued to break load records, including her own. Through the years, she suffered various casualties, including running aground, a collision with another ship, and multiple allisions with various locks, but nothing could stop her until November 1975, when the winter storms proved too much for the "Mighty *Fitz.*"

On the afternoon of November 9, 1975, the *Edmund Fitzgerald* sailed from the Burlington Northern Railroad dock in Superior, Wisconsin, loaded with 26,116 tons of taconite iron ore pellets bound for Zug Island on the Detroit River. Captain McSorley was her master. The trips were short, and at her normal operating speed of about sixteen knots, she would average just five days for a round trip.

Just nine minutes after her departure, the National Weather Service issued gale warnings for the waters in which she was sailing. Captain Cooper of the *Arthur M. Anderson* radioed the *Edmund Fitzgerald*, which was sailing just fifteen miles ahead, to discuss the weather. By 0100 the next morning, the winds had increased to over fifty knots, generating waves of ten feet or more. At 0700 November 9 the weather must have abated somewhat, as the *Edmund Fitzgerald's* weather report stated winds were at thirty-five knots. At 1515, the *Fitzgerald* rounded Caribou Island and the *Anderson's* Captain Cooper commented that the *Fitzgerald* was closer to Six Fathom Shoal than he'd want to be. He reported northwesterly winds at forty-three knots.

At 1530 Captain McSorley of the *Edmund Fitzgerald* radioed the *Anderson* to relay that he had sustained topside damage, had fence rail laid down, and that two vents were lost or damaged. He said the ship was listing and that he was "checking down."

McSorley asked the *Anderson* to stay by him until he got to Whitefish. Captain Cooper agreed and asked if McSorley had his pumps going. McSorely replied, "Yes. Both of them."

At 1610, the situation worsened when the *Fitzgerald* reported that both of her radars were not working and asked the *Anderson* to provide her with positional information.

For the next hour, the *Fitzgerald* searched in vain for the Whitefish Radio beacon, until another vessel, the *Avafors*, reported that it was not operating. Eventually, the *Avafors* reported that she saw Whitefish Light, but that the beacon was still not working.

When *Avafors* asked how the weather was at the *Fitzgerald's* location, because the wind was "really howling" where they were, the *Avafors* could only make out Captain McSorley's unintelligible voice, and then McSorely advising his watch officers not to let anyone on deck.

The *Fitzgerald* replied they had a bad list, both radars were down, they were taking heavy seas over the deck, and that it was one of the worst seas they had ever been in.

Sometime around 1900 the *Anderson*, still about ten miles behind the *Fitzgerald*, was hit by two huge waves and green water crashed on deck, thirty-five feet above the waterline, damaging the starboard lifeboat.

At 1910 there was another radio conversation and the *Anderson* notified the *Fitzgerald* that there was a ship contact about nine miles ahead, but that the *Fitzgerald* should clear her.

When asked how he was doing, McSorley replied he was holding his own in the gale force winds. That was the last time anyone heard from anyone aboard the *Edmund Fitzgerald*.

At 1925, the *Edmund Fitzgerald* disappeared from the *Anderson's* radar.

The *Anderson* informed the Coast Guard of the *Fitzgerald's* plight, and began to search for the now invisible ship. The Coast Guard search plane arrived on the scene at about 2300, almost three hours after the sinking.

The *Edmund Fitzgerald* sank at around 2000 on November 10, 1975. The NTSB's opinion, and more recent evidence, indicate she sank due to a sudden failure of a cargo hold hatch (or hatches) due to the weight of seas that crashed over her decks.

All twenty-nine men aboard were lost in 530 feet of Lake Superior's icy water, on the Canadian side of the big lake the Native Indians call Gichigami.

Aftermath

As a result of the investigations into the sinking, Great Lakes regulations were changed to require survival suits for all crew members. Additionally, vessels were to carry echo sounders and positioning systems. As a result of the casualty, 45 CFR §45 was amended to require closing of hatches and vent caps when underway. It was also recommended that 46 USC be amended to rescind 1969, 1971, and 1973 changes to load line regulations. As a result, regulations governing required freeboard were enhanced. The NTSB also recommended vessel construction standards be amended to require ore carries have watertight bulkheads.[5]

The MV *Argo Merchant*

The tanker *Argo Merchant* was particularly poorly maintained and operated, not atypical for tankers flying flags of convenience during this period. Her blemished record began in 1964, eleven years after her launch, when she grounded and damaged her propeller and cracked her shaft. Over the course of the next twelve years, before she grounded and was lost completely in 1976, she had four name changes and four different owners—she was passed around and used like a strumpet, poorly kept and poorly run. During this period, she had about twenty notable incidents, including some collisions, a few minor oil spills, four groundings, and numerous machinery casualties. In ten years, she had fourteen reported casualties, over five times the average rate. Goodness knows what went unreported.

In December 1976, the *Argo Merchant*, while en route from Puerto La Cruz, Venezuela, to Salem, Massachusetts, ran aground on Fishing Rip Shoal, northwest of the Nantucket Lightship, which they had intended to pass well east. Though she was a mid-sized tanker carrying only 27,000 tons of oil (about 8 million gallons), the location of her grounding and subsequent spill caused public outcry, as it threatened the economically critical and environmentally sensitive fishing grounds of Georges Bank, as well the New England coastal summer resorts.

A Liberian Marine Board of Investigation (meeting in New York, London, and then Rotterdam) was convened to investigate the incident. What they found was an almost perfect example of how *not* to run a ship and how *not* to run a navigational watch. At the time, it was one of the worst spills ever to threaten the coast of the United States.

Like many other irreputable ships of her day, she was owned by a tangled web of Liberian and Greek shell companies, all designed to be an impenetrable mesh shielding her unscrupulous owners. The ship was essentially a floating accident waiting to happen.

In 1976, the Netherlands Maritime Institute Report of her grounding labeled her a "sub-standard tanker," and apparently the navigational skills of her crew and officers matched her general sub-par condition. A U.S. Coast Guard officer engaged in salvaging the stricken vessel found her crew quarters horrible, her valves and porthole dogs rusted and inoperative.

She was outfitted with two radars, an RDF set (which some said was not working properly and had not been calibrated), and the only reliable gyro compass repeater was the steering station itself. She did not have a LORAN set. Her only external gyro repeater was on the flying bridge, but it had been inoperable for over a year before the grounding, rendering it almost impossible to observe an azimuth, which is done to check the master gyro compass for error.

So, the only way a watch officer could check the gyro error at sea, which is supposed to be performed each watch, was to either wait for a celestial object to be low and almost dead ahead (or change course to aim at it) so one could use the inside repeater at the forward bulkhead, or use the flying bridge repeater, and perform calculations based on relative bearings, which, given the natural motions of a vessel, are imprecise at best. In short, there was no viable way to properly and efficiently check the master gyro compass for error.

To say the vessel was poorly navigated the day of her demise is an understatement. Her navigational charts were six years old and uncorrected, with seemingly no one tasked with their upkeep. She also wasn't carrying the pilot chart for December, the month of the grounding, which would have indicated the onshore current she experienced. The ship was sailing short of two able seamen, the positions being temporarily filled by a deck-boy and a wiper. Despite a crew of thirty-eight, her manning situation was so unsatisfactory the third mate refused to stand a watch with the two crew who were not certified able bodied seamen, necessitating the chief mate rotate the watch bills around to ensure the third mate got the certified sailors he demanded.

The break rotation for the on-watch lookouts was so generous that it resulted in a lookout being on break 50 percent of the time, and not actually performing lookout duties. Compounding the already handicapped bridge team were language difficulties—some of the crew spoke neither Greek nor English, the primary languages spoken aboard. Leeway was applied mechanically, without actually calculating set and drift and without consideration to changing winds. Track lines had been laid out from dead-reckoned positions, ignoring a recent fix. Critical depth information, which should have alerted the watch that the vessel was seriously off track, was observed, but ignored. When steering by magnetic compass on the day of the grounding, the gyro having been recognized as unreliable, little if any consideration was given to the change in magnetic variation as the vessel made her way toward Nantucket. Indeed, by the time the RDF was consulted, the vessel was so far off track that what would normally be a simple resolution of the reciprocal (but not identical) bearings presented by RDF signals of the day, was misinterpreted to put the vessel exactly opposite of where she really was.

The vessel grounded on Fishing Rip Shoal on December 15, 1976, over twenty-four miles off track. As she ground herself apart over the next month, she spilled most of her cargo of roughly 8.5 million gallons of Venezuelan No. 6 fuel oil and cutter stock. Attempts to pump the remaining cargo off the ship, or set it on fire once it had spilled to the sea, proved ineffective.

Fortunately, offshore winds prevented the majority of the oil from reaching shore but the offshore slick was 100 miles long and sixty miles wide.

The majority of the oil ended up in the fishing area of George's Bank. It was fortuitous that the type of oil was too buoyant to enter the water column and that it was winter, when biological activity is lowest. Both aspects of the spill served to mitigate the environmental impact of the grounding, but numerous dead seabirds were washed up onto the shores of Nantucket and Martha's Vineyard and the damage to fisheries and seaborne life will never be known.

The MV *Argo Merchant. Collection of Doug Helton, NOAA/NOS/ORR.*

Aftermath

The Board of Inquiry, seemingly baffled by the master's ineptitude, opined that the master either intentionally navigated his vessel inside the lightship toward waters too shallow and confined for a ship of her size, or that he negligently failed to change the course of his vessel upon finding himself steaming into dangerous waters. In a failure of what is now called "bridge team management," the chief mate, who had been worried about the vessel's progress, remained silent, and never shared his concerns with the master.

Determining the cause of an incident, whether it be human error or unseaworthiness, can be critical. It determines who pays which costs and fines, and whether a ship owner can limit his liability or not. The Liberian government determined human error was the cause of the grounding.

As a result of this incident, the master's license was revoked, the chief mate's license was suspended for four years, and the second mate's license was suspended for nine months. The ownership of the oil was so muddled and convoluted that the insurance company who paid the claim for the lost cargo paid under an agreement allowing none of the involved companies to claim ownership.

During this decade, unprecedented numerous major tanker incidents were occurring worldwide, mostly involving tankers of Liberian flag or vessels flagged under other open registries. Many happened either in the United States or off the shores of our close allies.

Here is a sampling of the decade's incidents of direct concern to the United States, and the flags of the ships involved:

Arrow (major spill off Canada)—Liberian
Sansinena (blew up in Los Angeles Harbor)—Liberian
Olympic Games (ran aground in Delaware River, big oil spill)—Liberian
Grand Zenith (disappeared off Cape Cod)—Panamanian
Argo Merchant (major spill off Nantucket)—Liberian
Universe Leader (ran aground in Delaware river)—Liberian
Austin (spill in San Francisco Bay)—U.S.
Barcola (aground off Texas)—Liberian
Mary Ann (exploded off the Virginia coast while tank cleaning)—Liberian
Barge *New York* (spill in Tampa Bay due to ruptured tank)—U.S.
Chester A. Poling (broke apart off Massachusetts)—U.S.
Irenes Challenger (broke in half off Midway Island, oil spill)—Greek
Golden Jason (broke down at sea, towed in to Virginia before scrapping)—Liberian

Add to this the multitudinous casualties happening elsewhere in the world, again, with a disproportionate share happening aboard tankers registered with flags of convenience. Between 1970 and 1980, there were a total of 262 total losses of tankers worldwide, an average of 26 tankers lost each year—contrasted with 8 lost in 1996.

Even though the *Argo Merchant* spill had relatively minor (recorded) environmental and economic impact, it roused the attention of the U. S. Coast Guard. This incident, happening as it did in international waters, became the first exercise of the Intervention on the High Seas Act (IHSA) when the U.S Coast Guard undertook the salvage of the stricken vessel, despite the fact it was on the high seas.

It was really the *Argo Merchant* which prompted Congress, in an overdue response to the spate of tanker incidents, to initiate hearings and pass the Clean Water Act of 1977 and the Port and Tanker Safety Act of 1978.

The *Argo Merchant* incident prompted the Carter Initiative, and the United States delegation at the IMO to aggressively pursue additional safety and pollution regulations for tankers, and the

IMO agreed to convene the Conference on Tanker Safety and Pollution Prevention. A combined meeting of IMO's Marine Safety Committee (MSC) and the Marine Environment Protection Committee (MEPC) met in the summer of 1978.

A protocol was adopted that added provisions to MARPOL '73 expanding anti-pollution requirements for tankers. The new 1978 MARPOL protocol lowered the size limit of tankers that must have segregated ballast tanks from 70,000 DWT to 20,000 DWT, and required that segregated ballast tanks be located such that they could protect cargo tanks in the event of a grounding or collision. Tankers over 40,000 DWT would be required to have either segregated ballast tanks (which carried only clean water ballast and could never be used to carry oil) or a crude oil washing system.

Other tanker-specific measures were added (via a 1978 Protocol) to the International Convention for the Safety of Life at Sea 1974 (SOLAS '74), such as inert gas systems for cargo tanks, enhanced requirements for surveys and inspections, steering gear requirements (no doubt the result of the *Sea Witch* collision), and stricter requirements for radar and collision avoidance aids.

One month after the passage of the MARPOL '78 Protocol, on March 16, 1978, the Liberian-flagged tanker *Amoco Cadiz* ran aground off Brittany, resulting in the largest oil spill to date and dwarfing the spill of the *Argo Merchant*.[6]

The MV *Amoco Cadiz*

The stranding of the VLCC *Amoco Cadiz* off Ushant, an island off France at the southwest end of the English Channel (the Scilly Islands are to the north), in a gale on the night of March 16, 1978, resulted in the worst oil spill the world had seen to date. As she made her way across the Bay of Biscay, she endured forty-knot winds, but at over three football fields long and sixty-five feet in draft, her heft and size allowed her to ride the seas with relative comfort as she made her way along the Ushant Traffic Separation Scheme.

The ship, the namesake of Cadiz, Spain, where she was built in 1974, was owned by Amoco Transport Company of Monrovia, Liberia. She was operated by Amoco International Oil Company out of a head office in Chicago, while on a time charter to Shell Oil, which owned the cargo of Saudi and Iranian crude oil. She was chartered for $28,000 per day, a lucrative rate for the time. Like many tankers of her day, she flew a Liberian flag and was crewed by foreign nationals, in this case, Italians. On her final trip, she was under the command of Captain Pasquale Bardari.

The ship was only four years old and was considered one of the best-manned, best-operated, and best-equipped tankers in the world. She was bound for Rotterdam, laden with 223,000 tons (1.6 million barrels) of crude oil. Too large for the Suez Canal, she followed the route that led her around the southern tip of Africa, then north to Europe.

Except for some rough weather the last two days, the trip was uneventful until at 0946 on March 16, 1978, she lost steering, with the rudder stuck at hard port, swinging the vessel toward oncoming traffic. She was clear of the Ushant Traffic Scheme, but only eight miles north of Ushant, and a mile closer to the French shore than she should have been. The master left the bridge and went to the steering gear room himself to inspect the damage. The master returned to the bridge at about 1020.

When the engineer inspected the steering gear room, he found hydraulic oil spurting from a leak and the rudder slamming from side to side in the rough seas. Efforts to repair the ruptured hydraulic line failed, so the engineer left the steering gear room, securing the watertight door behind him, and the vessel was brought to a standstill. The master sent out securité messages (messages of urgency, not distress) on the VHF radio and other frequencies, and he hoisted "not under command" signals, indicating the vessel was unable to maneuver, but he did not request assistance. There is no evidence anyone heard or responded to the securité messages, perhaps because they were sent in English off a French coast.

As the gale worsened, the ship drifted to within ten miles of the rocky coast, yet the master still made no call for assistance. Ship's masters are prudently reluctant to call for assistance too soon, as such a request may result in a salvage claim against the vessel, her cargo, and freight, but waiting too long for a casualty to ripen is also perilous. Deciding when to call for help demands a delicate balance of economic, safety, and environmental considerations for which most ship's officers are poorly prepared.

By 1100, over an hour after the steering gear failure, the vessel had drifted a half-mile closer to the rocky shore and was broadside to the seas—the master finally called Brest radio to ask about assistance, but made no formal call for help. Just after his call to Brest Radio, the chief engineer informed him that the steering gear was not repairable, and the master finally asked for a tug (the nearest tug was fifteen miles away) to come and assist. The tug *Pacific* contacted the *Amoco Cadiz* and offered assistance under the terms of the world's most recognized salvage agreement, Lloyd's Open Form (LOF). The master's reluctance to agree to LOF without getting permission from the head office in Chicago, and his attempts to negotiate an hourly towage rate instead, was probably due to a common misunderstanding that LOF is unfair to vessel owners and frequently results in astronomical salvage awards to salvors, and unreasonable expense to the ship owners and insurers.

The tug, recognizing the immediacy of the problem, largely ignored the hesitations of the ship's master and got a line across to the stricken ship just after 1400.

Despite the raging seas and imminent danger to the helpless ship, the two vessels haggled in English (their non-native tongue) for almost three hours over the use of LOF or a straight towage contract. Finally agreement to use LOF was reached.

The tug tried to pull the ship around, with the towline almost perpendicular to the *Amoco Cadiz*. The tug was somewhat successful in slowing her drift, but the towline ultimately parted at 1615. Efforts to reattach the tow were hampered by language difficulties and accusations between the vessels that the other was, essentially, not trying hard enough. Despite the master's protests, this time the tug's operator suggested they tow the ship from the stern. Some think had this approach been taken from the start it would have prevented the towline from parting, and would have slowed the drift. (At the inquiry, the Commissioner felt the *Pacific* was too small to be of any meaningful advantage regardless of where or how she had been made up.)

Despite the worsening conditions, and the nearness of a rocky, lee shore, Captain Bardari had still not sent a distress.

The towline to the ship's stern was connected by 2100, seven hours after the first line had been passed, and by then the ship had drifted to within one-and-a-half miles of the Roche de Portsall buoy, in 120 feet of water. In an attempt to slow the drift of the vessel, the port anchor was paid out, but it had only momentary effect as both its flukes sheared off. The starboard anchor, never having been cleared, was not deployed, nor could it have been at that point, as green seas were breaking over the bow of the ship. (The master was later faulted for not having both anchors ready for letting go the moment he knew of the steering casualty.)

By the time the tug was made fast and ready to start trying to tow the foundering tanker, it was too late. The *Amoco Cadiz* struck ground on Men Goulven Rocks, off Portsall, France, at 2104, opening her hull plating, spilling cargo from the torn cargo tanks, and flooding the pump room. Thirty minutes later, she struck again, flooding the engine room and releasing more crude oil into the sea.

The tug kept trying to pull the vessel off the rocks, but to no avail, and the towline parted again. The ship's forty crew members were mustered to abandon ship. By then a second tug had arrived, but she was too late to be of any service. The seas were so rough that they carried away the port lifeboat the crew had been trying to launch. Just before midnight, it was determined the risk from fire and explosion was no greater than the risk of death by other means, so the decision was made use emergency power to send an SOS and to fire emergency flares. The first distress call was broadcast at 2326, over two hours after the first grounding.

The MV *Amoco Cadiz,* with her back broken, aground on Men Goulven Rocks. *National Oceanic and Atmospheric Administration.*

The only remaining means of rescue was by helicopter. The master and a company representative who was riding the ship stayed behind, while the crew was hauled to safety aboard French Navy helicopters. Four hours later the ship broke in two and the two remaining men were lifted off.

The *Amoco Cadiz* took two weeks to die, eventually breaking into three pieces on March 28 on the rocks of Roche de Portsall, just three miles from the coast of Brittany, France. Despite the ship's breaking apart, there was concern that some of her 223,000 tons (roughly 67 million gallons)of crude, as well as some of her 4,000 tons of bunker fuel still remained aboard, so the French Navy dropped depth charges in an attempt to release any remaining oil.

The massive spill covered over 1,400 square miles and oiled more than 130 beaches. In places, the oil was up to eleven inches thick.

According to the Center for Tanker Excellence,

> A slick 18 miles wide and 80 miles long polluted approximately 200 miles of Brittany coastline. Beaches of 76 different Breton communities were oiled. A 12-mile long slick and heavy pools of oil were smeared onto 45 miles of the French shoreline by northwesterly winds. Prevailing westerly winds during the following month spread the oil approximately 100 miles east along the coast. The isolated location of the grounding and rough seas restricted cleanup efforts for the two weeks following the incident.[7]

At the time, Dr. Wilmot Hess, director of NOAA's environmental research laboratory, declared the spill the "largest biological kill from any spill we've looked at."[8]

Ten thousand French servicemen were called upon to try and clean the mess, but cleanup was difficult due to the remoteness of the wreck and bad weather. Both fin fish and shellfish stocks were

ruined, as was the local seaweed crop, used by chemical and cosmetic manufacturers. The damage done to the economies of France and England, and the environment, was incalculable.

As an excellent example of how far the results of a complex error chain can reach, after the grounding of the *Amoco*

The impact of the MV *Amoco Cadiz* spill: a beach thick with oil. *National Oceanic and Atmospheric Administration.*

Cadiz, a Danish vessel, the *Henrietta Bravo*, was hired to remove oil-soaked seaweed from the shores of Roscoff and dispose of it in deeper water. However, due to the unstable nature of the cargo, it shifted and slid in the holds as the vessel worked in the rough seas, disrupting the vessel's stability and causing her to sink off of L'Aberwrac'h on April 14, 1978. No lives were lost.

Aftermath

The Liberian Board of Inquiry found irregularities in the recorded position of the vessel on the day of the grounding. Positions that had been recorded in the log were not supported by positions indicated on the chart. At one point the vessel had to change course in order to allow men on deck to secure some drums that had broken free, but it caused her to enter the wrong traffic lane, then she cut across the shipping lanes in order to get back on her proper side. Despite the availability of radar, visual navigational aids, and the availability of DECCA fixes, the Board had a difficult time teasing out the specifics of the vessel's navigation on the day of the grounding.

Failure of the steering gear, and lack of an auxiliary steering system, was a primary cause of the casualty, but a delayed and inept response by the master of the ship is what caused a simple mechanical failure to become one of the worst oil spills in history. The steering failure occurred at 0946, dangerously near a rocky lee shore. While steering failures are often readily corrected, and often occur where there's lots of sea room, by the time the master had inspected the failure himself and returned to the bridge at 1020, he knew that the steering failure was serious. Such a failure in such a location demands an acute and decisive response, not dithering and delay.

In summary, the Liberian Board of Inquiry found fault with the master on several counts, mostly for what he did not do. He did not ready the anchors, he did not call for assistance in a timely manner, he wasted time haggling over a salvage versus a towing agreement, and he delayed sending a distress call.

In contrast with the findings of the Board of Inquiry, Mr. Philip Bowen, the Commissioner of Maritime Affairs, found no real fault with Captain Bardari's failure to broadcast a formal request for help immediately. Mr. Bowen felt the first distress call should have been sent, at the latest, at 1615, when the first towline parted and it became obvious the tug *Pacific* would be ineffective towing the massive ship in the prevailing weather. He found it inexcusable that the first distress call was sent at 2326, almost two and a half hours after the first grounding.

Captain Bardari's license was impounded by the Board and was held in suspension for three years, but not revoked.

Interestingly, Shell Oil, the cargo owners, routinely did not insure its cargos, and the $20 million cargo was a total loss. The cost of cleanup and the financial damages sustained by the French soared into the hundreds of millions of French francs. Almost ten years after the incident, a U.S. court found the tanker's owners (Amoco is a U.S. corporation) liable for the spill and ordered Amoco to pay over $85 million in damages, almost half of which was allocated as interest payments, since the case took almost ten years to resolve. It took fourteen years of litigation against Amoco before the French Government was finally awarded approximately €190 million.

As a result of the *Amoco Cadiz* incident, the Lloyd's Open Form (LOF), which traditionally provided for "no cure, no pay" salvage agreement, was revised to address distressed ships that pose environmental threats. The goal was to encourage salvors to respond to environmental threats without worry that their efforts, if there was no traditional cure, would go uncompensated. The revised language allowed a salvor to recover his expenses plus up to 15 percent, even if he was unable to effect any salvaging of maritime property, but was successful in preventing or mitigating environmental damage. As of 1999, the LOF has a Special Compensation P&I Clause (SCOPIC) that allows recovery for prevention of environmental harm. Worldwide, recognizing the inherent fairness of such an agreement, distressed vessels agree to LOF roughly 100 times a year. It is, by far, the most used salvage agreement.

The French responded by changing their oil response plan (POLMAR) to require that stocks of spill equipment be maintained in various locations and to create traffic lanes in the channel. In the wake of the spill, the French created the Centre of Documentation, Research and Experimentation on Accidental Water Pollution (CEDRE), a nonprofit organization whose mission is to improve spill response preparedness and strengthen France's national response organization.

The Board also recommended that various industry organizations, such as the International Chamber of Shipping (ICS), the OCIMF, and INTERTANKO generate written guidance for masters facing salvage operations. They also urged that the story of the *Amoco Cadiz* be promulgated to ship's officers so they could learn from the disaster.

From 1965 to1980, the heyday of the supertankers, thirty-five tankers or combination oil-bulk-ore (OBO) carriers of over 100,000 DWT were victims of either fire or explosion. One such casualty that doesn't receive much attention is detailed as the last casualty in this chapter.[9]

The Standards of Training, Certification, and Watchkeeping (STCW) 1978

The STCW Convention was drafted in 1978 to standardize training and seatime requirements for mariners worldwide. It was the first major international convention to deal with the human element, augmenting multiple previous conventions that addressed equipment or construction standards, or specific operational practices.

The STCW convention entered into force in 1984 and applied to all crew members, officer and unlicensed alike. Since it basically imposed U.S. standards on the rest of the world, American mariners were not profoundly affected. Compliance with the provisions of the STCW convention can be required of any vessel that calls at a signatory nation's ports, even if the vessel's flag state never agreed to its provisions. This is rarely an issue since 157 nations representing over 99 percent of the world's tonnage have agreed to abide by the provisions of STCW. Nations abiding by STCW provisions are said to be on the "white list." See Appendix A for more information about STCW.[10]

The SS *Atlantic Empress* and the SS *Aegean Captain*

On the evening of July 19, 1979, two fully-loaded supertankers collided in rainy weather roughly ten miles off the Tobago Islands in the Caribbean Sea. The force of the collision locked the vessels together, and *Atlantic Empress* (290,000 DWT) was completely engulfed in flames.

Of the thirty-four crew members aboard the *Atlantic Empress*, only five survived, including her master. Thankfully, the fire only spread to the bow of the *Aegean Captain* (210,000 DWT), which, when the vessels finally broke apart, was able to be towed to safety. Despite some crew members being severely burned, all the crew members of the *Aegean Captain* survived. A few days later, the master of the *Aegean Captain* and three of his crew reboarded the ship, and were able to extinguish the fire.

The *Atlantic Empress*, however, continued to burn for days, despite multiple vessels attempting to quench the fire. On July 23 and 24 several explosions jolted the vessel, with another, more powerful, explosion on July 29. By then the vessel had been towed a safe 300 miles from Tobago. By August 2, the ship was listing, still engulfed in flames, and floating in an ever-increasing oil slick. Eventually, fifteen days later, almost a month after the original collision, she finally sank, leaving a silent oil slick behind. It is estimated she lost over 84 million gallons of oil, but no one knows how much oil burned, how much was emulsified with dispersants, and how much remained on the ocean surface.

There are no in-depth studies of this incident, nor is it widely known, probably because no shoreside pollution is recorded to have occurred as a result of the collision. We'll never know because no environmental studies were conducted—by anyone. The international community was still reeling and responding to the *Sea Witch* and the *Esso Brussels*, the *Argo Merchant*, and the

Amoco Cadiz, not to mention a much more newsworthy incident two weeks earlier when the oil drilling rig *Ixtoc* suffered a blowout on June 3, 1979, spewing tens of thousands of barrels of oil per day into the Gulf of Mexico. Nobody really cared what had happened in a relatively unpopulated part of the Caribbean, despite it being considered the fourth largest spill in history.[11]

Notes

1. Sources for VTS information: Michael T. Brown (NTSB Marine Transportation Safety Specialist), *Marine Voyage Data Recorders,* submitted at the International Symposium on Transportation Recorders, May 3–5, 1999; Richard A. Cahill, *Collisions and Their Causes*; U.S. Coast Guard Navigation Center History of Vessel Traffic Services, http://www.navcen.uscg.gov/?pageName=vtsHistory; *History of VTS Houston*, http://www.uscg.mil/vtshouston/docs/history.pdf.

2. Sources for *Oregon Standard* and *Arizona Standard* information: Richard A. Cahill, *Collisions and Their Causes*; National Transportation Safety Board Marine Casualty Report, *Collision Involving the SS* Arizona Standard *and SS* Oregon Standard *at the Entrance to San Francisco Bay on January 18, 1971;* U.S. Coast Guard Marine Board of Investigation Report and Commandant's Action released August 11, 1971.

3. Sources for *Esso Brussels* and *Sea Witch* information: *Proceedings of the Marine Safety Council*, May 1976, CG-129 Vol. 33 No. 5; U.S. Coast Guard/National Transportation Safety Board Casualty Report MAR-75-6 released March 2, 1976.

4. Federal Register FR-1996-06-04.

5. Sources for *Edmund Fitzgerald* information: David G. Brown, *White Hurricane: A Great Lakes November Gale and America's Deadliest Maritime Disaster* (New York: International Marine/McGraw-Hill, 2002); Robert J. Hemming, *Ships Gone Missing: The Great Lakes Storm of 1913* (Chicago: Contemporary Books, Inc., 1992); Norman Hooke, *Maritime Casualties*; William Ratigan. *Great Lakes Shipwrecks and Survivals* (Grand Rapids: William B. Eerdmans Publishing Co., 1987); Robert Shipley and Fred Addis, *Wrecks and Disasters: Great Lakes Album Series* (St. Catharines, Ontario: Vanwell Publishing Limited, 1992); NTSB Marine Accident Report on the SS *Edmund Fitzgerald* Sinking in Lake Superior on November 10, 1975, Report Number NTSB MAR 78-3 dated May 4, 1978, http://www.uscg.mil/history/WEBSHIP-WRECKS/EdmundFitzgeraldNTSBReport.pdf; U.S. Coast Guard *"Marine Board Casualty Report: SS Edmund Fitzgerald; Sinking in Lake Superior on 10 November 1975 With Loss of Life,"* dated July 26, 1977; http://www.ssefo.com/info/timeline.html.

6. Sources for *Argo Merchant* information: Richard A. Cahill, *Disasters at Sea*; Richard A. Cahill, *Strandings and Their Causes*; Norman Hooke, *Maritime Casualties*; Roger A. Peterson, *Maritime Oil Tanker Casualties*; Ron Winslow, *Hard Aground* (New York: Norton and Company, 1978); "Decision of the Committee of Maritime Affairs, R.L. and Final Report of the Marine Board of Investigation in the Matter of the Stranding of the Steam Tanker *Argo Merchant* (O.N. 3727) on December 15, 1976," *Bureau of Maritime Affairs*, Monrovia, Liberia, October 10, 1977.

7. Center for Tanker Excellence Document found at http://www.c4tx.org/ctx/job/cdb/precis.php5?key=19780316_001.

8. Carly Gillis, *Amoco Cadiz: A Brief History* (Counterspill: April 10, 2011), http://www.counterspill.org/article/amoco-cadiz-brief-history.

9. Sources for *Amoco Cadiz* information: Richard A. Cahill, *Disasters at Sea*; Richard A. Cahill, *Strandings and Their Causes*; Norman Hooke, *Maritime Casualties*; Roger A. Peterson, *Maritime Oil Tanker Casualties*; "Decision of the Commissioner of Maritime Affairs, R. L. and final and interim report of the formal inves-

tigation by the Marine Board of Investigation in the matter of the loss by grounding of the VLCC *Amoco Cadiz* (O.N. 4773), 16 March 1978," *Bureau of Maritime Affairs,* Monrovia, Liberia, December 30, 1980; Case Studies of the International Tanker Owners Pollution Federation, Ltd., http://www.itopf.com/information-services/data-and-statistics/case-histories; Centre of Documentation, Research and Experimentation (CEDRE) on Accidental Water Pollution, http://www.cedre.fr/en/cedre/index.php; NOAA Incident news on the *Amoco Cadiz,* http://incidentnews.noaa.gov/incident/6241; Counterspill Organization, www.counterspill.org; The Wrecksite Organization, www.wrecksite.eu; Lloyd's, www.lloyds.com.

10. Sources for STCW information: www.stcw.org; www.imo.org.

11. Sources for *Atlantic Empress* and *Aegean Captain* information: Richard A. Cahill, *Collisions and Their Causes*; Richard A. Cahill, *Disasters at Sea*; Norman Hooke, *Maritime Casualties*; Stuart A. Horn and Captain Phillip Neal, "The *Atlantic Empress* Sinking—A Large Spill Without Environmental Disaster," abstract, IOSC Proceedings, Mobil Oil Corp. New York, http://ioscproceedings.org/doi/pdf/10.7901/2169-3358-1981-1-429; Roger A. Peterson, *Maritime Oil Tanker Casualties*; Larry West, "The 10 Worst Oil Spills in History," *About.Com: Environmental Issues,* http://environment.about.com/od/environmentalevents/tp/worst-oil-spills.htm; CEDRE, Accidental Water Pollution, http://www.cedre.fr/en/spill/atlantic/atlantic.php; Case Studies of the International Tanker Owners Pollution Federation, Ltd., http://www.itopf.com/in-action/case-studies/.

Chapter 8
1980 to 1989

1983: MT *Castillo de Bellver,* explodes off Africa, one of the ten largest spills
1983: SS *Marine Electric,* sinking off the coast of Virginia
1987: The *Doña Paz* and MT *Vector,* historic loss of life aboard overloaded ferry
1987: The *Herald of Free Enterprise,* capsizing, leading to International Safety Management Code
1988: MT *Odyssey,* spill ten times larger than *Exxon Valdez*; no legislation pending
1989: MV *Exxon Valdez,* worst spill in U.S. history, leading to the Oil Pollution Act of 1990

The Iran-Iraq war brought dozens of tankers to their deaths, but non-war-related tanker losses of this decade averaged sixteen per year, still high, but fewer than in the previous decade. Most of the large tankers were involved with the Iran-Iraq war, and thus most of the losses of tankers during the war were of the VLCC class. Wartime losses are not the focus of this book, as usually no legislation is spawned by such tragedies.

The MT *Castillo de Bellver*

Despite valuable lessons learned in the 1970s, oil spills from large tankers continued to occur in the 1980s. In the wee hours of the morning of August 6, 1983, the Spanish tanker *Castillo de Bellver* (270,000 DWT) exploded off the coast of South Africa, spilling roughly half her load of approximately 79 million gallons of crude oil into the raging fire surrounding the vessel. Three crew members were killed. A day later, she broke in two and the stern section exploded again on its own, and sank, taking the rest of the cargo in her tanks to the ocean floor. The bow section, also with some remaining cargo still held up forward, was towed to deeper water and intentionally sunk.

Fortunately, light offshore winds and the expeditious use of dispersants kept the sixty-square-mile spill from damaging the sensitive shoreline and pristine beaches of the South African coast. Despite the fact that over a thousand sea birds (that they know of) were oiled as they flocked to their breeding grounds, and seals were seen surfacing in the oil slick and dispersant areas (apparently with no "visible" adverse affects), and that for twenty-four hours after the incident a "black rain" fell on crops and animal grazing areas ashore, reports were that "no significant damage" was recorded to the local fisheries and wildlife. This is considered the seventh largest spill in history. Hopefully, a similar incident today would prompt a more concerned response. It is included here due primarily to the size of the spill, and not due to any legislation prompted by the incident.[1]

The SS *Marine Electric*

During World War II, the United States built hundreds of handy-sized, roughly 500-foot-long, 16,000-DWT tankers, called T2 tankers. Several models were built, many prior to the war, but during the war the most popular model, the T2-SE-A1 tankers, were built with staggering speed at yards all across the country. The Marinship Boatyard in Sausalito, California, held the record, having built a T2 in just thirty-three days.

They were never intended to last very long and, probably due to logistical, economic, and time constraints, were often constructed with "dirty" steel, steel that was not of the highest purity or quality, and with a sulfur content that was too high, which rendered the steel brittle in cold temperatures.

After the war, most of these ships remained in service and were often converted for use in the commercial trade, but they began having problems as they aged.

So many T2 tankers broke apart in cold weather that mariners began to question their seaworthiness. After the *Pendleton* and the *Fort Mercer*, both T2 tankers, broke apart within four hours of each other during a gale off Cape Cod in February 1952, the Coast Guard held an investigation. Not only was it determined that substandard steel had been used to build the T2 tankers, but also that quite frequently the welds were suspect.

In response to these findings, commercial owners of T2 tankers tried to reinforce the hulls by belting or banding the ship with steel plates to nurse the ships along and keep them in service. By the 1980s, such ships, even with diligent attempts to maintain and repair them, were essentially rust buckets. They were forty years old and beyond their useful life, yet many remained in service.

The Marine Transport Lines' *Marine Electric* was just such a ship. She was built in 1961—well, not actually. Her bow and stern were from a T2 tanker built in 1944 (the *Muskgroves Mills*) and her midsection was built in 1962 at a German yard and installed in the United States at Bethlehem Steel. By 1983 she was an old girl, patched together to become a bulk ship, and even her "new" midsection was over twenty years old.

She shuttled coal on a thirty-two-hour run between Virginia and Massachusetts. On February 10, 1983, the ship's chief mate, Bob Cusick, who had worked the ship for five years and knew her intimately, was monitoring the big chutes that loaded the coal into the vessel's holds while she rested at her berth in Norfolk, Virginia. He loaded the ship to below her legal limit, a common procedure aboard vessels at fresh water berths, because he knew once the ship was out to sea, and floating higher in the denser salt water, she would float perfectly legally at her marks. The permanent master, James Farnham, was on vacation during this run, and the relief master, Philip Corl, himself a seasoned *Marine Electric* officer, was in command.

She had to be loaded carefully to prevent a non-uniform load of the heavy cargo from exceeding allowable stresses on the ship's tired bones or she could break her back. The chief mate, noting over ninety cracks in her hatch covers, knew the ship was falling apart.

The ship was "tired iron," and Cusick, concerned about her safety, had even once refused to take her across the Atlantic, opting instead to stay close to the U.S. shore and ready rescue should she go down. The mate even nicknamed the ship the *Marine Sidewalk*, because she had so much cement patching holes in her decks.

Another senior officer had also refused to take the ship offshore, and had even gone so far as to call the Coast Guard to report the ship's unsafe condition, but to no avail. He watched in disbelief as the Coast Guard inspectors, along with inspectors from ABS, the vessel's classification society, ignored obvious safety violations, stepping over cracks in the deck, despite the crew's having spray painted bright circles around them. Daylight beamed through some of the hatch covers, they were so rusted.

But the run was easy and the ship was a "feeder." Jobs were tight, the money was good, and best of all, the men were close to home and could see their families regularly, so they stayed. Most of the crew didn't complain openly about the condition of the ship. They wanted to keep their jobs and felt nothing would get fixed if they did speak up, so they nursed the rotten ship along, with patches made of glue, epoxy, some steel "doubler plates," and cement.

The post-incident Coast Guard investigation found the ship had over 400 holes in her decks and hatch covers, many of which had been patched by the crew.

What the crew didn't appreciate was that even if a hole was patched and made watertight by epoxy or cement, the steel was not properly repaired, and thus could not withstand the tremendous weights and stresses experienced when a ship takes green seas across her decks and hatches, or works and twists in a seaway. So the ship may have been watertight, but she was not flexible and she was not strong.

It was not uncommon for officer's wives to join them on the short, easy, coastwise run, but for some reason, on this one trip, Captain Corl, despite plans for her to come, told his wife to stay ashore and that he'd see her after they returned. That decision probably saved her life.

Two other crewmen reported to the ship but didn't sail with her, due to mix-ups with union hall assignments. Another seaman was fired before the ship sailed and an engineer failed to report for duty. The ship would sail anyway.

The ship was due to depart Norfolk with a full load of 24,800 tons of coal on February 10, 1983. Anticipating bad weather and knowing that a compromised hatch could sink the ship, the mate had all the hatch dogs secured. But the hatches had holes in them and some of the securing dogs didn't work. Just before midnight, the *Marine Electric* cast off her lines and headed north toward the pilot station.

At the Chesapeake pilot station, the harbor pilot climbed his way down the pilot ladder and, timing his jump with the growing waves, landed safely on the pilot boat. But the boat didn't leave immediately, and instead, a man got out and climbed aboard the *Marine Electric*—it was the missing engineer! Though the weather was bad, and worsening, everyone was in a cheerful mood.

By the next morning sea conditions had worsened. The ship was pounding through waves of up to forty feet and winding her way onward in sixty-knot winds. The ship was handling the weather and the crew settled in to their routines.

Around 1500 on February 11, the *Marine Electric* responded to a Coast Guard request to assist a nearby fish boat, the *Theodora*, which was south of their position and taking on water. It was a dangerous maneuver in such high seas, but Captain Corl turned the *Marine Electric* around and headed for the stricken vessel. After the turn, the *Marine Electric* started taking the pounding seas on her stern instead of her bow, and as a result she was rolling more, but taking less green water over her bow. By 1700 the radars of the *Marine Electric* had acquired the *Theodora* and the crew could hear the Coast Guard rescue helicopter hovering nearby. The Coast Guard helicopter lowered extra pumps to the *Theodora*, then headed back to shore with the assurance that the USCG cutter *Highland* was on its way and would be on scene before midnight. The *Marine Electric* was requested to stand by until the Coast Guard ship arrived.

International regulations require the rendering of assistance at sea, unless doing so presents an unreasonable risk to the rescuer's own vessel. Despite worsening conditions, the *Marine Electric* stayed on station, but she was taking a beating. The Coast Guard urged her to stay on station. By 1830, Corl radioed the Coast Guard and said he wasn't sure he could heave-to any longer, as he was taking green seas over the deck and having a rough time of it. The *Theodora* weighed in and said they would be OK, now that they had the extra pumps, and the cutter was on its way, so they were fine if the *Marine Electric* needed to leave. The Coast Guard concurred, and the *Marine Electric* was dismissed, turning once again northward in the heavy seas.

By 0100 February 12, some of the bridge officers sensed something was wrong with the way the ship felt, but they couldn't put their finger on it. The weather was so bad, and the visibility so low, they couldn't really see the bow. But something was wrong. By 0200 the bow was no longer explosively rising buoyantly from the waves and shedding water, and it seemed the ship was starting to trim down by the head, allowing green water to run increasingly farther down the deck. By now Captain Corl was awake and in the wheelhouse. The chief mate and chief engineer both came to the bridge to watch the bow, and what they saw horrified them. The ship was in trouble. She was not shedding off the boarding seas the way she should be.

The master immediately notified the Coast Guard, had the engineers redistribute ballast, and had the entire crew awakened and ordered the lifeboats made ready for launch.

The master had no intention of abandoning ship just yet. He knew the old adage about always "stepping up into a lifeboat" so one doesn't prematurely leave a huge floating object. But he wanted things ready just in case.

By 0300 things had become so dangerous the master called the Coast Guard and requested assistance. He wasn't sure exactly how bad things were, but he knew he wanted a chopper standing by to lift his crew off the ship if necessary.

He then mustered his crew in the wheelhouse to discuss abandoning ship. Launching boats in such heavy seas was more dangerous than staying aboard. The Coast Guard was to arrive in about twenty minutes, but walls of green water six feet deep were washing down the deck, covering the leaky hatches with tons of water. This was not normal. The ship was about eight degrees down by the head. The storm was not abating. Then the watch team saw the crack in the hatch of the forward-most cargo hold.

The engineers started pumps to empty the hold of seawater, but the ship began to list to starboard. The list, coupled with the rolling action of the waves, caused the ship to roll to fourteen degrees. The ship was listing and rolling so badly, it was doubtful the crew could launch the lifeboats, but they readied them anyway. The weakened, rusty condition of the ship was finally coming home to roost. One crew member reported he couldn't get the plug in the keel of the lifeboat because the fixture was too rusty. After using a wrench, the plug was finally inserted and the boat was made ready for launching. Meanwhile the radio officer hailed nearby ships and the crew threw liferings into the water in anticipation of abandoning ship. The *Marine Electric* was no longer responding to her helm, the list was worsening, and there was no hope of saving the sinking ship.

At 0414, Captain Corl radioed the Coast Guard that they were abandoning ship. Maddeningly, the Coast Guard, no doubt following some form, asked him what color the ship's lifeboats were!

Urgently, the crew scrambled to the lifeboat, one man falling overboard, when the ship suddenly lurched to starboard and capsized, taking everyone into the chaos of thirty-nine-degree water and twenty-foot waves. It was the worst storm the area had seen in forty years. There was little hope of survival in such a sea-state and freezing conditions. Hypothermia set in quickly as the crew frantically tried to get out from under the rolling, sinking ship.

Coast Guard cutters and a helicopter were dispatched to the scene, but the weather was awful and the cutters were hours away. The rescue would have to be made solely by the helicopter.

Though there were survivors in the water when the rescue helicopter arrived, they were too incapacitated by cold to grasp the baskets that the rescuers had lowered to them. A nearby ship reached the scene too late as well. As it had approached the scene, the crew thought they saw survivors waving in the sea and swell. But as they approached, they realized they had only seen dead bodies with their arms being tossed by the waves, as if they were waving.

The *Marine Electric*'s engineers were trapped below and went down with the ship, and all other crew who made it to the water died of hypothermia, except for three men. Ultimately, thirty-one of the thirty-four crew members perished. The *Marine Electric* sank at 1230 that day.

Aftermath

The incident exposed weak Coast Guard inspection policies and prompted the scrapping of dozens of tired and unsafe World War II vessels. The casualty was largely ignored by the mainstream media, but Robert Frump of the *Philadelphia Inquirer* relentlessly researched the case and published numerous articles exposing the rust buckets of World War II for the death ships they were.

The U.S. Coast Guard casualty report runs 154 pages. Recognizing the shortfalls in their shipboard inspection system, in July 1983, just six months after the *Marine Electric* sinking, the Coast Guard established a special inspection program, requiring senior surveyors with extensive experience, for inspections of vessels twenty years of age and older.

The Coast Guard also updated its training programs for marine safety inspectors and increased supervision of ABS surveyors acting on the Coast Guard's behalf in conducting load line and other inspections.

The hearing board in part blamed the *Marine Electric* crew for not directly pointing out safety violations to the marine inspectors, ostensibly because the crew wanted to keep their lucrative commercial maritime jobs, though there are accounts indicating reports were made and ignored by Coast Guard inspectors. To encourage reporting, the Coast Guard implemented a 24-hour hotline for mariners to report safety violations. The Coast Guard also determined, as a result of this incident, to promote the requirement for tankers and cargo ships in coastwise or ocean service to be fitted with closed lifeboats and automatic launching systems by 1991. The Coast Guard also proposed that inflatable liferafts be fitted with boarding ramps and that immersion testing for EPIRBs be implemented.

In February 1984, a final rule was published requiring an exposure (immersion) suit be carried for every person aboard on vessels sailing pole-ward of the 35th parallel. Though the Notice of Proposed Rulemaking to require exposure suits was in place before the *Marine Electric* sinking, this incident solidified and expedited the new requirement.

The Coast Guard investigation revealed the *Marine Electric* had over 400 "doublers," or patches over holes, in her deck and hatches. On January 25, 1985, the Coast Guard, determining correctly that a vessel owner bears primary responsibility for a vessel's seaworthiness, recommended criminal indictments for the Marine Transport Lines' marine superintendent Joseph Thelgie for sending such an unseaworthy ship to sea, and against the ship's permanent master, James Farnham (who was not aboard when the ship sank), for failing to report such gross safety violations to the Coast Guard or ABS, as required by law. The Coast Guard also began proceedings against Captain Farnham's license.

In response to the sinking, and the problems the Coast Guard had in rescuing survivors, a Congressional hearing was convened. As a result, on October 30, 1984, Congress directed the Coast Guard to begin a rescue swimmer program.

The company settled with the families for roughly $14 million, with each family receiving about $350,000.

The bodies of the ship's master and six engineers have never been found.[2]

The *Doña Paz* and the MT *Vector*

To date, this maritime tragedy remains the worst peacetime loss of life.

On December 20, 1987, the Philippine passenger ferry *Doña Paz* was headed to Manila for the holidays, packed with passengers. The *Doña Paz* was certified to carry 1,518 passengers. Despite an official passenger manifest indicating 1,493 passengers aboard, children under the age of four were not listed, nor were passengers who paid after boarding. In developing nations, with cultural values that often differ from modern western sensibilities, it is not unusual for vessel operators and scalpers to sell counterfeit tickets, often loading a vessel to its physical capacity—well in excess of its legal capacity—and regulatory enforcement of any sort is often lax. On the night

The ferry *Doña Paz* at Tacloban, Philippines. *lindsaybridge via Wikimedia Commons license.*

of December 20 hundreds of passengers sat on the deck and families crowded into cabins and lounges. Survivors reported that the ship was so crowded people had difficulty finding a place to lie down or even sit. The ship was so overloaded it was listing. Estimates put the total number of passengers aboard at well over 4,000—roughly four times the number of people the vessel was designed to carry.

At about 2200, while underway in the Tablas Straits, off the island of Mindoro in the Sibuyan Sea of the Philippines, the *Doña Paz* collided with the MT *Vector* (a tanker loaded with kerosene and gasoline) and both vessels instantly burst into flames. The *Doña Paz* had no radio, thus no way to call for help, and it was eight hours before authorities became aware of the disaster. It took another eight hours for search and rescue resources to locate the site of the incident. Given the ferocity of the fire and the speed of the sinking, it is doubtful a radio would have had much effect on the ultimate outcome of the tragedy.

Within two hours of the collision the burning ferry sank. Only twenty-four people of the thousands aboard the *Doña Paz* survived. Eleven crew members of the *Vector,* which also sank, were killed. Of the 4,047 people the Philippine government originally estimated were killed, only 180 bodies were recovered. The official final count of those lost ended up being a staggering 4,386 dead: 4,375 from the *Doña Paz*, and 11 from the *Vector.*

Due to the almost complete lack of evidence, little meaningful change resulted from the disaster. Though several Philippine Coast Guard officials were fired or reprimanded due to the bungled rescue response, the Philippine investigation report placed the blame entirely on the *Vector*, but it was never proven which ship was rammed. With typical third-world whitewash and twisted logic, the Philippine report also determined the *Doña Paz* was not overcrowded because her loadline was not submerged. When it was discovered that the *Vector* was on longterm charter to Cal-Tex Philippines, a wholly owned subsidiary of Cal-Tex Petroleum of Texas, family members of the deceased and injured brought suit in the United States, but due to jurisdictional issues, the case has never been adjudicated on the merits. It is considered the worst peacetime loss of life from a maritime disaster to date. The story was made into a National Geographic Special in 2009.

Seven years earlier, in a spot roughly forty miles from the *Doña Paz* disaster, another Philippine ferry, the *Don Juan*, collided with the motorized tank-barge *Tacloban City,* and sank, killing over 1,000. That so many lives are lost in the stretch of water between Mindoro and Marinduque is no surprise, as it is one of the busiest ferry and shipping lanes in the Philippines, and regulatory enforcement in this part of the world is notoriously weak.[3]

The *Herald of Free Enterprise*

Three minutes.

If the chief officer had lingered on the loading deck for three minutes more, none of this would have happened.

The Ro/Ro and freight ferry *Herald of Free Enterprise* was built in Bremerhaven in 1980 and was owned by Townsend Car Ferries Ltd., a subsidiary of Peninsular and Oriental Steam Navigation Company (commonly known as P&O). She was 433 feet long and had three controllable pitch propellers, each powered by an 8,000-horsepower engine. She was also fitted with a bow thruster and modern navigational aids. She was classed by Lloyd's Register, one of the world's most reputable classification societies, as a +100A2 ferry. The vessel did more than comply with the safety gear requirements for her size and route; she carried extra gear. Her Class II Passenger Ferry certificate had expired, but she was given a one-month extension before heading to the yard for her annual refit. So at the time of the incident, she had all required certificates and was in full compliance with existing regulations.

The number of passengers the ship could carry was dependant on her freeboard, and conversely, required freeboard depended on the number of passengers aboard. Depending on freeboard, the

The ferry *Herald of Free Enterprise* at her dock in Dover. Note the gaping vehicle doors.

Herald of Free Enterprise could carry between 630 and 1,400 passengers.

She was constructed of welded steel, with double bottoms below her eight decks. The lowest of her decks (H-Deck) was below the main deck, and was subdivided by thirteen watertight bulkheads with nine watertight doors to facilitate access between compartments. There were four watertight flats for passengers and stores. The main deck (G-Deck) was a "through-vehicle deck," with double weathertight doors at the bow and a single weathertight door at the stern, but no intermediate compartmentalization—it was basically one long, open deck. Along the sides of G-Deck was a mezzanine deck, which housed the crew accommodations. The next deck (F-Deck) was another vehicle deck, but this deck was open aft, and had only a weathertight door forward. D-Deck was a suspended vehicle platform, and C-Deck and decks above housed passengers, the bridge, and other non-vehicular areas.

Since this incident involved flooding, it is important to understand the construction of the lower vehicle deck and the meaning of the term "weathertight" as opposed to "watertight." A watertight door is meant to keep water out from pressure on either side. A weathertight door is designed to keep water out from one side only. Most doors on ships are actually "weathertight" doors, designed to keep water from the outside from getting in.

The doors on the *Herald of Free Enterprise* were weathertight, and designed to keep water that was external to the vessel, out. At her bow she had inner and outer doors. Her stern door was a single weathertight door. The steel doors were operated hydraulically, and the seal was a tubular neoprene gasket that was compressed by hydraulic dogs.

The lower vehicle deck had twenty drains on each side to drain away water that may accumulate due to weather, a leak, intentional hosing down, or even firefighting activity.

The usual run for the *Herald of Free Enterprise* was between Dover and Calais, a short run with very fast turnaround times, and a full crew was carried to accommodate the fast pace of operations. Because the ferry was changed to the longer run between Dover and Zeebrugge, the company, thinking the crew had longer to relax between ports, only hired a master, Captain Lewry, and two deck officers, instead of the usual three.

On arrival in Zeebrugge on March 6, 1987, after arriving passengers and vehicles had departed, the assistant boatswain prepared the forward vehicle doors for loading. After opening the forward doors, he worked with other crew members on routine cleaning and maintenance duties until the end of his shift, when he was relieved by the boatswain. The assistant boatswain then went to bed.

He slept so soundly he never heard the call to "harbor stations," which should have roused him to go secure the forward doors for sea. Despite a standing order requiring that a deck officer close the doors, the deck officers were performing other duties and no one double-checked to see that the doors had been closed. (Four years earlier, a similar incident had occurred on a sister ship.)

Zeebrugge, unlike other ports, had only a single-level loading dock, so the ship had to be creatively ballasted in order to get all the decks loaded with vehicles. So in addition to operating with a reduced crew, the deck officer on duty had to ballast and de-ballast, trimming the ship this way and that, in order to get the ship's loading ramps lined up with the single fixed dock at Zeebrugge.

There was an unspoken question between the two deck officers as to who was in charge of the loading cycle, and it was unclear exactly who was responsible for ensuring the doors were closed when loading was complete. Each officer probably assumed the other was responsible, as no guidance was found in the orders concerning operations with a reduced crew.

The boatswain, who had run the chain across the ramp after the last vehicle boarded, hadn't closed the doors afterward because it wasn't in his job description and he had never remained at the ramp on any previous trips to ensure the doors were closed.

In accordance with the standing orders (which assumed the ship had three deck officers), after loading was complete the chief officer was to take his post in the wheelhouse for departure. The standing orders read that the "O.O.W. (officer of the watch)/Master" be on the bridge fifteen minutes before departing, but it was unclear if one or the other, or both people were required. In the case at hand, the *Herald of Free Enterprise*'s chief officer felt compelled to be on the bridge before departure, and rushed from the cargo decks to the wheelhouse to be there before the ship got underway.

However, during the post-incident hearings, a senior master of the fleet said normal procedure is to have the chief officer at the bow, finalizing papers and closing doors, the second officer at the stern, ensuring the propeller is clear and letting go the stern mooring lines, and the master on the bridge.

It was normal procedure for the officer on duty at the end of loading to call the bridge just before loading was finished, and advise calling the crew to their departure stations. In an effort to stay on time, it was considered most efficient to call the crew just a bit early, as by the time they reported to their stations, the last vehicles would be aboard and the vessel could get underway immediately. It also was not unusual to untie the ship and get underway, closing the doors as the vessel was leaving the berth. She was, after all, in a protected harbor and a few minutes delay was not seen as any safety threat.

During the hearings, a memorandum surfaced indicating management's goal to have the ships sail fifteen minutes early, and to pressure the ship's officers if they were not moving fast enough. It was clear from both testimony and written evidence that the culture of Townsend Car Ferries, Ltd. was to pressure crews to decrease turnaround times.

As for the master's role, the standing orders stated that department heads were to notify the master if any condition would render the vessel unsuited for departure, and that absent such notifications, the master should assume the vessel was ready for sea and depart. So, absent any notifications that the ship wasn't ready that fateful day, Captain Lewry got the ship underway.

In order to accommodate the single-level loading dock at Zeebrugge, the *Herald of Free Enterprise* had to be trimmed down by the head. The crew accomplished this by filling the ship's forward ballast tank. As the *Herald of Free Enterprise* made her way from the dock, she was trimmed down by the head, as her forward ballast tank had not yet been emptied.

When the ship passed the outer breakwater, the master increased speed, which was premature, as the forward ballast tank was still full, and as the ship squatted down and the bow wave increased, water started coming in over the bow. The bow started digging in to the water, decreasing the forward freeboard, literally shoveling water into the vehicle deck like a gaping maw. The free surface effect from all the loose water on G-Deck caused negative stability, and the vessel rapidly listed to port about thirty degrees, which caused water to pool on the port side, further eroding her stability.

Almost instantly, the vessel reached neutral stability and came to a large angle of loll, yet icy water continued to pour in through the forward doors. With free communication with the sea, her stability was so badly compromised that she slowly rolled further to port, eventually capsizing to ninety degrees and coming to rest on the sea floor. She was prevented from sinking completely only because her port side grounded in the shallow water, leaving her starboard side above sea level.

She capsized about half a mile from the harbor entrance, just four minutes after she had passed

The Ferry *Herald of Free Enterprise* lying on her side, having capsized just beyond the harbor breakwater at Zeebrugge. *Associated Press / David Caulkin.*

the outer breakwater.

At least 150 passengers and thirty-eight crew were killed and hundreds more were injured. The official death toll was 193 lives lost. Though rescue arrived within fifteen minutes of the capsizing, it happened so suddenly that people trapped below decks were unable to free themselves.

There were problems with the rescue. The rescue helicopters' lights blinded the surface rescue crews, and the noise from the rotors and engines made communication almost impossible. Additionally, the downdraft from helicopters hovering above the scene made it difficult to stand or walk on the ship's side. None of the ship's lifesaving equipment had been deployed—the incident just happened too fast.

As a result of the incident, the vessel was declared a total loss and sold for scrap.

Elements of the Error Chain: The Company's Shortcomings

The confusion as to duties while in port arose because the standing orders had not been changed to address the reduced manning on the Zeebrugge run. The hearing board felt the reduced manning level would have been safe if the standing orders had been changed and duties redistributed to reflect the reduced manning level on the new run.

Despite five previous occurrences of their ferries sailing with the doors open, the company's standing orders remained confusing and woefully deficient in detail. The orders had no requirement for many safety checks, including ensuring the weathertight doors were closed. The company's standing orders were neither vessel nor route-specific, which meant no changes were made for differences between ports and runs.

Also exposed at the hearing was the lack of reliable stability data. The *Herald of Free Enterprise* had modifications and the addition of stores and other items that had not been added to the vessel's displacement values. The hearing board opined that since many of the vehicles' weights were underreported and erroneous lightship displacement values were used, the *Herald of Free Enterprise* was most likely significantly overloaded on the night of the incident. It was not felt, however, that this overloading contributed to the casualty.

It was discovered that other ferries had sailed with the doors accidentally left open, and another master had recommended to the company that indicator lights be installed. This suggestion not only was ignored, but was made light of by management. Interestingly, within a few days after the disaster, the company installed door indicator lights on the other vessels in the fleet.

On the Zeebrugge run, due to the single-level dock, all the ferries had to ballast significantly down by the head, yet no high-capacity pumps were fitted to expedite the handling of ballast water, which resulted in ships routinely departing while still significantly down by the head, sometimes even causing the forward doors to be immersed.

The *Herald of Free Enterprise* had a very high turnover of crew and masters, as well as frequent changes in her run. In short, most of the people who worked on her felt no sense of ownership or connection to the vessel, as vessels with more permanent crews enjoy. The company also had a history of undermining its masters by rescinding punishments that masters had issued against crew members. This resulted in masters losing credibility in the eyes of the crew.

The court stated, "From top to bottom, the body corporate was infected with the disease of sloppiness," and held the company responsible for the incident. The hearing report noted the company displayed "staggering complacency."

Elements of the Error Chain: The Master and Crew's Shortcomings

The assistant boatswain slept though the announcement to go to departure stations, but no one caught this. The chief officer assumed the second officer would close the doors, and vice versa. The court, finding the chief officer seriously negligent, suspended his license for two years.

The master, hearing no news to the contrary, assumed all was well. Despite passenger limits being set by freeboard, Captain Lewry never took the drafts of the vessel, nor did he determine if she was on an even keel. As it was, due to the configuration of the hull, drafts were difficult to read, and it appeared the industry practice was to guesstimate the drafts. Entries in the ship's official log had been falsified, and upon inspection revealed that the ship somehow miraculously always sailed on an even keel! The ship's smooth deck logbooks (a different log, kept in the wheelhouse) did not even have a spot to record departure drafts.

The court found the cause of the capsizing was due to serious negligence on the part of the master, and suspended his license for one year.

Aftermath

As a result of this tragic accident, weathertight door indicator lights are now required on all Ro/Ro ferries. Other recommendations included closed-circuit televisions in critical areas of the vessel, such as vehicle decks, exterior doors, and the engine room. The court recommended that ports servicing ferries should modify their facilities such that ferries can shut their doors prior to pulling away from the berth. Other recommendations included installing draft gauges, developing a more accurate way to weigh the vehicles aboard, installing emergency lighting that will continue to operate when submerged, and training in the donning of lifejackets.

Design modifications to allow for multiple escape routes, reconsidering the location of emergency gear lockers, and the addition of harnesses to gear lockers were also recommended.

A debate was held on the merits of laminated safety glass versus heat-treated, toughened, or tempered glass. Tempered glass is stronger than normal glass and will not break into shards, but will instead break into crumbles, which are less likely to cause injury and the glass can be knocked out of openings to facilitate escape. Tempered glass will also crack and break out during a fire. Tempered glass was used on the *Herald of Free Enterprise*, and, it being easily and safely broken, its use allowed rescue crews to more easily get passengers out of the vessel. Laminated safety glass, on the other hand, has a strong plastic film embedded in the glass, which will allow the glass to crack, but remain unbroken, and it will not crumble in a fire. The court called for a thorough debate on the glass issue, as some in the ferry industry were calling for laminated safety glass due to its increased ability to withstand fire.

The strongest recommendations concerned stability data for the ferries, the ability to calculate the loss of stability due to free surface, and that the existing conflicts between the stability regulations and interpretations of SOLAS be addressed. The court recommended that regulations be drafted requiring additional stability requirements, including that Ro/Ro ferries have up-to-date, meaningful stability calculations, that complete stability documentation be available to the ship's masters, and that logbook entries concerning stability are required.

The court's recommendations ran to sixty pages.

Largely in response to this incident, and with increasing recognition that people, and no longer equipment failures, were becoming the primary cause of maritime disasters, the IMO set out to amend SOLAS to address the "human element."[4]

The International Management Code for the Safe Operation of Ships and for Pollution Prevention (ISM) 1989

In 1989, in an effort to address the managerial component to safe vessel operations highlighted by the *Herald of Free Enterprise* and other disasters, the IMO adopted the "Guidelines on Management for the Safe Operation of Ships and for Pollution Prevention," which, in 1993 became the International Management Code for the Safe Operation of Ships and for Pollution Prevention, or International Safety Management (ISM) Code. The ISM Code was then incorporated into SOLAS and became mandatory in 1998.

The ISM Code addresses the way ships are operated and managed. Previous safety and pollution conventions focused on equipment, on the construction and outfitting of vessels, but not on operations and management. The ISM Code focuses primarily on people, practices, and behavior, not equipment. The purpose of the ISM Code is to support the ship master in the discharge of his duties. It requires management to provide masters and crews with the support and guidance they need to maintain high standards of safety and pollution prevention. The code was purposefully broadly worded so it could be applied to diverse companies and organizations.

Embedded within the ISM Code is a requirement for a Safety Management System (SMS), nudging the industry from a position of simple (often minimalist) compliance, to a more proactive "culture of safety" where employees at all levels are expected to make operations safer, rather than just do the minimum to comply. Safety management systems are now found in most industries. It is a systematic, proactive approach to managing risk.

The are several structural models for an SMS, usually generated by governmental agencies or industry-specific groups like the International Labor Organization (ILO), the Federal Aviation Administration (FAA) or, for the maritime industry, the International Maritime Organization.

Guidelines for implementing ISM were adopted in 1995 and revised again in 2001 and 2010. For more on the ISM Code, please refer to Appendix A.

The MT *Odyssey*

On November 10, 1988, in a raging winter storm, the seventeen-year-old loaded crude oil tanker *Odyssey* exploded and sank in the icy waters 700 miles off the coast of Nova Scotia, Canada. The explosion ripped the ship in two, and a fire started in the stern section, which sank shortly thereafter. The bow section remained afloat for some time until it too sank. The ensuing fire burned much of the cargo of North Sea Brent crude oil, but it is estimated she spilled over 43 million gallons of oil, and the slick was reported to be over a foot thick by the Russian research vessel that had responded to the scene. Two burned-out lifeboats were spotted by search and rescue aircraft, but no one was found alive. All twenty-seven crew members were presumed to have been lost.

The *Odyssey* disgorged over four times the volume of the much more publicized *Exxon Valdez* spill the following year. The lack of international outrage and legal fallout was no doubt due to the geographical remoteness of the incident and the lack of any recordable environmental damage. The *Odyssey* remains one of the ten largest oil spills in history.[5]

The MV *Exxon Valdez*

The trans-Alaska pipeline system (TAPS), run by the Alyeska Pipeline Company, carries Alaskan North Slope crude oil (ANS crude) from Prudhoe Bay to the Alyeska's loading facility at the port of Valdez, Alaska. Valdez was selected as the pipeline terminus because it is the northernmost ice-free port in Alaska. The pipeline was built largely in reaction to the Middle East oil embargos of the 1970s. The pipeline runs over the peaks of three mountain ranges, the highest point being Atigun Pass, with an elevation of 4,739 feet, and crosses several major rivers. Many miles of the pipeline are elevated above ground. Construction of the 800-mile pipeline started in 1974 and took three years to complete at a cost of $8 billion.

The first oil flowed through the pipeline on June 20, 1977, and since then over 16 billion barrels of crude oil have been loaded into tankers, with the average turnaround time taking just over twenty-two hours from docking to departure. Over 12,000 loads and transits have been safely completed at the Valdez terminal.

Since most of the supertankers carrying crude are too large for the Panama Canal, the typical destinations for tankers carrying ANS are either west coast refineries, or Puerto Armuelles, Panama, where the oil is offloaded to another pipeline, this one crossing the Panamanian isthmus to load tankers on the Gulf of Mexico side, which carry the oil to refineries in Houston and other U.S. cities along the Gulf of Mexico.

The *Exxon Valdez* was a single-hulled tanker built in 1986 specifically for the ANS trade. She was the largest ship ever built on the U.S. west coast and she ran primarily between Valdez and ports on the Pacific coast of the United States. She was 987 feet long and, if loaded to capacity, could carry 1.48 million barrels of cargo, just over 62 million gallons, in her eleven cargo tanks. She was a well-found vessel, in good condition and well outfitted, run by a reputable oil company, and as such, she had earned U.S. Coast Guard approval to operate with a reduced manning level. She was certified to carry a crew of only fifteen, four of them deck officers.

The *Exxon Valdez*, with Captain Joseph Hazelwood commanding, arrived at Alyeska's Marine Terminal berth #5 late in the evening on March 22, 1989, and began de-ballasting in order to lighten the ship so she could load her cargo of ANS crude oil. At 0505 the next day, loading of crude oil began. As was normal in those days, the chief mate, James Kunkel, was on duty around the clock during loading operations, and the two junior mates rotated on a six-hours-on/six-hours-off schedule.

At around 1000 on March 23, Captain Hazelwood headed ashore with the chief engineer and radio officer, leaving the chief mate and a junior mate to handle the loading of cargo. This was perfectly normal.

Joseph Hazelwood was a 1968 graduate of the State University of New York Maritime College, and upon graduation had hired on as a third mate with Exxon's predecessor, Humble Oil and Refining Company. Captain Hazelwood earned his master's license in 1977 and sailed as relief master in 1978. He earned a federal pilotage endorsement for the Prince William Sound between Cape Hinchinbrook and Rocky Point in 1987. He had served as master on nine different oil tankers with no breaks in service. While Hazelwood was serving as one of the two masters who took turns commanding the *Exxon Valdez*, the ship received service awards for being the best performer in the fleet for 1987 and 1988.

On March 23, while the ship was loading crude, Captain Hazelwood enjoyed lunch ashore in Valdez with his shipmates, and had a single beer with his meal. Later that afternoon, around 1600, he met them again at a local bar, where they played darts and had a few more alcoholic drinks. They left the bar at around 1900 and went to order pizza, and, while waiting for the pizza to bake, they went to another, nearby bar, where Captain Hazelwood had one more drink. They all returned to the ship shortly thereafter.

At 1924 loading was complete and the chief mate instructed the third mate, Gregory Cousins, to go to the bridge and begin the pre-departure gear tests. The third mate had sailed as an AB with Exxon for seven years before getting a third mate's position. He had been sailing as third mate since 1987 and had made six round trips into Valdez with Captain Hazelwood, so he was fairly seasoned and had been evaluated as "outstanding" on most of his evaluations. One noteworthy comment was that he seemed to be "reluctant" or "uncomfortable" keeping superiors posted as to his progress and/or problems in his assigned tasks.

The gear tests completed, third mate Cousins stayed on the bridge to communicate with the assist tugs, which would pull the vessel off the dock. The pilot who had brought the vessel to the dock reboarded at 2020 to take her out. When he knocked on the master's door, there was no answer, so the pilot proceeded to the wheelhouse on his own. Captain Hazelwood was reported to be back aboard at 2030, having spent most of the day ashore.

Ten minutes later, the chief mate, after securing the cargo systems, reported to the bridge and relieved the third mate of the watch. Shortly thereafter, the vessel let go her lines and departed, with two tugs assisting her off the dock. The pilot, master, and chief mate were in the wheelhouse, and an AB was at the helm. Last line was at 2112, making the vessel officially underway, and the pilot assumed the conn, with one tug remaining astern as an escort vessel.

The *Exxon Valdez*, loaded with over 53 million gallons of crude oil, departed Valdez bound for Long Beach, California. Her departure draft was fifty-six feet. The vessel proceeded toward Valdez Narrows, about six miles to the west of the terminal.

Just after the vessel had pulled away from the dock, the third mate, who had been handling lines on deck, returned to the bridge and relieved the chief mate of the watch. The master went below about twenty minutes after getting underway, while the vessel was still inside Valdez Bay, not yet to Valdez Narrows. The pilot later testified he smelled alcohol on the master's breath while he was on the bridge, but that he had not appeared intoxicated.

The pilot took the ship through the bay, then through Valdez Narrows and guided her to the pilot station off Rocky Point, just at the start of the Prince William Sound traffic lanes, slowing the ship for his departure. The pilot asked the third mate to call the master back to the bridge.

Once Captain Hazelwood returned, the pilot transferred control of the vessel back to the master, who then dispatched the third mate to escort the pilot down to the pilot ladder on the main deck. The bow lookout was also instructed to head aft to the pilot ladder, see the pilot off, and then assist with stowing the pilot ladder for sea. The pilot was logged off at 2324.

A minute later, Captain Hazelwood informed Valdez VTS that the pilot was away and that the ship was increasing to "sea speed" which was about sixteen knots. When VTS asked about the ice conditions (the nearby Columbia Glacier was calving, and ice extended into the outbound shipping lanes) Captain Hazelwood informed VTS that judging by his radar he expected to have to deviate from the outbound traffic lane, and use the inbound lane to get past the ice, as long as there was no incoming traffic. He told VTS he would notify them once he left the outbound lane, crossed into the separation zone, a buffer zone between inbound and outbound lanes, and again when he crossed back into the appropriate outbound lane. VTS concurred and responded that there was no reported inbound traffic.

The *Exxon Valdez* was just disappearing from VTS radar coverage when she left the outbound traffic lanes. It later turned out that the VTS radar was set to the 12-mile scale and had the VTS observer used the 24-mile scale, the vessel probably could have been tracked all the way to the grounding site. There were no written guidelines for VTS personnel regarding how far out a vessel should be monitored after it had left Valdez Narrows, or what radar settings should be used. While watch change was occurring aboard the *Exxon Valdez*, Coast Guard VTS personnel were also changing the watch at the Valdez VTS station.

At about 2330, Captain Hazelwood called VTS back and informed them he was dropping his speed to twelve knots to "wind his way through the ice."

Shortly after the pilot had departed, third mate Cousins returned to the bridge and the lookout returned to the bow. When Cousins had returned to the bridge, he noticed the engine telegraph was at full ahead sea speed of sixteen knots, not the twelve knots as Captain Hazelwood had told VTS. The electronic engine bell log also showed no decrease in speed had been ordered.

Just after Cousins returned to the bridge, Captain Hazelwood told Cousins he was bringing the ship to a course of 180° to avoid ice ahead in the outbound lane, and that Cousins should get a fix.

At about 2345, the master ordered the AB on the bow to go back to the house and tell the relief AB (on the on-coming 0000 x 0400 watch) to report to the bridge wing, instead of the bow, for lookout duties. The off-going 2000 x 2400 AB who was on the wheel testified that just before he was relieved, the master had instructed him to bring the ship to course 180° and put her in automatic pilot, which he said he did.

The off-going AB, who was on the helm, notified Cousins that the ship was on course 180° and on the automatic pilot. Cousins was surprised, as the vessel is normally hand-steered until clear to sea, but, assuming this status was at the master's request, he decided not to question the decision.

The vessel was now on course 180°, in autopilot, loading up to sea speed (not the twelve knots Captain Hazelwood had told VTS) and the unlicensed sailors of the bridge watch were getting relieved by the 0000 x 0400 watch.

The third mate had been instructed to start bringing the ship back into the outbound traffic lane when Busby Island Light was abeam, and that the master would return shortly, but that if he wasn't back on the bridge by the time the ship was returning to the outbound traffic lane, to call him to the bridge. Before heading below, Captain Hazelwood asked Cousins if he felt "comfortable" with what he was expected to do, and Cousins replied that he was. The master left the bridge at about 2352 to tend to paperwork.

The third mate recalled that the master, just before he went below, had started the load program to bring the engines to full sea speed. This comports with the handwritten entry in the bell book indicating that at 2352 the computer load program had been initiated to bring the vessel from full ahead maneuvering to full sea speed.

Exxon's policy required watch condition "C" in this area, which required either the master or chief mate conn the vessel, with a junior officer assisting, yet this requirement wasn't followed. Additionally, Cousins did not have a pilotage endorsement for this body of water and should not have been left conning the vessel alone.

The second mate, who normally stood the 0000 x 0400 watch, was scheduled to relieve Cousins at 2350, but Cousins decided to let him sleep in a bit, at least until the ship was clear of the ice. The vessel steamed on. Anticipating a course change after a few minutes, when he had passed the ice, Cousins took the vessel off the autopilot and put her back in hand-steering. He then proceeded to take a visual fix off Busby Island Light.

The oncoming 0000 x 0400 lookout, herself a third mate but who was sailing as an AB, reported to the wheelhouse, glanced at the chart and radars as was her custom, and then took up a lookout position on the starboard bridge wing.

A few moments later, she reported both the white light of Busby Island a few degrees forward of the port beam and the flashing red light of Bligh Reef buoy broad on the starboard bow. These were not where she had expected the lights to be, but it was unclear if she knew of the maneuver to avoid ice. Cousins, who was plotting a fix at the time, stated he knew about the red lighted buoy on Bligh Reef and had been tracking the buoy on radar.

Shortly after plotting his 2355 fix, Cousins ordered the helmsman to put the rudder at right ten degrees and called the master to inform him that the ship was starting its gradual right turn back into the outbound traffic lane. Cousins later admitted he did not monitor the rudder angle indicator to ensure the rudder was responding appropriately, and that, for about a minute and a half, his back had been facing the indicator while he was on the phone to the master. Captain

Hazelwood, probably surprised to hear Cousins' voice, asked if the second mate had arrived for watch, and Cousins informed him that the second mate had not yet been called for watch.

After he hung up with the master, Cousins returned to his radar. He noticed the ship had not deviated from its track, nor was the heading changing to the right as expected. The bridge wing lookout again reported the red flashing light on the starboard bow, and Cousins again acknowledged her. He stepped on to the port bridge wing, looked at Busby Island light, then at Bligh Reef light, then returned to his radar. Cousins then ordered the rudder increased to twenty degrees right. The vessel began to swing to starboard.

After another two minutes, not satisfied with the vessel's response, he ordered hard right rudder to increase the rate of turn. Shortly after the order for hard right rudder, he called the master and said, "I think we're in trouble."

The *Exxon Valdez* grounded on Bligh Reef in the pristine waters of Prince William Sound just after midnight, at 0004 on March 24, 1989. Her engines were still winding up to full sea speed. The impact ripped open eight of her eleven cargo tanks and three saltwater ballast tanks.

Immediately after the grounding, the master arrived on the bridge and proceeded to issue helm and engine commands, presumably trying to free the impaled vessel. Engines were finally stopped at around 0020.

At 0027 Captain Hazelwood called Valdez VTS on the radio to report the grounding. At roughly the same time, the chief mate called the master with updates on the condition of the cargo in the tanks, and began calculating hull stresses. Two minutes later the U.S. Coast Guard Marine Safety Office (MSO) closed Valdez to vessel traffic and the Alyeska tug *Stalwart* was sent to aid the grounded tanker. At around 0035 the master ordered the engines restarted and, against the advice of the local Coast Guard and the ship's chief mate, for the next hour he tried to free the stranded vessel from the reef by cycling the rudder and using various engine commands.

The MV *Exxon Valdez,* aground on Bligh Reef in Prince William Sound, Alaska, surrounded by oil boom. *NOAA Office of Response and Restoration.*

By 0100 a pilot boat with a Coast Guard investigator and an Alaska Department of Environmental Conservation representative was en route to the stricken ship.

Sometime later, the chief mate informed the master that hull stresses were beyond acceptable limits and that the vessel should not be moved. The vessel, now subject to free communication with the seas, was in a dangerously unstable condition and probably would have capsized had she come off the reef.

Despite this, in an 0107 call with the Coast Guard, Captain Hazelwood informed them that he was trying to work the vessel off the reef and that they were in "pretty good shape stability-wise." The Coast Guard wisely cautioned against any drastic moves. At 0141, after admitting to Cousins that his attempts to free the vessel probably weren't going to work, the engine bell log shows the master finally stopped trying to free the ship.

Coast Guard personnel finally made it aboard the vessel by 0335, over three hours after the grounding. The Coast Guard investigator, after speaking with the ship's crew who had gauged the tanks, announced that approximately 5.8 million gallons of crude had spilled into the seas, and the ship was continuing to leak.

Post-Incident Chemical Testing

The Coast Guard officer reported that the master smelled of alcohol, and, not having any testing equipment, requested a toxicology test be run. Captain Hazelwood explained he had had two Moussy beers (at 0.05 percent alcohol, it is considered a non-alcoholic beer) upon his return to the ship, and two empty cans were seen in his trash.

The Coast Guard then called the Alaska State Troopers' office to come to the vessel and conduct drug and alcohol testing, but when they arrived at 0630, they too didn't have any testing equipment. It wasn't until after 1000 that Coast Guard personnel realized the ship itself had toxicology sampling and testing equipment aboard, but when they attempted to test him, the master stated he was unable to urinate. Finally, at 1030 a separate Coast Guard medical team arrived to take blood and alcohol samples from all involved crew members.

Meanwhile, oil continued to drain from the stranded ship.

All crew members' test results came back negative, except for Captain Hazelwood, whose blood and urine indicated blood alcohol content of between 0.061 percent (blood) and 0.094 percent (urine), ten and a half hours after the incident.

It later surfaced that Captain Hazelwood had entered a hospital in 1985 for treatment of an alcohol problem, and that Exxon only found out about it accidentally. Captain Hazelwood also had convictions for driving while intoxicated in 1985 and 1988. He ultimately had been placed on disability and given a leave of absence to deal with his alcohol issue. Exxon stated it monitored Captain Hazelwood closely after his return to service, but documentation proving this was sketchy at best. During the period surrounding the accident, Captain Hazelwood was in the middle of divorce proceedings.

Spill Mitigation and Cleanup

Attempts to contain the spill were plagued with misadventure.

Alyeska was unable to comply with its own spill contingency plans, as its spill barge was undergoing repairs and was stripped of its equipment. There were other equipment casualties, some personnel were absent on holiday, and chaos was beginning to reign.

By 0400 it was realized that the ship's stability was of utmost concern, for if she capsized and sank she'd spill her entire cargo. Arrangements were made to call in another vessel, the *Exxon Baton Rouge*, to lighter cargo off the *Exxon Valdez*. At 0530 March 24 it was estimated the ship had lost over 10 million gallons of her cargo of crude oil, but 43 million gallons (about 80 percent of the cargo) remained aboard.

Alyeska was the first group to offer meaningful aid. By 0730 Alyeska had a helicopter in the air over the site, and mapped the spill as 1,000 feet wide and four miles long and spreading. As daylight broke, other assets were brought to bear on the scene from various federal, state, and corporate sources.

Response and cleanup efforts were hampered by the remoteness of the location and the massive area covered by the slick. The initial response by both government and industry was bungled and confused. The available equipment was not up to the task and conflicts in command and organization led to confusion and leadership gaps, all of which delayed the cleanup and salvage effort. The federal government had contingency plans in place for oil spills—as did Alyeska Pipeline Company, Exxon, the U.S. Coast Guard, the State of Alaska, and the Captain of the Port of Valdez. No one, including the government, was prepared for a spill of this magnitude in such a remote location, and coordination of the various plans was nearly impossible.

In addition to a lack of a coordinated, organized response, cleanup activities were hampered by a lack of useable equipment (including the fuel to run the equipment) and bad weather. Equipment and personnel were flown in from around the world and it seemed money was no object. By late March 1989, thousands of feet of oil boom had been deployed, hundreds of vessels were on site, over 1,700 tons of equipment had been delivered, over 1,000 personnel were on site, and over a dozen aircraft were available

Clean-up efforts on the shores of Prince William Sound, Alaska. *Taken March 28, 1989, by U.S. Coast Guard District 17; from the Defense Video and Imagery and Distribution System (DVIDS).*

to assist. Aircraft from the U.S. Air Force's Military Airlift Command brought in supplies and equipment from Exxon, the U.S. Navy, and Coast Guard from places as diverse as Oregon, Texas, California, Virginia, Denmark, and Finland. By late March the resulting oil slick had spread over 3,000 square miles, oiling over 350 miles of once pristine beaches and coastline.

On April 15, thirteen days after the spill, the *Exxon Valdez* was carefully refloated.

The cleanup continued for weeks.

Aftermath

Myriad agencies were involved with the subsequent investigations.

The U.S Coast Guard investigated the causes of the accident, including the role of VTS, coordinated cleanup and salvage efforts, and determined if license suspension and revocation hearings should proceed against any of the ship's officers. The U.S. Coast Guard, as is usual, shared its findings with other law enforcement groups and state and local agencies. The National Transportation Safety Board, primarily a fact-finding body, also investigated the cause of the incident, and made recommendations as to how to prevent future spills. The Alaska State Attorney General's Office and the FBI were both primarily interested in fault-finding and bringing civil and criminal actions against involved parties.

Joseph J. Hazelwood, left, master of MV *Exxon Valdez,* and Gregory Cousins, at right rear, the ship's third mate, who was conning the tanker when it ran aground, leave Coast Guard offices in Valdez, Alaska, March 28, 1989, with an unidentified Exxon official. The men met with officials of the National Transportation Safety Board, who were investigating the grounding of the tanker and the subsequent oil spill. *Associated Press / Rob Stapleton.*

Ultimately, the National Transportation Safety Board concluded the causes of the accident were:

- The third mate's failure to properly maneuver the vessel, caused by fatigue and excessive workload
- The master's failure to provide a proper navigation watch due to impairment from alcohol
- Exxon's failure to provide a fit master, and a rested and sufficient crew for the ship
- A lack of an effective VTS due to a lack of equipment, inadequate manning levels, inadequate personnel training, and deficient management oversight
- Lack of effective pilotage services

On April 1, Captain Hazelwood was arrested and criminally charged with operating a vessel while intoxicated, reckless endangerment, negligent discharge of oil, and felony criminal mischief. He faced roughly seven years in jail and fines of $61,000 if convicted on all four charges. He pleaded not guilty to everything.

An Alaska jury ultimately found him guilty of negligent discharge of oil, a misdemeanor, which carried a fine of $1,000 and up to six months in jail. He received a suspended sentence and had to perform 1,000 hours of community service, which he performed over a five year period in Alaska, picking up trash and working at a soup kitchen. He also had to pay $50,000 in restitution. Administratively, the U.S. Coast Guard did not revoke Captain Hazelwood's license, but agreed to only suspend it for nine months, after he pleaded no contest to charges of drinking alcohol within four hours of a navigational watch and to negligently leaving the bridge when he should have been conning.

Gregory Cousins was not pursued legally, but his license was suspended for nine months after he pleaded no contest to charges of failing to maintain an accurate record of the vessel's position, and failing to ensure steering commands to return the vessel to the Prince William Sound Traffic Separation Scheme were executed in a timely manner, thereby placing the vessel in danger of grounding. During Cousins' appeal to an administrative law judge, the hearing officer (properly) refused to consider new evidence which should have been presented at the original hearing, and rejected every claim for relief presented by Cousins. Ultimately, Cousins' nine-month license suspension was upheld.

Exxon itself faced both federal and state criminal charges, as well as hundreds of civil suits, including charges of violating the U.S. Dangerous Cargo Act, the Ports and Waterways Safety Act, and for knowingly allowing an "incompetent" person to operate its vessel.

Cleanup efforts took roughly three years, cost well over $2 billion, and involved the efforts of over 11,000 people.

The spill, seemingly massive at 10 million to 32 million gallons, doesn't even rank in the top thirty largest spills in history, but it was the largest spill the United States had experienced. Worldwide, the *Exxon Valdez* spill ranks below the largest fifty spills in history. Its occurrence in a pristine, environmentally sensitive area generated intense media attention and public outcry, which prompted swift and dramatic action by U.S. lawmakers.

Exxon's primary liability sprang from violating the Clean Water Act (CWA) but many felt the CWA was insufficient to address major oil spills of this nature because, unless "willful negligence" or "misconduct" could be proven, Exxon's liability was limited to $150 per gross ton of the vessel, or in this case, about $14.3 million—which to Exxon, was peanuts.

Using novel (and some feel inappropriate) legal theories, Exxon ended up being held criminally and civilly liable for much, much more. The lawsuits and counter-suits lasted for years and involved hundreds of parties (including at one point over 100,000 private parties), multiple courts, and billions of dollars. Years after the incident, legal claims were even brought by the cleanup personnel, claiming injury from the toxic oil and detergents used in the cleanup efforts.

The *Exxon Valdez* spill, more than any other incident, raised awareness of the need for comprehensive oil spill liability and compensation legislation—and The Oil Pollution Act of 1990 (OPA '90) was born. The OPA '90 changed the shipping industry in myriad and unprecedented ways. It will be explored in the next chapter.[6]

Notes

1. Sources for *Castillo de Bellver* information: Norman Hooke, *Maritime Casualties*; Case Studies of the International Tanker Owners Pollution Federation, Ltd., http://www.itopf.com/information-services/data-and-statistics/case-histories/clist.html; CEDRE case study, http://www.cedre.fr/en/spill/castillo_de_bellver/castillo_de_bellver.php; Laura Moss, "The 13 Largest Oil Spills in History," *Mother Nature Network*, July 16, 2010, http://www.mnn.com/earth-matters/wilderness-resources/stories/the-13-largest-oil-spills-in-history.

2. Sources for *Marine Electric* information: U.S. Coast Guard, *Marine Board of Investigation Report and Commandant's Action: SS* Marine Electric *O.N. 245675 Capsizing and Sinking in the Atlantic Ocean on 12 February 1983 With Multiple Loss of Life*, Report No. 16732/001 HQS 83, http://www.uscg.mil/hq/cg5/cg545/docs/boards/marineelectric.pdf; Robert Frump, *Until the Sea Shall Free Them: Life, Death, and Survival in the Merchant Marine* (Annapolis, MD: Naval Institute Press, 2007); Lt. Stephanie Young, *The* Marine Electric *Tragedy: So Others May Live*, blog of the U.S. Coast Guard, February 13, 2012, http://coastguard.dodlive.mil/2012/02/the-marine-electric-tragedy-so-others-may-live/.

3. Sources for *Doña Paz* information: Richard A. Cahill, *Disasters at Sea*; Howard Chua-Eoan, "The Philippines off Mindoro: A Night to Remember," *Time/CNN*, January 4, 1998, http://web.archive.org/web/20071209182552/http://www.time.com/time/magazine/article/0,9171,966394,00.html; Norman Hooke, *Maritime Casualties*; *The Associated Press*, "1,500 Are Feared Lost as 2 Ships Collide and Sink Near Philippines," December 21, 1987, http://www.nytimes.com/1987/12/21/world/1500-are-feared-lost-as-2-ships-collide-and-sink-near-philippines.html; www.donapaz.com/.

4. Sources for *Herald of Free Enterprise* information: "*U.K. Department of Transport Investigation Court Report # 8074*," (Marine Accident Investigation Branch (MAIB)), http://www.maib.gov.uk/publications/investigation_reports/herald_of_free_enterprise/herald_of_free_enterprise_report.cfm.

5. Sources for *Odyssey* spill information: Norman Hooke, *Maritime Casualties*; http://www.oilspillsolutions.org/majorspills.htm; Case Studies of the International Tanker Owners Pollution Federation, Ltd.,

http://www.itopf.com/information-services/data-and-statistics/case-histories/indexold.html#Odyssey.

6. Sources for *Exxon Valdez* grounding and spill information: Richard A. Cahill, *Disasters at Sea*; Norman Hooke, *Maritime Casualties*; National Response Team, *The* Exxon Valdez *Oil Spill Report to the President*, 1989, http://docs.lib.noaa.gov/noaa_documents/NOAA_related_docs/oil_spills/ExxonValdez_NRT_1989_report_to_president.pdf; National Transportation Safety Board, *Marine Accident Report of the Grounding of the U.S. Tankship* Exxon Valdez *on Bligh Reef, Prince William Sound, near Valdez, Alaska March 24, 1989, Government Accession Number PB90-916405 NTSB/MAR-90/04* (July 31, 1990), http://docs.lib.noaa.gov/noaa_documents/NOAA_related_docs/oil_spills/marine_accident_report_1990.pdf; *Exxon Valdez* Oil Spill Trustee Council, *In the Matter of the Investigation of the Accident Involving the Grounding of the Tankership* Exxon Valdez *in Prince William Sound, Alaska on March 24, 1989, Proposed Probable Cause, Findings and Recommendations of the State of Alaska, Docket No. DCA 89 MM 040*, Report Before the National Transportation Safety Board, http://www.evostc.state.ak.us/index.cfm?FA=main.home; Environmental Protection Agency, *The* Exxon Valdez *Spill: A Report to the President, Executive Summary* (May 1989), http://www2.epa.gov/aboutepa/exxon-valdez-oil-spill-report-president-executive-summary; EPA National Response Team, *Update of Implementation of Recommendation of the NRT Following the* Exxon Valdez *Oil Spill*, http://www.epa.gov/emergencies/docs/chem/evupdate.pdf; Gregory Cousins' appeal to the U.S. Coast Guard regarding his license, http://www.uscg.mil/legal/CDOA/Commandant_Decisions/S_and_R_2280_2579/2515%20-%20COUSINS.pdf.

Chapter 9
1990 to 1999

1990: The Oil Pollution Act of 1990
1990: *Scandinavian Star*, possible arson, leading to SOLAS Amendments
1991: MT *Haven* and the ABT *Summer*, leading to the Haven Law
1991: MV *Kirki*, leading to exploration of liability of classification societies
1993: *Mauvilla* and the AMTRAK Sunset Limited, leading to the Towing Officers' Assessment Record (TOAR)
1994: *Estonia* and the International Safety Management Code (ISM)
1995: MV *Royal Majesty*, grounding due to overreliance on electronics
1995: The International Convention on Standards of Training, Certification, and Watchkeeping for Seafarers (STCW) 1995
1999: MV *Erika*, leading to accelerated phase-out of single-hull "pre-MARPOL" tankers

The Oil Pollution Act (OPA) 1990

The Oil Pollution Act of 1990 (OPA '90) was a direct response by the United States to not only the *Exxon Valdez* disaster of 1989, but to other domestic spills that year, including:

- The *World Prodigy* grounding and spill in Narragansett Bay in June 1989 (spilling 290,000 gallons of heating oil)
- The grounding of the *Presidente Rivera* in the Delaware River in June 1989 (spilling 306,000 gallons of oil)
- The collision of the *Rachel B* and Coastal Towing tank barge 2514 in the Houston Ship Channel in July 1989
- The grounding of the *American Trader* in Huntington Beach, California, in February 1990 (spilling over 416,000 gallons of crude)
- The explosion of the Norwegian tanker *Mega Borg* fifty miles off the Texas Gulf coast (spilling 4.5 million gallons of light Angolan Palanca crude oil)

The OPA '90, which amended the Clean Water Act, consolidated the liability and compensation schemes previously set forth in the Federal Water Pollution Control Act, the Deepwater Port Act, the Trans-Alaska Pipeline System Authorization Act, and the Outer Continental Shelf Lands Act, just to name a few. Prior to the OPA '90, vessels in the United States had to comply with a dizzying patchwork quilt of state and federal pollution liability regulations, interpreted through a kaleidoscope of maritime cases, with attorneys performing legal gymnastics trying to keep their corporate clients in compliance.

The OPA '90 required volumes of regulations to clarify its text and facilitate compliance. Naturally, most of the regulations, which were generated by the U.S. Coast Guard, are codified in various sections of the Code of Federal Regulations (CFR). OPA '90 mandated numerous sweeping changes to tanker operations, which include:

For Mariners:
- New requirements for manning and tanker crew credentials
- Mandated rest hours for mariners working on tankers

- Limits permissible blood alcohol level to 0.04 percent while aboard and disallows any alcohol consumption within four hours of assuming watch

For Operating Companies:
- Established new and higher liability limits for oil spills
- Increased the type of recoverable damages to include damages for environmental harm
- Increased operators' financial responsibility requirements and required vessels and petroleum handling facilities to carry a Certificate of Financial Responsibility (COFR)
- The Oil Spill Liability Trust Fund (OSLTF) was created in 1986 but was never authorized to spend or collect monies. After the *Exxon Valdez* incident, the OSLTF was finally authorized by Congress to create a $1 billion fund (generated from taxes on the petroleum industry) to pay for damage assessments, oil cleanup, and damages not covered by other sources, up to $1 billion per incident. The U.S. Coast Guard's National Pollution Funds Center administers the fund.
- Mandated the phasing out of single-hull tankers and specified new construction standards, including double hulls (46 USC §3703(a) and 33 CFR §157, Appendix G)
- Required participation in Vessel Traffic Systems
- Mandated vessels and maritime facilities generate pollution contingency plans
- Criminalized most maritime oil pollution incidents, as well as clarified and enhanced civil liabilities for polluters
- Created new research programs
- Generally broadened enforcement authority
- And in a bizarre, emotional, illogical stroke of legalese, the Oil Pollution Act (in 33 USC §2737) prohibits any ship that has had a spill (anywhere, after March 22, 1989) of over 1,000,000 gallons from operating in Alaska's Prince William Sound (mind you, the people who caused the spill are not prohibited)

The United States encouraged the IMO to adopt changes to MARPOL to reflect the requirements of OPA '90, such as requiring double-hulls on tankers. The IMO's MEPC agreed and discussions began on how the U.S. proposals requiring double-hulls for tankers could be implemented worldwide.

Changes to MARPOL ensued with the IMO's 1990 drafting of the International Convention on Oil Pollution Preparedness, Response and Co-operation (OPRC '90). This new convention addressed oil pollution preparedness and cooperation between nations and industries when addressing pollution incidents. Parties to the convention are required to assist each other when responding to pollution incidents, and there are provisions in OPRC for compensation for the costs of rendering such aid.

The OPRC also calls for stockpiles of equipment and supplies to be strategically located. The OPRC requires ships to maintain a shipboard oil pollution emergency plan (SOPEP), to conduct pollution incident drills, and to report pollution incidents to national authorities. As of 2007, the OPRC also applies to hazardous and noxious substances releases.[1]

The *Scandinavian Star*

Despite the many advances that had been made in the area of fire safety by the 1990s, fire safety provisions of SOLAS had not been thoroughly revisited since the fifth SOLAS Convention in 1974, which entered into force in May of 1980.

The devastating fire aboard the passenger vessel *Scandinavian Star*, which occurred during the very early morning of April 7, 1990, swung the IMO's attention back to issues of fire safety aboard passenger ships.

The fire left roughly 158 people dead. The exact count is uncertain, as many children were not listed on the passenger manifest. The investigation revealed, as is often the case, multiple contributing factors to the casualty.

The ship, originally a casino ship, was converted to a passenger ferry and she ran between Denmark and Norway. The crew was only given ten days of training (and apparently no drills were ever held) before being tasked with running the vessel and handling her passengers. Despite most of the passengers being Danish or Norwegian, most of the crew, many of them new to the vessel, were Portuguese and didn't speak English, Danish, or Norwegian. (Fortunately, during the fire, the master was able to issue instructions in both English and Norwegian over the ship's loudspeaker system.)

The fire was apparently deliberately set (some sources indicate six fires were set) and consisted mostly of piles of clothing and blankets being set afire in passageways. Insurance fraud was suspected, as the vessel had recently been insured for more than her market value, and there were reports some crew seemed prepared for the fire, refused to help panicked passengers, and had their luggage already packed as they boarded lifeboats.

Multiple issues contributed to the loss of life and increased the scale of the disaster. Automatic fire doors, strategically placed to halt the spread of fires, did not close remotely, and the fire spread quickly throughout the vessel. The master ordered the air conditioning secured, which was prudent as it is common practice to secure ventilation when fighting a fire. But in this case, securing the air conditioning meant smoke was now free to enter cabins that had previously been slightly pressurized by the air conditioning system. Many passengers did not hear the fire alarm, despite reports that the alarm had operated properly, and many never woke up before suffocating in their cabins. People who were awake and were trying to escape had trouble finding escape routes due to the dense black smoke and lack of deck-level escape lighting. In addition to the normal harmful byproducts of fires in living spaces, the bulkheads were covered in melamine, which released hydrogen cyanide when they burned.

Of the 158 bodies found aboard the ship, ninety-nine were found in their cabins. Most died not from burns, but from a lack of oxygen, and from carbon monoxide and inhalation poisoning from the hydrogen cyanide (also called prussic acid) released when the bulkheads burned. The Swedish medical report stated that in eighteen victims, hydrogen cyanide concentrations were high enough to indicate hydrogen cyanide poisoning as the cause of death.

After the fire, investigators also found the body of a four-time convicted Danish arsonist among the dead.

Two years later, in response to this and previous fires aboard ships, the IMO amended SOLAS' fire and safety requirements to mandate the same sort of protections as are found in modern hotels. The new amendments required:

- Non-flammable bulkhead materials
- Automatic smoke- and fire-detection systems
- Automatic sprinkler systems
- Protected, well-marked and well-lit escape routes, with signs and lighting placed near the deck
- Remotely operated fire doors
- An effective public address and alarm system
- Hose ports in fire doors so doors could remain closed while water was sprayed into a space
- That the crew be able to communicate effectively enough to assist passengers in emergencies

Another improvement was clarification in SOLAS Chapter II-2 of the phase-in schedules for the (now multitudinous) amendments and a streamlined structure for the entire chapter dealing with fire safety, with additional focus on human factors. Although the changes came too late for the people aboard the *Scandinavian Star*, the changes were a huge step toward increased safety aboard ship.

Captain Hugo Larsen, the ship's Norwegian master, Henrik Johansen, the majority shareholder of the shipping line, and Ole Hansen, the company's director, were each convicted of violating Danish ship safety laws, namely for not adequately training the crew, nor adequately checking the ship's safety equipment. Rather than being fined, for the first time in Danish history these three violators of Danish ship safety laws were put in jail, albeit briefly. Captain Larsen received sixty days in jail, and the other two men received forty days each.[2]

The MT *Haven* and the ABT *Summer*

These two VLCC incidents are noteworthy because they are both in the top-ten worst oil spills in history, and they happened within a month of each other, both occurring after the passage of OPA '90.

The MT *Haven*

The MT *Haven* (ex–*Amoco Milford Haven*), built in Spain in 1973, was a VLCC flying the Cypriot flag of convenience. She was owned by Amoco and operated by Trodos Shipping, a father-and-son enterprise of Greek nationals Loucas Haji-Ioannou and his son Stelios, who later started Britain's easyJet airline.

The MT *Haven* had offloaded about a third of her cargo of crude oil to a floating platform off the coast of Genoa, Italy, when she disconnected and began to transfer cargo internally between her tanks. On April 11, 1991, during this internal transfer operation, she exploded, broke into three parts, burned for three days, exploded again on April 13, and ultimately sank on April 14, releasing approximately 44 million gallons of crude into the Mediterranean Sea.[3] The spill ranks in the top ten worst oil spills in history. It is an eerie coincidence that the MT *Haven* was a sister ship to the *Amoco Cadiz*, which grounded, sank, and caused a massive spill in 1978.

Fortunately, the seas were calm, and the authorities decided to burn the oil from the sea surface, rather than risk it getting ashore. Despite these efforts, large swaths of the Italian and French coastlines were oiled, including the French Riviera, and fishing reserves were impacted heavily.

Most of her crew had jumped overboard to avoid the flames, but five (some accounts say six) of her thirty-five crew members died in the explosion.

Allegations were that the eighteen-year-old ship was in a terrible state of disrepair. In 1988, during the Gulf War between Iran and Iraq, the ship had been hit by a missile. Repairs took roughly eighteen months in a Singaporean shipyard. Some felt the ship should have been scrapped as a result of the missile hit. After repairs were completed, she was put back in service, only to explode and sink, four months later.

The father-and-son owners of the ship were charged by Italian prosecutors with manslaughter, and then later with intimidating witnesses and bribery attempts, though they were ultimately acquitted of all criminal charges.

Governments of the affected nations lodged compensation claims to various pollution funds, but there were differing interpretations of the rules for compensation, and some of the claimants had not yet fully assessed or quantified the environmental damage. A major issue was that environmental damage was ongoing, as oil continued to seep from the sunken tanker, making exact damage assessments almost impossible.

There were also squabbles about which courts and which sets of laws should be used to interpret the language of various international compensation and liability conventions that applied to the case. As a result of the legal morass, claims for compensation were ultimately simply denied.

Finally, in 1995, some monies were paid to the Italian government and it was determined they needn't have justified quantifiable environmental damages at all. The ship owners and their insurers offered a voluntary amount, not admitting guilt, but the offer was rejected by the Italians.

Eventually the Italians accepted the money, with the stipulation that a new law, the "Haven Law" be applied. The "Haven Law" stated that some of the proceeds must be used for environmental purposes. A convention was signed in 2001 ensuring that a fund would be created to pay for the ongoing cleanup and study of the environmental impact of the disaster.[4]

The ABT *Summer*

The VLCC ABT *Summer*, having loaded crude oil at Kharg Island, Iran, was en route to Rotterdam, when, on May 28, 1991, she exploded, killing five of her thirty-two crew members. The explosion happened about 900 miles off the coast of Angola. The ship burned for three days and the spill spread over eighty square miles before she finally sank. Due to the remoteness of the incident, the spill posed no measureable environmental threat. An estimated 51 million to 81 million gallons of crude was spilled, ranking this spill in the top ten worst in history.[5]

The MV *Kirki*

On July 21, 1991, the *Kirki*'s bow fell off.

The Greek-flagged, Liberian-owned tanker *Kirki*, which had six previous names, was laden with crude oil from Jebel Dhanna in the United Arab Emirates. She was almost to her destination, the British Petroleum refinery in Kwinana in Western Australia, when, just fifty-five miles off the Australian coast, her bow section broke off and sank in heavy weather. She was to be Australia's largest oil spill.

The *Kirki* was built in Spain in 1969 to Lloyd's specifications. She was a single-screw vessel of 97,000 DWT, fitted with four rows of cargo tanks. She was transferred to ABS for classification, and then, in 1986, to Germanischer Lloyd.

During the evening of July 20, the vessel was laboring in thirty-five-knot winds and heavy seas and the weather was worsening. The master tried to ease the vessel's motion, as she was taking green water over the bow, by changing course forty-five degrees (which took twenty minutes). The vessel was behaving unusually sluggishly, even given the prevailing conditions, and the master ordered the forepeak sounded. When the crewman opened to door to the forepeak, a "whoosh" of air was felt. Soundings indicated the water in the forepeak tank was even with sea level.

When attempts to pump the forepeak empty were ineffective, and the water level remained the same, the master knew the space was in free communication with the ocean. He reduced speed and tried to get the bow up by transferring weight aft, but at 0220 the next morning, he noticed the forward masthead light disappear as the ship's bow fell off.

Twenty minutes later the master stopped the engines and transmitted a distress call. Weather conditions made launching of a lifeboat impossible, but by early morning the Australian search and rescue teams had evacuated all thirty-seven crew members off the vessel, leaving her to flounder in rough seas.

An agreement was reached under the terms of Lloyd's Open Form, and a salvage tug was dispatched. By the time the salvage tug arrived, the vessel had drifted to within eight miles of the Australian coast and barrier reefs.

It wasn't until after 0800 that the authorities understood the bow had fallen off the vessel. Because oil had only leaked from the forward cargo tanks, and the flow was diminishing, concern for a major pollution incident was lessened, but discussions ensued about the best course of action. Options included sinking the vessel, trying to tow it to port, even lightering to another vessel. The owner of the cargo, British Petroleum, was very helpful and provided invaluable assets, equipment, and maritime expertise to the Australian authorities.

By late afternoon, the vessel was towed roughly fifty miles off the coast, mostly to buy time while additional decisions were made and to keep her away from sensitive coastlines. The weather was easing, which allowed salvage crews to board the vessel. Once aboard, it was determined the *Kirki* was in no immediate danger of sinking and posed no ongoing pollution risk. There was concern that the roughly 65,000 barrels of oil spilled from the forward bulkhead, which had been fractured when the bow fell off, would drift ashore.

Salvors towed the ship for 11 days, getting her beyond the 100 miles authorities requested she stay offshore. On August 7, salvors towed the *Kirki* to the Dampier Archipelago, which provided the shelter necessary to safely effect necessary lightering. Weather hampered the rendezvous, but by August 14 the *Kirki* was connected to the lightering vessel *Flying Clipper*, and pumping operations began. Once empty of oil, the *Kirki* was towed by her salvors to Singapore, where she was broken for scrap.

Findings

The primary cause of the hull failure was determined to be severe corrosion and lack of maintenance. Significant and obviously long-standing defects were found in the safety and survival equipment, and in the overall poor condition of the engine room and cargo equipment. A crude attempt to camouflage a canvas patch on a cargo tank lid was an obvious attempt to fool inspectors as to the poor condition of the vessel's steel.

After a thorough survey of the vessel, fault was placed squarely at the feet of Germanischer Lloyd, the classification society selected to inspect and certify the seaworthiness and fitness of the vessel. But other inspections by BP Vetting (the charterer), Mayamar Marine Enterprises (the ship's managers) and port state inspections by the Australian Maritime Safety Authority also should have exposed the *Kirki*'s substantial defects.

But Germanischer Lloyd, as the issuer of the compliance certificate, bore primary responsibility for the failure to discover severe structural corrosion in several tanks. Such corrosion, which could not have happened in the time period between inspections, indicated a systemic, repeated failure to properly survey the vessel.

The master was not faulted for his ship-handling or actions taken after the incident, except for his premature decision to abandon ship. The investigation concluded that a skeleton crew should have remained aboard to help prepare the vessel to be taken in tow and to assist the salvors. The master was also chided for not establishing adequate communications with shoreside authorities.

The *Kirki* incident highlighted the troubling conflict of interest between classification societies and the ship owners who pay for their services.

Other lessons learned:

- There was confusion as to which agency had primary control over an incident occurring in offshore waters. This type of problem is not only an Australian problem, but no doubt is experienced by other nations facing similar situations.
- There was squabbling within the Australian environmental agencies about a suitable safe haven to which to tow the ship, which would facilitate transferring oil both within the ship and lightering to another vessel. This wasted valuable time and added an unnecessary layer of inefficiency to the decision-making process.
- The office from which the disaster was being handled was not secure, and it quickly became crowded with too many people who had thin connections, at best, to the incident

- There was so much media coverage and air activity, that helicopter operations in the area became hazardous. In the future, it was recommended, clear air zones should be created immediately after a casualty.
- Before abandoning the vessel, the crew made no arrangements to facilitate taking the vessel in tow or to accommodate salvors
- Most of the ship's labeling was in Greek, making it difficult for salvage crews to understand machinery placards
- Failure to advise the locals in advance that the ship was to be towed off their coast caused public outcry, and led to antagonism between the local inhabitants, the salvor, and the federal agencies involved

Fortunately, the *Kirki* incident resulted in no loss of life and no major pollution incident.

Classification societies remain largely immune from liability for oversights during surveys or inspections.[6]

The *Mauvilla* and the AMTRAK Sunset Limited

Over 5,000 tugs and towboats handle roughly 25,000 barges on the United States' 25,000 miles of inland waterways. A typical barge can carry as much cargo as sixty semi trucks, so transportation by water is one of the most economical of shipping methods. Over 800 million tons of goods and commodities are carried on the nation's river system each year, but not without incident. One particularly catastrophic accident prompted the U.S. Coast Guard to significantly amend the regulations covering uninspected towing vessels and the mariners who operate them.

At roughly 0245 on September 22, 1993, the operator of the pushboat *Mauvilla*, an uninspected towing vessel pushing a cluster of barges, got lost in the fog on the Mobile River and mistakenly turned down a non-navigable cut, right where a railroad swing bridge crosses over Big Bayou Canot in Alabama. The *Mauvilla* had a radar, but the boat's operator was not trained in its use.

The allision dislodged the tracks by fourteen inches. Eighteen minutes later, unaware of the danger ahead, the AMTRAK Sunset Limited passenger train, en route from California to Florida, reached the twisted tracks of the swing bridge and derailed. She had 220 people aboard.

The three locomotives and four other cars, two of them passenger cars, fell into the water below. Forty seven people died and over one hundred were injured. The four crew members of the *Mauvilla* were unharmed.

The tug *Mauvilla* allides with a bridge near Big Bayou Canot, Alabama, causing the derailment of the AMTRAK Sunset Limited passenger train. *Associated Press.*

The NTSB, which investigated the incident, made recommendations to the U.S. Coast Guard, as well as to the U.S. Department of Transportation, the U.S. Army Corps of Engineers, the American Waterways Operators, AMTRAK, FEMA, the Association of American Railroads, the American Short Line Railroad Association, and, lastly, the owners of the *Mauvilla*.

The NTSB concluded the cause of the accident was the towboat operator's failure to properly use and interpret the information from the vessel's radar, and the U.S. Coast Guard's lack of a rigorous licensing scheme for towboat operators.

The legislative reaction and industry response to this incident was broad and far-reaching.

Aftermath—The Towing Officers' Assessment Record (TOAR) Endorsement

It used to be that if a mariner had a license to operate a vessel of a given tonnage, it didn't matter what type of vessel it was. That meant that a person with, say, an unlimited-tonnage third mate's license (which is earned by a typical graduate of a maritime academy, who has almost no experience) could operate a towboat pushing fifteen massive barges up the Mississippi River. This made no sense. Different types of vessels and different bodies of water require different skill sets and knowledge. On rivers especially, local knowledge is essential.

The U.S. Coast Guard, in cooperation with the towing industry, developed new regulations that completely changed how tug operators in the United States are trained, qualified, and licensed. No longer is tonnage alone the determiner of an operator's qualifications. As a result of significant regulatory changes in the wake of the AMTRAK Sunset Limited derailment, towboat operators need experience on the specific classes of towing vessels and the specific waterways on which they hope to operate. Under the new regulations, separate parts of the Code of Federal Regulations (46 CFR §27 and 33 CFR §164) were developed just for towing vessels.

Now, a mariner must progress from deckhand to master, documenting sea time experience and passing skill assessments administered by designated examiners (themselves towboat mariners) along the way. Currently, in order to be a master of towing vessels, a mariner needs forty-eight months of service, with eighteen months of service as mate, plus multiple certificates and assessments. Special route endorsements for operations on the Western Rivers are also required.

The Towing Officers' Assessment Record (TOAR) was created to record a mariner's experience and assessments and it has been a requirement for towing vessel personnel since May 21, 2001.

Despite the new regulations affecting the mariners aboard towing vessels, most tugs and towboats are "uninspected" vessels, with few requirements, and are not subject to U.S. Coast Guard inspections because they usually fall below threshold tonnage requirements. This raised the question of which, if any, agency has authority to regulate working conditions aboard an "uninspected" vessel.

In 2002, much to the chagrin of the towboat industry, the result of the Supreme Court case *Chao v. Mallard Bay Drilling, Inc.* (534 U.S. 235 (2002)) was to allow the Occupational Safety and Health Administration (OSHA) to fill the gap, and have jurisdiction where the U.S. Coast Guard doesn't already have preemptive regulations. This means if there is no Coast Guard regulation that applies to a given condition aboard an uninspected towing vessel, OSHA can promulgate regulations. This was a sea change for the towing industry, a sector considered by many to be the last "wild west" of the maritime industry.

Several other noteworthy changes occurred because of this tragedy:

- U.S. Coast Guard now requires immediate reporting of casualties and notice of hazardous conditions
- A radar observer endorsement is now required for all operators of uninspected towing vessels equipped with radar

- Requirements were updated for safety, navigation, and towing equipment aboard towing vessels, including fire-detection and fire-suppression devices
- Towing vessels are now required to have charts in the wheelhouse (what a concept)

The Responsible Carrier Program was initiated in 1994, and became a condition of membership in the American Waterways Operators (AWO); it requires members to comply with operating practices and policies representing the best practices of the industry.[7]

The *Estonia*

The sinking of the *Estonia* was another catastrophic ferry disaster that, similar to the capsizing of the *Herald of Free Enterprise,* involved a problem with the forward doors.

On September 27, 1994, the Ro/Ro ferry *Estonia* was making her way from Estonia across the Baltic Sea to Stockholm, with almost 1,000 people aboard. She was listing a little to port due to uneven weight distribution. The weather was bad, with winds from twenty-eight to forty knots and seas up to twenty feet high, as was typical for the fall.

The ferry *Estonia. From a Finnish casualty report (http://www.onnettomuustutkinta.fi/ uploads/x9tzewssr.pdf) by Accident Investigation Board Finland.*

At around 0100 September 28, while off the coast of Finland, a loud metallic bang was heard in the forward section of the ferry. When the crew checked the indicator lights for the forward doors, they found nothing wrong, but no close physical inspection was made of the forward door system. The bangs continued for another ten minutes or so, until at 0115 the forward visor separated, the ship's forward door opened, and icy, cold seawater rushed in, flooding the main deck. Five minutes later the alarm was sounded, but the list was increasing so rapidly, most people couldn't react quickly enough. Within twenty minutes, the ship had rolled completely to her side, similar to the *Herald of Free Enterprise.*

She sank at 0150, taking 852 lives with her.[8] Rescue craft, including helicopters, rushed to the scene but were only able to rescue roughly 137 people, while others who had also escaped the vessel had succumbed to the frigid waters and died of hypothermia.

Findings

The ensuing investigation determined the bow door visor had failed to lock, probably due to the strain of rough sea conditions, and that the design of the forward doors was for protected waters, not the rigors of the Baltic Sea. Basically, the failure was caused by a design flaw, or an inappropriate route for a vessel with doors designed for protected waters.

Accusations flew in myriad directions, some blaming the classification society, Bureau Veritas, for classing the ship despite it not having a watertight bulkhead at the car deck. Others accused the flag state of not conducting rigorous inspections of the vessel's safety equipment and not inspecting the bow doors more closely, especially since the vessel's sister ship, the *Diana II,* had a similar bow door problem, and still others accused the ship's personnel of negligence. The master was faulted for not contacting rescue authorities, and for not notifying passengers of the problem in a timely manner, though most doubt that would have made much difference.

According to maritime author Norman Hooke, naval architect Anders Bjorkman doubted the bow door failed before the vessel took on a list. According to Hooke, Bjorkman thinks the vessel was holed below the waterline, causing the initial list, and that the bow doors were then torn off by aggressive wave action at the bow. Bjorkman felt the investigation was incomplete, and that legislation in reaction to disasters like the loss of the *Estonia* should be supported by more thorough investigations than what happened in this case.[9]

Aftermath

As a result of this incident:

- SOLAS '90 (effective in 2010) specified enhanced stability requirements for passenger ships
- Voyage Data Recorders were mandated for certain vessels
- SOLAS regulations requiring lifeboat systems that would allow launching even in very rough seas were introduced
- Ferry crews are now required to get training in crowd control and crisis management
- EPIRBs must deploy and activate automatically, rather than require manual activation

Most importantly, the *Estonia* incident prompted expedited implementation of the International Safety Management Code (ISM), which deals with the human element, training, and management.

The *Estonia*, having sunk in relatively shallow waters, was never raised, but was instead eventually encased in concrete, and turned into a sacred burial site for the 852 souls she took with her.[10]

The MV *Royal Majesty*

The grounding of the passenger ship *Royal Majesty* is a story about complacency—the complacency that sets in when a system has worked flawlessly for months. The investigators determined that "cues of reliability," such as brilliant, crisp, detailed graphics and numerical displays, can bias human decision-making. Humans are easily induced to trust equipment if it is fancy, very precise, (but not necessarily accurate), and, in a word, bewitching.

The *Royal Majesty* left Bermuda on June 9, 1995, for the forty-one-hour run back to Boston, where she was due to arrive the morning of June 10. Prior to departure, the navigator had tested the bridge equipment and had found everything in working order. After the harbor pilot disembarked, the navigator compared the GPS and LORAN positions, and found the positions indicated by the two systems to be within a mile of each other. (That level of accuracy was acceptable given the crossing angles of the LORAN lines in the area. As the vessel approached the coast of the United States, LORAN accuracy was expected to increase.)

The ship had an integrated bridge and could be steered by an automated system called the navigation and command system (NACOS) 25, which took information from the GPS and other sensors, and steered the ship along a route that had been entered into the system. The NACOS 25 would account for set and drift to keep the vessel along its pre-programmed track. According to the watch officers, the system accurately followed the pre-planned route, as they monitored the vessel's progress on the electronic chart overlay on the ship's ARPA.

On the ocean-crossing leg of the voyage, positions from the GPS were plotted hourly. The LORAN was checked a few times by the chief mate during his watch, and on each occasion the LORAN position was about a mile to the southeast of the GPS position. The weather and visibility were excellent.

At 1845 on June 9, the chief mate picked up the "BA" buoy on radar, which marked the traffic lane into the Boston area. The buoy was acquired on the radar at the time and location he had expected, and its position coincided with the indication on the electronic chart display. At 1920 the buoy appeared (electronically) to pass down the ship's port side at a range of one-and-a-half miles, but was never visually sighted, possibly due to glare from the setting sun.

The master was notified that the "BA" buoy had been passed, but the chief mate did not explain that he hadn't visually seen the buoy, and the master had not asked.

At 2000 the second officer relieved the chief mate of the watch with the usual turnover discussions about traffic, course, speed, position, and weather. No discussion of the "BA" buoy indicated it had never been seen visually.

The second officer plotted hourly GPS fixes, but he considered the LORAN a backup system and did not use it to confirm GPS positions. He dropped the radar scale from twelve miles to six as the ship got closer to land. At about 2030 the lookout reported a yellow flashing light off the ship's port side—the second officer acknowledged the report, but took no action. The NACOS 25 and electronic charts showed the ship was past the "BA" buoy and halfway to the next buoy in the inbound traffic lane—right on track.

Shortly thereafter, both lookouts reported red lights high in the sky off the port side. Such lights are usually seen on shoreside antennas and towers. The master arrived on the bridge just after the reporting of the red lights and checked the vessel's position on the NACOS 25 chart overlay. Both the GPS and chart overlay indicated the vessel was within 200 meters of the intended track. It never occurred to anyone that the GPS provides position input to the chart overlay, so it would be no surprise that they always agreed. No one mentioned the red and yellow lights and, thinking all was well, the master left the bridge.

Shortly after he went below, the master called the bridge to see if the second officer had yet sighted the second traffic lane buoy, the "BB" buoy, and the second officer said he had—but he hadn't. The second officer had not visually sighted the "BB" buoy, but actually had only seen the ship's icon next to it on the electronic chart.

Based on the reported sighting of the "BB" buoy, the plotted positions on the chart, the GPS positions, and the position indicated by the chart overlay, the master had no indication the vessel was off her track-line. A moment later, a lookout reported seeing blue and white water dead ahead, usually a sign of shallow water, but the second officer again took no action.

At 2220, still being conned by the NACOS 25 system, the ship suddenly veered to port, then to starboard, and then heeled to port.

The second officer immediately took the helm and switched from the autopilot to hand steering. The master felt the ship's violent motion, ran to the bridge, and ordered one of the helmsmen acting as lookout to take the helm from the second officer. The master took a radar fix and ordered hard right rudder, but at 2225, before the helm could respond, the ship was aground.

For the first time the master had the GPS and LORAN positions compared, and he realized the GPS position was off by fifteen miles. The LORAN had the ship correctly positioned on Rose and Crown Shoal about ten miles off Nantucket Island.

Fortunately the bottom was hard sand and not rocky. The vessel remained intact but hard aground.

Efforts to free the ship and evacuate the 1,509 people aboard were unsuccessful due to deteriorating weather conditions. It eventually took five tugboats to free her.

Findings

As a result of this grounding, there were no injuries, no loss of life, and no pollution incidents. The casualty is interesting because of the NTSB's post-accident recommendations to the U.S. Coast Guard and the IMO. The grounding highlights the dangers of overreliance on complicated electronic systems, and the changing role of the modern navigator from one of active navigation to that of a relatively passive monitor of colorful, brightly lit screens.

The NACOS 25 integrated system took position inputs from GPS and LORAN, and was designed to sound an alarm if the two systems' positions differed by a specified distance, but the *Royal Majesty's* unit had not been configured to do this.

The NACOS 25 would sound an alarm if the vessel deviated significantly from her preprogrammed track, but there were electronic language issues between the integrated system and the GPS, as well as glitches with the GPS set itself, and watch officers had learned to bypass some of these issues in order to keep the electronic chart display up and useful. Problems with the GPS signal had been recorded by the automatic bell logger as early as June 9, but no one noticed.

Findings of the ensuing investigation revealed:

- The ship's echo sounder was on, but the recording feature was not on at the time of the grounding. The investigation revealed that the depth alarm on the fathometer, normally set for three meters of under-keel clearance, had been set to zero. Had the safety depth been properly set, the watch officers would have had multiple alerts (both aural and visual) that the ship was standing into shoal waters.
- Though watch officers got on-the-job training on the NACOS 25 and other bridge equipment from other officers, there was no formal curriculum, no checklist, nor any assessment to ensure watchstanders fully understood the complex equipment and systems on the bridge.
- Company policy required the vessel's position be checked every thirty minutes, at a minimum, yet the master had ordered positions be plotted every hour. No record of the positions was maintained, nor was any guidance given on what methods should be used to obtain a position fix. The watch officers did not verify their plotted positions by any secondary means, and no one did any cross-checking.
- It was discovered during the investigation that the GPS cable had separated from the antenna base. This would account for the erroneous GPS position fixes and the automatic switch into dead reckoning (DR) mode when satellite information was no longer available. The NACOS 25 system was driving the ship based on dead reckoning estimates, not GPS position information.
- The NACOS 25 system had no way of recognizing the GPS position information it was receiving was based on a DR.
- The NACOS 25 was not configured to compare positions from multiple inputs.

- The GPS had been providing either no position information or incorrect information for roughly *thirty-four hours*. The GPS set indicated it was in DR mode and that it was not giving a reliable satellite position, but no one noticed the small icon on the GPS indicating it was in DR mode.
- The GPS audible alarm indicating DR mode only lasted one second, and the on-screen DR alert display was too small to be easily noticeable.
- Both the GPS and LORAN sets were located not at the main console, but back in the chartroom. The NTSB felt this contributed to their being overlooked. A loud external GPS/DR alarm could have been fitted, but was not.
- The ship's officers were not provided with any manufacturer-based training on the integrated bridge system, despite it being available, and none of the officers, except perhaps the navigator, was proficient with it.

Aftermath

The NTSB was so concerned with the increasing reliance on poorly understood, highly complex integrated systems, and the potential for great loss of life and environmental harm, that it issued urgent recommendations to the U.S Coast Guard, the International Council of Cruise Lines, the International Chamber of Shipping, the American Institute of Merchant Shipping, the International Association of Independent Tanker Owners, STN Atlas Elektronik (makers of the autopilot), and the National Marine Electronics Association urging them to share the story of the *Royal Majesty* and take steps to review the design of their systems and to identify potential failure modes. All of the NTSB recommendations were acted upon.

The hearing board concluded the primary cause for the grounding was the watch officers' overreliance on the automated features of the integrated bridge system, and their lack of training on it. Also specifically faulted was the second officer, who failed to take corrective action despite multiple indications the vessel was off course. Of greatest concern was that none of the officers, including the master, verified the vessel's position by any means other than the GPS. Simply looking at the electronic chart, which uses the same GPS position to place the ship's icon on the chart, is not an independent verification of position.

The investigators opined that modern technology has changed the role of the watch officer from one of proactively acquiring information, to a more passive role, where they are "out of the control loop." As a result of passive monitoring, the crew missed multiple opportunities to discover that the ship had deviated dangerously from her track. The NTSB commented that such passivity is not new and has manifested in the marine and aviation industries, and that humans are "poor monitors of automated systems." They found this especially true when a system has a history of working flawlessly.

The investigation report went on to hold that international training standards for vessels equipped with such equipment were inadequate, as were the international standards for the design, installation, and testing of such systems.[11]

The International Convention on Standards of Training, Certification, and Watchkeeping for Seafarers (STCW) 1995

The horrific ferry incidents, the tug and barge allisions, and other casualties of previous decades indicated that human factors, rather than equipment failures, were becoming the primary cause of maritime accidents. It became clear to the international maritime community that the existing STCW convention, originally drafted in 1978, needed updating.

Largely at the prompting of the U.S. Coast Guard, sweeping changes were made to the convention in 1995. Because these changes were amendments to a convention that had already been ratified, changes did not require a second ratification process, so passage of the amendments was relatively simple. More details can be found in Appendix A.[12]

The MV *Erika*

The 1992 amendments to MARPOL requiring double-hulls replace single-hull tankers were coming into effect when the single-hulled tanker *Erika* broke in half during a winter storm off the coast of France.

The *Erika*, a 578-foot, 37,000-DWT tanker, was built in 1975 as a "pre-MARPOL" ship. She was single-hulled and did not have segregated ballast tanks. She was one of eight sister ships built at bargain rates. It is reported that these "pre-MARPOL" ships were built with 10 percent less steel than was customary. Financially, it would make sense to make a cheaper ship that would come to the end of her useful life just before being rendered obsolete by the new MARPOL regulations that were being phased in, though it is doubtful such was the motivation for the *Erika*'s scantlings, given her build date. As it turned out, three of her sister ships also suffered structural failure. The ships were popular with charterers because they were cheaper than the other newer vessels that had to comply with increasingly stringent safety standards.

The *Erika* departed Dunkirk on December 8, 1999, bound for Italy with a load of approximately 9.7 million gallons of #2 fuel oil. She was old and at the end of her service life, and as such, she came cheap, her charter rate being roughly half the going rate. On December 11, as she entered the Bay of Biscay, the weather worsened and the ship began to list to starboard. The winds were upwards of forty knots with sea and swell to eighteen feet. The ship was taking on water and her hull and deck plating were giving way as her internal structure failed. Green seas were boarding and sweeping down the deck. The master, Captain Karun Mathur, tried to correct the list.

On the morning of December 12 she broke her back, split in two, and sank, spilling her cargo. The entire crew was successfully rescued by helicopter, but the oil drifted toward the Brittany coast, oiling seabirds and marine mammals on the way.

Captain Mathur was arrested by French authorities and spent a week in jail before being released on bail. He felt, naturally, that the fault lay with the owner of the ship and the vessel's Italian classification society, Registro Italiano Navale. Various other nations had found deficiencies when they had inspected her under the port state control (PSC) program when she called at their ports. The *Erika* was able to continue sailing, since no PSC inspectors surveyed her structural members. This is expected, as when the vessel is in port and available for inspection, she is usually working cargo, rendering interior tank inspections almost impossible.

The master had not, however, followed the procedures set forth in the vessel's SOPEP, and the French Commission investigating the casualty faulted him for this. The Commission also, however, determined that the number of statutory documents to be complied with was too numerous to be effectively handled in a time of emergency. Modern mariners would concur that too many checklists, binders, and documents render them ultimately less than helpful in times of crisis.

The *Erika*'s managers also did not follow procedure. After the incident they diligently notified everyone that had a financial stake in the event, but they failed to notify the relevant maritime authorities who could most effectively address the casualty.

Findings

When investigators tried to locate the owners of the vessel, they were led on a paper chase through seven different countries, clearly an attempt by the owners to limit liability and shield exposure. The owner was determined to be Tevere Shipping, a Maltese company controlled by two Liberian entities, which, it turned out, were owned by an Italian national. There was also an Italian ship management company (Panship) which answered to the owner. An agent located in Switzerland gave the ship her sailing orders. The French time charterer was registered in the Bahamas, but operated out of Switzerland. The British P&I club was actually registered in Bermuda, and the freight brokers were in Venice and London.

The *Erika*, for her part, was built in Japan, and was currently flagged out of Malta, though she had previously been flagged under the open registries of both Panama and Liberia. She was manned by Indian officers and crew recruited by Herald Maritime Services of Bombay. The incident happened off the coast of France.

Intentionally creating a legal and jurisdictional quagmire by cloaking a vessel's operations in multiple countries and shell companies was (and is) not an uncommon practice of unscrupulous vessel operators and owners.

Eventually Giuseppe Savarese, an Italian, was determined to be the actual owner and he was criminally charged by France for owning such a poorly maintained and unseaworthy vessel. But he argued it was the classification society, RINA, that he paid to certify the ship as seaworthy, which should be held responsible, not him. RINA accepted some responsibility, but it in turn pointed its finger at the flag state, Malta, as being responsible for the ship's poor condition. Malta, of course, said that if a ship's owner and its classification society say a ship is safe, then the flag state can assume the ship is safe.

Investigators finally determined the probable cause of the structural failure began with the conversion to segregated ballast tanks. The corrosion caused structural deficiencies that should have been noted and acted upon. The French Co-

The tanker MV *Erika*, her hull broken, sinks off the coast of northwestern France, releasing thousands of tons of fuel oil into the ocean. *AP-Photo / French Navy / The New York Times.*

mmission determined that because ships carrying "black" cargoes, like heavy fuel oil and tar, have less stringent tank cleaning and carriage requirements, they tend to be carried by less safe ships. They found that ships carrying "black cargoes" were, on average, seven years older than the fleet average for ships carrying clean cargoes like gasoline or naphtha.

Aftermath

As a result of the *Erika* incident, in 2001 the IMO accelerated implementation of the 1992 amendments to MARPOL which phased out single-hull tankers. The new timetable came into force on September 1, 2003. The incident also prompted European Union legislation requiring audits by the European Maritime Safety Agency of classification societies every two years. In 2008 a French court found both Total (the owner of the vessel) and RINA (the ship's classification society) guilty of negligence. Total was fined €375,000 and ordered to pay France €200 million.

Later attempts to overturn the French verdict failed. In 2010, however, RINA was cleared of liability when the appeals court determined RINA was performing a "public function" and thus had immunity.[13]

Notes

1. Sources for Oil Pollution Act of 1990 information: 33 USC §2701 et seq. (the complete text of the Act is available at http://www.epw.senate.gov/opa90.pdf); Eric A. DeGroff, "The Application of Strict Criminal Liability to Maritime Oil Pollution Incidents: Is There OPA for the Accidental Spiller?," *Loyola Law Review* 50 (2004): 827–868; Alan Neuhauser, "Oil Spills Aplenty Since Exxon Valdez," *U.S. News and World Report*, March 25, 2104, http://www.usnews.com/news/blogs/data-mine/2014/03/25/us-racks-up-dozens-of-oil-spills-in-25-years-since-exxon-valdez; Alan Khee-Jin Tan, *Vessel-Source Marine Pollution,* 320; Environmental Protection Agency, *Oil Pollution Act Overview,* http://www.epa.gov/osweroe1/content/lawsregs/opaover.htm; Proceedings of the Marine Safety and Security Council: *The Coast Guard Journal of Safety and Security at Sea,* "Oil Spill Liability and Compensation: A National Pollution Funds Center Regulatory Perspective" (Spring 2010), http://www.uscg.mil/npfc/.

2. Sources for *Scandinavian Star* information: Norman Hooke, *Maritime Casualties;* Testimony of Chairman of the National Transportation Safety Board before the Committee on Transportation and Infrastructure Subcommittee on Coast Guard and Maritime Transportation, House of Representatives, Regarding Cruise Ship Safety on October 7, 1999, http://www.ntsb.gov/news/speeches/hall/jhc991007.htm; Swedish National Board of Health and Welfare (Socialstyrelsen) Report, http://www.socialstyrelsen.se/publikationer1993/thefireonthepassengerlinerscandinavianstarapril7-1990kamedo-report60; "Survivors Hail New Willingness to Re-examine *Scandinavian Star* Fire," *News In English,* (April 13, 2013), http://www.news-inenglish.no/2013/04/13/survivors-hail-new-willingness-to-reexamine-scandinavian-star-fire/; http://www.cruiseshipfires.com/Fires/Scandinavian_Star_Fire_April_7_1990.html; Nyheter Innernicks, "Fagfolk: Mannskap stiftet Scandinavian Star-brann," *Norwegianat* April 5, 2013 (translated for the author by Christian Adelbo), http://www.vg.no/nyheter/innenriks/artikkel.php?artid=10115445; *Scandinavian Star* investigation video, http://www.youtube.com/watch?v=n-fYX4b7g6s; www.imo.org.

3. Some accounts indicate the ship's crew was washing tanks when the explosion occurred.

4. Sources for MT *Haven* information: Norman Hooke, *Maritime Casualties;* CEDRE, http://www.cedre.fr/en/spill/haven/haven.php; Oil Spill History, http://www.oilspillhistory.com/mt-haven-oil-spill/; Joy Research Group, University of Georgia Department of Marine Sciences, http://www.joyeresearchgroup.uga.edu/public-outreach/marine-oil-spills/other-spills/mt-haven; Joanna Walters, "Making It All Look Easy," Comment and Leaders: *The Guardian,* April 21, 2002, http://observer.theguardian.com/comment/story/0,,687834,00.html.

5. Sources for ABT *Summer* information: CEDRE, http://www.cedre.fr/en/spill/abt_summer/abt_summer.php; Case Studies of the International Tanker Owners Pollution Federation, Ltd., http://www.itopf.com/information-services/data-and-statistics/case-histories/alist.html; Joy Research Group, University of Georgia Department of Marine Sciences, http://www.joyeresearchgroup.uga.edu/public-outreach/marine-oil-spills/other-spills/abt-summer.

6. Sources for *Kirki* information: Donald Brodie, "The *Kirki* Incident" (presented at the International Oil Spill Conference Proceedings March 1993), http://ioscproceedings.org/doi/pdf/10.7901/2169-3358-1993-1-201; Norman Hooke, *Maritime Casualties;* Australian Maritime Safety Authority, Report "*Kirki* Western Australia 21 July 1991," http://www.amsa.gov.au/environment/major-historical-incidents/Kirki/index.asp. For a spoof on the *Kirki* incident, see Clark and Dawe's "The Front Fell Off," https://www.youtube.com/watch?v=IQKjj_FDI_M.

7. Sources for TOARs and Tug *Mauvilla* information: National Transportation Safety Board, "Report RAR-94/01," http://www.ntsb.gov/investigations/summary/rar9401.htm; U.S. Fire Administration, "Technical Rescue Incident Report: The Derailment of the Sunset Limited September 22, 1993 Big Bayou Canot, Alabama," http://www.usfa.fema.gov/downloads/pdf/publications/fa-163b.pdf; Federal Emergency Management Agency, "The Derailment of the Sunset Limited September 22, 1993, Big Bayou Canot, Alabama," http://www.usfa.fema.gov/downloads/pdf/publications/fa-163b.pdf; *Proceedings,* Vol. 59, U.S. Coast Guard (April-June 2002), http://www.uscg.mil/proceedings/archive/2002/Vol59_No2_Apr-Jun2002. pdf; U.S. Coast Guard NVIC 4-01 on TOARs, http://www.uscg.mil/nmc/regulations/NVIC/NVIC_4-01_encl_1.pdf.

8. Some accounts put the loss of life as high as 912 souls.

9. Norman Hooke, *Maritime Casualties*, 200.

10. Sources for *Estonia* information: Norman Hooke, *Maritime Casualties*; Finnish Joint Accident Investigation Commission (JAIC) final report, http://www.turvallisuustutkinta.fi/en/index/tutkintaselostukset/vesiliikenneonnettomuuksientutkinta/mvestonia/mvestonianloppuraporttiyhdessapdf-tiedostossa.html; http://www.estoniaferrydisaster.net/estonia/index.html.

11. Sources for *Royal Majesty* information: National Transportation Safety Board, "Marine Accident Report PB97-916401 NTSB/MAR-97/01," http://www.ntsb.gov/doclib/reports/1997/mar9701.pdf.

12. For information on STCW '95, see www.stcw.org.

13. Sources for *Erika* information: French Permanent Commission of Enquiry into Accidents at Sea (CPEM),"Report of the Enquiry into the Sinking of the *Erika* off the Coasts of Brittany on 12 December 1999," http://www.beamer-france.org/BanqueDocument/pdf_87.pdf; "The Scandal of the *Erika*," *BBC News*, August 16, 2000, http://news.bbc.co.uk/2/hi/programmes/correspondent/883110.stm; "Court Upholds Total Conviction in 1999 *Erika* Oil Spill," *France 24 International News*, September 25, 2012, http://www.france24.com/en/20120925-france-appeals-court-upholds-total-conviction-1999-oil-spill-erika-environment-disaster-atlantic; U.S. Coast Guard vessel information, https://cgmix.uscg.mil/PSIX/PSIXDetails.aspx?VesselID=224572; Europa: Summaries of EU Legislation, "Commission communication of 21 March 2000 to Parliament and the Council on the safety of the seaborne oil trade (not published in the official journal)," http://europa.eu/legislation_summaries/transport/waterborne_transport/l24230_en.htm; "France upholds Total verdict over *Erika* oil spill," *BBC Europe,* Sept. 25, 2012, http://www.bbc.com/news/world-europe-19712798; *The* Erika *Decision,* Paris Court of Appeals, Area 4, Division 11e, General Register No. 8/02278, March 30, 2010, p. 325.

Chapter 10
2000 to 2009

The MV *Jessica*

What do the U.S. Coast Guard, the Grand Duke of Luxembourg, Princeton University, Petroecuador (the state-owned Ecuadorian petroleum company), the U.S. National Oceanographic and Atmospheric Administration, the Charles Darwin Research Station, the Heriott Watt University of Edinburgh, Scotland, and the Sea Shepherd organization have in common? They were all involved with the oil spill in the Galápagos Islands from the grounding of the tanker *Jessica* in 2001.

The *Jessica* set sail from Guayaquil, Ecuador, with a load of diesel and bunker fuel bound for the Galápagos Islands. The fuel depot on Baltra Island was expecting 160,000 gallons of diesel fuel #2, and the *Galápagos Explorer II*, a local tourist boat, was waiting to receive 78,900 gallons of intermediate fuel oil. It was the only vessel in the Galápagos that burned this type of heavy bunker fuel, as opposed to lighter (and cleaner) diesel.

The *Jessica* ran aground at approximately 2200 on January 16, 2001, on Schiavoni Reef in San Cristóbal Island's aptly named Wreck Bay, just half a mile from her destination of Puerto Baquerizo Moreno.

The tanker MV *Jessica* aground in the Galápagos. Members of the Coast Guard Gulf Strike Team and local contractors work aboard the *Jessica,* trying to seal port side fuel tanks for possible re-floating of the vessel. Large swells made oil removal operations dangerous as seawater washed over the deck, soaking clean-up workers. *U.S. Coast Guard by PACS Tod Lyons.*

At the time of the grounding, no petroleum products had been spilled. The Sea Shepherd vessel *Sirenian*, with Galápagos National Park personnel aboard, was the first on the scene. They started pumping fuel from the stranded ship before any of it spilled, but their efforts were allegedly hampered by Petroecuador, the San Cristóbal Port Captain, and the Ecuadorian Navy, who apparently were concerned with protecting the (uninsured) cargo.

A day later the ship had listed to twenty-five degrees (some blame a crew mistake for this).

Within days of the grounding, an international effort, including the Galápagos National Park Service, the Ecuadorian Ministry for the Environment, the Ecuadorian Navy, the U. S. Coast Guard, the U.S. National Oceanic and Atmospheric Administration, and Petroecuador, had joined forces to address the deteriorating situation. The various groups started working together to keep the vessel intact and get her towed off the reef, but there was bickering amongst the various agencies as to how to proceed.

Some felt Petroecuador, who owned the shipment of oil, was more concerned about preserving as much of the cargo as possible than preserving the environment; the Galápagos National Park Service was against the use of certain dispersants; others recommended the fuel tanks be back-filled with seawater to prevent further listing, but that required prior approval of the Port Captain of San Cristóbal.

With the help of a very low tide, which no doubt helped to stabilize the vessel, the Ecuadorian Navy, U.S. Coast Guard, and NOAA crews were able to seal some of the leaking tanks and extract roughly 50,000 gallons of oil from the stricken vessel.

Animal rescue and cleanup efforts were coordinated by the Galápagos National Park Service. Meanwhile, experts, scientists, cleanup teams, and salvage crews arrived from around the world.

An oil containment boom was deployed around the vessel. Calm seas and light winds facilitated efforts to prepare for emptying the ship of her cargo. Time was of the essence, as stronger winds and higher waves were predicted within a week.

While spill prevention and mitigation efforts were being carried out, others were busy cataloging the flora and fauna of the area in order to establish an environmental baseline in advance of any damage caused by the now increasingly imminent spill.

By January 19, two days after the grounding, part of the ship's fuel system ruptured (either a tank or a fuel line) causing another spill of about 2,000 gallons, with more expected as the bunker tank drained. By January 20, heavy bunker fuel was spilling from a cargo tank. Recognizing the new fuel leak would overwhelm the containment booms, the Galápagos National Park Service assigned sixty of their park wardens to work with the Charles Darwin Foundation, local fishermen, tourist groups, and local citizens to try to contain and mitigate the damage from the spill. People were collecting fuel that floated on the water, rescuing coated wildlife, and building corrals to contain as yet unaffected animals and keep them from entering the oiled areas.

Extra crews, bringing specialized equipment to empty the ship's tanks, oil booms, and huge inflatable storage bladders, began arriving by the morning of January 21. Ecuadorian naval aircraft began delivering oil dispersants and sorbents. Meanwhile, the Galápagos National Park staff worked round-the-clock washing and saving oil-soaked animals. Teams of scientists monitored the migration of the spill and its effect on the local vegetation and animal life. By January 23, the spill had reached Santa Cruz Island.

By January 24, scientists had recorded multiple sea lion pups with eye infections due to oiled eyes, heavily oiled, sick pelicans, lots of dead fish and dead green sea urchins, but luckily so far, no oiled iguanas had been reported. Fuel continued to leak from the vessel and emptying the tanks was proving difficult.

The oil slick was predicted to move along the eastern coast of Santa Cruz Island. Experts from around the world, including specialists from the International Bird Rescue Research Center and the

Sea Research and Rescue Center, continued to arrive. Oiled sea lion pups were found on Santa Fe, but severe contamination of that island was averted by the use of mesh nets, sorbents, and dispersants.

Meanwhile, the Ecuadorian navy tried to stabilize the leaking ship, but efforts to deploy anchors to hold her steady were hampered by a deteriorating sea state. Other teams tried to off-load the oil, but didn't yet have an appropriate place to collect and store it. Still other teams tried to seal leaking parts of the ship, but the ship needed to be returned to an almost upright position to effect such remedies.

Everything the cleanup and salvage teams needed, including food and water for all the extra people now on the islands, which now included the media, had to be flown in, or arrive by ship. Then, there remained the question of what to do with the stricken ship once it was re-floated.

Eventually, the slick separated into floating patches of oil, which traveled independently around and between the islands. Teams on small craft outfitted with GPS and satellite imagery devices were mobilized to follow these oil patches and contain them where they could. By January 25, so many sorbent pads had been used that the supplier in Ecuador was running out of them. As the foundering ship continued to leak oil, efforts to stabilize her remained unsuccessful. Experts from around the world continued to arrive, including Dr. Paul Kingston of Heriott Watt University, Edinburgh, Scotland, an expert in oil spill analysis.

On February 1, 2001, His Royal Highness Henri, the Grand Duke of Luxembourg, member of the Board of the Charles Darwin Foundation, arrived at the Galápagos to survey the damage. This was not a publicity stunt. The Grand Duke founded the Galápagos Darwin Trust, an endowment fund to help the work of the Charles Darwin Research Station and the Galápagos National Park.

A day later, on February 2, after two weeks of trying, the U.S. Coast Guard salvage team gave up their efforts to right the vessel or re-float her, and headed home. Efforts to remove the remaining oil, about 1,000 gallons, also proved fruitless; the majority of the ship's 240,000 gallons of cargo oil and fuel had already spilled into the sea.

Fortunately, several mitigating factors lessened the environmental impact of the spill. Despite five major islands being impacted, the prevailing weather carried most of the oil west and north, away from sensitive islands and out to sea, and intense sunshine helped evaporate the lighter diesel fuel. Also, bunker fuel is thick, nasty stuff, which meant it leaked more slowly, and much of the spilled bunkers drifted offshore. When the bunkers mixed with the diesel, it softened the bunker fuel and broke up the bunker globules. Some experts viewed this as a bad thing, since it renders a once semi-solid blob more easily dispersed, ingested, and more likely to coat wildlife, but others viewed the mixing as a positive effect, allowing the heavy bunkers to be more quickly broken down by the elements, thus returning things to normal faster.

Another positive aspect of the spill was the international interest and response. The world took notice and experts and crews came from around the world to help clean up and contain the spill.

Aftermath

On February 8, 2001, not even a month after the spill, the Galápagos National Park filed suit against the people responsible for the grounding and subsequent spill from the *Jessica*. The suit named Mr. Tarquino Arévalo Escandón (the master of the ship), Acotramar C.A. (the owners of the ship), Petrocomercial (a state-owned Ecuadorian company responsible for the safe transport of petroleum products within Ecuadorian territory), and Terra Nova Insurance Co. Ltd. (a London-based insurance company that insured the *Jessica* against fuel spills).

In addition to being sued, the beleaguered master of the *Jessica*, Captain Tarquino Arévalo Escandón, and his crew were confined pending criminal charges. They faced years in prison if found guilty of environmental crimes.

Some felt the *Jessica* had no business sailing the sensitive waters of the Galápagos, let alone Wreck Bay of San Cristóbal Island. She was supposed to deliver her cargo to Baltra, a deep sea harbor free of perilous reefs, but instead ended up grounding in Wreck Bay. There are allegations that she was decrepit, uninsured, had no local charts aboard, and that her master was not a deep-sea master and was unsuited for the job. So how did she land the contract? Some think it was because the vessel's controlling company was partly owned by a relative of the Minister of Defense.

Ecuadorian authorities launched an investigation to determine the responsible parties in the case. At the hearings, Hugo Unda, the Minister of Defense, testified that the *Jessica* was in a seaworthy condition and was safe to transport fuel. He said the ship had all appropriate documentation in place and affirmed that Captain Escandón had suitable licensure and experience for the trip. There was testimony that the *Jessica* had all requisite permits and safety certificates in place, wasn't due for inspection until March 30, 2001, and had no restrictions to operating in international waters, including the territorial waters of Ecuador. Representatives from Petroecuador, the Ecuadorian navy, and even the Ecuadorian Attorney General also testified that the *Jessica* was sound. Also pointing to her fitness, it was argued, was the fact that she sustained a hard grounding and held her cargo for three days before leaking any oil.

As a result of this spill, the Ecuadorian government generated contingency plans should such a disaster strike again, and heavy bunker fuel is no longer allowed in the Galápagos Islands.

The master of the *Jessica* was ultimately sanctioned. Monitoring of wildlife and other environmental systems continued for two to three years after the spill.

Though it was a substantial spill by any measure, its occurrence in such an environmentally sensitive location renders it especially noteworthy. The vessel *Jessica* remains aground in Bahia Naufragio near San Cristóbal Island.[1]

Tug and Barge Problems Persist

In the United States between 1992 and 2001, there were over 2,600 incidents of bridges being hit by towboats, tugboats, and their tows. While this seems surprisingly high, the rate calculates out to about six allisions per 10,000 towboat passes. In all the recorded hits mentioned above, the vast majority of allisions (65 percent) resulted in little or no reported damage. Not surprisingly, 90 percent of investigated cases were determined to have been caused by human error, predominantly poor decisions by the towboat operator (78 percent due to piloting error causing a poor approach, and 12 percent operational error, such as miscommunication by a deckhand, or tow misconfiguration). Mechanical failures accounted for 5 percent of all allisions, and the remaining 5 percent were due to indeterminate causes. Of the cases studied, 94 percent resulted in no fatalities, no injuries, no environmental harm, and relatively minor damage if any.

Surprisingly, the bridges most frequently hit by towboats or their tows are not the bridges most frequently passed, suggesting that the location of the bridge, river features, and the maneuvering techniques required to transit the bridge area may be the most determinative factors in predicting, and ultimately preventing, bridge allisions. Interestingly, bridge construction, fendering, approach layout, and design clearances are not dictated by the U.S. Coast Guard or the U.S. Army Corps of Engineers, but by the American Association of State Highway Officials (for vehicle bridges) and the American Railway Engineering and Maintenance Association (for railroad bridges). The U.S. Coast Guard does not have any authority or responsibility for the structural integrity of bridges. The U.S. Coast Guard does, however, have a permitting process to approve bridge locations and the clearances of bridges over commercial waterways.

In the early 2000s, less than a decade after the *Mauvilla* and the AMTRAK Sunset Limited disaster, two deadly allisions with bridges refocused the U.S. Coast Guard's attention on the towboat industry.[2]

The MV *Brown Water V*

During the early morning hours of September 15, 2001, relief master David D. Fowler was the only one awake in the wheelhouse of the *Brown Water V*. He was pushing four loaded hopper barges, in line straight ahead (also called "strung-out"), as they made their way eastward from Brownsville, Texas along the Gulf Intracoastal Waterway. The on-duty deckhand, Levie Old, was asleep in the wheelhouse. All the other off-duty crew members were asleep below. Captain Fowler was an experienced vessel operator, having held his Operator Uninspected Towing Vessels license for twelve years, and he had made this particular transit approximately fifty times. Despite his experience, however, Captain Fowler had two previous incidents: a grounding in 2000, and another grounding a year later of the vessel's propeller, which caused an engine to stall, which caused his vessel to strike a bridge.

At 0200 on September 15, 2001, the lead barge of the *Brown Water V*'s tow struck the Queen Isabella Causeway Bridge, which connects Port Isabel with South Padre Island, Texas. The barge hit the bridge almost head on, about 375 feet west of the channel. The allision took out two eighty-foot sections of the bridge, leaving a 160-foot gap in the roadway, and decoupling the lead barge. Nine vehicles fell into the waterway, resulting in eight deaths and three injuries. Later that day, a third eighty-foot section of the bridge collapsed, but no one was injured from the collapse.

Aftermath

In October 2003, the Coast Guard conducted a one-person formal investigation into the incident. During the investigation, Captain Fowler exercised his Fifth Amendment rights and declined to testify, but some information had been gleaned from his responses to Coast Guard investigators immediately after the incident. Those conversations were taped by the responding Coast Guard personnel. Several interesting facts surfaced during the investigation.

Though the vessel had the appropriate chart of the area aboard, it was found hidden away, tightly folded, and apparently unused. Also, there was a television set located in the wheelhouse, but all testimony indicated it was not in use at the time of the allision. The starboard tachometer (it was a twin-engine vessel) had been inoperative since July 2000.

After all the evidence was considered, the cause of the accident was found to be failure to respond appropriately to hard-running cross-currents in the area. Captain Fowler was unaware of the cross-currents and had failed to set up for them. Captain Fowler was found at fault for not considering existing current conditions but it was found that the current itself was not a contributing factor. The Coast Guard determined the cause of the allision, and ultimate loss of life, was Captain Fowler's "failure to exercise reasonable care according to the standards of the ordinary practice of good seamanship" and concluded there were "no contributing factors" to the casualty. The lone investigator's recommendations included a suspension and revocation hearing against Captain Fowler's license, as well as criminal charges.

Despite the Coast Guard's findings of no contributing factors to the casualty, several recommendations resulted (indicating to this author that there may have been at least *some* contributing factors), including:

- Installation of current meters in critical areas
- Closure of the channel when currents are particularly strong
- Installing better fendering on bridges
- Limiting the lengths of the tows

In April 2005, the Commandant of the U.S. Coast Guard reviewed the findings of the investigation report, and disagreed with some of its findings and recommendations. Notably, the

Commandant disagreed that the current was not a contributing factor, and indeed found the current to be a contributing cause of the accident. The Commandant also found the configuration of the tow, with deeper barges forward, to be a contributing factor. The Commandant's memo also instructed the involved Coast Guard District Commander to examine the issue of horsepower limitations on towing vessels of the area.

Most important was the Commandant's concurrence with the initial investigator's recommendation that the Coast Guard consider applying voyage planning requirements to all towboats. This had not been a common practice in the towing industry.

Back in 1997, in a Notice of Proposed Rulemaking (NPRM), the U.S. Coast Guard proposed requiring towboats to employ voyage planning, as do ocean-going ships. This would require towing vessels to have a bona fide voyage plan, including requirements to carry necessary charts and publications (or excerpts of pertinent publications) in the wheelhouse, to calculate tides and currents for the route, and to predetermine ETAs and waypoints along the route. Also required as a result are standing orders from the vessel's master (or, in the case of uninspected towboats, the operator) outlining operational details like closest points of approach and critical maneuvers.

Before implementation, however, the proposed rule requiring voyage planning for tugs and barges had softened, with the resulting 2003 interim rule only requiring voyage planning if the tow vessel traveled beyond the protected waters of the territorial sea. As a result of the *Brown Water V* allision, where such a rule could have positively influenced the transit, the U.S. Coast Guard proposed revisiting the relaxation of earlier proposals and suggested including voyage planning requirements for inland towing vessels as well.

The Commandant ultimately recommended removing the current exemption from voyage planning and requiring inland towboats to comply with the provisions of the regulations, (33 CFR §164.80), but simply making the regulation apply to inland boats would also include application of unwanted or unnecessary regulations to the entire inland industry. As a remedy to this sweeping, imprecise approach, the Commandant suggested issuing a Navigation and Vessel Inspection Circular (NVIC), which would offer guidance on generating voyage plans. The Commandant also recommended publishing a "lessons learned" document, and amending 33 CFR §164.78 (Navigation Underway: Towing Vessels) specifically for inland towing vessels. The Commandant also wisely reached out to the towing industry through the American Waterways Operators' Responsible Carrier Program to help generate procedures and guidance for vessels transiting under and through bridges.

The MV *Robert Y. Love*

On May 26, 2002, the towboat *Robert Y. Love*, pushing two empty asphalt barges, was making its way up the Arkansas River when it veered, swinging over 200 feet beyond the channel limits, and allided with the I-40 Highway bridge near Webbers Falls, Oklahoma. A 500-foot span of the bridge collapsed, falling on top of the barges below. A nearby recreational fisherman fired a warning flare into the air to alert motorists that something was wrong. A truck driver jackknifed his truck in order to stop in time, and, fortuitously, the maneuver effectively blocked other oncoming vehicles from going over. By the time the vehicular traffic had stopped, eight automobiles and three semi trucks had already fallen onto the barges below, fallen into the river, or driven over the edge.

Fourteen motorists lost their lives. Five more were injured. The incident caused over $30 million in damage to the bridge, and $276,000 in damage to the barges. The investigation determined the probable cause of the incident was the loss of consciousness of the operator, possibly due to an irregular heart rhythm. Exacerbating the loss of life was the inability of oncoming motorists to see the missing parts of the bridge and stop in time.

Aftermath

The NTSB made recommendations to the U.S. Coast Guard, the Federal Highway Administration, and the American Association of State Highway and Transportation Officials. This incident prompted the formation of a joint working group between the U.S. Coast Guard and the American Waterways Operators (AWO) to study bridge allisions, their causes, and possible solutions. As a result, in 2003 the USCG-AWO Bridge Allision Work Group was formed to develop best practices for towboat operators, and to address ongoing concerns with the safety and operation of uninspected towboats in general, and the result was a recommendation for an inspection regime for towing vessels. The group approached Congress to get the authority to promulgate the new regulations. Congress approved.

The Coast Guard then formed the Towing Safety Advisory Committee (TSAC) to pull together a team of advisors with the breadth and depth of maritime expertise necessary to generate effective and appropriate regulations. Over 160 experts participated and contributed their knowledge to the group.

The Maritime Transportation Security Act of 2002 (MTSA), which became effective in 2004, included towboats as vessels that needed to be inspected by the Coast Guard. It also required that towboats employ a safety management system as is required of larger, inspected vessels. As a result, in 2007 a new subchapter, Subchapter M of 46 CFR, was generated specifically to address towboats.

The MV *Prestige*

The *Erika* spill had already persuaded the international community to accelerate the phase-out of single-hull tankers. The *Prestige* incident, another spill from a single-hulled tanker, motivated regulators even more and led to the 2003 MARPOL amendments.

Like the *Flying Dutchman*, the ship which eternally roamed the seas looking for a safe haven, the *Prestige* was repeatedly denied entry due to pollution concerns.

The *Prestige*, built in 1976, was a single-hulled crude carrier flagged out of the Bahamas. She was operated by a Greek company (Universe Maritime Limited) and was under the command of a Greek master, with crew from the Philippines and Romania. Her corporate owner (Mare Shipping) was a registered Liberian firm, probably owned by Russians. She was bound from Riga, Latvia, on her way to Singapore via the Straits of Gibraltar with a load of heavy heating oil carried for charterers Crown Resources of Switzerland. At twenty-six years old, the *Prestige* was deep into her sunset years. Despite recent rules requiring new tankers to have double hulls, due to her build date she would not have been required to comply until 2015. Under the previous convention, she would have been forcibly retired at age thirty, well before 2015.

The *Prestige* had been classed by ABS, one of the world's most reputable classification societies, and her name had never appeared on any "black lists" maintained by port state control authorities. Thus, as an apparently well-maintained and well-run vessel, for three years before her casualty she had avoided any port state control inspections, which might have noticed her failing condition.

On November 12, 2002, during heavy weather about thirty miles off the coast of Galicia in northwest Spain, one of her cargo tanks split open and cargo started spilling out of a forty-five-foot crack in the shell plating.

By November 13 she was still being hammered by strong gale winds and monstrous seas, and she had developed a significant list. After a call to Spain for help, a Spanish search and rescue helicopter lifted off twenty-four crew members, leaving the master, chief engineer, and chief mate aboard. Four Spanish tugs tried unsuccessfully to take her in tow.

On November 14, a salvage tug was finally able to get her under tow, but the ship was in danger of spilling her entire cargo, and no local authorities wanted to allow the stricken ship into their ports. Spanish authorities would not allow the ship into their ports and urged her salvors to take her elsewhere. So she was towed northward toward France. The French also made the tug turn around. She then was towed south and headed toward Portuguese waters, but the Portuguese Navy kept the languishing ship from approaching their shores as well.

By November 15, after being relentlessly battered by the storm and denied shelter by every nearby country, a forty-foot section of the hull broke away from the starboard side.

On November 18 the salvage tug was towing the vessel in a southwesterly direction, away from land, as neither the French, Spanish, nor Portuguese authorities had allowed the vessel into their ports, but the leaking oil was being driven ashore anyway by the winds and seas.

This was not the first case of ships being denied entry due to pollution concerns. In 1979, the tanker *Andros Patria* was denied entry by every port she tried to enter and she spent fifty days at sea looking for a safe haven. Also in 1979, the *Atlantic Empress* also was ordered out to sea and was eventually lost, though, granted, she was on fire. Legal problems plagued the tanker *Tarpenbec* when she went looking for a salvage port after a collision in 1972.

By November 19 the *Prestige* was listing badly, and the crack in her midships area was widening, being exacerbated by the constant working of the vessel in heavy seas. She finally gave up, split in two, and sank about 130 miles off the coast of Spain, releasing 20 million gallons of oil into the sea. Some of her cargo of oil, thick and fudge-like in the cold water, stayed in the tanks and sank with her. The spill eventually oiled the coasts of six countries.

Aftermath

After the sinking, the ship's master, Captain Apostolos Mangouras, was promptly taken into custody and charged with an environmental crime. He was also charged with interfering with the salvage crews because he initially refused to head back out to sea when denied entry by Spanish authorities. The master had not abandoned his vessel or his crew, but had desperately tried to find a safe haven, to then hopefully be able to boom the ship and contain the spill. He was held for eighty-five days in a high security prison, until being released after posting a €3 million bail. Twenty-two months later he was allowed to return to Spain.

A lone soul stands with an umbrella on a beach in Finisterre in Galicia, Spain, dwarfed by oil sludge from the stricken tanker *Prestige. Associated Press / Carmelo Alen.*

The original court case featured over 1,500 claimants and over 300,000 pages of documents.

After the sinking, the ship continued to leak oil. The coastline of Galicia and parts of the French coastline were so badly affected that fishing had to be suspended for six months. Hundreds of thousands of sea birds washed up dead. Years after the sinking, salvage and environmental crews tried to seal the ship's tanks to prevent continued seepage of oil. They also tried to remove the remaining oil completely. Some success was had, but estimates for the cleanup of the Galician coast determined the cost would exceed the *Exxon Valdez* cleanup. Cost estimates ran as high as €4.4 billion.

In October 2003, largely in response to this incident, the European Community finally joined the United States in prohibiting single-hulled tankers carrying heavy fuels from entering European ports.

In October 2012, ten years after the spill, the *Prestige*'s master, her chief engineer, and the former head of Spain's Merchant Marine Department (who ordered the ship to sea) still faced charges from a court in Spain. The Spanish prosecutors wanted a twelve-year prison sentence for the ship's master, who by then was seventy-seven years of age, primarily for refusing to turn his ship around and head to sea when he was denied a port of refuge from Spain. The Philippine chief mate was also charged, but was not in Spanish custody. Spanish and French authorities also sought billions in compensation from the ship's insurers for the costs of the cleanup and the environmental harm caused by the spill.

A legal issue arose as to whether the classification society, in this case ABS, could be held responsible when a ship it certified as being "in class" has a casualty due to corrosion or lack of maintenance that should have been noted in a survey report.

Other legal battles arose between countries, with the French accusing the Spanish of incompetence in handling the affair.

In 2013, after an eight-month trial with hundreds of witnesses, a Spanish court ultimately found no one criminally responsible for the disaster, and acquitted the captain, chief engineer, and Spanish maritime official who had ordered the stricken ship back to sea.[3]

The MV *Tricolor*

The *Tricolor* incident is somewhat similar to the *Herald of Free Enterprise* disaster of 1987, in that it involves the failure of forward doors on a Ro/Ro vessel and rapid capsizing and stranding of a massive ship. The incident is included because it is noteworthy. The *Tricolor* (she was not actually tri-colored, but was painted orange) was operated by Wallenius Wilhelmsen Lines and had a Norwegian master and a crew of Philippine nationals.

At around 0230 on the foggy morning of December 14, 2002, the *Tricolor* was underway in the English Channel, specifically in the Pas-de-Calais, twenty miles northwest of Dunkirk, on her way from Zeebrugge, Belgium, to Southampton, England. She was carrying almost 3,000 luxury automobiles (worth about $48 million) and other rolling stock consisting of tractors and other heavy equipment. She was about twenty miles off the coast of France when she collided with the *Kariba*, a Bahamian-flagged container ship.

The impact damaged the hull of the *Kariba* above the waterline, but the *Kariba* was still operational and continued on her voyage to Antwerp. The *Tricolor*, on the other hand, capsized within minutes and sank, lying on her side, stuck in the mud in 100 feet of water. The crew of twenty-four was rescued by the *Kariba* and a nearby tug, but the vehicles were a total loss. No oil had yet escaped the vessel.

The primary concerns, beyond the loss of the valuable cargo, were a potential pollution incident from the vessel's fuel and lubricating oil tanks and from the vehicles she carried, and her perilous location right on the edge of a traffic separation scheme, just beyond French and British monitoring zones, in one of the world's busiest traffic lanes.

Aftermath

The French authorities immediately placed warning buoys around the stranded *Tricolor*, and posted picket boats to keep other vessels from hitting the hulk. The Dutch salvage company Smit International was assigned to coordinate salvage efforts, and they placed two barges around the stricken ship to help mark the site. The *Tricolor* lay with her flat beam just barely breaking the surface of the water. Every effort was made to broadcast the location of the wreck and clearly mark it so vessels proceeding along the traffic lanes wouldn't hit it.

Despite all these precautions, on December 16 the cargo ship *Nicola* rammed the *Tricolor*, firmly lodging herself atop the *Tricolor*'s hull. With the help of two Belgian tugs and a rising tide, the *Nicola* re-floated herself after a few hours. After this, two patrol boats were added to the wreck site and the marking system around the *Tricolor* was enhanced to include several lighted cardinal marks and a RACON.

From late December to mid-February salvage vessels pumped as much of the *Tricolor*'s fuel off as possible, minimizing the pollution risk, but they were hampered by rough winter weather. Two weeks later, on January 1, despite warnings from the French Navy, another ship, the *Vicky*, carrying light petroleum products from Antwerp, plowed into the stranded wreck. She too was able to refloat herself and carry on to her destination in New York.

On January 15 an oil slick was noticed in the area around the *Tricolor*, and it was discovered a salvage tug had accidently knocked a plug from the ship's fuel tanks, spilling some fuel oil. In a final humiliating blow, on January 22 while pumping fuel from the *Tricolor*, a salvage barge hit two valves of the *Tricolor*'s fuel piping, resulting in another oil spill.

Environmental damage was difficult to assess, but over 5,500 birds were killed by the oil spilled from the *Tricolor*.

Once the *Tricolor* was as empty of fuel and oil as possible, Smit salvors began cutting the ship apart into manageable pieces. Cutting the wreck began in late July 2003. The Smit salvors sliced the huge ship into 3,000-ton sections using long wires embedded with diamonds, called "Kursk" wires because they were used in salvage operations of the Russian submarine *Kursk*, which sank in the Barents Sea in 2000. The wires sliced through the ship like it was a loaf of bread. Wreck removal operations were finally completed in late October 2004.[4]

The *Tricolor*, a Ro/Ro ferry, capsized and sank in the English Channel, one of the busiest shipping lanes in the world. Her salvors, Smit International, cut her up and removed her a piece at a time. She was sliced like lunch meat, using a carbide-encrusted cutting wire, a technique similar to the method used to slice up the Soviet sub *Kursk* after she sank in the Barents Sea. *Associated Press.*

The *Le Joola*

The *Le Joola* was a relatively well-equipped ferry, owned and operated by the Senegalese navy, which ran from south Senegal to Dakar. She capsized in heavy weather seventeen miles off the coast of Gambia late at night on September 26, 2002. Reportedly, the ship capsized and sank within five minutes.

The disaster killed at least 1,800 people—over 300 more than were lost on the *Titanic*, but very few have ever heard of this tragedy. After the 1987 *Doña Paz* ferry disaster, the loss of the *Le Joola* represents the second greatest loss of life in a peacetime maritime accident. (In 1948, the Chinese ferry *Kiangya,* while steaming in the Huangpu river, hit what probably was a Japanese mine, and exploded, killing as many as 3,900 people. But this could be more appropriately considered a casualty of war, and no legislation was spawned by the incident.)

The *Le Joola* was only certified for 550 passengers (statistics vary) and she was supposed to stay near the coast. It is unknown exactly how many people were aboard because, like other ferries in developing nations, not all passengers had tickets and the ferry was overloaded.

Causes of the casualty included the vessel sailing beyond the protected coastal waters for which she was designed, lack of maintenance, lack of stability calculations performed before leaving port, too few life rafts, broken radio equipment, and the overcrowding that drove many passengers to seek the cool air of the open decks, which adversely affected the vessel's stability.

The ferry MV *Le Joola* resting at her moorage.
Yaamboo (Own work) via Wikimedia Commons.

Aftermath

Some officials were fired, and families of victims were offered a paltry figure as compensation for their loss, but no Senegalese criminal charges were levied and no laws were changed as a result of this disaster. Because some of the dead were French nationals, the French conducted an investigation and the families of the French victims brought suit in a French court. The French court found nine Senegalese officials guilty of crimes and issued international arrest warrants, but the French had no effective control over Senegalese nationals and the charges were eventually dismissed. The Senegalese government reacted to the French convictions by threatening to charge the French judge with a crime.

Some estimates put the number of passengers at over 2,000. People from at least fifteen nations were aboard. Many drowned while trapped inside the hull. Others were thrown into the sea. Rescue crews took hours to respond. Some bodies were eaten by fish and were beyond recognition when they were finally recovered. There were only sixty-four survivors, many of them orphaned children.[5]

The *Andrew J. Barberi*

This ferry incident was one of New York's worst transportation accidents.

On the afternoon of October 15, 2003, Assistant Captain Richard Smith was standing at the controls of the ferry *Andrew J. Barberi* on a routine run between Manhattan and Staten Island. The ferry was going full speed, about fifteen knots, when she hit the maintenance pier at Staten Island.

Normally, the ferry would slow to make its approach, but on this day Captain Smith never slowed the boat. At the time, the senior mate was sitting in the pilothouse, aft of the helm station, reading a newspaper. At around 1520 he felt a heavy vibration, heard Captain Smith say, "Jesus" and saw the ferry hit the concrete pier, south of where they should have docked. Immediately after the allision, Captain Smith throttled back and tried to back the ferry away from the concrete pier and another nearby vessel.

The master then came to the bridge and relieved Richard Smith of the con. He told the chief engineer at one point that Smith had "lost it" and was pacing around in a daze. Later, when asked what happened, Smith had said he "passed out."

The master eventually turned the ferry around so the undamaged end could be used to disembark passengers, and about twenty minutes after the allision, successfully docked at St. George.

The scene was chaotic; passengers were screaming and yelling, and debris blocked passageways. Immediately upon docking, emergency responders boarded and began tending to the injured passengers. When the director of ferry operations saw Smith and asked what happened, Smith said, "I'm sorry. I blacked out. It's all my fault. I killed these people." He then ran to the dock.

The director of ferry operations then found the master in the pilothouse and asked for his version of the events. The master told him that right after the allision he had entered the pilothouse to find Smith slumped over the controls, and that he had to pull him off to get control of the ferry. Prior to this incident, Smith's performance reviews had been consistently "superior" or "outstanding."

It is unknown exactly how many passengers were aboard because in 1997 the ferry stopped charging passengers for the ride and, satisfied with a rough estimate, stopped counting the exact number of people aboard. Of the roughly 1,500 passengers aboard, eleven died, seventy were injured, and physical damages to facilities and ferry were estimated at $8 million.

The work schedule for the two masters was typically four-days-on, three-days-off, with hours of 1330 to 2130 during the work days, but extra hours were sometimes worked for overtime. One master would drive the northbound route, and the other would drive southward.

The NTSB determined the cause of the accident to be the assistant master Richard Smith's sudden incapacitation, the lack of oversight by the ferry owners and operators (New York City Department of Transportation), the failure of the regular master to ensure safe operations, and the

U.S. Coast Guard's poor oversight of the medical qualifications of mariners. The investigators also indicated that navigation technology may have contributed to the casualty.

Immediately after the accident, Richard Smith called his wife and then drove home. He locked himself in a bathroom and refused to come out. Later that afternoon, two New York Department of Transportation employees arrived at his house and broke

The interior of the ferry *Andrew J. Barberi* after it rammed the Staten Island pier. *United States Coast Guard, PA2 Mike Hvozda.*

down the bathroom door to find him bleeding from cuts to his wrist and what appeared to be a gunshot wound to his chest. He had apparently tried to commit suicide, first by slitting his wrists, and then shooting himself with a pellet gun. Emergency medical personnel arrived ten minutes later and, determining his wounds were life threatening, transported him to a hospital where he underwent emergency surgery. Upon arriving at the hospital, blood and urine samples were collected. Traces of tramadol, an opioid pain medication, and diphenhydramine, an antihistimine, were found in his system.

While in the hospital, he underwent a battery of tests and it was determined he had significant narrowing of his coronary arteries and a congenital heart abnormality.

The NTSB tried to determine his medical condition at the time of the incident by retrieving his medical records. Though they were able to retrieve complete medication histories from various pharmacies, they discovered that no record of his medication history was maintained by either the U.S. Coast Guard or his employer, the New York City Department of Transportation.

Information from his medical history was confusing because the primary physician's records did not match the actual prescriptions filled at a pharmacy. However, according to what they could piece together with certainty, Richard Smith had been continuously treated for multiple medical conditions, including chronic back pain (for which he had been prescribed a narcotic analgesic) and insomnia (for which he'd been prescribed a sedative). He had been taking both drugs regularly since 2000. He also had high blood pressure and high cholesterol. He (oddly) also had prescriptions after dental work for psychoactive drugs, which can alter mood, behavior, and cognition.

Despite this rather lengthy medical history, on his last license renewal Smith stated he had no health conditions, was not taking any medications, and signed the oath page, swearing that his statements on the form were true. In short, he lied. In August 2004 he pled guilty to knowingly making a false report to the Coast Guard, which is a crime. He told the court he was worried that telling the truth about all his conditions might jeopardize his job.

Richard Smith refused to appear before investigators until forced to do so by subpoena. When he finally did appear, he pled the Fifth Amendment and refused to respond to questions.

Smith, who pleaded guilty to charges of negligent manslaughter, was sentenced to eighteen months in prison. The former director of the Staten Island Ferry, who had failed to enforce a rule requiring two pilots in the wheelhouse when ferries were docking, was sentenced to one year and a day.

Aftermath: New U.S. Coast Guard Medical Evaluations

Mariners typically only need a medical exam when submitting an application for license issuance, renewal, or upgrades. Otherwise, a medical exam was required every five years when one renewed his or her license. Mariners can pick their own doctors, and will typically "forum shop" to find a provider who will characterize any health issues in a positive light.

As a result of the accident, the NTSB recommended the U.S. Coast Guard revise 46 CFR §10.709 (the medical section) to require results of all medical examinations of mariners be reported to the Coast Guard, and to review their own medical oversight process, specifically as regards to:

- Inconsistent medical interpretations and standards between medical providers
- The lack of efficient tracking of mariners' medical exams
- The lack of any requirement for mariners to report changes to their medical condition between exams
- The Coast Guard's limited ability to review exams performed by a mariner's own provider

The medical guidelines had not been updated since 1998. Guidelines to those standards were set forth in NVIC 2-98. As a result of this incident, the Coast Guard, after lengthy comment periods and input from various constituents within the maritime industry, responded to the NTSB's recommendations and extensively modified the medical requirements for mariners. The Coast Guard issued NVIC 04-08 (a seventy-five-page NVIC, which replaced NVIC 2-98) offering guidance to medical providers and mariners on the new medical guidelines.

For the first time, conditions such as attention deficit disorder (ADD), sleep apnea, stuttering, breast cancer, having a body mass index (BMI) over 40, and even gender reassignment were listed as conditions needing further review. Even some over-the-counter medications (like antihistamines, which are mildly sedative) were listed as substances that may require a waiver, or at minimum, additional medical review. Mariners now have to report all dietary supplements, even vitamins they have taken within ninety days of signing the medical form.

Additionally, the U.S. Coast Guard, in conformance with the 2010 amendments to STCW, now requires mariners subject to STCW (and pilots) to carry a medical certificate, which is valid for two years.[6]

The *al-Salam Boccaccio 98*

Yet another Ro/Ro ferry disaster. The Egyptian Ro/Ro ferry *al-Salam Boccaccio 98* sank in the Red Sea, roughly fifty miles from the Egyptian coast in the early morning hours of February 3, 2006. Of the roughly 1,400 people aboard, mostly Egyptians, only 388 were rescued.

The *al-Salam Boccaccio 98* was flagged out of Panama and her RINA classification certificate was valid. Neither the flag state, nor the classification society, had any reason to doubt the ferry's safety, yet some people at Lloyd's had doubts about the vessel's integrity.

A letter to *Fairplay* magazine by an inspector (who chose to remain anonymous to protect his job) indicated he had inspected vessels for the ferry's operator and found numerous deficiencies throughout the fleet, all the while being plied with cigarettes and whisky. And, despite all the deficiency notations he made on the *al-Salam Boccaccio 98*, the vessel remained in class and was given port state control clearance. He felt the entire industry, from insurers to classification societies to owners and operators, and even the port state, were all complicit in an ongoing, industry-wide sham.

After the incident, families of the victims stormed the Safaga offices of El Salam Maritime Transport Company, the owner of the vessel, breaking windows and tossing furniture into the street.

Survivors reported that about two hours after departing Dubah, Saudi Arabia, a fire had broken out aboard the ship. Data recovered from the ship's voyage data recorder indicated that the ferry's owner knew there was a fire on board but gave orders to continue the voyage toward Safaga, Egypt, despite the master's request to turn the ship around and head back to port.

The fire was difficult to extinguish and kept relighting. The smoke got so thick that passengers became concerned and started donning life jackets despite the crew's admonitions to keep calm and not worry.

Eventually, the ship began taking on a starboard list and the master ordered passengers to assemble on the port side. As the ship continued to list, the master jumped over the side. No one had been given any instructions on how to deploy the ship's life rafts. Minutes later, the ship rolled and sank.

A vessel was sighted passing by, but it did not turn to render aid. No abandon ship alarm had been sounded, and no distress message had been received by any shoreside authorities (though apparently a VHF mayday call had been sent).

It was the EPIRB signal that finally alerted authorities. Egyptian authorities initially declined offers of assistance from both a British warship and an American aircraft, but finally accepted the assistance of an American P3-Orion patrol plane.

Based on crew members' statements, it is suspected that firefighting water collecting inside the ship due to inoperative bilge pumps and clogged drains reduced the vessel's stability to the point she capsized. Two surviving crew members said the ship basically sank herself.

Aftermath

In July 2008, an Egyptian court acquitted Mr. Mamdouh Ismail, who owned the *al-Salam Boccaccio 98*. He was a well-connected businessman and member of parliament, and his acquittal enraged survivors and the families of the victims. A conviction may have been pointless, however, as shortly after the disaster Mr. Ismail had left the country. The only person to see any jail time as a result of the disaster was the master of a vessel who didn't stop to help the ferry. He was sentenced to six months in an Egyptian jail.

A year later, a parliamentary panel of Egyptian officials investigating the incident found there was "wicked collaboration" between the Egyptian maritime authorities and the owner of the vessel, and Mamdouh Ismail was sentenced to seven years in prison for involuntary manslaughter, but he was, reportedly, in London, and the UK has no extradition treaty with Egypt.[7]

The MV *Cosco Busan*

The *Cosco Busan* was a 900-foot Chinese container ship in the Pacific Far East trade. At 0784 on November 7, 2007, she cast off her lines from berth 56 in the Port of Oakland, California. The San Francisco Bay was shrouded in very thick fog, with visibility ranging from an eighth to a quarter of a mile. Bar Pilot Captain John Cota was directing the movement of the ship as she made her way from the berth under the "D-E" span of the Oakland Bay Bridge, and out to the pilot station, eleven miles west of the Golden Gate Bridge.

The ship was equipped with all the usual equipment, including two radars, an electronic charting system, AIS, and a bow thruster. On the bridge was the bar pilot, the ship's master, a third mate and the unlicensed helmsman. This is considered "watch condition four" by most bridge team management plans. It is the highest watch condition and is the normal manning contingent for a harbor transit such as this.

On most merchant vessels, the chief mate and the boatswain traditionally man the bow and stand by the anchors in case they need rapid deployment during harbor transits. The chief mate, had, in this case, left his post and allegedly headed aft for a "meal and a smoke" shortly before the allision. (He later allegedly lied about this to the Coast Guard.) The boatswain was left alone to man the bow and the anchors. The second mate was on the stern, probably stowing lines for sea. Trailing the ship on a slack towline was the tractor tug that had helped the ship off the dock.

The *Cosco Busan* had just left the harbor entrance channel and was shaping up to pass under the Oakland Bay Bridge when, at 0828, San Francisco VTS radioed the pilot and told him his ship was running parallel to the bridge, and inquired if he still intended to use the "D-E" span. A minute later the bow lookout reported sighting the bridge support.

A minute after that, at 0830, the *Cosco Busan* allided with the D-span's fendering system, slicing open her port side. The roughly 200-foot gash breached two of her fuel tanks and a ballast tank. Roughly 53,000 gallons of the ship's heavy bunker fuel spilled into San Francisco Bay. The pilot informed VTS he had "touched" the bridge and that he was proceeding to anchorage 7, just off Treasure Island, where he planned to anchor. By 0850, with the tug still tethered to her stern, the *Cosco Busan* arrived at Anchorage 7 and a few minutes later a relief pilot boarded to relieve Captain Cota of his pilotage duties.

Coast Guard investigators boarded the vessel after she anchored, just over an hour after the allision. By nightfall, an armada of eight oil-skimming boats, twenty other support vessels, and roughly 150 people were on scene to assist. Over 19,000 feet of boom was deployed. Due to the extraordinary response and efficient techniques used to address the spill, roughly 43 percent of the spilled oil was recovered.

The damage estimates to the vessel and bridge were in the low millions of dollars, but the environmental cleanup was estimated at over $70 million, as the spill contaminated twenty-six

The MV *Cosco Busan*'s hull was torn open after alliding with the Oakland Bay Bridge in San Francisco Bay. *Unified Command Photo by Petty Officer Second Class Prentice Danner, U.S. Coast Guard.*

miles of shoreline. There were no injuries or fatalities, other than wildlife, mostly birds. The San Francisco crab season was delayed and a local fishery was closed until the cleanup and environmental assessments were completed.

Aftermath

While not particularly noteworthy by international standards, the case resulted in one of the longest criminal sentences ever handed down for an environmental crime, and may be one of the harshest sentences ever for an unintentional act. It was the first time in U.S. history that a ship's pilot was charged criminally for an accident and sentenced to federal prison.

This is remarkable because a pilot's legal status is one of an advisor, with the ship's master retaining ultimate authority over the vessel's movements.

The inconsistencies of this case are brought to the fore when contrasted with the 2006 case of the *Zim Mexico III,* which crashed into a shoreside crane in Alabama due to a thruster malfunction while under pilotage, killing a shoreside worker. The pilot in that case, determined to be only an advisor, faced no criminal charges, but the vessel's master, Captain Wolfgang Schröder, was jailed for the accident. This awful case will be explored more in Chapter 12.

On November 30, 2007, just twenty-three days after the *Cosco Busan* spill, the United States filed a lawsuit in federal court against Regal Stone Limited (the owner of the ship), Fleet Management Ltd. (the operator of the ship), and pilot John J. Cota seeking damages for resource injuries caused by the spill and for cleanup costs. The United States asserted claims under the Oil Pollution Act, the National Marine Sanctuaries Act, the Park System Resource Protection Act, and the Clean Water Act.

On December 10, 2007, the City and County of San Francisco filed an action (which the city of Richmond later joined) in the Superior Court of California seeking damages and injunctive relief under both state statutory and common law.

After investigating the myriad impacts of the spill, on January 7, 2009, the California Department of Fish and Game, the California State Lands Commission, and the Regional Water Quality Control Board–San Francisco Bay Region, filed a complaint in Superior Court that included causes of action for natural resource damages under the Lempert-Keene-Seastrand Oil Spill Prevention and Response Act, the Oil Pollution Act of 1990, various other state law provisions, and common law. California asserted claims for civil liability, civil penalties, and state costs incurred responding to the spill.[8]

As is usual with marine casualties, a multitude of causal factors contributed to the incident. The NTSB concluded the major cause of the accident was a breakdown of communications between the pilot and the ship's Chinese master, including the lack of a pre-departure meeting.

The pilot was found to have negligently elected to depart despite fog so thick he couldn't see the bow of the ship. (Six other pilots had refused to maneuver ships due to the fog that morning.) When the pilot determined that both the ship's radars were unreliable, he did not notify VTS, but instead he and the ship's master chose to rely entirely on the ship's electronic chart display. (Screen captures of the ship's radar images from the vessel's VDR indicated the ship's radars were functioning properly.) When Cota asked the master to point out the center span of the bridge, the master had allegedly pointed to a bridge tower, not the center span, and that may have been what Cota aimed for. (A vertical bridge tower, absent any electronic aids or markers, would not be visible as a discrete item on a ship's radar. A ship's radar does not display objects in 3-D and only shows horizontal returns.) The recording of the conversation in the wheelhouse that morning indicated the pilot was confused about the chart symbol on the ship's electronic chart.

John Cota had also ordered full ahead maneuvering speed despite the fog and the ship was going approximately eleven knots when it hit the bridge. Excessive speed was found to be a contributing factor to the allision.

Despite no evidence that John Cota had drugs in his system at the time of the incident, the NTSB cited his use of prescription drugs as a contributing cause of the accident. The NTSB found evidence that in the two months before the accident, John Cota had obtained relatively large quantities of the following drugs:

- Generic equivalents of the painkillers Vicodin, Valium, Darvon, Talwin
- Imitrex and sumatriptan, both migraine medications
- Lorazepam, an anxiety medication
- A sleep disorder medication called Provigil
- Zoloft, an antidepressant
- Diphenoxylate and atropine, for gastrointestinal problems
- Compazine, which treats nausea, vomiting, schizophrenia, and anxiety

The NTSB found fault with the Coast Guard for not effectively monitoring Cota's medical conditions and his prescription medications.

Other contributing factors included the bow lookout not being on the bow, the foghorns on the Bay Bridge being inoperative, and the failure of San Francisco VTS to notify the pilot in a timely manner that he was getting too close to the bridge.

In 2008, the Hong Kong–based operator of the *Cosco Busan* was indicted on six felony counts for falsifying documents and interfering with a federal investigation, as well as misdemeanor counts for contributing to the spill. They paid $10 million in restitution to resolve the charges. The owner of the ship pleaded guilty to obstructing justice and falsifying documents after the casualty, and paid $44 million toward cleanup costs and a $10 million criminal fine.

Pilot John Cota had already surrendered his pilot's license and retired by the time he faced federal prosecution from the Environmental Crimes Section of the Justice Department's Environment and Natural Resources Division for the oil spill and the environmental damage, primarily the killing of birds.

John Cota pled guilty to two misdemeanor charges of negligently causing discharge of a harmful quantity of oil in violation of the Clean Water Act and to violating the Migratory Bird Treaty Act, by causing the death of protected species of migratory birds, specifically the Brown Pelican and the Marbled Murrelet. Six crew members of the *Cosco Busan* were granted immunity if they agreed to stay in the United States and act as witnesses.

The *Cosco Busan* was John Cota's fourteenth piloting incident, and the tenth incident for which he'd been personally held responsible by the San Francisco Bar Pilot's Association. On July 17, 2009, John Cota was sentenced to the maximum possible sentence, ten months in federal prison. He was the only person charged with a crime. It was the first time a U.S. pilot had been sentenced to federal prison for negligence. He later sued the Coast Guard in an attempt to regain his license, but his case was dismissed. The Coast Guard also dismissed his administrative appeal for reinstatement. He completed his sentence and was released on August 17, 2013.

In the July 2009 edition of *The Pilot,* an official publication of the United Kingdom Maritime Pilots' Association, editor John Clandillon-Baker expressed his concern regarding the criminalization of accidents:

> Although the [NTSB] report catalogues "Human element" failures, in my opinion it doesn't identify any actions which could be identified as criminally negligent. It is therefore all the more worrying that in sentencing John Cota to prison, the prosecutors have set a precedent that will encourage other legal teams around the world to criminalise [sic] the pilot.

As a result of this incident, new regulations for San Francisco Bay were drafted requiring half-mile visibility for vessels travelling in certain newly-designated maneuvering areas, including approaches to the Oakland Harbor. San Francisco pilots also now carry their own GPS receivers and their own laptops and electronic charts, so they are less reliant on the varying models and brands of navigational equipment found aboard ships.

Also recommended by the U.S. Coast Guard was expedited replacement of NVIC 2-98, which addressed physical evaluations of mariners, with NVIC 4-08 (brought about largely in the wake of earlier ferry and towboat accidents caused by medical issues with operators), which enhanced medical screening and reporting requirements.

The *Cosco Busan* was repaired at a cost of $1.5 million, placed back in service, and renamed *Hanjin Venezia*. She departed San Francisco for Korea in December 2007. Despite changes to federal law, state law, and local rules in the wake of the *Cosco Busan*, in January 2013, while shrouded in thick fog, another ship, the *Overseas Reymar*, allided with the Oakland Bay Bridge while under pilotage. Luckily, no injuries or pollution resulted, and no one went to jail.[9]

Notes

1. Sources for *Jessica* information: Diego Bonilla Urbina and Robert Bensted-Smith, and press releases from the Galápagos Islands, a compound document, http://www.galapagos.to/TEXTS/JESSICA.HTM; "NOAA Provides Oil Expertise in Galapagos Islands Spill," NOAA Newspaper, http://www.noaanews.noaa.gov/stories/s569.htm; European Union Task Force, "Accident of the Oil Tanker 'Jessica' Off the Galapagos Islands (Ecuador), January 16, 2001," Final Report to the European Commission DG Environment ENV.C.3—Civil Protection, http://ec.europa.eu/echo/files/civil_protection/civil/marin/reports_publications/jessica_report.pdf; The Charles Darwin Foundation, http://www.darwinfoundation.org/oilspill.html/_report.pdf.

2. Sources for tug and barge allisions information: U.S. Coast Guard, "Formal Investigation into the Circumstances Surrounding the Allision Between the Barge Tow of the *Brown Water V* and the Queen Isabella Causeway Bridge on September 15, 2001, in Port Isabel Texas, Resulting in Multiple Loss of Life," April 28, 2005, http://www.offsoundings.com/WEB%20PDF/MV_BROWN%20_WATER_V_v._CAUSEWAY.pdf; National Transportation Safety Board, Highway/Marine Accident Report, "U.S. Towboat *Robert Y. Love* Allision With Interstate 40 Highway Bridge Near Webbers Falls, Oklahoma May 26, 2002," http://www.ntsb.gov/doclib/reports/2004/HAR0405.pdf; report of the joint U.S. Coast Guard/American Waterways Operators Bridge Allision Workgroup (May 2003), https://homeport.uscg.mil/cgi-bin/st/portal/uscg_docs/MyCG/Editorial/20071102/bawgr.pdf?id=77b40ea4d9d61272020e941a6d3be844cd79ed0e.

3. Sources for *Prestige* information: U.S. Coast Guard, Ship Structure Committee, report on the *Prestige*, http://www.shipstructure.org/case_studies/Prestige.pdf; IMO Maritime Knowledge Centre, "Information Resources on the *Prestige*," London: January 28, 2010, http://www.imo.org/KnowledgeCentre/InformationResourcesOnCurrentTopics/InformationResourcesOnCurrentTopicsArchives/Documents/PRESTIGE%20_28%20January%202010.pdf; CEDRE, http://www.cedre.fr/en/spill/prestige/prestige.php; Giles Tremlett, "*Prestige* Oil Tanker Spill: Three Go On Trial in Spain," *The Guardian*, October 15, 2012, www.theguardian.com/environment/2012/oct/15/prestige-oil-tanker-spill-trial-spain; "The *Prestige* Oil Spill: How It Happened," *The Guardian*, 2011, slideshow, http://www.theguardian.com/flash/0,5860,843370,00.html; "Spanish court to hear accusations over *Prestige* oil disaster," *Lloyd's List*, October 15, 2012, www.lloydslist.com/ll/sector/regulation/article409443.ece; "Spain Worsened Tanker Tragedy," *BBC,* November 13, 2003, http://news.bbc.co.uk/2/hi/europe/3265929.stm; "Spain: *Prestige* oil spill disaster case in court," *BBC*, October 16, 2012, http://www.bbc.co.uk/news/world-europe-19952329; Fiona Govan, "*Prestige* oil tanker sinking: Spanish court finds nobody responsible," *The Telegraph,* Nov 13, 2013, http://www.telegraph.co.uk/news/worldnews/europe/spain/10447185/Prestige-oil-tanker-sinking-Spanish-court-finds-nobody-responsible.html; Roger A. Peterson, *Maritime Oil Tanker Casualties*; Elizabeth R. DeSombre, *Flagging Standards: Globalization and Environmental, Safety, and Labor Regulations at Sea* (Cambridge: MIT Press, 2006).

4. Sources for *Tricolor* information: CEDRE Report, http://www.cedre.fr/en/spill/tricolor/tricolor.php; Bureau d'Enquetes sur les Evenements de Mer (BEAmer),"Supplementary Report to the Inquiry into the Collision Between the Car Carrier *Tricolor* and the Container Vessel *Kariba* on 14th December 2002 near Westhinder," http://www.beamer-france.org/BanqueDocument/pdf_129.pdf; "Salvage of Sunken Car Carrier *Tricolor*," Smit, http://www.smit.com/projects/project/salvage-of-sunken-car-carrier-tricolor.html; Soumyajit Dasgupta, "Worst Maritime Accidents: The *Tricolor* Cargo Ship Accident," *Marine Insight*, July 20, 2011, http://www.marineinsight.com/marine/life-at-sea/maritime-history/worst-maritime-accidents-the-tricolor-cargo-ship-accident/; "Kerosene-filled tanker strikes sunken vessel," *CNN*, January 2, 2003, http://www.cnn.com/2003/WORLD/europe/01/01/ship.accident/; The Law Offices of Countryman and McDaniel, "Thrice Bitten," March 2003, http://www.cargolaw.com/2003nightmare_tricolor.html.

5. Sources for *Le Joola* information: Pat Wiley, *The Sinking of the* MV Le Joola*: Africa's* Titanic (First Steps Publishing, 2012, e-book); "Hundreds Lost as Senegal Ferry Sinks," *BBC News,* September 27, 2002, http://news.bbc.co.uk/2/hi/africa/2285092.stm; Sheriff Bojang Jnr, "*Le Joola*—seven years since Africa's worst maritime disaster," *Radio Netherlands Worldwide Africa,* September 29, 2009, http://www.rnw.nl/africa/article/le-joola-seven-years-africa%E2%80%99s-worst-maritime-disaster; "Q&A: What caused the *Joola* ferry disaster?" and "Search Ends Under Senegal Ferry," *BBC News,* October 1, 2002, http://news.bbc.co.uk/2/hi/africa/2290490.stm; "Senegal Army 'Left' Ferry Survivors," *BBC News*, November 6, 2002, http://news.bbc.co.uk/2/hi/africa/2409087.stm; Scott Bob, "Senegal Marks Anniversary of Ferry Disaster Amid Court Cases," *Voice of America*, November 1, 2009, http://www.voanews.com/content/a-13-2008-09-26-voa39/400523.html; "Senegal: Families Demand Justice for *Joola* Ferry Deaths," *IRIN Humanitarian News and Analysis*, September 19, 2008, http://allafrica.com/stories/200809220161.html; Hamadou Tidiane,

"Senegal: Country and France in Legal Battle Over Ferry Disaster," *The Daily Nation*, September 29, 2008, http://allafrica.com/stories/200809300211.html; "Senegal's *Le Joola* Victims Seek Answers," *AFP News Agency*, September 25, 2012, video, http://www.youtube.com/watch?v=GXKaWAtffm0.

6. Sources for *Andrew J. Barberi* information: National Transportation Safety Board, Marine Accident Report "Allision of Staten Island Ferry *Andrew J. Barberi* St. George, Staten Island, New York, October 15, 2003 NTSB MAR/05-01 PB 2005-916401 Notation 7628A," http://www.ntsb.gov/doclib/reports/2005/MAR0501.pdf; Federal Register Vol. 71, No. 188, (71FR56998), Notices, September 8, 2006, http://www.gpo.gov/fdsys/pkg/FR-2006-09-28/pdf/06-8305.pdf; "Pilot in ferry accident sentenced to 18 months," *Associated Press,* reported by *NBC News,* January 9, 2006, http://www.nbcnews.com/id/10778306/ns/us_news-crime_and_courts/t/pilot-ferry-accident-sentenced-months/; U.S. Coast Guard medical standards, NVIC 4-08, http://www.uscg.mil/nmc/regulations/NVIC/NVIC_4_08_with_enclosures.pdf.

7. Sources for *al-Salam Boccaccio 98* information: Panama Maritime Authority, General Directorate of Merchant Marine Casualty Investigation Branch, "Preliminary Investigation Report on the sinking of the MV *al Salam Boccaccio 98*," August 17, 2006, http://www.naviecapitani.it/gallerie%20navi/Ro-Ro%20%20e%20%20Ro-Pax%20%20----%20Ro-Ro%20%20and%20%20Ro-Pax/foto/B/Boccaccio/Relazione%20sul%20naufragio.pdf; Daniel Williams, "Survivors Say Egyptian Ferry Was on Fire Before Sinking," *Washington Post Foreign Service*, February 6, 2006, http://www.washingtonpost.com/wp-dyn/content/article/2006/02/04/AR2006020400473.html; "Egyptian ferry sinks in Red Sea," *BBC News*, February 3, 2006, http://news.bbc.co.uk/2/hi/middle_east/4676916.stm; Miriam Fam, "Most of 1,400 on Doomed Ferry Feared Lost," *Associated Press*, February 3, 2006; Heba Saleh, "Egypt ferry probe raps officials," *BBC News*, Cairo, April 19, 2006; Octavia Nasr, "Grief and Outrage in Egypt," *CNN*, July 31, 2008, http://edition.cnn.com/CNNI/Programs/middle.east/blog/2008/07/grief-and-outrage-in-egypt.html; "Anger at Egyptian ferry verdict," *BBC News* July 27, 2008, http://news.bbc.co.uk/2/hi/middle_east/7527652.stm; "Mamdouh Ismail to jail for seven years," *Egyptian Chronicles*, http://egyptianchronicles.blogspot.com/2009/03/mamdouh-ismail-to-jail-for-seven-year; "Jail term for Egypt ferry owner," *BBC News,* March 11, 2009, http://news.bbc.co.uk/2/hi/middle_east/7937035.stm; Maggie Michael, "Owner of sunken Egyptian ferry gets 7 years prison," *Associated Press*, Cairo, March 11, 2009, http://www.foxnews.com/printer_friendly_wires/2009Mar11/0,4675,MLEgyptSunkenFerry,00.html; *Lloyd's List* (various dates) No. 59098–59104, 59149, 59150; Letter by anonymous inspector, *Fairplay*, Vol. 356, 14, February 16, 2006; IMO Knowledge Center, http://www.imo.org/KnowledgeCentre/InformationResourcesOnCurrentTopics/InformationResourcesOnCurrentTopicsArchives/Documents/AL%20SALAM%20BOCCACCIO%2098%20_January%202010.pdf.

8. U.S. Department of Justice, "Ship Owners and Operators to Pay $44 Million in Damages and Penalties for 2007 San Francisco–Oakland Bay Bridge Crash and Oil Spill," press release, September 19, 2011, http://www.justice.gov/opa/pr/2011/September/11-enrd-1209.html.

9. Sources for *Cosco Busan* information: National Transportation Safety Board, "Allision of Hong Kong-Registered Containership MV *Cosco Busan* with the Delta Tower of the San Francisco-Oakland Bay Bridge San Francisco, California November 7, 2007, NTSB/MAR-09/01 PB2009-916401," http://www.ntsb.gov/doclib/reports/2009/MAR0901.pdf; U.S. Coast Guard, "Report of Investigation into the Allision of the *Cosco Busan* with the Delta Tower of the San Francisco-Oakland Bay Bridge in San Francisco Bay on November 7, 2007," March 2, 2009, www.uscg.mil/foia/coscobuscan/coscobusanfinal030609.pdf; U.S. Department of Justice, "Prison Sentence for *Cosco Busan* pilot: Pilot Sentenced to Serve 10 Months in Federal Prison," press release, July 17, 2009, http://www.justice.gov/opa/pr/2009/July/09-enrd-698.html; Capt. Michael R. Watson, "The Evils of Criminalization," *Professional Mariner*, October 6, 2009, http://www.professionalmariner.com/October-2009/The-evils-of-criminalization/; Bob Egelko, "Felony charges for ship's management," *San Francisco Chronicle/SF Gate*, July 24, 2008, http://www.sfgate.com/bayarea/article/

Felony-charges-for-ship-s-management-3275963.php; Paul Elias, "Captain involved in SF oil spill pleads guilty," *Associated Press*, December 31, 2009, http://www.foxnews.com/wires/2009Mar06/0,4670,BaySpi ll,00.html#ixzz2cG9eDOXO; "Ship pilots still avoid some drug tests," *San Francisco Examiner*, August 16, 2010, http://www.sfexaminer.com/sanfrancisco/ship-pilots-still-avoid-some-drug-tests/Content?oid=2162178; "*Cosco Busan* Pilot Loses in License Reinstatement Attempt," *The Maritime Executive*, December 5, 2013, http://www.maritime-executive.com/article/Cosco-Busan-Pilot-Loses-in-License-Reinstatement-At-tempt-2013-12-05; John Clandillon-Barker, "*Cosco Busan*: Criminalization of Pilots Is Confirmed!," *The Pilot,* No. 298, July 2009, http://www.pilotmag.co.uk/wp-content/uploads/2008/06/Pilotmag-298.final-web.pdf; Dan Noyes, "Exclusive: Ship pilot laughs after *Cosco Busan* oil spill," *ABC Channel 7 News,* February 14, 2012, http://abc7news.com/archive/8542308/; *Safer Seas 2013* National Transportation Safety Board, go.usa.gov/Vd7k.

Chapter 11
2010 to 2015

2012: MV *Costa Concordia*, grounding and capsizing off Giglio Island, Italy; 32 dead
2012: MV *Rabaul Queen*, capsizing off Papua New Guinea; four times the loss of life as *Costa Concordia*
2013: *Seastreak Wall Street* hits pier in Manhattan January; SMS plans required on ferries
2015: MV *Sewol*, capsizing; 304 dead

Selecting recent casualties to include in this chapter was difficult because some final reports have not yet been issued, and legislative outcomes, if any, are as of yet undetermined. That being said, I have included the most noteworthy casualty of the decade so far, the grounding of the *Costa Concordia*, and a ferry capsizing off the coast of South Korea that resulted in the loss of ten times as many lives as from the *Costa Concordia* capsizing. Also included is a domestic ferry accident that may finally have prompted the U.S. Coast Guard to require Safety Management Systems aboard ferries.

The MV *Costa Concordia*

The majestic *Costa Concordia*, a sumptuous 114,000 GRT Italian passenger ship, was built in 2004 for Carnival Cruise Lines, the parent company of her operator, Costa Crociere. She sailed a weekly Mediterranean cruise, calling at ports in Italy, France, and Spain, and the islands of Majorca and Sicily.

It was the evening of January 13, 2012. The *Costa Concordia*, with 4,229 persons aboard, was en route from Civitavecchia to Savona, Italy, under the command of her master, Captain Francesco Schettino. He had almost seventeen years of seagoing experience, over half of them sailing with Costa Crociere. He held his first command in June 2004. He had never attended a bridge resource management (BRM) course, nor had any of his officers.

The weather was fair, visibility was good, and the seas were calm to moderate. The ship had suffered no mechanical breakdowns and her state-of-the-art navigation systems were all functioning. The crew of 1,023 was composed of people from thirty-eight different nations, and the passengers hailed from over twenty-five different countries. Italian was the official working language of the ship, but when crew couldn't understand each other, they would revert to English. Several American passengers later testified that language barriers were a major problem during the emergency, as most people aboard did not speak Italian.

Upon departing Civitavecchia, the master had informed the navigator of his plan to deviate from the normal route, and pass the nearby Isola del Giglio. The ship did not carry the appropriate scale chart for this area, as it was not an area along her planned route. The navigators should have referred to chart #119, which has a scale of 1:20,000, appropriate for navigation near the island. The ship didn't have chart #119 aboard; they had chart #6, which showed Giglio, but at a scale of 1:100,000, which is a dangerously small scale for navigation so near to land.

The vessel was steaming at over fifteen knots as she passed within half a mile of Giglio, while navigating on a chart of dangerously improper scale.

At 2139, as the vessel approached the island, the master arrived on the bridge and relieved the chief officer, Ciro Ambrosio, of the watch, but data recovered during the investigation indicated no formal watch turnover or assumption of the conn had been properly announced. Also in the wheelhouse were three deck officers, the cadet, a helmsman, and lookout. Contrary to the provisions of the ISM code, two non-watchstanders were also in the wheelhouse—one of whom was the master's lover, a charming, twenty-five-year-old Maldovan dancer, Miss Domnica Cemortan.

Just after he arrived on the bridge, the master was on his cell phone, and not really focusing on navigating the vessel. Possibly due to all the distractions in the wheelhouse, the master overshot his turn, and then when he finally initiated the maneuver, the helmsman made several errors on the helm. The helmsman, an Indonesian, later testified he had trouble understanding the helm commands that Captain Schettino had issued in English. Basically, he botched the turn.

According to the chief mate's testimony, the bridge watch urged Captain Schettino not to pass so close to the island, but this was not supported by the audio recordings on the voyage data recorder (VDR), which had no evidence of anyone warning the master of any danger during the time period before impact. The evidence actually showed that no one on the bridge was taking careful measurements of the vessel's proximity to land, either by radar or visually. Apparently, no one was correctly parallel indexing.

At 2145, while headed in a northerly direction, the *Costa Concordia* struck Scole Rocks with her port quarter. The impact ripped open her hull (the breach ran roughly 159 feet down the port side), flooding five contiguous watertight compartments, including the engine room. She quickly lost propulsion and electrical generation—in fact, almost all of the vessel's critical machinery was located in the spaces that flooded. She started to list to port and the spaces below decks went dark.

Fortunately, most of the bridge equipment continued to function on power from backup batteries. At 2154 the bridge issued an announcement to the passengers that the blackout was under control and that technicians were working to restore functionality to the ship. Three minutes later, the master contacted the company to inform them the ship had hit a rock on her port side, aft, and that water was flooding machinery spaces, had reached the main electrical panel, and that the ship was in blackout. The master did not send a distress.

The damaged ship began to drift, being gently pushed back toward the shore to the southwest by the prevailing breeze and current.

At the company headquarters, chaos reigned, and misinformation was repeatedly passed along with details of the casualty changing with every telling. Initial contact with search and rescue authorities was made at 2200, but not by the ship. A person ashore whose mother had called him from the ship was first to notify authorities. Seven minutes later, the Civitavecchia SAR organization contacted the ship, but the master downplayed the casualty.

At 2205 Captain Schettino again contacted the company, and reassured them that he told the authorities only that the ship had a blackout. Passengers were told to muster in the lounges, but were not given any other instructions, and the ship was drifting slowly back toward land. Many crew and passengers took it upon themselves not to go to the lounges, but to instead head for their muster stations. By then, the Livorno SAR group contacted the vessel. At around 2215, the list shifted from port to starboard. Neither the master nor the company officials had yet notified shoreside authorities as to the true nature of the problem. Captain Schettino only informed the authorities, when they contacted the ship at 2216, that he had hit a rock. The Italians, fortunately, had already initiated rescue activities.

At 2222, Captain Schettino contacted the Civitavecchia Coast Guard and requested two tugs, but indicated nothing serious was wrong. He then made a few more calls to the company. Four minutes later, the chief mate notified SAR authorities of the breach and flooding problems—this was the first notification the authorities had that the ship was flooding and not simply experiencing a blackout.

By 2230, some enterprising passengers had decided to board the lifeboats themselves, without being told by anyone to abandon ship. While this was going on, the chief engineer suggested to the master that he should issue the abandon ship signal, but the master wanted to wait. At 2233 the general emergency alarm was sounded, but the master again reassured passengers the situation was under control. At 2236, Captain Schettino finally issued instructions for passengers to go to their muster stations, but it was unclear if a formal "abandon ship" was ever issued.

Captain Schettino didn't send a distress call until 2238, and then, only at the insistence of the shoreside authorities. The official order to abandon ship was verbally issued by the staff captain via the public address system (in English) at 2254, about an hour after the initial allision, but many passengers didn't hear the announcement. The first lifeboat was lowered a minute later, while the ship continued to drift toward Giglio Island.

During the investigation it was discovered that many of the crew assigned to manage lifeboats and liferafts either did not have the proper certifications and training for the task, or had expired certificates.

The *Costa Concordia* finally ground to a stop at 2300, impaled on a rocky outcropping and listing badly to starboard. By then, the starboard list had worsened to fifteen degrees and most of her starboard side was submerged. She was fortunate to have grounded so close to shore, because with such a severe list, it was almost impossible to launch the lifeboats. By 2311 the list had worsened to between twenty-five and thirty degrees.

The master and most of the crew left the wheelhouse by 2320, leaving one crew member to coordinate the rescue efforts since most passengers were still aboard, but he too left the bridge twelve minutes later as the list continued to worsen. By then, roughly 300 people still remained aboard.

Once the order to abandon ship had been given, it took over six hours to get the remaining passengers disembarked. By midnight the list had increased to forty degrees and kept worsening. Many people who had not made it into the lifeboats jumped into the sea, and were picked up by the local vessels and rescue craft which had swarmed to the area to assist.

At 0034 the next morning, Captain Schettino notified rescue authorities that he was in a lifeboat with several other crew members (roughly eighty people were still stuck on the ship). Seven minutes later, the ship had heeled to eighty degrees. Schettino refused to reboard his vessel, despite multiple urgent pleas from rescuers to reboard and coordinate the evacuation. Captain Schettino arrived on shore at roughly 0253, leaving roughly fifty people still stranded aboard the now capsized ship.

Rescue operations were completed at 0617 January 14. Fortunately, the ship was very close to shore and the weather remained calm, so most of the vessel's complement made it to shore alive, but twenty-seven passengers and five crew members lost their lives, and 157 were injured. Over forty-three vessels and eight helicopters had taken part in the rescue operation.

The MV *Costa Concordia*, capsized on Giglio Island, Italy. *paolodefalco75 via Wikimedia Commons.*

Findings

The entire list of things done wrong is too long to list here, but fault was plainly laid at the master's feet, as well as the chief officer, for not running a tighter bridge watch. The ultimate cause of the incident, according to the Italian

Marine Casualty Investigation Central Board (MCICB), was a human element, namely the catastrophic failure of bridge team management both before and after the accident, specifically:

- Using a poorly planned route that brought the ship within a half-mile of shore
- Demonstrating an overall passive attitude on the bridge watch, and failure to advise the master of an inadequate rate of turn and turn radius
- Fully-manned bridge team not paying attention to the ship's progress
- Selection of an inappropriate reference point to guide the turn
- Use of charts of an inappropriate (and dangerous) scale
- Failure to use nautical publications
- Master was distracted by non-essential persons on the bridge and taking a non-navigational-related phone call
- Master was giving the helmsman a course to steer, rather than a rudder command, for a significant course change
- Traveling too fast near a poorly lit shoreline
- Sloppy watch turnover between master and chief officer
- Fully enclosed bridge obscured night viewing of the surrounding area

After the incident, the poor operational practices of the crew continued, including:

- No emergency alarm was sounded after the initial impact
- Inconsistencies on the muster lists led to some crew members being confused as to their duties
- No orders to the crew were issued from the bridge post-incident
The master repeatedly minimized the severity of the casualty to authorities
- The master did not follow the ships SMS procedures

Aftermath

Again, the investigating body found the cause of the incident was entirely due to the human element. The investigating body recommended that international treaties be amended to require that bridge team members be given very specific roles for various watch conditions. They also recommended a complete ban to non-essential crew in the wheelhouse, especially during critical maneuvers. The board found no lack of competency, alertness, or physical ability amongst the crew. What they discovered were lapses, slips, and bad decisions caused by distractions, lack of training, and violations of numerous ISM provisions.

Shortly after the casualty, Captain Schettino was detained and put under house arrest while he awaited trial. By late February, four ship's officers and three shoreside managers had been arrested and charged for their contributions to the disaster. The trials began in July 2013.

An Italian court, after accepting their various plea bargains, sentenced chief officer Ciro Ambrosio to one year and eleven months, third officer Silvia Coronica to eighteen months, and helmsman Jacob Rusli Bin to twenty months. Two company officials also received sentences, also as a result of plea bargains. It is unlikely any of them will see the inside of a cell, as Italy typically suspends sentences that are less than two years, and helmsman Jacob Rusli Bin is reportedly back in Indonesia. The company's Crisis Coordinator, Roberto Ferranini, who was not aboard but was found guilty of downplaying the crisis and not providing adequate or timely support, received a sentence of two years and ten months. The ship's Hotel Director, who was aboard, received a sentence of two years and six months for not providing better leadership during the chaotic evacuation.

In 2013, Costa Crociere, the ship's operating company, agreed to pay a fine of just over €1 million to avoid criminal charges. Captain Schettino's trial began in July 2013, with his case heard by a three-judge panel in Grosseto, Tuscany. The prosecutor asked for a sentence of twenty-six years. Despite efforts by his attorneys to place some blame on crew and other factors, on February 11, 2015, Captain Schettino was sentenced to a total of sixteen years: ten years for manslaughter and the death of thirty-two people, five years for causing a shipwreck, one year for abandoning his vessel, and an additional month for giving false information to authorities. He may never see the inside of a cell, however, as he is entitled to two appeals which may take years to resolve. Each of the 110 civil plaintiffs were awarded €30,000 and €300,000 was awarded to the island of Giglio and the Tuscany region.

As a result of this tragedy and recommendations articulated in the final investigation report, lawmakers are already looking at ways to improve safety aboard passenger ships, including the following amendments to SOLAS:

- Collecting additional passenger information, such as nationality, to facilitate communications in emergencies
- Requiring ships to submit their voyage plans to their operating companies before departure
- Providing passengers a flyer in both their own language and the working language of the vessel detailing emergency procedures and locations
- Ensuring safety information is posted throughout the vessel, including in cabins, and is available on the vessel's TV system
- Conducting muster drills in any ports where new passengers embark, not just the original departure port
- Requiring that lifejackets are stowed at the embarkation points, not just in staterooms
- Creating a system of standards and audits for international manning agencies
- The updating and addition of technical and mechanical requirements regarding subdivision and stability, redundancy of critical systems, flooding detection systems (interfaced with stability programs), and building vessels with double skins around vital areas of the vessel
- Requiring revised evacuation plans for new ships, requiring plans similar to those required on Ro/Ro ships
- Considering increasing the number of embarkation ladders (currently one per side is required)

The report made numerous other recommendations, mostly concerning the location of critical components, and lighting, and communications systems.

In addition to the international response, the cruise lines, through their industry group, the Cruise Lines International Association (CLIA), passed new guidelines requiring ships to:

- Require all passengers to participate in a muster drill before departure
- Limit access to the wheelhouse to only those on watch
- Carry more lifejackets

CLIA has also created a passenger's bill of rights, which includes requirements to inform passengers of schedule or route changes, transport and lodge passengers whose trips are interrupted, provide emergency medical services, and refund fares for voyages that are cut short or cancelled.

The body of the last victim, Russel Rubello, an Indian waiter, was finally recovered by salvage workers on November 3, 2014, almost three years after the accident.[1]

The MV *Rabaul Queen*

The *Rabaul Queen,* a passenger ferry plying the waters of the Solomon Sea, capsized and sank on February 2, 2012, in a gale off Morobe in Papua New Guinea. Similar to other ferry disasters, the vessel had been designed for protected waters, not the often rough seas found around Papua New Guinea. She, as is not unusual in developing parts of the word, was probably overloaded, possibly carrying as many as 500 people, despite her certificate allowing only 295 passengers. What is different about this story is that this vessel was owned by a westerner from a family with a long and varied (and in some cases illustrious) seafaring history. Though exact numbers are still uncertain, it is estimated that many more than the 162 known dead perished when the ship capsized.

To say this story is fraught with intrigue, corruption, and conflicts of interest, is an understatement. An acquaintance who fished the waters of Papua New Guinea has called the area "the last wild west," citing corruption and dirty dealings as the norm.

Peter Sharp comes from a long line of Scottish seafarers. He owned the *Rabaul Queen* ferry, one of many vessels of his Starships (PNG) Limited Line (also known as Rabaul Shipping). Peter Sharp's company is reportedly the largest passenger ship operator in Papua New Guinea.

Peter Sharp's children are also in the maritime industry; his son, Alexander, manages one of his shipping companies and his daughter, Christine, is a chief engineer with Teekay Shipping.

At the time of the incident, Peter's younger brother, Hamish Sharp, owned Bismark Maritime Pty. Ltd., another local vessel operator. In 2006, Hamish Sharp was appointed (some think unfairly) chairman of the Papua New Guinea National Maritime Safety Authority (NMSA), which had been formed only three years earlier in 2003. According to news sources, two of Hamish's vessels later sank while he was NMSA chairman and the wrecks were not cleared away quickly, but were left to rust, creating not only navigational hazards, but quite a local scandal. Eventually Hamish was able to sell the wrecks for a pittance, and remove his name from the vessels.

Peter Sharp's grand-father, Captain Rudolph Sharp, however, is a maritime hero. Captain Rudolph Sharp was master of the *Lancastria* on June 17, 1940, when she was sunk by Nazi bombers, killing over 4,000, most of them civilians, but Captain Sharp survived. Captain Rudolph Sharp was also the master of the ill-fated RMS *Laconia* when she was sunk by a German U-Boat off the west coast of Africa just two years later. Fewer than half of the more than 2,700 people aboard, who were mostly non-combatants, survived. Captain Sharp survived the torpedo, but allegedly elected to go down with his ship.

Despite the seafaring blood coursing through Peter Sharp's veins, he has a somewhat checkered history, his vessels having been involved in numer-ous other incidents, some resulting in deaths. He also had a rather conten-tions interview during the investigation of the sink-ing of the *Rabaul Queen*.

The ferry *Rabaul Queen* in better days. *Michael Pennay (derivative work) via Wikimedia Commons.*

The examiner accused him of allowing passengers to be crammed on the ship so tightly as to be comparable to the transportation of cattle. The ship was so crowded that passengers allegedly could not lie down, or stretch their legs if they were sitting. Many were reportedly sitting on the steel decks.

The Commission of Inquiry determined the *Rabaul Queen* was not seaworthy and never should have departed on its final voyage—Peter Sharp was arrested in August 2013 in East Britain and charged with 162 counts of manslaughter and other charges, such as taking an unseaworthy ship to sea. The ferry's master and chief mate were similarly charged. Company officials and a Papua New Guinea national safety manager were also charged with manslaughter.

Despite desperate attempts by his family and attorney to secure his release, Peter Sharp was denied bail. In October 2014 his case was delayed pending amendments to evidence.[2]

The *Seastreak Wall Street*

On January 9, 2013, the 141-foot *Seastreak Wall Street* ferry, which speeds commuters between New Jersey and New York, struck Manhattan's Pier 11 while cruising at twelve knots, injuring eighty people, four of them seriously.

On his approach, as ferry operators had done hundreds of times, the master intended to switch from the centerline steering station to the starboard station, which had better visibility for docking. He also intended to reduce speed for docking. After he transferred to the starboard control station, the master stated he felt a vibration and then lost control of the vessel.

The master, Jason Reimer, was an experienced and senior operator. The NTSB found that responsibility fell primarily on the master of the vessel, but that mechanical and operational shortcomings were also a proximate cause of the accident. As a result of the investigation, the NTSB determined the following caused or contributed to the accident:

- The master lost control of the vessel and had not allowed enough time to react in case something went wrong with the docking maneuver. He had not successfully returned the propulsion control system to "combinatory" mode after switching to "backup" mode earlier in the voyage, which resulted in the vessel accelerating forward when he put the controls astern.
- The design of the control station was such that controls were ambiguous, and operators could be confused as to which station was engaged, and which controls for engine RPM and propeller pitch were active.
- The managerial oversight and training provided by Seastreak LLC, the ferry's owner and operator, were lacking and should have included more safety training, clearer assignment of crew members' duties during approach and docking, specific procedures for switching control stations, and better documentation of the new propulsion system that had recently been retrofitted on the *Seastreak Wall Street*.
- Passengers were allowed to use the stairways during docking and approach and there were no formal policies on passenger location during transits, nor were crew members formally trained in vessel operations or modern safety practices.
- No passenger safety announcements were made during the ferry's approach. Company policy at the time did not address this.
- The procedure manual had not been updated since after the vessel's propulsion was changed from water jet to controllable pitch propellers in July 2012.

Aftermath

As a result of this, and other ferry accidents, the NTSB recommended (again) that domestic ferries, which are not subject to the ISM code, have SMS plans. The NTSB pointed out that an SMS plan may have averted this and other ferry accidents, simply be requiring, for example, a pre-arrival checklist. The U.S. Coast Guard agreed, and is drafting such a rule.

The NTSB also recommended that VDRs be installed on ferries to aid in post-incident investigations, but this recommendation was dismissed by the U.S. Coast Guard as being cost prohibitive. Domestic vessels are not subject to many international requirements, but the NTSB argued they should be subject to some of the provisions of ISM, found in Chapter IX of SOLAS.[3]

The MV *Sewol*

When analyzing casualties, one thing stands clear—culture matters. Not only do different cultures treat safety, corruption, and integrity with varying degrees of seriousness, but post-disaster reactions vary widely around the globe. In some cultures, bribes are a normal and expected part of doing business, and no one is surprised, let alone mortified, by a bulging brown envelope. In many Asian cultures, speaking "uphill" within a hierarchy is discouraged. Different cultures also place varying importance on the correctness of forms, logbooks, and official documents. Interestingly, cultures that seem to have a historic tolerance for graft, seem to have the most draconian punishments for transgressions when something goes wrong—especially when the mishap is exposed by the international media.

In the report on the 2013 Asiana airline crash in San Francisco, the NTSB cited cultural issues, such as it being impolite to wear sunglasses in the presence of a senior officer, and reluctance to make operational suggestions to a superior, as contributing factors. Professor Najmedin Meshkati, an expert in aviation industry human factors research, determined there are two main areas affected by cultural factors: human interactions with each other, and the human interface with equipment and machinery.

The story that follows illustrates what can only be described as a cultural failing, and many South Koreans are clamoring for change in its wake.

Sources on this casualty differed and even conflicted in some cases, so all values, including times, are necessarily approximate. Weights are in metric tons (tonnes).

In the Beginning

Decades prior to running the *Sewol* ferry, the patriarch of the family, Yoo Byung Un, was an evangelical Christian pastor of a religious cult called Gu Won Pa (the Salvation Sect). On August 29, 1987, the bodies of thirty-three sect followers were found bound and gagged, stacked in two piles in a factory south of Seoul, in what appeared to be a murder-suicide linked to the cult. The crime was never solved. In 1992, Yoo was found guilty of various financial crimes associated with organized crime, including fraud, and was imprisoned for four years. At the time, Yoo had close ties with then South Korean President Chun Doo-Hwan. (President Chun was later sentenced to death in 1996 for his role in the spring 1980 Gwangju massacre, where hundreds of people protesting martial law were killed by Korean army troops. He was later pardoned.)

After that adventure, Yoo became the CEO of the Semo ferry company, which operated on the Han River in Seoul until 1997, when it went bankrupt under a debt of roughly $200 million. His new company, Chonghaejin Marine, absorbed Semo and its debt, which was ultimately forgiven.

The Korea Development Bank then loaned Yoo $10 million, presumably to help start a new ferry service. Yoo Byung Un still ran his cult and maintained a compound with hundreds of devoted followers.

Chonghaejin Marine was one of several holdings of parent company I-ONE-I Holdings, controlled by Yoo Byung Un's family. The eldest son, Yoo Dae Kyun, and his brother Yoo Hyuk Ki were majority shareholders, and Yoo Byung Un's wife also owned shares.

In 2012, Chonghaejin Marine purchased a 479-foot, eighteen-year-old, dilapidated passenger ferry from Japan for $9.8 million. Under the Lee Myung Bak administration, shipping had been largely deregulated in order to help Korea compete economically. One aspect of the regulatory changes was that passenger ship life was extended from twenty years to thirty, meaning that the ferry could still work for another ten years.

So the vessel was bought on the cheap with borrowed funds, renamed MV *Sewol*, classed under the Korean Registry (KR), and almost immediately modified to carry 240 additional passengers and more cargo than her original plans allowed for. She then had to pass safety and stability inspections by the Korean Registry, which she did without any issues. After modifications, she was issued a recommended load of 987 tons of cargo by the Korean Registry.

Investigators later determined that KR inspections, which are done on behalf (and under the oversight) of the flag state (Korea), are often lax. It was opined this may be because government maritime regulators often seek employment with KR when they leave government service.

Another circumstance fostering lax compliance was the fact that coastwise vessels are inspected and monitored by an industry group, the Korea Shipping Association, a group of two hundred shipping businesses, and not by the Korean Coast Guard. (This is similar to the conflict of interest seen in the United States where the American Bureau of Shipping, a private, for-profit industry group, is paid by ship owners to perform governmental inspections.)

In March 2013, with governmental and industry blessing, the *Sewol* started shuttling passengers and cargo between Incheon and Jeju, a volcanic island known for white sand beaches and waterfalls. It was a short, fourteen-hour trip. The only tricky part of the run was a three-mile stretch of treacherous water called Maeng Gol Soo Ro, or the Maenggol Channel. The Maenggol Channel is a shortcut between the islands off South Korea, and is plagued by rapid, swirling currents.

On April 15, 2014, at about 2100, the *Sewol*, loaded with 476 passengers, 315 of whom were high school students on a four-day field trip to Jeju, departed Incheon, with the relief master Lee Joon Sook in command. Captain Lee was 69, well past retirement age, and was paid a paltry $2,600 per month, about a third less than normal wages for such a post.

Unlike previous ferry trips passengers had taken, on this trip, no pre-departure safety announcements were made explaining where life jackets were stowed. No one was overly concerned, and the passengers enjoyed the onboard entertainment and prepared for bed as the ship departed.

The Capsizing

On the morning of April 16, 2014, at around 0830 the ship was in the Maenggol Channel, cruising at her usual speed of approximately eighteen knots. Only the third mate, twenty-five-year-old Park Hyun Kul, who was conning the vessel, and helmsman Cho Joon Ki, were in the wheelhouse. Captain Lee was in his cabin. Third mate Park had roughly a year of sea time, and had only been with the company six months. She had never navigated the Maenggol Channel before. By any measure, she was inexperienced and should not have been left alone to navigate the tricky pass.

What none of the passengers (and probably few of the crew) knew, was that the ship was overloaded, top heavy, dangerously tender, and that her cargo was poorly secured.

At around 0845, the ship made a turn to starboard, sending dishes and furniture flying. People were thrown against bulkheads as the ship suddenly, violently listed to port. There were reports that some on-deck containers broke loose and instantly tumbled to the low side, the extra off-center weight making it impossible for the vessel to right herself. Water started pouring into the ship. The senior prosecutor later stated his investigation had determined cargo lashings were loose and some crew didn't even know how to use them properly. Later it was discovered that 180 cars and 1,100 tons of containers in the hold had also shifted, causing the unrecoverable list.

At the trial, the third mate testified she was maneuvering to starboard to avoid another vessel and that she had only ordered a change of five degrees. It is unclear if she ordered five degree right rudder, or a five degree course change. Either way, data recorder evidence indicated a contact was ahead of the *Sewol* and that Park had initiated a turn to starboard. Evidence indicated it as a sharp and sudden turn. Passenger testimony was that the ship shuddered and shook, but there is no evidence the vessel struck anything. The helmsman corroborated Park's testimony, and stated he had only followed the third mate's helm instructions, and there is no evidence to the contrary. Data recorder evidence shows the *Sewol* changing to starboard and coming to an almost reciprocal heading, almost as if it were pushed by an external force. There was evidence of past steering gear problems. Regardless, even at sea speed, a vessel should be able to handle any degree of rudder without capsizing.

Right after the incident, Captain Lee rushed to the bridge and issued the orders for passengers to stay put. An announcement was made over the ship's PA system advising, "Stay where you are. It's dangerous if you move." Most passengers obeyed.

By 0850 the ship had listed to thirty degrees.

The first call for help was made at 0852 when a passenger, a high school student named Choi, called the local emergency number on his cell phone and told them the ferry was sinking.

At 0855, an officer on the *Sewol* radioed Jeju island VTS (which was much farther away than the nearby Jindo VTS) stating that the ship was listing and in danger. When the VTS station asked for the ship's location, the caller only asked them to hurry and that the ship had listed a lot. The VTS station in Jindo, an island on the southern tip of the South Korean mainland which was much closer to the incident site, responded and asked about passengers. Someone on the *Sewol* responded that passengers were not in lifeboats because of the list.

Between 0830 and 0900 passengers heard two announcements advising them to don their lifejackets but remain at their locations. (It is generally considered unwise to don floatation while still inside, as it could render it more difficult to escape a flooding vessel and can even pin a person against an overhead surface.) The ship was listing badly and was filling with water. During interviews, Captain Lee said he advised passengers to stay put because the rescue boats had not yet arrived, the water was very cold, and the currents were extremely fast. Basically, the passengers had nowhere to go.

By 0900 the ship had listed to forty-five degrees, prompting some passengers to ignore the order to stay put and make their way to the deck. All forty-four lifeboats, except for one, were unusable due to the extreme list. Most passengers remained in their cabins, waiting for instructions.

At 0900 Jeju VTS told an unidentified crew member to get lifejackets on people as they may need to evacuate, but the crew member replied that it was hard for people to move, presumably due to the list. During the next thirty-eight minutes, the crew member reiterated that passengers could not move about, the vessel was listing so badly.

At 0906 Jindo VTS asked a nearby vessel to assist, but twelve minutes later the vessel reported no one was evacuating and that they couldn't help if people were not evacuating.

By 0924 the *Sewol* was listing to over 50 degrees, but even then, expert testimony demonstrated she could still theoretically have been evacuated in under ten minutes, had the crew only reacted correctly. I doubt that any vessel listed to 50 degrees, and full of terrified passengers, who are unfamiliar with the ship, could be easily evacuated in ten minutes. At such an angle, doors jam shut, openings become blocked with fallen equipment, and panic sets in as one has no flat place to walk and, in this case, the vessel was flooding.

Jindo VTS urged the *Sewol* to get passengers into life jackets and extra clothes, but the *Sewol* responded that the captain needed to make the decision to evacuate. A minute later, the *Sewol* explained if the Coast Guard could arrive right away they could they save everyone, but that there were too many for a helicopter evacuation.

The Rescue

At about 0940, public announcements were made over a loudspeaker at a Jindo harbor asking for people with boats to assist the stricken ferry. By 1000, fishing and recreational vessels swarmed the area to assist. Witnesses reported that local vessels arrived to help about thirty minutes before the Coast Guard arrived.

But not everyone was worried. While waiting for the Coast Guard, some crew drank beer, later testifying it "calmed the excitement." Most passengers stayed put.

Eventually, Coast Guard vessels arrived on scene. The Coast Guard, in what hopefully was optimistic zeal, initially reported to South Korea's President that it had rescued 370 passengers and crew. However, this contradicted phone transcript evidence in which just ten minutes earlier, the Coast Guard said it was not evacuating passengers and that they were just observing because "no passenger had jumped from the ferry yet."

When they finally did start evacuating passengers, unbeknownst to Coast Guard rescuers, Captain Lee was one of the first to be rescued, leaving hundreds behind to fend for themselves. There is a photo of the Captain Lee being helped off the sinking ship by Coast Guard rescuers, while hundreds remained obediently below. None of the fleeing crew identified themselves to rescuers, and any uniforms were hidden by life vests. Later it emerged that the master, chief engineer, chief mate, and second mate were among the first to be rescued.

By 1120, the bow was submerged, but portions of the hull were still visible. The *Sewol* took two and a half hours to submerge completely.

The vessel eventually rolled over and sank, taking 304 lives with her. Of the twenty-nine crew, twenty-two (76%) survived the disaster, which contrasts sharply with passenger statistics. Of the 447 passengers aboard that day, only 152 (or 34%) survived.

Recovery Operations

There are claims the Korean Coast Guard bungled the response so badly that it actually increased the loss of life. The Korean Coast Guard apparently did not encourage passengers to evacuate the vessel, and instead rescued the waiting crew. Also, the Coast Guard did not have its barge ready for use and had not properly availed itself of a nearby barge, which delayed and confused rescue efforts. Even the local VTS was condemned for not properly managing the scene. As a result, three Coast Guard officials were indicted for interference with the exercise of rights, interference with business, and breaches of the Ship Safety Act.

During later recovery operations, it was discovered the renovation drawings had been forged, which further hampered rescue efforts, especially for the divers.

Panicked parents swarmed to the area shoreside. Websites and social media were swamped with images of the event and surviving children and parents trying to find each other. A Jindo school gymnasium was turned into a massive staging area where survivors were brought to try to be matched with family members. Color posters and lists of names were posted to facilitate reunions.

Two days after the incident, on April 18, Kang Min Kyu, the Vice Principal in charge of the student group, was found hanged behind the gymnasium staging area. A suicide note was found in which he asked parents to place all the blame on him, since he had been in charge of the trip. He asked for his ashes to be spread where the ship had sunk, so he could be a teacher for the missing children in the "other world"—another casualty of the disaster.

Aftermath

A two-month investigation by South Korea's Board of Audit and Inspection yielded an interim report finding that lax governmental regulation and corruption contributed to the catastrophe. Over twenty government agencies were called before investigators.

Within days of the incident, police raided offices of the Coast Guard, the Korea Shipping Association, the Korean Register of Shipping, and the offices of Chonghaejin Marine. The investigation discovered a tangled web of oversights, intentional misdeeds, and corruption that, acting in concert, ultimately doomed the small ship.

The ferry had been illegally modified so she could carry more cargo, modifications made with the collusion of shoreside regulators, but which left the ship dangerously unstable. Korean safety surveyors had looked the other way. The regular master had complained more than once about the unstable condition of the vessel, but was threatened with losing his job if he didn't quiet his concerns. On the day of the sinking, the *Sewol* was carrying triple the cargo load she should have been.

The owners earned much more money carrying cargo than people. She was certified for 978 tons of cargo, mostly carried on cargo trucks that drove aboard the ferry, but on this fateful day, she carried 3,608 tons of cargo, over three times her recommended load. The *Sewol* earned about $68,000 in freight charges for that run, two and a half times what she earned from carrying humans. She also carried 180 vehicles, 32 more than her legal limit. Each cargo truck was worth an average of eight times more than a human passenger. In order to load more cargo, most of her ballast had been discharged, which rendered her dangerously unstable.

This wasn't new. According to investigators, on 139 of 241 previous trips (57%), the ship carried cargo in excess of the recommended limits, which had thus far earned them an extra profit of $2.9 million.

Charges Against Officials

Forty-three officials were charged with various criminal offenses. Lee In-Soo, former head of the Korea Shipping Association (KSA) and then a top official of South Korea's Ministry of Oceans and Fisheries, was charged with embezzlement. He later resigned.

KSA's vice president was charged with taking public money. Another KSA official was charged with telling safety inspectors to overlook illegal actions by shipping companies.

The CEO of the Korean Registry resigned in April, less than one month after taking the post.

The South Korean Prime Minster, laboring under accusations the Korean government did not do enough to help the victims, resigned April 27, 2014. Culturally in Korea, resignations are often tendered to alleviate the emotional suffering of victims' families, and are not necessarily considered a sign of guilt.

According to reporter Jae Jung Suh of the *Asia Pacific Journal*, another governmental agency was involved—the Korean National Intelligence Service (NIS). Oddly, he reports the NIS, and not the Korean Coast Guard, was listed on the vessel's safety documents as the primary contact in case of an accident. A list of work items planned for the passenger area was found on a laptop computer recovered from the sunken ferry. It indicated 100 repair items ordered by the NIS. The repair orders included paint and vending machine installations, not items typically associated with security interests.

According to Jae Jung Suh, there is speculation the NIS was actually intimately involved with the management and operation of the company and its ferries. The *Sewol* ferry sank a day after a damning press conference during which the head of the NIS had to make a public apology concerning an espionage incident involving a suspected North Korean defector. About a month after the sinking, supposedly as public suspicion grew, Nam Jae Joon, the head of the intelligence agency, and Kim Jang Soo, the Korean president's national security advisor, both resigned. But this may all be quite innocent, as in the Korean culture it is not unusual for political leaders to resign in the wake of national disasters.

Charges Against the Coast Guard

The Coast Guard was slow to arrive and bungled the evacuation once it got there. Expert witness testimony, supported by simulation demonstrations, proved the ship, even when listed to thirty degrees, could have been evacuated in just over five minutes. Even thirty minutes afterwards, when the *Sewol* had listed farther and a nearby ferry captain warned the *Sewol* crew to evacuate the passengers, some experts argue they could have all escaped in under ten minutes.

The Coast Guard rescued thirty-five passengers by helicopter. Most of the crew was rescued by patrol boat, which returned to rescue passengers who had made their way topside. Most surviving passengers were rescued by private boats and fishing vessels. After roughly 1025, no more people were rescued by the Coast Guard. Navy and Coast Guard salvage and rescue teams arrived too late to be helpful. Though some Coast Guard personnel boarded the ferry, no one from the Coast Guard advised passengers to evacuate. Video of this period shows Coast Guard boats slowly circling the foundering ferry, even hampering local and navy vessels that were approaching to provide assistance.

A South Korean Coast Guard officer, Kim Kyung-Il, who was one of the first to arrive at the scene, was convicted of professional negligence and sentenced to four years in prison for failing to order the ferry's evacuation promptly enough, and for then lying about it. Sergeant Kim had earlier testified he didn't think the Coast Guard had adequately trained them for large scale rescues or rescues from stranded ships.

Five safety inspectors were charged with allowing overloaded vessels to sail.

In reaction to this tragedy, and overwhelming public pressure, on November 19, 2014, South Korea established the Ministry of Public Safety and Security, consisting of more than 10,000 officials, to take over the safety and rescue duties of the Coast Guard and respond to future disasters more efficiently. South Korea also plans to review its sea safety rules.

Charges Against the *Sewol*'s Owners

It was later shown that Yoo Byung Un, the 73-year-old chairman of Chonghaejin Marine, which owned the ferry, knew of the safety problems and allowed the ferry to be overloaded. When the court issued summonses on May 12, 2014, for the family to appear, not only did they all fail to respond—they disappeared. Yoo was indicted for embezzlement, financial malpractice, and evasion of taxes but went missing shortly after the incident.

There were reports he had sought political asylum at a foreign embassy, but had been denied. While the police search for Yoo raged on in May, hundreds of sect followers obstructed police efforts to find him. As part of a massive manhunt, 5,000 riot police were stationed at his compound. Six cult followers were arrested, suspected of helping Yoo evade police. By June, Yoo had a half-million-dollar bounty on his head.

Yoo was found dead in a field in June 2014, after a nationwide manhunt. His brother, Yoo Byung II, was found, and arrested for embezzlement. Korean law enforcement then pursued Yoo's eldest son, Yoo Dae Kyun, but he went on the run almost immediately. Yoo Dae Kyun was finally caught and arrested, along with an assistant, who was also arrested for allegedly helping Yoo Dae Kyun avoid capture. Yoo's eldest daughter, Sum Na, fled to Paris. She was arrested for embezzlement by French police in May, and is awaiting extradition. The younger son, Hyuk Ki, is in the United States. The total amount of money supposedly embezzled by the family, or tied to financial malpractice or tax avoidance, is about $136 million.

Chonghaejin Marine CEO Kim Han Sik was arrested and charged with death by negligence and violating the Korean Ship Safety Act after the regular captain testified that he had told Kim of the compromised stability on multiple occasions. Four other Chonghaejin Marine employees were arrested and charged similarly.

Charges Against the Crew

On the twentieth day of testimony, the helmsman testified that the master had told him to make the passengers stay in their cabins, even as the ferry took on a dangerous list, claiming it was too dangerous to make them move. Other crew testified they felt the Coast Guard was better prepared to evacuate passengers, so there was no need for them to stay aboard and help. At the trial, several crew members, including the first engineer, were quick to accuse the captain of mishandling the whole affair.

For his part, at the trial of the Chonghaejin Marine executives, Captain Lee stated that the pre-departure safety checklists were regularly completed in a careless manner, and pointed blame towards the third mate who completed the form for the doomed trip, and the regular master. Captain Lee admitted he had previously operated the ferry overloaded and with less than recommended ballast, but stated that was really the chief mate's fault, not his, because the chief mate had told him it was okay to sail.

Captain Lee, the chief mate, second mate, and chief engineer were formally charged on May 15 with a type of homicide, which carries the death penalty. Eleven other crew, including the third mate Park, were charged with abandoning ship, a violation of Korean maritime law, and negligence. Third mate Park stated there were problems with the steering gear and that she didn't make the hard turn.

The master, Captain Lee Joon Sook, was sentenced to thirty-six years for gross negligence and dereliction of duty. He avoided the equivalent of a murder charge and its associated death penalty, only because it had not been proven he acted with foresight or intent to kill. The prosecutor, who had sought the death penalty, was disappointed in the ruling, as were some victims' families. Others, including the International Federation of Shipmasters' Associations (IFSMA), which publicly held the conviction to be a "travesty of justice," think the sentence unduly harsh.

The chief engineer, who pled guilty to criminal abandonment, was sentenced to thirty years for failing to assist others. Thirteen other crewmembers, including third mate Park Hyun Kul and her helmsman Cho Joon Ki, were found guilty of accidental homicide and/or criminal negligence, and received sentences of between five and twenty years.

It doesn't end here—this tragedy extends to the rescuers. A 53-year-old civilian diver died while searching for bodies in the sunken wreck. On July 17, 2014, a helicopter loaded with five rescue workers who had been working on the *Sewol* salvage crashed, killing all five.

Captain Lee and eight other convicted crew members have appealed.[4]

Notes

1. Sources for *Costa Concordia* information: (Italian) Ministry of Infrastructures and Transports: Marine Casualties Investigative Body, "Preliminary Report on the Safety Technical Investigations Cruise Ship Costa Concordia Marine Casualty on January 13, 2012," http://www.ifsma.org/tempannounce/CostaConcordia.pdf; (Italian) Ministry of Infrastructures and Transports: Marine Casualties Investigative Body, "Complete Report on the Safety Technical Investigations Cruise Ship Costa Concordia Marine Casualty on January 13, 2012," http://www.safety4sea.com/images/media/pdf/Costa_Concordia_-_Full_Investigation_Report.pdf; Silvia Ognibene, "Prosecutors target cruise ship captain, Costa executives," *Reuters*, February 23, 2012, http://uk.reuters.com/article/2012/02/23/us-italy-ship-idUSTRE81M1NS20120223; "Costa Concordia captain Francesco Schettino says he'll plead guilty in return for lenient sentence," *Metro News* (UK), July 17, 2013, http://metro.co.uk/2013/07/17/costa-concordia-captain-francesco-schettino-says-hell-plead-guilty-in-return-for-lenient-sentence-3886828/; "Costa Concordia Trial Intensifies: Recordings of Captain Are Damning," *The Maritime Executive*, December 9, 2013, http://www.maritime-executive.com/article/Costa-Concordia-Trial-Intensifies-Recordings-of-Captain-Are-Damning-2013-12-09; Nick Squires, "Helmsman from Costa Concordia disaster fails to turn up for trial of captain," *Daily Telegraph*, March 12, 2014, http://www.telegraph.co.uk/news/worldnews/europe/italy/10691614/Helmsman-from-Costa-Concordia-disaster-fails-to-turn-up-for-trial-of-captain.html; Barbie Latza Nadeau and Laura Smith-Spark, "5 convicted over deadly Costa Concordia cruise liner wreck in Italy," *CNN*, July 22, 2013, http://edition.cnn.com/2013/07/20/world/europe/italy-costa-concordia-trial/; Marnie Hunter, "Cruise passengers get bill of rights," *CNN*, May 23, 2013, http://edition.cnn.com/2013/05/23/travel/cruise-passengers-bill-of-rights/; Michael Day, "Costa Concordia trial: Dancer Domnica Cemortan admits Captain Francesco Schettino was her lover and tells court she was on ship's

bridge when it capsized," *The Independent* (UK), October 29, 2013, http://www.independent.co.uk/news/world/europe/costa-concordia-trial-dancer-domnica-cemortan-admits-captain-francesco-schettino-was-her-lover-and-tells-court-she-was-on-ships-bridge-when-it-capsized-8911492.html; Jim Walker, "Crying Captain Schettino Shows No Remorse: Sentenced to Sixteen Years," *Cruise Law News,* February 11, 2015, http://www.cruiselawnews.com/2015/02/articles/crime/crying-captain-schettino-shows-no-remorse-sentenced-to-sixteen-years/; Chris Pleasance, *"Costa Concordia's 'Captain Coward' sentenced to 16 years in jail on manslaughter charges over 2012 cruise ship disaster which killed 32,"* Mailonline, February 11, 2015, http://www.dailymail.co.uk/news/article-2949670/Costa-Concordia-s-Captain-Coward-sentenced-16-years-jail-manslaughter-charges.html; Coleen Barry and Francesco Sportelli, "Italy: 5 convicted for *Costa Concordia* shipwreck," Associated Press, July 20, 2013; "Five Costa Concordia staff convicted over shipwreck in Italy," The Guardian July 20, 2013, http://www.theguardian.com/world/2013/jul/20/five-costa-concordia-guilty-shipwreck-italy; Josephine McKenna, "Costa Concordia: Last victim found in wreckage," The Telegraph, November 3, 2014, http://www.telegraph.co.uk/news/worldnews/europe/italy/11205374/Costa-Concordia-body-of-final-victim-found-on-board.html.

2. Sources for *Rabaul Queen* information: Papua New Guinea Commission of Inquiry, Report into the "Capsizing and Sinking of the MV *Rabaul Queen*," June 28, 2012, http://www.mvrabaulqueen.com/Report/fullreport.pdf; "Final Report Released Over *Rabaul Queen* Sinking in PNG," *The National*, September 4, 2012, http://pidp.eastwestcenter.org/pireport/2012/September/09-05-08.htm; B. J. Skane, "Arrests made and charges laid over MV *Rabaul Queen*," *Vanuatu Daily Post*, September 9, 2013, http://www.dailypost.vu/content/arrests-made-and-charges-laid-over-mv-%E2%80%9Crabaul-queen%E2%80%9D-sinking; Liam Fox, "PNG election delays public release of ferry report," *Australia News Network*, June 29, 2012, http://archive.today/JrOau; News reports found in: https://pngexposed.wordpress.com/tag/peter-sharp/; Martin Cox, "Passenger Ferry MV Rabaul Queen Sinks—Updated" *Maritime Matters*, February 1, 2012, http://maritimematters.com/2012/02/passenger-ferry-mv-rabaul-queen-reported-sunk/; Jo Chandler, "Ferry captain admits series of failures," *Sydney Morning Herald*, May 1, 2012; Leonce Peillard, *The Laconia Affair* (New York: Putnam, 1963); Cedric Patjole, "Peter Sharp case delayed again," *PNG Loop,* October 1, 2104, http://www.pngloop.com/2014/10/01/peter-sharp-case-delayed/.

3. Sources for *Seastreak Wall Street* information: National Transportation Safety Board, "Preliminary Marine Accident Summary," http://www.ntsb.gov/investigations/2013/new_york_ny/Seastreak_Wall_Street_Preliminary.pdf; National Transportation Safety Board, "Investigative Update on the *Seastreak Wall Street Ferry* Accident," press release, January 17, 2013, http://www.nysb.gov/news/2013/130117.html; National Transportation Safety Board Public Meeting April 8, 2014, http://www.ntsb.gov/news/events/2014/nyferry/2014abstractseastreakaccident.pdf; Bart Jansen, "NTSB: Ferry captain blamed for New York crash," *USA Today,* April 8, 2014, http://www.usatoday.com/story/news/nation/2014/04/08/ntsb-ferry-seastreak-wall-street-new-york-crash/7456525/; Dale K. DuPont, "Seastreak ferry accident due to captain's error, says NTSB," *Workboat Magazine,* April 8, 2014, http://www.workboat.com/Online-Features/2014/Seastreak-ferry-accident-due-to-captain-s-error,-says-NTSB/.

4. Sources for MV *Sewol* information: Jae-Jung Suh, "The Failure of the South Korean National Security State: The *Sewol* Tragedy in the Age of Neoliberalism," *Asia Pacific Journal,* Vol. 12, Issue 40, October 6, 2014, http://japanfocus.org/-Jae_Jung-Suh/4195; "*Sewol* captain sentenced to 36 years for gross negligence," All About Shipping.Co.U.K. Nov. 12, 2014, http://www.allaboutshipping.co.uk/2014/11/12/ Sewol-captain-sentenced-to-36-years-for-gross-negligence/; "South Korean prime minister resigns over ferry sinking," *The Guardian,* April 27, 2014, http://www.theguardian.com/world/2014/apr/27/south-korea-chung-hong-won-resigns-ferry-sinking; "Civilian diver dies in South Korea ferry search," *The Guardian,* May 6, 2014, http://www.theguardian.com/world/2014/may/06/diver-dies-in-south-korea-ferry-search; Malcolm Moore, "South Korea ferry disaster: third mate at wheel was navigating route for first time," *The Telegraph,* April 19, 2014, http://www.telegraph.co.uk/news/worldnews/asia/southkorea/10776250/South-Korea-

ferry-disaster-third-mate-at-wheel-was-navigating-route-for-first-time.html; "Greed Was Biggest Culprit in Ferry Disaster," *The Chosunlibo,* February 25, 2015, http://english.chosun.com/site/data/html_dir/2014/05/06/2014050600343.html; Andrew Stevens, "Images of ferry captain abandoning ship are shocking," CNN, April 29, 2014, http://www.cnn.com/2014/04/29/world/asia/south-korea-captain-video-stevens/; Crystal Chan, "Coastguard officer jailed over *Sewol* disaster," IHS Maritime 360, February 11, 2015, http://www.ihsmaritime360.com/article/16620/coastguard-officer-jailed-over-Sewol-disaster; Moyoun Jin, "South Korea reviews 300 sea safety rules," IHS Maritime 360, February 10, 2015, http://www.ihsmaritime360.com/article/16600/south-korea-reviews-300-sea-safety-rules; Moyoun Jin, "S Korea's Minister of Oceans and Fisheries steps down," IHS Maritime 360, December 28, 2014, http://www.ihs-maritime360.com/article/15946/s-korea-s-minister-of-oceans-and-fisheries-steps-down; Titus Zheng, "*Sewol* captain appeals conviction," IHS Maritime 360, November 17, 2014, http://www.ihsmaritime360.com/article/15465/Sewol-captain-appeals-conviction; Titus Zheng, "IFSMA: *Sewol* captain's sentence is too severe," IHS Maritime 360, November 12, 2014, http://www.ihsmaritime360.com/article/15384/ifsma-Sewol-captain-s-sentence-is-too-severe; Moyoun Jin, "*Sewol* prosecutors accuse coast guard of bungling rescue op," IHS Maritime 360, October 7, 2014, http://www.ihsmaritime360.com/article/14882/c-prosecutors-accuse-coast-guard-of-bungling-rescue-op; Moyoun Jin, "*Sewol* Passengers kept aboard, court hears," IHS Maritime 360, October 2, 2014, http://www.ihsmaritime360.com/article/14833/Sewol-passengers-kept-aboard-court-hears; Crystal Chan, "*Sewol* trial: crew too slow to evacuate," IHS Maritime 360, September 25, 2014, http://www.ihsmaritime360.com/article/14724/Sewol-trial-crew-too-slow-to-evacuate; Crystal Chan, "*Sewol* crew member points finger at captain," IHS Maritime 360, September 3, 2014, http://www.ihsmaritime360.com/article/14408/Sewol-crew-member-points-finger-at-captain; Moyoun Jin, "*Sewol* captain: Lax checks 'habitual'," IHS Maritime 360, September 1, 2014, http://www.ihsmaritime360.com/article/14377/Sewol-captain-lax-checks-habitual; Moyoun Jin, "*Sewol* trial; coastguard 'lacked training'," IHS Maritime 360, August 13, 2014, http://www.ihsmaritime360.com/article/14087/Sewol-trial-coastguard-lacked-training; Moyoun Jin, "Officials charged with *Sewol*-linked corruption," IHS Maritime 360, August 8, 2014, http://www.ihsmaritime360.com/article/14024/officials-charged-with-Sewol-linked-corruption; Moyoun Jin, "*Sewol* owner's son arrested," IHS Maritime 360, July 28, 2014, http://www.ihsmaritime360.com/article/13838/Sewol-owner-s-son-arrested; Moyoun Jin, "Prosecution shifts focus to *Sewol* owner's family," IHS Maritime 360, July 23, 2014, http://www.ihsmaritime360.com/article/13777/prosecution-shifts-focus-to-Sewol-owner-s-family; Moyoun Jin, "Five dead in *Sewol* rescue helicopter crash," IHS Maritime 360, July 18, 2014, http://www.ihsmaritime360.com/article/13713/five-dead-in-Sewol-rescue-helicopter-crash; Crystal Chan, "Audit report: Lax regulation, corruption led to *Sewol* disaster," IHS Maritime 360, July 9, 2014, http://www.ihsmaritime360.com/article/13561/audit-report-lax-regulation-corruption-led-to-Sewol-disaster; Crystal Chan, "Korea Coast Guard underestimated *Sewol* incident," IHS Maritime 360, July 3, 2104, http://www.ihsmaritime360.com/article/13461/korea-coast-guard-underestimated-Sewol-incident; Moyoun Jin, "Search for *Sewol* owner and followers continues," IHS Maritime 360, June 12, 2014, http://www.ihsmaritime360.com/article/13145/search-for-Sewol-owner-and-followers-continues; Moyoun Jin, "*Sewol* owner denied political asylum," IHS Maritime 360, June 4, 2014, http://www.ihsmaritime360.com/article/13028/Sewol-owner-denied-political-asylum; Moyoun Jin, "*Sewol* owner's followers obstruct arrest," IHS Maritime 360, May 21, 2014, http://www.ihsmaritime360.com/article/12806/Sewol-owner-s-followers-obstruct-arrest; Crystal Chan, "Chonghaejin CEO arrested over *Sewol*," IHS Maritime 360, May 8, 2014, http://www.ihsmaritime360.com/article/12615/chonghae-jin-ceo-arrested-over-Sewol; "*Sewol* trial: South Korea coast guard was 'ill equipped'," *BBC News Asia,* August 12, 2014, http://www.bbc.com/news/world-asia-28752727; Sam Kim, Cynthia Kim, and Heesu Lee, "Two hours turned school excursion into horror at sea," *Bloomberg Business,* April 20, 2014, http://www.bloomberg.com/news/articles/2014-04-21/two-hours-turned-school-island-excursion-to-horror-at-sea; Julian Ryall, "South Korea ferry captain charged with manslaughter," *The Telegraph,* May 15, 2014, http://www.telegraph.co.uk/news/worldnews/asia/southkorea/10832527/South-Korea-ferry-captain-charged-with-manslaughter.html; Madison Park, "What went wrong on the *Sewol*?" CNN, May 15, 2014, http://www.cnn.com/2014/05/15/world/asia/Sewol-problems/; Geoffrey Thomas and Jerome Greer Chandler, "Boeing and experts question NTSB's Asiana 214 findings," The West Australian Airlineratings. com, June 25, 2014, http://www.airlineratings.com/news/316/controversy-in-the-wake-of-ntsbs-asiana-214-findings; "Asiana Crash Probe Renews Debate Over Culture in Aviation," The Associated Press, December 12, 2013, http://sanfrancisco.cbslocal.com/2013/12/12/asiana-crash-probe-renews-debate-over-culture-in-aviation/; Kim Jung-Yoon, "Offices of *Sewol* owner searched," *Korea Joonang Daily,* April 19, 2014, http://koreajoongangdaily.joins.com/news/article/Article.aspx?aid=2988141; Park Hyong-ki, "Key suspects revealed in deadly *Sewol* sinking," *Korea Herald,* April 21, 2014, http://www.koreaherald.com/view.php?ud=20140421001183.

Chapter 12
The Criminal Liability of Mariners

The alarming global trend toward increasing criminalization of accidents is sobering and mariners are well advised to understand their legal rights and obligations under various domestic and international environmental laws. Corporations, like vessels, are considered legal "persons" and can be charged with crimes, as can their officers.[1]

Under the Responsible Corporate Officer Doctrine, some corporate officers and managers can be found guilty of environmental crimes even if they had nothing to do with the accident, had no knowledge it occurred, and had done nothing wrong! The logic behind extending criminal sanctions to corporate officers who had no direct involvement with an incident is that a corporation found guilty of a crime can simply pass on the expense of the fines to its customers, which would yield no deterrent effect. Corporate criminal fines can be considered simply a cost of doing business, and sometimes are cheaper than the cost of compliance with the law. Charging corporate officers with crimes that happened "on their watch" definitely gets their attention, and, as a result of personal criminal and civil exposure, managers are more inclined to take a proactive interest in ensuring company policies and operational practices are responsive to environmental laws. Thus, the logic goes, criminally charging corporate officers for crimes committed by their company results in the desired deterrent effect.

Crimes versus Torts

The difference between a crime and a civil wrong, called a tort, is normally a difference in mindset, or intentionality. To find someone guilty of a crime the government usually has to successfully prove a *mens rea,* or a criminal state of mind, or intent to do the bad act, and it is this intent that differentiates a crime from a tort. For example, if you intend to hurt someone and punch them in the nose, that's a crime. If you accidentally slip and punch someone in the nose, with no intent to hurt them, that's not a crime because there was no intent to do harm and you weren't being reckless. Some unintentional behaviors, if bad enough, can rise to the level of criminal negligence.

Another big difference between crimes and torts is that criminal charges are levied by government prosecutors, and the guilty person (criminal) will have to pay a fine or serve a jail and/or federal prison sentence. For a civil tort, the person who was harmed files a civil lawsuit, and if successful, the injured party will usually be awarded some amount of money (called damages) as compensation. Civil damages are meant to make the injured party whole, to fix the damage done, and compensate for actual expenses, as well as for pain and suffering. Criminal penalties, in contrast, are meant as punishment and, theoretically, to act as deterrents.

Let's break this down. There are primarily two types of incidents that could cause criminal charges to be levied against a mariner:

• Incidents involving death, severe injury, or significant property damage
• Incidents involving pollution

If an incident results in death, injury, or significant property damage, state and federal general criminal statutes may apply. An example of such a charge is operating a vessel while intoxicated, or reckless endangerment. Generally, to be found guilty of a crime, a mariner would have to be proven to have some criminal state of mind, such as these (in decreasing order of "badness"):

- Willful bad conduct is just what it says; a person willfully chooses to act badly
- Recklessness is to understand a substantial and unjustifiable risk, ignore it, and do the act anyway
- Criminal negligence (as opposed to civil negligence, which is failure to use reasonable care) means to have no perception of a substantial and unjustifiable risk, when a reasonable person would have, and would have taken steps to address the risk
- Willful ignorance or willful blindness means one closed one's eyes to obvious wrongdoing, or intentionally elected not to become aware of it when one should have. This concept can also be applied to corporate officers who refuse to acknowledge safety problems that result in death or serious injury.

Criminal State of Mind Is Not Required for "Environmental Crimes"

The criminal prosecution of maritime environmental accidents, where no one did anything intentionally wrong, and no one was negligent, is fairly recent. Some environmental statutes are almost "strict liability" statutes, requiring simply that the event happened, and carry no requirement that the government prove anyone did anything wrong.

An example of a strict liability crime is statutory rape. One can be found guilty of statutory rape simply by having sex with an underage person, even if it was performed with the good faith belief (or even extraordinary measures taken to confirm) that the person was of the age of consent, but actually was not.

Modern environmental criminal statutes require a frighteningly minimal proof of negligence, and little or no requirement to prove a criminal state of mind. In other words, prosecutors need not prove criminal negligence, which is normally required to prove a crime has been committed, but need only prove "simple negligence," a much lower threshold normally applied to civil torts.

If a casualty results in a pollution incident, criminal and civil penalties, at both the federal and state levels, may be levied. This means a mariner (and corporate officers) can face prison time, criminal fines, as well as civil penalties, at both the state and federal levels.

For example, the Oil Pollution Act of 1990, passed in response to the *Exxon Valdez* spill of 1989, provides for criminal penalties, including jail and fines, and also for unlimited civil liability, including liability for punitive damages if there was willful or reckless conduct. Unlike civil "compensatory" damages, which are monies collected to fix the harm done, make the victim whole, or remediate environmental damage, punitive damages are just that, punishment meant to teach a lesson and act as a deterrent.

Environmental Statutes Are Public Welfare Statutes

Environmental crimes don't require proof of criminal intent because they fall under a set of laws called "public welfare" statutes, which were originally drafted in the 1920s to address dangers of tainted or adulterated food and drugs. Public welfare statutes eliminated the requirement to prove bad intent. The courts felt that since average citizens had no ability to protect themselves from tainted food, and since they relied entirely on the government and the food industry to provide products that were safe to consume, the public interest outweighed concerns about due process or fairness to the producers.

The potential for harm was considered so great, that if a food producer made a mistake, even by accident, he should be held criminally liable. The thinking was that this would create a deterrent effect, and make people running highly regulated industries, who are in positions to do tremendous public harm, really, really careful.

Since citizens can't protect themselves from an environmental incident, it was reasoned that environmental protection laws should be drafted as "public welfare" statutes.

As a result, simple negligence, and not criminal negligence, is enough to trigger criminal liability for environmental accidents. The result is that there is a lower criminal threshold for causing an oil spill than for negligently killing someone.

Post-Incident Investigations

Criminal Investigations

It is not unusual, post incident, to have representatives of the U.S. Coast Guard, NTSB, EPA (both civil and criminal branches), FBI, as well as state and local agencies, all arriving on-scene. The U.S. Coast Guard, as well as agents of other law enforcement agencies, may arrive in plain clothes, in an effort to put mariners at ease.

The U.S. Coast Guard has a multifaceted role as on-scene coordinator in charge of rescue, cleanup efforts, and salvage efforts. The Coast Guard is also the lead investigating body for other agencies conducting criminal investigations.

As the lead investigating agency, anything the Coast Guard discovers, it will turn over to the EPA, FBI, and other local, state, and federal law enforcement agencies. Evidence the Coast Guard collects is funneled to the U.S. Attorney, the Attorneys General of the states involved, and/or the District Attorney, who represents a county or municipality. Each agency will then decide whether to prosecute a crime on behalf of the particular governmental entity they serve. It is possible to have the federal government and the state prosecute for the same crime, and it is possible to have one federal agency decide to prosecute, while another does not.

Understand that law enforcement agencies are not there to help—they are there to investigate a crime scene. Unlike the U.S. Coast Guard, with their multifaceted role, state and federal law enforcement agencies, as a rule, are not involved with cleanup or rescue efforts, nor are they interested in mitigating the damage from an incident, or even saving lives. Their sole purpose is to enforce criminal laws.

Coast Guard Investigations

The Coast Guard's primary investigative focus is determining what happened for statistical and educational reasons, and determining a mariner's fitness to hold a mariner's credential and its various endorsements. Coast Guard hearings are held before an administrative law judge (and without a jury) and result in rulings that can include civil fines and license or credential suspension or revocation. Mariners can be represented by counsel at Coast Guard hearings, and would be well advised to do so, as regular rules of evidence and other legal protections may not apply. The Coast Guard is not usually interested in pursuing mariners criminally—but other federal, state and even local agencies may be. That being said, the Coast Guard, despite being a military agency, is also a law enforcement agency and has full arrest and subpoena powers.

The outcome of a Coast Guard hearing is not necessarily dispositive. A mariner can appeal the results of a Coast Guard administrative hearing to the Commandant of the Coast Guard, and then to the National Transportation Safety Board, and ultimately to the U.S. Courts of Appeal.

In the frenzy of an incident, it is understandable that mariners would want to be as cooperative and helpful as possible, but they would be prudent to seek legal counsel before offering any statements beyond what is necessary to address the immediate operational concerns or mitigation efforts. If a question involves, say, which valve to shut off to stem the flow of a spill, the mariner should answer, as it is an operational necessity and declining to answer may be construed as interference with the investigation or mitigation efforts.

Under the authority of 46 CFR, the Coast Guard conducts two types of investigations: Part 4 and Part 5.

A Part 4 investigation is a casualty investigation and usually is done first and is performed to determine what happened, and why. During these types of investigations, a mariner usually has no right to remain silent or to wait until counsel arrives before answering questions, as the questions are usually dealing with the exigencies of the situation, such as what type of cargo is in the tanks, or who is on watch. Mariners are encouraged to respond quickly (and thus usually without the protections of counsel) to the investigator's questions, as often the questions concern mitigating damage or facilitating rescue or salvage. Delay in answering may be construed as hampering the investigation. Typically, since a Part 4 investigation is administrative in nature, mariners are not read their Fifth Amendment rights (or "Miranda warning").

A gray area is created, however, when a mariner is responding to questions posed during a Part 4 investigation, but his answers lead the investigator to probe into areas he would not have otherwise probed, and/or the mariner's responses may indicate criminal activity. Typically, Coast Guard investigators will not Mirandize a subject until criminal activity is suspected. At the first hint that criminal activity may have occurred, the investigator is supposed to stop and Mirandize the subject. That being said, since so many environmental accidents are now "strict liability" crimes, the mere fact there was a spill is enough to trigger a criminal investigation, so ideally mariners should be read their rights right away.

According to a Coast Guard Investigative Services attorney, information gathered during a Part 4 investigation is not admissible as evidence nor (technically) is it allowed to be used in future discovery efforts by other agencies.

Part 5 investigations are administrative investigations to determine fault, and to determine if a mariner's credential or license should be suspended or revoked.

During a Part 5 investigation, a mariner may be able to postpone questioning until his or her attorney arrives, especially if the questions don't directly affect rescue or cleanup efforts. Although the post-incident investigators want to gather information and evidence as soon as possible, often there is no exigency to their questions (for example, "Did you have wine with dinner last night?"). Ideally, a mariner should secure legal representation before answering questions during Part 5 investigations, and if confused, a mariner should ask which type of investigation is being conducted.

There is a fine line between hampering an investigation and requesting a reasonable delay in answering non-operational, non-exigent questions. If the mariner is reasonable in his or her requests, odds are the Coast Guard will be too. If a request to delay questioning is denied, careful notes should be made as to the circumstances of the situation.

Fifth Amendment (Miranda) warnings apply only to criminal cases, not civil suits. Thus, a mariner can't remain silent or "take the Fifth" if potential sanctions are only civil in nature.

During an administrative hearing, mariners retain their Fifth Amendment rights and can decline to testify if testimony is sought that could later be used as evidence of a crime. However, unless a mariner has first secured immunity, any statements made by a mariner during a casualty investigation may result in his accidentally waiving his right to later "plead the Fifth." Generally, information gathered before a person has been read his or her rights will not be admissible in a criminal trial. This is not true of voluntary statements or actions made before the start of a formal investigation. Once a mariner has spoken, those statements can later be used in a criminal proceeding, even if the mariner was never read his rights.

Additionally, if a mariner is compelled to testify by way of a court order, that testimony cannot later be used against that person in a criminal trial. So, in some ways, not receiving a Miranda warning is a good sign. It means that at least the Coast Guard doesn't suspect criminal activity. It also means that the information given by the mariner who was under a compulsion to speak can most probably not be used against him should there be a subsequent criminal trial.

Mariners need to understand that any voluntary statements made to the U.S. Coast Guard, whether the mariner has been read his Miranda rights or not, may be admitted as evidence in criminal as well as administrative hearings.

Here are some guidelines for mariners to follow if involved in a marine casualty investigation:

- Ask to see identification before answering questions, regardless if the questioner appears to be in uniform. Investigators often arrive in civilian clothes in an effort to put mariners "at ease." There will be all sorts of people aboard (attorneys and others who represent competing interests, such as the ship owner, charterer, insurance agencies, pilots, etc.). Recognize that most of the people aboard post-incident do not have the mariner's best interest at heart. In the chaos, it is not unusual for aggressive attorneys to not identify themselves and just start asking questions and trying to collect evidence.
- Contact an attorney who specializes in maritime affairs and mariner's defense. If you have license insurance, contact your carrier. Licensed officers are well advised to maintain license defense insurance.
- Don't volunteer any information, unless offering information would facilitate cleanup efforts, mitigate damage, or save property or lives. When answering questions, respond simply and factually, without injecting opinions or suppositions, and answer only what they asked, fully and truthfully. Remember, voluntary admissions are admissible as evidence, even if you have not been read your rights.
- Don't do anything that might interfere with post-incident drug and alcohol testing. Refusal to comply with a chemical test has serious ramifications.
- Ask questions if you are confused as to the type and purpose of the questions. Coast Guard investigators are not out to trick you and should answer truthfully.
- Ask the investigator to explain what type of investigation is being conducted and ask what your rights are. If you think you are in custody, meaning you are not free to leave, ask. Being in custody has serious legal ramifications and if you are in custody that status should always be made clear to you.
- Maintain notes, or preferably a recording, of any interview. Record the date, time, place, and circumstances on tape. Have everyone identify themselves on tape so their voices can be properly identified. There should be no objections to a mariner making his own recording of the investigation and inviting a third party to act as a witness.
- Investigators may write down notes after an interview and most will show the subject the notes to ensure statements were accurately recorded. You should review and get a copy, if possible, of whatever notes were taken.
- If you are advised you have the right to remain silent, exercise that right and get an attorney. It means you are likely the subject of a criminal investigation.

One of the best sources I've found of advice for mariners regarding post-incident behavior is the Chamber of Shipping of America's 2000 publication *Environmental Criminal Liability in the United States: A Handbook for the Marine Industry* by the attorneys at Venable, Baetjer, Howard, and Civiletti, LLP. It includes simple checklists of behaviors and actions one should take post-incident.

Trend Toward Increasing Criminalization

In a 2012 survey conducted by Seafarers' Rights International (SRI) of over 3,400 mariners from sixty-eight countries, over 50 percent of mariners said they were reluctant to cooperate with casualty investigators for fear of being prosecuted criminally.[2] Granted, due process and the consequences of a criminal conviction may be harsher in developing countries, but similar reluctance is found in mariners of the westernized nations. This is in spite of the fact that the International Labor Organization and IMO have adopted Guidelines on Fair Treatment of Seafarers in the Event of a Marine Accident. Mariners just don't trust the system to give them a fair shake.

Since criminal laws are crafted to address a nation's own citizens, mariners, if they are foreigners, are often caught in the middle of an international legal nightmare. Their concerns are not unfounded. Worldwide, there is a lack of reasonably priced legal representation (especially for mariners from developing nations), a lack of employment protections, widely varying degrees of due process, and a lack of uniformity in the laws and procedures governing mariners' rights.

The Guidelines on Fair Treatment of Seafarers in the event of a maritime accident was generated by a joint working group of the IMO and ILO, with input from industry groups such as the International Federation of Shipmasters Association (IFSMA). In April 2013, the IMO's Legal Committee reviewed a Seafarers' Rights International survey of the rights of seafarers facing criminal prosecution, which was submitted by delegations of the International Transport Workers' Federation (ITF) and the IFSMA. After reviewing the survey, the IMO Legal Committee asserted their position that mariners involved in maritime accidents should be treated in accordance with the adopted guidelines, but that the guidelines were often not followed. They agreed the problem persists and that the issue would remain on its agenda. Interested organizations were encouraged to offer proposals as to how to increase compliance with the IMO/ILO Guidelines, but in neither the 2014 nor 2015 Legal Committee agendas was the topic specifically addressed.[3]

Following is a list of some of the most noteworthy incidents involving the criminalization (or not) of mariners involved with operational accidents. What is especially alarming is the disparity in how pilots and ship masters are treated within the United States. Though the stories and circumstances are dramatically different, compare the disparate handling of the pilot and master in the 2006 *Zim Mexico III* case in Alabama and the 2012 *Cosco Busan* allision in San Francisco Bay. Most importantly, the reader will note the global trend toward increasingly draconian treatment of masters whose ships suffered casualties resulting in environmental damage or loss of lives.

1976—*Argo Merchant*: grounding and spill, 7.7 million gallons off Nantucket
No criminal penalties were levied. Liberian authorities revoked the master's license, suspended the chief mate's license for four years, and suspended the second mate's license for nine months.

1976—*Amoco Cadiz*: spill, 67 million gallons off France
The master's license was held in suspension for three years, but not revoked.

1990—Ferry *Scandinavian Star*: fire, 158 dead
Despite arson being the most probable cause of the fires, the Norwegian master and two Danish ship owners were convicted of crimes for improperly training the crew and not adequately checking the ferry's safety equipment. The master was sentenced to sixty days in jail. The company's director and the majority shareholder were sentenced to forty days each. This was a first in Danish history.

1990—*Exxon Valdez*: spill, 10–32 million gallons in Alaska
Captain Joe Hazelwood was convicted of criminal misdemeanor negligent discharge of oil, received a nine-month suspension of master's license, $1,000 fine, and 1,000 hours of community service. He also had to pay $50,000 in (civil) restitution.

1993—Towboat *Mauvilla*: barge strikes AMTRAK railroad bridge, 47 dead, 103 injured
Captain William Odom had his license revoked; no criminal charges were levied.

1997—*Nissos Amorgos*: grounding, spill resulted, approximately 105,000 gallons in Venezuela's Maracaibo Channel
The ship was under compulsory pilotage at the time. Greek master Konstantinos Spiropoulos was detained for roughly six months without charges, then found guilty of negligence, but the charges

were eventually dismissed on appeal on procedural grounds. No charges were brought against the pilot nor the authorities who had the responsibility to keep the channel dredged and clear. Two other ships also went aground in the same channel during this period.[4]

1999—*Erika*: spill, 30,000 gallons off France

The ship's owner was criminally charged by France for owning such a poorly maintained and unseaworthy vessel. The *Erika*'s owner, her handler, the charterer, and RINA, the classification society certifying the ship as seaworthy, were all convicted by a French court. The *Erika*'s owner, Total (owned by Giuseppe Savarese), was ordered to pay €200 million to France as well as criminal fines of €375,000. The master, initially arrested, was released a week later and, in 2008, was cleared of all charges.

2001—*Jessica*: spill, 240,000 gallons in the Galápagos

The master was sanctioned.

2002—*Prestige*: spill, 20 million gallons off Spain

Immediately after the incident, the master was arrested and charged with environmental crimes. The master was held for eighty-five days in a high-security prison until eventually being released on €3 million bail. Twenty-two months later, the master was allowed to leave Spain and return to Greece, as long as the Greek government promised he would return to face criminal charges in Spain. Ten years after the spill, in October of 2012, the *Prestige*'s master, the chief engineer, and the former head of Spain's Merchant Marine Department (who ordered the ship to sea) still faced charges from a court in Spain. The Spanish prosecutors were seeking a twelve-year prison sentence for the ship's master, primarily for refusing to turn his ship around and head to sea, when he was denied a port of refuge from Spain. The master was seventy-seven when the Spanish charges were levied. The Philippine chief mate was also charged, but was not in Spanish custody. All ship's officers were ultimately found not guilty of any crime. The master, however, was charged with disobedience and given a nine-month suspended sentence.[5] Spain also brought suit against ABS in the United States, the ship's classification society, but the suit was dismissed.[6]

2002—Ferry *Le Joola*: capsizing, over 1,800 dead

In mid-October 2009 a French judge issued international arrest warrants for nine senior Senegalese officials, charging them with negligent manslaughter and failure to help people in danger. In reaction, the Senegalese government charged the French judge with abuse of authority.

2002—Ferry *Andrew J. Barberi*: hits dock, 11 dead, 70 injured

Captain Smith, who pleaded guilty to charges of negligent manslaughter, was sentenced to eighteen months in prison. Smith, who suffered a cardiac event which caused the accident, had lied on a a a U.S. Coast Guard medical form. The former director of the Staten Island Ferry, who had failed to enforce a rule requiring two pilots in the wheelhouse when ferries were docking, was sentenced to one year and a day.

2006—Ferry *al-Salam Boccaccio 98*: fire, capsizing, and sinking, over 1,000 dead

The Egyptian owner of the vessel was sentenced to seven years in prison for involuntary manslaughter, but he was, reportedly, in London, and the UK has no extradition treaty with Egypt.

2006—*Zim Mexico III*: under pilotage, during an undocking maneuver in Mobile, Alabama, the ship's bow thruster failed, the bow swung around and knocked over a shoreside crane, killing an electrician ashore

No charges were levied on the ship's pilot, it being determined the pilot served in an advisory capacity only. The ship's master, Captain Wolfgang Shröder, was arrested a month later in Houston, Texas. He was then transferred to Alabama to await trial. Allegedly, the Coast Guard investigators had extracted statements about the incident from crew members without giving any Miranda warnings, and mariners assumed the purpose was for a civil, not criminal, investigation.

Prior to this incident, Captain Shröder not only had an unblemished career—he had a decorated one. He had earned national commendations and awards in England for his actions during the 1987 *Herald of Free Enterprise* disaster. He was in command of the MV *Gabriele Wher*, one of the first vessels at the scene, and is credited with saving hundreds of lives.

Upon his arrest, his passport and papers were confiscated, and he was allowed out on bail to await trial. At the trial, the judge, bound by statute and legal precedent, instructed the jury to apply a standard of simple negligence to the case, and, per statute, since a ship's master is responsible for the actions of those below him (including the harbor pilot) the master must be held responsible for the actions of his subordinates. Absent jury nullification, the jury had almost no choice but to find Captain Shröder guilty (after a six-day trial in October of 2006) of violating the Seaman's Manslaughter Statute (18 USC §1115) which reads:

> Every captain, engineer, pilot, or other person employed on any steamboat or vessel, by whose misconduct, negligence, or inattention to his duties on such vessel the life of any person is destroyed, and every owner, charterer, inspector, or other public officer, through whose fraud, neglect, connivance, misconduct, or violation of law the life of any person is destroyed, shall be fined under this title or imprisoned not more than ten years, or both.
>
> When the owner or charterer of any steamboat or vessel is a corporation, any executive officer of such corporation, for the time being actually charged with the control and management of the operation, equipment, or navigation of such steamboat or vessel, who has knowingly and willfully caused or allowed such fraud, neglect, connivance, misconduct, or violation of law, by which the life of any person is destroyed, shall be fined under this title or imprisoned not more than ten years, or both.

His bail was immediately revoked and he spent the next four months as a maximum-security prisoner in the Baldwin County jail. He was allowed two thirty-minute visits a week, in handcuffs and leg shackles. After two months at this status, he was reduced to a medium-security risk. At his sentencing hearing in February, he was finally charged with negligence, the judge gave credit for time served, and he was released, whereupon he returned to Europe. He died in Ireland in 2010. Interestingly, two years earlier on February 21, 2004 the *Zim Mexico III* was involved with another fatal accident. Captain Shröder was not aboard at the time. The ship collided with a towboat OSV *Lee III* on the Mississippi river's Southwest Pass, capsizing the towboat, killing all five crewmembers. To date, the captain of the *Zim Mexico III* involved with that incident has not been criminally charged.[7]

2007—MV *Hebei Spirit*: loaded supertanker anchored off Korea, hit by a barge that had broken free from its tug in bad weather, puncturing three tanks
South Korea detained the Indian master and chief officer of the *Hebei Spirit* for roughly 550 days, some of it spent in a South Korean prison. They were ultimately acquitted by the South Korean Supreme Court.[8]

2012—MV *Cosco Busan*: bridge allision, spill, 53,000 gallons in San Francisco Bay
Pilot Captain John Cota voluntarily surrendered his license, pleaded guilty to misdemeanor conviction for violation of the Clean Water Act and the Migratory Bird Act, and was sentenced to ten months in federal prison; this was the first time a US pilot has been imprisoned for a maritime accident. Here, in stark contrast to the *Zim Mexico III* outcome, the pilot (legally considered an advisor), not the ship's master, was held directly responsible for the ship's movements. The U.S. Department of Justice, the State of California, the City and County of San Francisco, and the City of Richmond lodged a consent decree that required Regal Stone Limited and Fleet Management Limited, the owners and operators of the *Cosco Busan*, to pay $44.4 million for natural resource damages and penalties and to reimburse the governmental entities for response costs incurred. An $18.8 million portion of the settlement is set aside to compensate for the lost use of the shoreline and the bay. It constitutes one of the largest human use recoveries for any oil spill in the United States. Six Chinese crew members were detained in the United States for over a year during the investigation.[9]

2012—MV *Costa Concordia*: grounding and capsizing off Giglio, Italy, 32 dead
The master was arrested on preliminary charges of multiple manslaughter in connection with causing a shipwreck, failing to assist passengers, failing to be the last to leave the wreck, failing to describe the scope of the disaster to authorities, and with abandoning incapacitated passengers. On February 11, 2015, Captain Schettino was sentenced to a total of sixteen years: ten years for manslaughter and the death of thirty-two people, five years for causing a shipwreck, one year for abandoning his vessel, and an additional month for giving false information to authorities. He is entitled to two appeals which may take years to resolve. Each of the 110 civil plaintiffs were awarded €30,000, and €300,000 was awarded to the island of Giglio and the Tuscany region.

2012—Ferry *Rabaul Queen*: sinking off Papua New Guinea, over 162 dead
The ferry's owner (Peter Sharp), master, and chief mate were charged with allowing/taking an unseaworthy vessel to sea, and with 162 counts of manslaughter. Company officials and a Papua New Guinea national safety manager were also charged with manslaughter. Peter Sharp was arrested in August 2013. He was denied bail. As of mid-2014 the trials are still pending.

Criminal Sanctions Are Unlikely Deterrents

The trend toward increasing criminalization of maritime accidents is of great concern. Equally concerning is the disparity between how pilots and masters have been treated here in the United States, and the disparity among how different states characterize maritime accidents. The idea that fining or imprisoning a mariner after a disaster will somehow deter others from having a similar mishap, and will somehow make mariners more careful, is absurd. There should be a bright line between intentional acts, or behavior that is so reckless as to be criminal, and accidents where the mariners behaved as normal, prudent mariners in their position would have behaved. Jailing corporate officers, absent the showing of any fault, for accidents that simply happen "on their watch" is equally absurd.

If criminalizing accidental behavior is a truly effective deterrent, shouldn't everyone who played a part in the incident, no matter how remote, be brought up on charges? After all, the competent, fully compliant shoreside manager who was asleep in his bed when an incident happened on one of his ships arguably has less culpability than the governmental authorities, including "Recognized Organizations" such as classification societies, who inspected the ship and her equipment, and who licensed the officers on whom he relies. Despite the understanding that the ship owner, not the surveyor, warranties a vessel as seaworthy, and that the duty to deliver a seaworthy vessel is not delegable, there have been sporadic instances worldwide where classification societies have been found liable for negligence or even breach of contract, but it is rare. Liability of a classification society for tort in negligence, breach of contract, and even criminal sanctions varies widely among nations, but there is evidence the longtime immunity enjoyed by classification societies is eroding.

If one looks at other industries, the absurdity of the mariner's plight becomes more obvious. When a NASA flight fails, astronauts die, and debris gets scattered, so far no one at NASA is pursued criminally. If a faulty ignition switch results in the deaths of multiple drivers across the nation, the engineer who designed the faulty switch is not sent to jail, nor are innocent automotive executives imprisoned.

It appears the "public welfare statutes" are unevenly applied, with governmental authorities and some industries enjoying immunity for their honest mistakes.

I am absolutely confident that time will show no change in casualty statistics due to the aggressive pursuit of mariners for "strict-liability" environmental crimes—but even so, it is doubtful such draconian sanctions will be repealed. If proof of efficacy were a requirement for strict-liability crimes to stay on the books, I would, perhaps, be more supportive. But it isn't. Until it is, mariners will continue to fall on the mercy of the courts, which largely have their hands tied by sentencing guidelines. Perhaps, if the defense is persuasive enough, jury nullification may afford some relief.

Casualty and Near-Miss Reporting

There are now increasing avenues for the confidential reporting of casualties, unsafe conditions, and near misses. Since 2003, mariners worldwide may avail themselves of the Confidential Hazardous Incident Reporting Programme (CHIRP), a United Kingdom–based reporting system for maritime and aviation conditions and incidents that nearly result in injury or damage. Reports are confidential, but not anonymous. Reports can be submitted online at www.chirp.co.uk or by phone at +44 (0) 1252 378947. Reports can also be directly emailed to CHIRP at reports@chirp.co.uk.

Once verified, CHIRP will investigate the issue and notify pertinent authorities of the safety concern, but will redact all of the reporter's identifying information.

The mission of CHIRP is not to affix blame or seek to levy penalties, but to investigate and remedy unsafe situations and then to disseminate lessons learned to the maritime industry, all while protecting the identity of persons reporting the unsafe condition or incident. Once a report has been made, its veracity and source must be verified. Once verified, CHIRP will conduct an investigation and generate a report. Reports deemed by a panel of experts to be of benefit to the maritime industry at large are then included in a publication called *Maritime Feedback*, which has a current distribution of over 65,000. CHIRP can also be followed on Facebook at CHIRP Maritime, and subscription to its quarterly newsletter is free.

Another similar reporting mechanism is the Nautical Institute's Mariner's Alerting and Reporting Scheme (MARS). MARS is a confidential reporting scheme for reporting unsafe practices, dangerous occurrences, personal accidents, near miss situations, or equipment failures. The MARS program is open to commercial, naval, fishing, and pleasure users. Its goal is to allow safe, confidential reporting without fear of identification or litigation. MARS does not investigate reports of unsafe conditions or incidents, but does maintain an anonymous, searchable public database available in their *Seaways* publication, as well as online. MARS can be found online at www.nautinst.org/en/forums/mars/index.cfm.

The Coast Guard maintains a boating safety hotline, which will assist boaters in completing necessary reporting forms in the case of a boating accident. The U.S. Coast Guard hotline is 800-368-5647.

Whistleblower Protection

A consideration for mariners contemplating reporting pollution incidents is a provision in the United State's codification of MARPOL that persons involved in reporting violations of the code may receive an award up to half the fine incurred by the offending company (33 USC §1908(a)). Whistleblowers are one of the primary ways offending vessels are caught. According to Marine Defenders (www.marinedefenders.com) roughly one-third of convictions for pollution violations have been secured due to notifications from whistleblowers, and awards have ranged from $40,000 to over $400,000. Mariners wishing to report cases of illegal dumping, falsifying of logs, or other criminal activity should report to the nearest Port State Control officer, the U.S. Coast Guard in the United States. Reports are best when substantiated by photos, videos, and logs.

To report pollution incidents in the United States or aboard U.S. flag vessels, contact the National Spill Response Center at 800-424-8802 or 202-267-2675, or complete an online spill-report form at http://www.nrc.uscg.mil.

To contact the Center for Seafarers' Rights, email them at csr@seamenschurch.org or call 973-589-5828.

What Can Be Done?

International organizations, such as the IMO and Seafarer's Rights International, as well as pilotage organizations and other mariners' groups, are becoming increasingly active in their efforts to stem the tide of criminalization. Time and statistics will indicate if harsh criminal penalties for accidents will indeed lessen their frequency and severity, but it seems unlikely that criminally punishing mariners for unintentional acts will make them any more careful or make equipment any less likely to fail. The airline and automotive industries do not seem to be laboring under a similar burden.

Notes

1. General information and statistics on criminalization worldwide gathered from Seafarers' Rights International, https://www.seafarersrights.org/ and specifically from https://www.seafarersrights.org/seafarers_subjects/criminal_law_topic/high_profile_cases; Information on environmental crimes was found at U.S. Department of Justice Environment and Natural Resources Division, http://www.justice.gov/enrd/2951.htm; Information on Responsible Corporate Officer Doctrine was found in Sean J. Bellew and Daniel T. Surtz, "Criminal Enforcement of Environmental Laws: A Corporate Guide to Avoiding Liability," 8 Vill. Envtl. L.J. 205 (1997), http://digitalcommons.law.villanova.edj/elj/vol8/iss1/5; Information on Coast Guard investigations was found in the U.S. Coast Guard Marine Safety Manual, Volume V: Investigations and Enforcement, http://www.uscg.mil/directives/listing_cim.asp?id=16000-16999. Additional generalized sources include: Fr. Sinclair Oubre, J. C. L., "Panel Presentation on Criminalization," *Sidelights: the Magazine of the American Council of Master Mariners* 37, no. 2 (2007): 8–10; Michael Grey, "Criminalization and its Consequences," *Sidelights: the Magazine of the American Council of Master Mariners* 37, no. 2 (Summer 2007): 5–7; Skuld Crew Newsletter (November 2013): 3–10, http://www.skuld.com/Documents/Library/Crew%20newsletter/Crew_Newsletter_November13.pdf.

2. "Seafarer's Rights International Survey: Seafarers and Criminal Law," *Marine Link*, April 24, 2013.

3. http://www.imo.org/MediaCentre/MeetingSummaries/Legal/Pages/LEG-100th-session.aspx.

4. Sources for *Nissos Amorgos* information: "Gard takes action regarding *Nissos Amorgos* incident," *The Maritime Executive*, March 19, 2014, http://www.maritime-executive.com/article/Gard-Takes-Action-Regarding-Nissos-Amorgos-Incident-2014-03-19; "Greek captain gets furlough: Captain Konstantino Spyropoulos of oil tanker *Nissos Amorgos* is furloughed from jail for 30 days after his arrest for oil spill," *The Oil Daily*, August 19, 1997, http://www.highbeam.com/doc/1G1-19693042.html.

5. Additional sources for *Prestige* information: "*Prestige* Captain Innocent of Environmental Crimes," *The Maritime Executive*, November 13, 2013, http://www.maritime-executive.com/article/Spain-Court-Clears-Captain-Merchant-Navy-in-Prestige-Oil-Spill-2013-11-13; https://www.seafarersrights.org/seafarers_subjects/criminal_law_topic/high_profile_cases.

6. Southern District of New York case docket SDNY #03-cv-03573.

7. Sources for *Zim Mexico III* information: Michael Chalos and Eugene O'Connor, "The *ZIM MEXICO III* Incident and the Trial of Captain Schroeder: The Complete Saga," *Gard News*, no. 187 (August/October 2007), http://www.gard.no/ikbViewer/page/iknowbook/section?p_document_id=52713&p_subdoc_id=52726; Captain C. E. "Chick" Gedney, "Sentencing Day: Captain Schröder's hearing after convicted for the *Zim Mexico III* Accident," *Sidelights: the Magazine of the American Council of Master Mariners* 37, no. 1 (Spring 2007): 11–12; Captain C. E. "Chick" Gedney, "The *Zim Mexico III*: The Facts You didn't Know," *Sidelights: the Magazine of the American Council of Master Mariners* 37, no. 1 (Spring 2007): 13; Robert Frump, "Criminalization on the Bridge: More Than Unjust; It's Unsafe," *Sidelights: the Magazine of the American Council of Master Mariners* 37, no. 1 (Spring 2007): 10–11; https://www.seafarersrights.org/seafarers_subjects/criminal_law_topic/high_profile_cases; Gulf Coast Mariners Association Report #R-438, February 13, 2007, http://www.nationalmariners.us/images/R-438.pdf; U.S. Coast Guard Report of Investigation into the Collision and Five Fatalities Onboard the M/V *Zim Mexico III* and the OSV *Lee III* in the Southwest Pass of the Mississippi River on 02/21/2004, https://homeport.uscg.mil/mycg/portal/ep/editorialSearch.do#.

8. Sources for *Hebei Spirit* information: The Government of India, "The Officers of MV *Hebei Spirit* Felicitated by the Shipping Minister," press release #51318, July 31, 2009, http://pib.nic.in/newsite/erelease.aspx?relid=51318; https://www.seafarersrights.org/seafarers_subjects/criminal_law_topic/high_profile_cases.

9. Additional sources for *Cosco Busan* information: U.S. Department of Justice: Office of Public Affairs, "Ship Owners and Operators to Pay $44 Million in Damages and Penalties for 2007 San Francisco–Oakland Bay Bridge Crash and Oil Spill," news release, September 19, 2011, http://www.justice.gov/opa/pr/2011/September/11-enrd-1209.html; https://www.seafarersrights.org/seafarers_subjects/criminal_law_topic/high_profile_cases.

Looking Forward:
What Will Future Casualties Look Like?

The general casualty trend through the decades indicates that casualties are increasingly not caused by equipment malfunctions, but by human failures. Most common seem to be failures to cross-check vessel positioning information with truly independent systems, over-reliance on electronic information, and overload of information provided by advanced equipment that is working properly. Regulations limiting work hours and more stringent health and training requirements will no doubt continue to improve casualty statistics. Additionally, if classification societies are to lose immunity for negligence, their surveys may become more rigorous, which would positively impact casualty rates caused by equipment and hull failures.

A new class of casualty that is looming in the future is intentional remote interference with vessel operations. Integrated bridge systems, and some communication equipment, are completely reliant on GPS inputs, and thus vulnerable. It is now possible to interfere with the GPS signal and either jam the signal or control the signal and literally take over maneuvering the vessel. All one has to do is confuse the timing signal received by the GPS receiver. Any intentional interference will be experienced by all the vessel's sets.

Though illegal in the United States, GPS jammers can be had for about $100 virtually worldwide. Since the GPS signal is so weak, an inexpensive jammer close enough to a GPS receiver could easily disrupt its signal. In the July 27, 2013, article in the *Economist*, "GPS Jamming: Out of Sight," it was reported that every day, for about ten minutes, from a position near the London Stock Exchange, someone blocked the GPS signal, frazzling vehicle GPS navigation sets and interfering with bank trades. The most likely culprit was a truck driver trying to undermine his company's tracking system. There have been cases of truckers inadvertently jamming the GPS sets on Ro/Ro ferries when the trucks drive aboard.

Nation states have used GPS jamming to harass their enemies. In 2012, powerful North Korean GPS jammers interfered with GPS sets for sixteen days, and over 1,000 planes and 254 ships reported disruptions.

A simple solution for nations worried about GPS jamming and spoofing is to revitalize LORAN, and many nations are doing just that. South Korea, in response to the GPS-jamming threat posed by North Korea, is instituting a regional eLORAN system that should be functional by 2016, for use by ships and aircraft. Britain did the same, and for the same reasons, and its eLORAN stations came online in October 2014. In areas where LORAN is available, most vessels are now opting for DGPS as the primary navigation system, but eLORAN as the automatic backup data source if DGPS signal is lost, rather than a second GPS set or manual fixes. Now, ground-based eLORAN signals, a million times stronger than GPS signals, can be used to safely guide ships around busy European waters should GPS signals become unreliable. Full implementation in the area is expected by 2019.

LORAN, being a hyperbolic ground-based navigation system that generates very precise time differences (especially if the system employs local differential receivers) would be a useful substitute for the GPS time data currently used by financial and communication sectors.

Dr. Todd Humphreys directs the Radionavigation Lab at the University of Texas, Austin, campus. He has focused his research on defending against intentional GPS spoofing (inserting a false signal mimicking the real signal) and jamming. These types of threats are possible today. If one thinks of the havoc that could be caused by a meddler simply sitting on a coastline with a handheld VHF radio, posing as vessel traffic, think of what a sophisticated criminal could do with technology capable of interfering with and mimicking GPS signals.

Absent true mechanical breakdowns and intentional acts, human error remains the single greatest source of maritime casualties. In the United Kingdom's Marine Directorate's 1991 study "The Human Element in Shipping Casualties," it was determined that, "the behaviors leading to accidents were most likely violations of established rules and codes, rather than mistakes, errors of judgment, or faulty assessment of risk." After reviewing multiple casualties of all sorts, the investigators found a major contributing factor to be "the torpor" that comes from hours upon hours of uneventful watchstanding.

In March 2010, the Japanese classification society NK published a document titled *Guidelines for the Prevention of Human Error Aboard Ships Through the Ergonomic Design of Marine Machinery Systems*. The document assigns 80 percent of all maritime accidents to human error, usually lack of knowledge of or confusion with equipment—not equipment failure.

As shipboard equipment gets increasingly complex, offering ever-increasing options and features, and the differences between brands widens, accidents due to confusion are likely to increase. The difference in "knobology" between radar or ECDIS sets of differing brands poses increasing demands on a mariner's brain.

Before the advent of trackballs and touch screens, the number of buttons and knobs on a radar set, for example, was limited to the physical size of the unit. Until the 1990s, a navigator could walk aboard any ship and get up to speed on a particular brand of radar fairly quickly. It was not unusual to sign on to a ship and stand one's first watch just a few hours later. It was literally a "have license, will travel" mindset and it worked for decades.

With the introduction of screen-based "buttons" and selections made by mouse or trackball, the choices suddenly became almost infinite, with the user now given dozens of choices of colors and even what icon he'd like to use for "own ship." On a modern ECDIS, there are literally dozens, if not hundreds, of choices, limits, selections, and parameters that now must be understood, selected, and then properly entered. The buttons, boxes to click, virtual setting knobs, limits, and even the terms used to describe different features vary from manufacturer to manufacturer. Gone are the days of being able to simply walk aboard a ship and know how to use all the bridge equipment.

Yet, despite volumes of information on the human element, redundant and robust construction and equipment, and unprecedented positional accuracy, modern, well-equipped ships continue to suffer needless casualties at the hands of their human handlers. The 2012 grounding and capsizing of the passenger liner *Costa Concordia*, a fully modernized vessel that went aground in perfect weather, with a full complement of officers, and all equipment working properly, is a prime example of how humans can still create catastrophe from perfection.

Undoubtedly, international regulations will be drafted to address the shortcomings exposed by the *Costa Concordia* incident, but no matter how detailed the rules, humans, susceptible to their neurological and psychological shortcomings, will find a way to mess things up.

Appendix A
International Maritime Organization (IMO)
Conventions and Codes

The International Maritime Organization (IMO) conventions deal primarily with operational and technical aspects of shipping.[1] Issues such as international jurisdiction and territorial rights are covered by the United Nations Convention on the Law of the Sea (UNCLOS) and are largely beyond the scope of this book.

The majority of IMO conventions fall into three main categories:

- Maritime safety and prevention and mitigation of casualties
- Maritime pollution prevention and response
- Post-casualty liability and compensation programs to address who pays, and for what

There are a number of other types of conventions, but these three categories compose the majority of international maritime agreements. The three most comprehensive maritime conventions (to which 99 percent of the world's tonnage has agreed) are also the three that most directly impact the operations of the maritime industry and seafarers. They are:

SOLAS—The International Convention for the Safety of Life at Sea, ratified by 159 nations[2]

MARPOL—The International Convention for the Prevention of Pollution from Ships, ratified by 150 nations[3]

STCW—The International Convention on Standards of Training, Certification and Watchkeeping for Seafarers, ratified by 154 nations[4]

SOLAS—The International Convention for the Safety of Life at Sea

The International Convention for the Safety of Life at Sea (SOLAS), generated in 1914 by five nations, largely in response to the sinking of the RMS *Titanic*, was the first comprehensive, internationally embraced set of standards governing the safe construction, equipping, and operation of commercial vessels. Each ratifying flag state is responsible for enforcing the provisions of SOLAS on its own vessels, and on vessels calling at its ports. Under Port State Control, nations who are signatories to SOLAS may inspect the ships of other signatory nations calling at their ports to ensure compliance. Certificates are issued to vessels which comply with the provisions of SOLAS, and these certificates are the first things inspectors usually ask to see.

SOLAS is now the backbone upon which hang many other codes and protocols, and the Convention was (and is) constantly amended to keep pace with changing technology and advances in the industry. When it becomes obvious that the amendment process is too cumbersome, and too many amendments render the instrument confusing, a new conference is usually held to draft a new Convention. Amendments are usually drafted by the Maritime Safety Committee of the IMO.

Lengthy explanation of the Convention and all its amendments is too detailed for this narrative. What follows is an abbreviated SOLAS timeline, indicating events that motivated the timing of conferences and revisions of the Convention.

SOLAS Timeline

1914
- The first SOLAS Convention (immediate response to the sinking of the RMS *Titanic* in 1912)
- First international agreements on fire protection requirements

1929
- The second SOLAS Convention (entered into force 1933)

  Eighteen nations signed the second SOLAS Convention, which set forth sixty articles on ship construction, lifesaving equipment, fire prevention and fire fighting, wireless telegraphy equipment, navigation aids, and rules to prevent collisions. The United States, initially concerned about "control language," finally signed the second SOLAS Convention in 1936.

1948
- The third SOLAS Convention (lessons learned from the fire aboard the *Morro Castle* in 1934)

  In response to advances in technology, the third SOLAS Convention was more detailed than previous versions, and covered more types of vessels. In part, it:
    - Established three methods of construction for passenger ships
    - Established basic fire protection requirements for cargo ships
    - Placed greater emphasis on the use of non-combustible materials in ship construction

  New parts (D, E, and F) were added to deal specifically with fire safety.

1960
- The fourth SOLAS Convention (entered into force 1965)

  This was the first convention promulgated by IMCO (now IMO) since it was formed in 1948. This revised Convention brought the code up to date with existing technology, and new requirements applied some passenger ship fire standards to cargo ships.

1972
- The 1972 Amendments, Convention on the International Regulations for Preventing Collisions at Sea ('72 COLREGS)

  The 1972 Amendments updated the COLREGS, the first time since 1960, and set forth mandatory behaviors in and around the relatively newly implemented vessel traffic schemes. These amendments entered into force in July 1977.

1974
- The fifth SOLAS Convention (entered into force in 1980, largely prompted by the *Sea Witch/Esso Brussels* collision of 1973)

  Several disastrous fires on passenger ships showed that the previous Convention's provisions on fire safety were not effective.

  This conference divided SOLAS Chapter II (Construction) of the 1960 SOLAS Convention into two new chapters: Chapter II-1 (structure, subdivision and stability, machinery, and electrical requirements) and Chapter II-2 (fire protection, fire detection, and fire extinguishment).

It required all new passenger ships to be built of non-combustible materials, and to have either a fixed fire sprinkler system or fixed fire detection system installed.

Requirements for cargo ships were updated.

Special regulations for specific types of ships, such as tankers, were added.

This is the Convention document currently in force. It also changed how the instrument is to evolve by adding a "tacit amendment" provision, which means that an amendment will enter into force unless a specified number of parties object. This streamlines the amendment process and significantly shortens the time necessary to make changes to the Convention. As a result, SOLAS '74 as a Convention is unlikely to be replaced, since instead, it is updated or amended as required. This is why, despite significant changes, people still refer to the Convention as "SOLAS '74" and why, from 1974 on, one will only find amendments to SOLAS '74, rather than a new Convention.

1978

➤ The 1978 Protocol incorporated measures affecting tanker design and operations (in response to the *Sea Witch / Esso Brussels* collision of 1973 and the *Argo Merchant* spill in 1976)

1988

➤ Amendments: The Global Maritime Distress and Safety System (GMDSS) replaced the Morse code operators of past years with newly required automated radio systems. Phasing in of the system began in 1992.

1992

➤ Amendments (lessons learned from the fire aboard the *Scandinavian Star* in 1990) required:
- The installation of fire protection systems, such as automatic sprinklers and smoke detectors
- That fire safety bulkheads to be constructed of non-combustible materials
- Enhanced escape signage and lighting near the decks
- Clarified vague language and emphasized focusing on the human elements of casualty prevention

1996

➤ Amendments required the International Code for Application of Fire Test Procedures (FTP Code) to be used by flag states when testing and approving systems for installation aboard their flag ships. It provides guidance on testing procedures.

1998

➤ Amendment: International Lifesaving Appliance Code

2000

➤ Amendments:
- Complete revision of the fire protection requirements of Chapter II-2. Changes included requirements to employ modern fire detection and extinguishing systems. The revisions focused on advances in fire prevention, rapid detection of fires, and the swift extinguishment of fires.
- Vessel design was also addressed, specifically with an eye toward evacuation routes

- Added new Part E to Chapter II-2, dealing with human elements such as training, drills, and maintenance issues
- Added new Part F to Chapter II-2, which details methods for approving alternative or unusual designs and arrangements
- Refers shipbuilders to the International Fire Safety Systems (FSS) Code for technical details. The fifteen-chapter FSS is required by and incorporated by reference into the SOLAS Convention.

2004
- ➢ Amendments: International Ship and Port Facility Security Code (ISPS) amendment developed in response to the terrorist attacks in the United States on September 11, 2001

The SOLAS Chapters

SOLAS is currently divided into twelve chapters, most of which require compliance with an embedded code.

Current SOLAS Chapters
Chapter I—General Provisions
Surveying of Ships
Documents
Control of ships of other signatory nations
Chapter II-1—Construction
Subdivision
Stability
Machinery Installations
Electrical Installations
Chapter II-2—Fire Protection, Detection, and Extinguishment
Passenger Ships
Cargo Ships
Tankers
Chapter III—Lifesaving Appliances
Life Saving Appliances (conform to International Life Saving Appliance [LSA] Code)
Chapter IV—Radio Communications
GMDSS
EPIRBs
SARTs
Chapter V—Safety of Navigation (applies to all vessels regardless of tonnage or route)
Manning Levels
Voyage Planning
Duty to Render Aid
Ice Patrol
Maintenance by Nations of Search and Rescue Services
Automatic Identification System (AIS) Carriage Requirements
Voyage Data Recorder (VDR) Carriage Requirements
Chapter VI—Carriage of Cargoes
Securing Containers
International Grain Code

Chapter VII—Carriage of Dangerous Goods (compliance with various codes are required)

International Maritime Dangerous Goods (IMDG) Code

International Bulk Chemical Code (IBC Code)

International Gas Carrier Code (IGC Code)

International Code for the Safe Carriage of Packaged Irradiated Nuclear Fuel, Plutonium, and High-Level Radioactive Wastes on Board Ships (INF Code)

Chapter VIII—Nuclear Ships

Code of Safety for Nuclear Merchant Ships

Chapter IX—Management for the Safe Operation of Ships (lessons learned from the ferry disasters *Herald of Free Enterprise* in 1987 and *Estonia* in 1995)

International Safety Management (ISM) Code

Chapter X—Safety Measures for High Speed Craft

International Code of Safety for High-Speed Craft (HSC Code)

Chapter XI-1—Special Measures to Enhance Maritime Safety

Chapter XI-2—Special Measures to Enhance Maritime Security

International Ship and Port Facilities Security Code (ISPS Code)

Chapter XII—Additional Safety Measures for Bulk Carriers

MARPOL—The International Convention for the Prevention of Pollution from Ships

Great Britain organized the International Convention for the Prevention of Pollution of the Sea by Oil, 1954 (OILPOL '54), one of the first international agreements dealing with oil pollution from ships. OILPOL '54 addressed the fact that most of the oil in the seas came from routine operations, like tank washing and the practice of pumping bilges and slops overboard. The practice seems unthinkable to a modern mariner, but it was common practice in those years to pump oily wastes overboard, as well as to discharge all manner of solid wastes.

The IMCO (now the IMO) became active in 1958, ten years after its creation by the UN in 1948. IMCO's activation occurred just a few months before OILPOL '54 was to enter into force, and thus, OILPOL '54 was one of the first conventions managed by IMCO.

The provisions of OILPOL '54 defined an "oily mixture," which under the terms of the convention was not to be discharged overboard, as a mixture having more than 100 parts heavy oil per million parts of water. OILPOL '54 prohibited oily discharges in certain protected "special" areas, such as the Adriatic and North Sea zones, where discharges occurring from 100–150 miles from shore were prohibited, and other areas where discharges were only prohibited within fifty miles of land.

OILPOL '54 mandated the use of an oily water separator, and required that ships maintain an oil record book. It also required shore side facilities to accept oily mixtures from ships (though shoreside reception facilities turned out to be in short supply).

There were other, relatively mild admonitions not to pollute the oceans. The Geneva Convention on the High Seas of 1958, for example, had two provisions on marine pollution; one simply articulating that oil pollution had harmful effects and the other requiring nations to take steps to prevent pollution from radioactive materials. In the late 1950s, international interest in pollution was still lukewarm at best.

In 1962, OILPOL '54 was amended to include more stringent requirements, including provisions for the "load on top" method of decanting water from oil. By then oil pollution was increasingly becoming an international concern, and in reaction IMCO created the Sub Committee on Oil Pollution within its Maritime Safety Committee to address the growing, but still relatively mild, concerns about pollution.

In 1967, the massive spill from the *Torrey Canyon* catapulted oil pollution abruptly into the international spotlight, and IMCO met again to address the multifaceted consequences of the incident.

MARPOL '73

The 1973 International Convention for the Prevention of Pollution from Ships (MARPOL '73), organized directly in response to the *Torrey Canyon* spill, superseded OILPOL '54. MARPOL incorporated most of the provisions of OILPOL '54 into what became Annex 1 (which covered only oil pollution) of MARPOL. But MARPOL didn't solely address oil pollution. Its provisions included additional annexes that covered sewage, garbage, chemical pollution, and dangerous substances carried in packaged form.

To clear the ratification threshold, MARPOL needed ratification by at least fifteen states, which had to collectively represent at least 50 percent of the world's tonnage. There was difficulty getting many nations to ratify MARPOL, as the convention required compliance with both Annex I (oil) and Annex II (bulk chemical). Compliance with the other Annexes was voluntary, thus not problematic.

Annex I set limits on the rate (dilution) and total quantity of oil that could be discharged, and required ships to monitor the discharge of oily water mixtures. Other requirements mandated that shoreside facilities accept oily and dirty water from vessels. Additionally, all new tankers over 70,000 DWT were required to have segregated ballast tanks, which eliminated the need for ships to pump clean ballast water into dirty cargo tanks, effectively eliminating "dirty ballast" completely. Some see the requirement for segregated ballast tanks as one of the most effective oil pollution provisions of MARPOL. Annex I also set forth "special areas," environmentally sensitive areas where oily discharges from ships were either prohibited completely, or if allowed, were tightly controlled.

Fearing the cost of compliance and the inability to meet technical guidelines and time frames for implementation, many nations were reluctant to ratify MARPOL. In 1973, many nations did not have the monitoring equipment and shoreside reception facilities required by Annex I.

Compliance with the Annex II requirements for chemical tankers was even more problematic for many nations. By 1976, only Jordan, Kenya, and Tunisia had ratified MARPOL—far below the necessary threshold. To put it mildly, in the 1970s the provisions of the new MARPOL convention were cumbersome and expensive, and in some cases, the technology necessary to comply wasn't readily available.

While negotiations languished within IMCO, ships continued to pollute the oceans, both as a result of normal operations, and accidentally. In 1978, in response to a cluster of tanker casualties in the 1970s (most notably the *Amoco Cadiz* and the *Argo Merchant* incidents) a conference on Tanker Safety and Pollution Prevention was held to address the unprecedented losses. The losses of the 1970s were more environmentally devastating than casualties of past decades, largely due to the exponential increase in the size of the average oil tanker during this time period. The conference led to the 1978 Protocol, which amended MARPOL '73.

One of the most important changes from the 1978 Protocol was the elimination of the requirement to comply with both Annex I and Annex II. The 1978 Protocol amended MARPOL to only require compliance with Annex I. To facilitate ratification of MARPOL '73/'78, under the 1978 Protocol, nations could ratify the convention, which would require compliance initially only with Annex I. The (apparently objectionable) requirements of Annex II were not mandatory until three years after ratification. This gave nations the time they needed to accommodate the technical obligations of Annex II.

Since MARPOL '73 had not yet become effective when the 1978 Protocol was adopted, the Protocol simply absorbed MARPOL '73, hence MARPOL is now often referred to as MARPOL '73/'78. It entered into force in 1983 and had five annexes.

Also in response to the many tanker casualties of this period were changes to the SOLAS convention, specifically new provisions that dealt with the design of tank ships.

Since then, MARPOL has been amended and now includes six Annexes. States which are parties must adopt Annexes I and II, but all other Annexes are still voluntary. Currently, over 150 nations, representing over 99 percent of the world's tonnage, have ratified two or more of the MARPOL Annexes. As with most other IMO Conventions, jurisdictional and enforcement issues are addressed in Law of the Sea (LOS) conventions. Violations of MARPOL can be enforced by any contracting party as well as the flag state of the vessel.

MARPOL Timeline

1967
➤ The *Torrey Canyon* disaster occurred (which was followed by multiple, massive pollution incidents in the 1970s).

1973
➤ MARPOL adopted.

1978
➤ MARPOL Protocol adopted.

1983
➤ MARPOL Annex I (oil) entered into force.

1984
➤ Amendments to Annex I; created "special areas," modified oily water discharge requirements.

1985
➤ Amendments to Annex II; embraced modern technological advances, set forth chemical ship construction standards, and required ships carrying noxious liquid substances to comply with the International Code for the Construction and Equipment of Ships Carrying Dangerous Chemicals in Bulk (IBC Code).
➤ Amendments to Protocol I made reporting of discharges to sea of harmful substances in packaged form mandatory.

1987
➤ Annex II (noxious substances in bulk) entered into force.

1988
➤ Annex V (garbage) entered into force.

1989
➤ Amendments to the IBC Code and other rules revised lists of chemicals.

1990
➤ Harmonized System of Survey and Certificates (HSSC) amendments; harmonized MARPOL, SOLAS, and Load Line Convention requirements.
➤ IBC amendments; introduced the HSSC into the IBC Code.

1991
> Amendments included requiring ships to carry an oil pollution emergency plan.

1992
> Amendments reduced the amount of oil that could be discharged into the sea from 60 liters/mile to 30 liters/mile and increased dilution rates for some vessels; introduced phased-in requirements for tankers to have double hulls, or another approved type of construction to mitigate pollution by oil in case of a hull breach; also included some new subdivision and stability requirements for tankers over 20,000 DWT.
> Annex III entered into force.

1994
> Amendments affected Annexes I, II, III, and V; extended port state control by allowing other parties to the convention to inspect foreign ships calling at their ports to ensure operational practices comply with pollution prevention requirements.

1995
> Amendments clarified Annex V garbage placard and recording requirements.

1996
> Amendments clarified reporting requirements for harmful substance incidents and brought IBC and Code for the Construction and Equipment of Ships Carrying Dangerous Chemicals in Bulk (BCH) components of MARPOL more in concert with SOLAS.

1997
> Protocol of 1997 adopted Annex VI concerning air pollution, specifically sulfur oxide, nitrogen oxide, ozone depleting substances, and incineration of certain products.

1999
> Amendments made ships carrying "persistent oils" subject to crude oil tanker rules; also added rules for venting systems covered by the IBC and BCH codes.

2000
> Amendments removed products originally classed as marine pollutants solely because they were capable of "tainting" the smell or flavor of seafood.

2001
> Amendments accelerated the phase-out of single hull tankers.

2003
> Amendments further accelerated phase-out of single hull tankers.
> Annex IV (sewage) entered into force.

2004
> Amendments revised Annex IV sewage treatment provisions.
> Amendments clarified and simplified Annex I (oil); classed Annex II (noxious liquids) into four groups, depending on the level of hazard; lowered discharge

limits made possible by improvements in technology; required vegetable oil to be carried in chemical tankers.

2005
➢ Annex VI (air pollution) entered into force.

2006
➢ Amendments to Annex I (oil) addressed protection of fuel oil tanks; changed some language to encompass more types of oils; allowed for port state inspections for compliance with Annex IV (sewage).

2007
➢ Revised Annexes I and II entered into force.

2008
➢ Amendments to Annex VI (air pollution) phased in decreasing limits of airborne pollutants.

2009
➢ Amendments to Annex I concerning ship-to-ship (STS) transfers; also included definitions of "sludge" and other terms.

2010
➢ Amendments enacted stricter air pollution limits for North America than apply globally; also addressed the carriage of oil in Antarctic areas.
➢ Amendments mandated changes to Annex II to coincide with the International Dangerous Goods (IMDG) Code.

2011
➢ Amendments to Annex VI added mandatory Energy Efficient Design Index (EEDI) requirements for new ships and the Ship Energy Efficiency Management Plan (SEEMP) for existing vessels; Annex V (garbage) was revised, expanded and brought up to date.

2012
➢ Amendments dealt with reception facilities to accept waste.

The MARPOL Annexes
Annex I—Regulations for the Prevention of Pollution by Oil
- Covers accidental and operational discharge of oil
- Sets forth allowable rates of discharging of oily substances for operational purposes
- Requires use of an oil discharge monitor and oil/water separators
- Requires new tankers to have segregated ballast tanks
- Sets forth requirements for an Oil Record Book
- Specifies certain "special areas" with more stringent control of oily discharges
- Specifies survey intervals for tankers
- Sets forth ship design characteristics to minimize accidental discharge of oil
- Requires shoreside facilities to accept oily waste, and sets forth specifications for an international fitting to facilitate discharge at any port

- Ships issued an internationally recognized International Oil Pollution Prevention (IOPP) Certificate if they pass survey

Annex II—Regulations for the Control of Pollution by Noxious Liquid Substances in Bulk
- Details discharge criteria and measures for the control of pollution by noxious liquid substances carried in bulk
- Requires most discharges be made to shoreside facilities
- Requires a Cargo Record Book be maintained
- Sets forth survey requirements
- No discharge of residues containing noxious substances is permitted within twelve miles of land

Annex III—Prevention of Pollution by Harmful Substances Carried by Sea in Packaged Form
- Addresses substances listed as marine pollutants in the International Maritime Dangerous Goods Code (IMDG Code) or which meet the criteria in the Appendix of this Annex
- General requirements for standards on packing, marking, labeling, documentation, stowage, quantity limitations, exceptions and notifications

Annex IV—Prevention of Pollution by Sewage from Ships
- Discharge of sewage into the sea is prohibited, except through an approved sewage treatment plant, or if discharging pulverized and disinfected sewage using an approved system at a distance of more than three nautical miles from land.
- Sewage which is not pulverized or disinfected has to be discharged at a distance of more than twelve nautical miles from land.

Annex V—Prevention of Pollution by Garbage from Ships
- Complete ban on discharging of plastics into the sea
- Other types of garbage may be discharged, depending on distance from land
- Amended to prohibit the discharge of all garbage into the sea, except as provided otherwise, under specific circumstances

Annex VI—Prevention of Air Pollution from Ships
- Sets limits on sulphur oxide and nitrogen oxide emissions from ship exhausts
- Prohibits deliberate emissions of ozone depleting substances
- Designated "emission control areas" can have more stringent standards
- Amended to include mandatory technical and operational energy efficiency measures which will reduce greenhouse gas emissions from ships

STCW—The International Convention on Standards of Training, Certification and Watchkeeping for Seafarers

The 1978 STCW Convention (STCW '78) was the first international maritime convention that addressed the human element as a primary cause of maritime casualties, and that set minimum levels of competency for seafarers. Prior to this, every nation established its own standards, and, as you can imagine, standards varied widely.

Estimates vary, but one can comfortably ascribe over 80 percent of all maritime casualties to some sort of human error caused by the people aboard the vessel. Human error includes shortcomings caused by lack of training, lack of familiarity, incompetence, fatigue, illness or injury, impairment from alcohol or drugs, and attitudinal postures such as complacency or overconfidence.

If one really thinks about it, even an equipment malfunction or breakdown is fundamentally caused by human error. If a piece of equipment fails, it is because some human didn't design the item correctly, or there was some problem with its manufacture. Even an improper cast of a metal part is ultimately a human failure. During the 1970s there was increasing recognition that the human element is the primary cause of casualties and failures, regardless of the industry or circumstance. During the 1970s, the focus began to shift from equipment to people.

It is now widely recognized that to safely operate modern large and complex vessels, maritime nations need to adopt a required set of skills, familiarities, and competencies to address the human part—the most important part—of the operational equation.

The STCW '78 standards set forth minimum levels of proficiency, but many maritime nations require skills and competencies in excess of these requirements.

In 1995, largely in response to pressure from the United States to clarify enforcement provisions and ambiguous phrases, changes were made to STCW '78 which updated enforcement provisions and clarified competency standards. Since the 1995 changes were amendments to the existing convention, they did not need the formal ratification the original convention required.

As a result of the 1995 amendments, specific requirements of compliance were teased out of the convention, and put into a Code. Currently, the STCW Convention (17 Articles and 18 Resolutions) sets forth broadly worded requirements, such as "a deck watch officer must know how to navigate." The Code, composed of the technical annexes of the original convention, details specifically how to comply with the requirements of the convention, and how to assess and record competency. The Code sets forth mandatory regulations in Part A, while the provisions of Part B are recommendations.

This revision streamlined the organization of the convention and made technical requirements of the convention easier to update and administer, since regulations can be easily amended without having to call an entirely new conference. The STCW '95 Convention sets forth regulations, which are then detailed and clarified in the STCW Code.

The 1995 amendments also, for the first time, required states to report on how they were complying with the convention, including how mariners are trained and assessed.

STCW '95 requires mariners to display both knowledge of various subjects, usually proven by way of paper examinations, as well as practical competency of various physical skills, such as tying a knot or launching a lifeboat, to the satisfaction of an assessor.

The 1995 amendments required signatory nations to issue a paper certificate to seafarers indicating they met training and competency requirements. Currently, mariners operating only in domestic U.S. waters need not carry international STCW certificates. Mariners venturing offshore must carry and present current STCW certificates before signing aboard ship if the vessel is routed overseas.

STCW certificates look like passports, in which are placed various stickers listing the positions, jobs, routes, and types and sizes of vessels for which a mariner is certified. In the United States, STCW '95 had a modest substantive effect on how mariners are trained and assessed, but the convention has impacted both record keeping and academic curriculums at the maritime academies. For other nations, with perhaps less formalized maritime training and recordkeeping systems, the impact was more acute.

In January 2006, a comprehensive review of the convention began, culminating in a 2010 conference in Manila, Philippines. As a result of those meetings, major revisions, called the Manila Amendments, were adopted, which included upgraded standards of training for seafarers. The Manila Amendments became effective in 2012. Some of the more important provisions of the Manila Amendments (which shall be fully implemented by 2017, but may have different phase-in dates, depending on the country) include:

- Enhanced provisions to prevent fraudulent certificates of competency
- New rest hour rules, more in harmony with International Labor Organization rules, require minimums of:
  - Seventy-seven hours rest in any seven-day period
  - Ten hours rest in any twenty-four-hour period
  - Onboard records of crews' rest periods
- Rest requirements apply to masters as well as watchstanders
- New Able Seafarer requirements and requirements to maintain on-board training record books
- Requirements for engineering officers to competently operate pollution prevention equipment
- New Electro-Technical officer and ratings endorsements
- Change of medical certificates validity to two years, required of all U.S. mariners subject to STCW
- Basic safety training required every five years (first aid, lifesaving, firefighting, personal safety)
- International 0.05 percent blood alcohol level limit, and provisions to prevent drug abuse
- Required bridge and engine room resource management training, relating to teamwork, leadership, and managerial competencies
- Mandatory tanker training for crew of oil, gas, and chemical tankers
- Guidance for offshore support vessels and dynamic positioning vessels
- Guidance for vessels operating in polar regions
- Mandatory electronic chart and information display system (ECDIS) training
- Security training for non-vessel security officer (VSO) crew members, including anti-piracy training

Nations which can demonstrate full compliance with STCW '95 are listed by the IMO on a "white list." Vessels from nations that are not on the white list may be denied entry or be heavily scrutinized when they come into port. Crew bearing documents from non-white-listed nations may be denied equivalency recognition by other nations, or may also be carefully scrutinized before being allowed to man a vessel flying a white list flag.

STCW Timeline

1978
➢ STCW adopted.

1984
➢ STCW '78 entered into force.

1995
➢ STCW '95 Amendments adopted by the IMO.

1997
➢ STCW '95 Amendments entered into force.

2007

➤ IMO begins comprehensive review of entire STCW; meetings in Manila, Philippines.

2010

➤ IMO adopts the Manila Amendments.

2012

➤ Manila Amendments enter into force.

The STCW Code Chapters

Chapter I—General Provisions

Regulation I/7 Communication of Information

Regulation I/8 Quality Standards

Regulation I/9 Medical Standards

Regulation I/10 Recognition of Certificates

Regulation I/11 Revalidation of Certificates

Regulation I/12 Use of Simulators

Regulation I/13 Conduct of Trials

Regulation I/14 Responsibilities of Companies

Regulation I/15 Transitional Provisions

Chapter II—Master and Deck Department

Regulation II/1 Requirements for Navigational Watch Officers on Vessels of 500 GRT or more

Regulation II/2 Requirements for Masters and Chief Mates on Vessels of 500 GRT or more

Regulation II/3 Requirements for Navigational Watch Officers on Vessels Less than 500 GRT on Near-Coastal Voyages

Regulation II/4 Requirements for Ratings Forming Part of a Navigational Watch

Regulation II/5 Requirements for Ratings as Able Seafarer Deck

Chapter III—Engine Department

Regulation III/1 Requirements for Engineering Officers in Charge of a Watch

Regulation III/2 Requirements for Chief Engineer and Second Engineer on Vessels of 3,000kW Propulsion Power or More

Regulation III/3 Requirements for Chief Engineer and Second Engineers on Ships with Machinery between 750kW and 3,000kW Propulsion Power

Regulation III/4 Requirements for Engineering Ratings

Regulation III/5 Requirements for Ratings as Able Seafarer Engine

Regulation III/6 Requirements for Electro-Technical Officers

Regulation III/7 Requirements for Electro-Technical Ratings

Chapter IV—Radio Communication and Radio Personnel

Regulation IV/1 Application

Regulation IV/2 Requirements for GMDSS Radio Operators

Chapter V—Special Training Requirements for Personnel on Certain Types of Ships

Regulation V/1—1 Requirements for Masters, Officers, and Ratings on Chemical Tankers

Regulation V/1—2 Requirements for Masters, Officers, and Ratings on Liquefied Gas Tankers

Regulation V/2 Requirements for Masters, Officers, and Ratings on Passenger Ships

Chapter VI—Emergency, Occupational Safety, Medical Care, and Survival Functions

Regulation VI/2 Requirements for the Issue of Survival Craft, Rescue Boats, and Fast Rescue Boat Certifications

Regulation VI/3 Required Training in Advanced Firefighting

Regulation VI/4 Required Training in Medical First Aid and Medical Care
Regulation VI/5 Requirements for Ship Security Officers
Regulation VI/6 Requirements for Security-Related Training for All Seafarers
Chapter VII—Alternative Certification
Regulation VII/1 Issue of Alternative Certificates
Regulation VII/2 Certification of Seafarers
Regulation VII/3 Principles Governing the Issue of Alternative Certificates
Chapter VIII—Watchkeeping
Regulation VIII/1 Fitness for Duty
Regulation VIII/2 Watchkeeping Arrangements and Principles to Be Observed

Other International Conventions and Protocols Relating to Safety and Casualties

1948
> ➢ Convention on the International Maritime Organization

1965
> ➢ Convention on Facilitation of International Maritime Traffic (FAL)

1966
> ➢ International Convention on Load Lines (LL)

1969
> ➢ International Convention on Tonnage Measurement of Ships (TONNAGE)
> ➢ International Convention Relating to Intervention on the High Seas in Cases of Oil Pollution Casualties (INTERVENTION)
> ➢ International Convention on Civil Liability for Oil Pollution Damage (CLC)

1971
> ➢ Convention relating to Civil Liability in the Field of Maritime Carriage of Nuclear Material (NUCLEAR)
> ➢ Special Trade Passenger Ships Agreement (STP)

1972
> ➢ Convention on the International Regulations for Preventing Collisions at Sea (COLREG)
> ➢ International Convention for Safe Containers (CSC)
> ➢ Convention on the Prevention of Marine Pollution by Dumping of Wastes and Other Matter (LC) (and the 1996 London Protocol)

1973
> ➢ Protocol on Space Requirements for Special Trade Passenger Ships1974
> ➢ Athens Convention relating to the Carriage of Passengers and their Luggage by Sea (PAL)

1976
> ➢ Convention on the International Maritime Satellite Organization (IMSO C)

1977

➢ The Torremolinos International Convention for the Safety of Fishing Vessels (SFV) (superseded by the 1993 Torremolinos Protocol; and the Cape Town Agreement of 2012 on the Implementation of the Provisions of the 1993 Protocol relating to the Torremolinos International Convention for the Safety of Fishing Vessels, International Convention on Standards of Training, Certification and Watchkeeping for Fishing Vessel Personnel [STCW-F], 1995)

1979

➢ International Convention on Maritime Search and Rescue (SAR)

1982

➢ United Nations Convention on the Law of the Sea (UNCLOS), and amendments

1988

➢ Convention for the Suppression of Unlawful Acts Against the Safety of Maritime Navigation (SUA)
➢ Protocol for the Suppression of Unlawful Acts Against the Safety of Fixed Platforms located on the Continental Shelf (and the 2005 Protocols)
➢ The International COSPAS-SARSAT Programme Agreement (COS-SAR 1988)

1989

➢ International Convention on Salvage (SALVAGE)

1990

➢ International Convention on Oil Pollution Preparedness, Response and Co-operation (OPRC)

1992

➢ 1992 Protocol to the International Convention on Civil Liability for Oil Pollution Damage (CLC), 1969, on the Establishment of an International Fund for Compensation for Oil Pollution Damage (FUND 1992)

1994

➢ UN Convention on the Law of the Sea (UNCLOS)

1995

➢ International Convention on Standards of Training, Certification and Watchkeeping for Fishing Vessel Personnel (STCW-F 1995)

1996

➢ International Convention on Liability and Compensation for Damage in Connection with the Carriage of Hazardous and Noxious Substances by Sea (HNS) (and its 2010 Protocol)
➢ Agreement concerning specific stability requirements for Ro/Ro passenger ships undertaking regular scheduled international voyages between or to or from designated ports in North West Europe and the Baltic Sea (SOLAS AGR 1996)

1999
- ➢ International Convention on the Arrest of Ships

2000
- ➢ Protocol on Preparedness, Response and Co-operation to Pollution Incidents by Hazardous and Noxious Substances (OPRC-HNS Protocol)

2001
- ➢ International Convention on the Control of Harmful Anti-fouling Systems on Ships (AFS)
- ➢ International Convention on Civil Liability for Bunker Oil Pollution Damage

2004
- ➢ International Convention for the Control and Management of Ships' Ballast Water and Sediments

2007
- ➢ Nairobi International Convention on the Removal of Wrecks

2009
- ➢ The Hong Kong International Convention for the Safe and Environmentally Sound Recycling of Ships

Notes

1. Sources for IMO Conventions information: www.imo.org; www.uscg.mil.

2. Sources for SOLAS information: www.imo.org.

3. Additional sources for MARPOL information: Alan Khee-Jin Tan, *Vessel-Source Marine Pollution*; Scott Powell, *Great Lakes: Implementing MARPOL V*, Environmental Policy Report, State University of New York, April 27, 2007.

4. Additional sources for STCW information: U.S. Coast Guard web page, http://www.uscg.mil/nmc/stcw/; *The STCW Convention and STCW Code Including the Manila Amendments*, U.S. Coast Guard, National Maritime Center, Virginia, US SNPRM Docket ID: USCG-2004-17914.

Appendix B
Timeline

Pre-1912 Events

1688—Lloyd's of London founded

1707 Oct 22—Four British ships aground on Scilly Islands, presumably because they could not determine their longitude; 1,400–2,000 dead

1714—Britain passes the Longitude Act in response to the devastating losses of naval vessels in 1707

1760—Committee formed by Lloyd's of London for independent inspection for seaworthiness of hulls and machinery of vessels (first stages of a classification society)

1828—Bureau Veritas (BV) Classification Society founded in Antwerp

1830—Lloyd's classification society became Lloyd's Register of British and Foreign Shipping, a true classification society

1834—Lloyd's Register of British and Foreign Shipping became a stand-alone classification society, publishing rules for the construction and survey of vessels

1835—Lloyd's sets forth "Lloyd's Rule," a set of loading limits for cargo ships, first hints of loadline regulations

1852—U.S. Steamboat Act of 1852, authorized the Steamboat Inspection Service to license pilots and engineers of steam vessels carrying passengers

1861—Registro Italiano Navale (RINA) classification society founded in Italy

1862—American Bureau of Shipping (ABS) founded in the United States

1864—Det Norske Veritas (DNV) classification society founded in Norway

1867—Germanischer Lloyd (GL) classification society founded in Germany

1869—Suez Canal opened

1872—Samuel Plimsoll pleads with British Parliament to save mariners' lives by requiring ships not be overloaded

1872—The establishment of the Royal Commission on Unseaworthy Ships (in response to Samuel Plimsoll's efforts)

1875—Egypt sold its interest in the Suez Canal to Britain, due to debt problems

1876—The United Kingdom Merchant Shipping Act required the first load line (Plimsoll marks) to be displayed on ships, requiring minimum freeboard

1888—The 1888 Convention of Constantinople, signed by European nations to ensure the Suez canal remained open during times of war

1899—Nippon Kaiji Kyokai (ClassNK, or NK) classification society formed in Japan

1912 to 1929

1912 Apr 14—*Titanic* allided with iceberg, sank on April 15, only 706 of 2,228 survived, roughly 1,522 dead

1913—The First International Conference for Safety of Life at Sea (SOLAS) meet in response to the *Titanic* disaster

1913—Russian Register of Shipping (RS) formed

1913 Nov—"Deadly White Hurricane" on the Great Lakes, 19 ships lost, 19 stranded, 250 dead

1914 to 1918—World War I

1914 Jan 20—SOLAS signed by thirteen nations, including the U.S.; International Ice Patrol established, in response to the *Titanic* disaster

1915—U.S. Act to Promote the Welfare of American Seamen in the Merchant Marine of the United States or Longshore and Harbor Workers' Compensation Act (The La Follette Seaman's Act), passed in the wake of the *Titanic* disaster. It was later amended by the U.S. Merchant Marine Act of 1920 (46 USC §688)

1915—U.S. Revenue Cutter Service merged with Life Saving Service to become the U.S. Coast Guard

1915 May 7—*Lusitania* torpedoed by German submarine off Ireland, approximately 1,198 dead

1915 Jul 24—The *Eastland* sank at the dock; her full complement of passengers went to one side while moored at the dock in the Chicago River; she rolled over and sank; over 830 dead

1919—League of Nations formed under the Treaty of Versailles, in response to World War I, and an effort to prevent any future such conflicts (dissolved after it failed to prevent World War II)

1920s—Oil companies beginning to experiment with inerting cargo tanks

1920—U.S. Merchant Marine Act passed

1921—International Chamber of Shipping formed

1922—Echo sounders installed aboard ships

1929 Apr 16—Eighteen nations (not including the United States) signed second SOLAS convention; United States, concerned about "control language," finally signed on August 7, 1936

1930 to 1939

1930—International Load Line Convention passed

1933—The second SOLAS convention entered into force

1934 Sep 8—*Morro Castle* caught fire (or was set on fire); arson suspected; 135 dead

1936—The Anglo-Egyptian Treaty of 1936 made Egypt fundamentally independent, but gave Britain the right to maintain military control of the entry points to the Suez Canal

1936—U.S. Congress passed the Merchant Marine Act of 1936, largely in response to the *Morro Castle*

1936 Aug 7—United States signed second SOLAS convention

1937—The Steamboat Inspection Service renamed the Bureau of Marine Inspection and Navigation, responsibilities expanded to include approval of construction plans for passenger vessels

1939—U.S. Coast Guard took over the Lighthouse Service

1939—First major conference of classification societies hosted by RINA (attended by ABS, BV, DNV, GL, LR, and NK)

1940 to 1949

1939–1945—World War II

1940s—Welding replaced riveting of new steel ships

1940s—LORAN, an electronic, hyperbolic navigation system established

1940 Jun 17—The *Lancastria* sunk by German bombers off the coast of St. Nazaire, France; 4,000–6,000 dead

1941 Dec 12—The *Normandie* burned and sank

1942—U.S. Coast Guard absorbed the duties of the Steamboat Inspection Service and began inspecting merchant ships

1944—DECCA, an electronic, hyperbolic navigation system established

1945—United Nations formed

1945 Jan 30—The *Wilhelm Gustloff* sunk by Soviet submarine during WWII, largest single maritime loss of life; roughly 9,400 dead; some estimates put the loss of life at over 10,000

1946—U.S. Coast Guard inherited Bureau of Marine Inspection and Navigation, placed merchant marine licensing and vessel safety under purview of U.S. Coast Guard

1947 Jul 17—Ferry *Ramdas* capsized ten miles from Mumbai, over 600 dead

1948—The UN created Israel; Egypt responded by closing the Suez Canal to any vessels headed to or from Israel

1948—Inter-Governmental Maritime Consultative Organization (IMCO) established, came into force in 1958, meeting first in 1959

1948—Federal Water Pollution Control Act passed

1948—The third SOLAS convention held, later superseded by the 1960 SOLAS convention

1948 Dec 4—The passenger steamship *Kiangya* exploded and sank in mouth of Huangpu River south of Shanghai, supposedly hit a WW II mine left behind by Japanese Navy; 2,750–3,920 dead, with 700–1,000 survivors

1949—Croatian (ex-Yugoslav) Register of Shipping formed

1949—China Classification Society (CCS) formed

1949—First record of Vessel Traffic Service (in Liverpool)

1950 to 1959

1950—U.S. Maritime Administration (MARAD) formed

1951—Egypt demanded Britain repudiate the 1936 Anglo-Egyptian Treaty, which gave Britain military control of Suez Canal entry and exit points

1954—Britain signed seven-year agreement allowing Egypt to take over British military posts on the Suez Canal

1954—The International Convention for the Prevention of Pollution of the Sea by Oil, 1954 (OILPOL '54) adopted

1955—Second major classification society conference held, led to the establishment of Working Parties

1956—Egypt nationalized the Suez Canal, expelled all British oil workers and embassy officials

1956—Israel, France, and Britain invaded Egypt to reopen the Suez Canal. Egypt sank forty ships and blocked the canal.

1956—U.N "peacekeeping" troops landed in Egypt to reopen the Suez Canal

1956—Korean Register (KR) classification society formed

1956—Suez Canal closed briefly

1956 Jul 25—*Andrea Doria* collided with *Stockholm* off Ambrose, New York, 51 dead

1957—The International Association of Marine Aids to Navigation and Lighthouse Authorities is formed

1958—The Automated Mutual Assistance Vessel Rescue System (AMVER) became operational; it was articulated in SOLAS, in reaction to the *Titanic* disaster; long delay was due to lack of equipment for meaningful worldwide coverage and coordination

1958—IMCO came into force ten years after its formation, in 1982 IMCO changed its name to the International Maritime Organization (IMO)

1959—First meeting of IMCO held

1959—First tanker of over 100,000 DWT delivered

1960 to 1969

1960s—VHF radio became more commonplace on ships for ship-to-ship communications

1960s—U.S. Navy, Esso, and other companies experimented with cargo tank inerting

1960—The fourth SOLAS convention adopted by IMCO

1960—First international Collision Regulations adopted

1962—OILPOL '54 amended to mitigate operational pollution from ships

1963—British Petroleum inerted its tankers

1964—First transit satellite navigation system (SatNav) became available to navy ships

1965—Radar was made mandatory by SOLAS convention provisions

1965—The fourth SOLAS convention entered into force

1965—IMCO Sub-Committee on Oil Pollution formed to address vessel-source oil pollution

1966—IMCO Load Line Convention set forth international minimum freeboard requirements

1966—First tanker of over 200,000 DWT launched

1967—First transit satellite navigation system (SatNav) became available to merchant ships

1967—First (voluntary) traffic separation scheme adopted in Dover Strait

1967—Suez Canal closed (this time for eight years); reopened in 1975

1967 Mar 18—*Torrey Canyon* grounded, massive spill on Seven Stones Reef, UK

1968—First Very Large Crude Carrier (VLCC) of 180,000 DWT entered service

1968—Nonprofit International Tanker Owners Pollution Federation (ITOPF) formed, in response to *Torrey Canyon,* to administer the Tanker Owners Voluntary Agreement concerning Liability for Oil Pollution (TOVALOP)

1968—International Association of Classification Societies (IACS) established by the seven leading societies

1968—First vestige of VTS started in San Francisco Bay (nineteen years after Liverpool) called Harbor Advisory Radar

1969—International Association of Classification Societies given consultative status with IMCO (it remains the only non-governmental organization with "observer status" which is able to develop and apply rules)

1969—ARPA was introduced (but was not mandatory)

1969—Three VLCCs exploded in a three-week period (the *Marpessa, Mactra,* and *Kong Haakon VII*)

1969—The International Convention on Civil Liability for Oil Pollution Damage (CLC) 1969, and the International Convention Relating to Intervention on the High Seas in Cases of Oil Pollution Casualties (INTERVENTION) 1969 passed, in response to the *Torrey Canyon* disaster

1970 to 1979

1970—OCIMF formed

1971—Inerting of cargo oil tanks required on U.S. tankers

1971—IMCO Assembly resolution required mandatory participation in traffic separation schemes

1971—IMCO adopted the International Convention on the Establishment of an International Fund for Compensation for Oil Pollution Damage (FUND), established a pool of money from which to compensate victims, (amended 1992)

1971 Jan 18—*Arizona Standard* and *Oregon Standard*, both Chevron tankers, collided in San Francisco Bay, spilling roughly 800,000 gallons; spawned Bridge to Bridge Radiotelephone Act (33 USC §1201) of 1971

1972—Amendments to SOLAS adopted the International Regulations for Preventing Collisions at Sea ('72 COLREGS), which replaced the 1960 Collision Regulations, enhanced safety at sea by recognizing traffic separation schemes, and redefined "safe speed" (became effective in 1977)

1972—San Francisco and Seattle got first official VTS run by U.S. Coast Guard

1972—U.S. Vessel Bridge to Bridge Radio Telephone Act required VHF radios on vessels over 300 GRT sailing on inland waters

1972—Federal Water Pollution Control Act (33 USC § 1251 et seq.) passed

1972—Ports and Waterways Safety Act (PWSA) of 1972 (33 USC §1221) passed

1973—The International Convention for the Prevention of Pollution from Ships 1973 (MARPOL '73) adopted

1973 Jun 2—*Sea Witch* lost steering and collided with anchored *Esso Brussels* in New York Harbor; 1.3 million gallons were spilled, sixteen crew members dead

1974—The fifth SOLAS convention (became effective in 1980)

1974—INTERVENTION codified into U.S. law as the IHSA, 33 USC §1471

1975—Indian Register of Shipping (IRS) formed

1975—The International Convention on Civil Liability for Oil Pollution Damage (CLC) 1969 became effective

1975—International Convention Relating to Intervention on the High Seas in Cases of Oil Pollution Casualties (INTERVENTION) 1969 became effective

1975 Nov 10—*Edmund Fitzgerald* sank on the Great Lakes, taking all of her 29-man crew with her (amended Title 45 CFR §45 to require closing of hatches and vent caps when underway, recommendation that 46 USC be amended to rescind 1969, 1971, and 1973 changes to load line regulations)

1976—Convention on the International Maritime Satellite Organization (IMSO), created a global search and rescue system, greatly enhanced communications at sea

1976 Dec 15—*Argo Merchant* ran aground off Nantucket, spilling 8 million gallons, partly due to 180° error in RDF sense antenna

1977—Clean Water Act (U.S.) (passed largely in response to the *Argo Merchant* grounding)

1977—International Regulations for Preventing Collisions at Sea ('72 COLREGs) in effect

1977—First crude oil flowed through the Trans-Alaska Pipeline System (TAPS)

1978—1978 Protocol to MARPOL, became MARPOL '73/'78, also made amendments to SOLAS, reaction to the *Sea Witch / Esso Brussels* collision of 1973 and the *Argo Merchant* spill of 1976

1978—IMCO drafted the International Convention on the Standards of Training, Certification and Watchkeeping for Seafarers (STCW '78), established training and certification requirements for seafarers

1978—Congress passed the Port and Tanker Safety Act of 1978 (after a rash of tank vessel accidents in the latter part of 1976 and early 1977 (33 USC §1221 et seq.)

1978 Mar 16—VLCC *Amoco Cadiz* stranded off Ushant, an island off France (one month after passage of MARPOL '78), massive spill of roughly 68 million gallons

1978 Oct 20—USCG *Cuyahoga* collides with loaded coal freighter in Chesapeake Bay, sinking the *Cuyahoga*; 11 died

1979—International Convention on Maritime Search and Rescue (SAR) adopted

1979—*Energy Determination* (320,000 DWT), exploded while in ballast, in the Strait of Hormuz; this was Lloyd's largest ship lost to date

1979 Jul 19—Super-tankers *Atlantic Empress* and the *Aegean Captain* collided off Tobago, causing a spill of approximately 84 million gallons

1980 to 1989

1980—The fifth SOLAS convention (SOLAS '74) entered into force

1980 Jan 28—USCG *Blackthorn* collides with tanker *Capricorn* in Tampa Bay, Florida; 23 dead

1980 May 9—*Summit Venture* rammed the Sunshine Skyway Bridge by in Tampa Bay, Florida

1981 May 6—*LASH Atlantico* and *Hellenic Carrier* collided off Kitty Hawk, North Carolina

1982—IMCO changed its name to the International Maritime Organization (IMO)

1983—MARPOL '73/'78 Annex I (oil) entered into force

1983 Feb 12—Bulker *Marine Electric* sank off Virginia coast, killing 31

1983 Aug 6—Tanker *Castillo de Bellver* exploded off South Africa, spilling 79 million gallons

1984—STCW '78 came into force

1986 Jul 24—*Mobil Endeavour* grounded in Torres Strait, due to ignored passage plan, ship's squat

1986 Aug 31—*Admiral Nakhimov* collided with *P. Vasey,* an ARPA-assisted collision

1987—MARPOL Annex II (noxious liquid substances in bulk) entered into force

1987 Mar 6—Ferry *Herald of Free Enterprise* sank, 193 people died, prompted creation of International Safety Management Code (ISM)

1987 Dec 20—Passenger ferry *Doña Paz* collided with tanker *Vector* in the Tablas Strait, fire and sinking, over 4,300 dead, worst peacetime loss of life

1988—MARPOL Annex V (garbage) entered into force

1988—Global Maritime Distress and Safety System (GMDSS) adopted, incorporated into SOLAS, phase-in began in 1992

1988—Protocols to the International Convention on Load Lines

1988—Convention for the Suppression of Unlawful Acts (SUA) Against the Safety of Maritime Navigation

1988 Nov 12—Tanker *Odyssey* exploded and sank in a storm off Canada (the spill, at 43 million gallons, was more than double the spill from the *Exxon Valdez*)

1989—IMO adopted the Guidelines on Management for the Safe Operation of Ships and for Pollution Prevention in response to the *Herald of Free Enterprise* disaster

1989—ARPA made mandatory

1989 Mar 24—The *Exxon Valdez* ran aground on Bligh Reef in Prince William Sound, Alaska, spilling 10–32 million gallons; spawned the Oil Pollution Act 1990 (33 USC §2701 et seq.) which, among other things, required participation in VTS

1990 to 1999

1990—U.S. Oil Pollution Act of 1990 (33 USC §2701 et seq.) passed in response to the *Exxon Valdez* spill

1990—IMO drafted the International Convention on Oil Pollution Preparedness, Response and Co-operation (OPRC '90), which changed MARPOL, addressed cooperation between nations and industries in addressing pollution incidents, passed largely at the request of the United States to mimic provisions of OPA '90

1990 Apr 7—Ferry *Scandinavian Star* burned, arson suspected, roughly 158 dead, mostly due to poisoning from cyanide gas generated when melamine-clad bulkheads burned

1991 Apr 11—The *Haven* (sister ship to the *Amoco Cadiz*) exploded during internal cargo transfer operation spilling over 1 million gallons, burned for three days, and sank in the Mediterranean Sea

1991 May 28—The *Summer* exploded off Angola, massive spill of 51–81 million gallons, five dead

1991 Jul 21—Tanker *Kirki*'s bow fell off while off the coast of Australia, raised issues of conflict of interest and efficacy of classification societies

1992—Amendments to oil spill treaties of 1969 and 1971

1992—MARPOL Annex III (harmful substances in packaged form) entered into force

1992—GMDSS requirements began phase-in period

1992—The 1992 Civil Liability Convention and the 1992 Fund Conventions superseded 1969 CLC and FUND conventions

1993—The Guidelines on Management for the Safe Operation of Ships and for Pollution Prevention (passed in response to the *Herald of Free Enterprise* disaster) became the International Safety Management (ISM) Code, which addressed management and operational practices, effective in 1998

1993 Sep 22—Towboat *Mauvilla* allided with AMTRAK bridge near Big Bayou Canot, Alabama; caused the derailment of the AMTRAK Sunset Limited passenger train, lead to the Towing Officers' Assessment Record (TOAR), see NVIC 4-01

1994—American Waterways Operators initiated the Responsible Carrier Program

1994—GPS system became fully operational

1994—UN Convention on the Law of the Sea (UNCLOS) 1994

1994 Sep 28—Ro/Ro ferry *Estonia* sank off the coast of Finland; problems with the front doors; 852 dead

1995—Amendments to STCW '78 adopted by IMO, separated technical requirements and placed them into the STCW Code

1995—SOLAS Conference (reaction to *Estonia* loss by allowing regional agreements between member states (rather than requiring full international agreement) and seven European states agree to follow an agreement regarding the safety of passenger ferries operating between their countries)

1995 Jun 9—Passenger ship *Royal Majesty* ran aground outside of Boston; her GPS signal feed line had become disconnected

1996—Amendments to SOLAS dealing with fire protection passed

1997—1995 Amendments to STCW '78 came into force (now STCW '95)

1997—TOVALOP and CRISTAL were allowed to expire, replaced by the 1992 CLC and FUND conventions

1998—International Safety Management Code (ISM) in effect and mandatory (implemented fully by 2002)

1998—International Lifesaving Appliance Code added to SOLAS

1999—GMDSS became fully operational

1999 Dec 12—Twenty-five-year-old tanker *Erika* sank off the west coast of France, spilling 9.7 million gallons of heavy fuel; a sister ship also broke in half

1999—Lloyd's Open Form (salvage agreement) added a Special Compensation P&I Clause (SCOPIC) that allows recovery for prevention of environmental harm

2000 to 2014

2000—Amendments to oil spill treaties of 1969 and 1971

2000—SOLAS amendments completely revised fire protection systems, made Voyage Data Recorders (VDR) mandatory on new ships

2000—ISM Code revised, full implementation by 2002

2001 Jan 16—Tanker *Jessica* ran aground in the Galápagos, spill

2001 Sep 11—Terrorist attack on the World Trade Center (United States)

2001 Sep 15—Towboat *Brown Water V* struck the Queen Isbabella Causeway Bridge in Texas; eight dead

2002—United States passed the Maritime Transportation Security Act of 2002 (MTSA) (effective 2004) in response to terrorist attacks

2002—SOLAS amended to cover security issues, created the ISPS Code

2002—Voyage Data Recorders required on all newly built passenger ships and ships over 3,000 GRT

2002 May 26—Towboat *Robert Y. Love* struck I-40 Bridge over the Arkansas River; fourteen dead, several injured

2002 Sept 26—Overloaded Senegalese ferry *Le Joola* capsized in heavy seas, roughly 1,800 dead

2002 Nov 13—Tanker *Prestige* broke apart in a bad storm off Spain spilling her cargo of 20 million gallons and was denied entry by all ports; she eventually broke her back and sank

2002 Dec 14—Ro/Ro ferry *Tricolor* collides with the *Kariba* off the coast of France

2003—Amendments to the International Load Line Convention concerning hatch covers

2003—MARPOL Annex IV (sewage) entered into force

2003 Oct 15—New York commuter ferry *Andrew J. Barberi* allided with Staten Island pier, eleven dead and over 70 injured; led to enhanced medical screening of U.S. mariners (NVIC 4-08)

2004—International Ship and Port Facility Code (ISPS) made mandatory under the 2002 amendments to SOLAS

2004—The Maritime Transportation Safety Act of 2002 (MTSA) became effective

2004—Automatic Identification Systems (AIS) for vessels became functional

2005—MARPOL Annex VI (air pollution) entered into force

2005—Suppression of Unlawful Activities (SUA) adopted protocols to allow boarding of other nation's vessels when violations of SUA are suspected

2006—IACS Common Structural Rules for Tankers and Bulk Carriers implemented

2006 Feb 3—Egyptian Ro/Ro passenger ferry *al-Salam Boccaccio 98* sank in the Red Sea, approximately 1,020 lost

2007—IMO performed comprehensive review of STCW, meeting took place in Manila, Philippines

2007 Nov 7—*Cosco Busan* hit Oakland Bay Bridge in San Francisco Bay, ruptured fuel tanks causing 53,000-gallon spill; resulted in first criminal charges against U.S. ship's pilot

2009—Draft guidelines for Ships Operating in Polar Waters approved by IMO

2010—IMO adopted the Manila Amendments to STCW

2012—STCW Manila Amendments entered into force

2012—ECDIS became mandatory

2012 Jan 13—Passenger ship *Costa Concordia* grounded and capsized off Giglio, Italy; thirty-two dead

2012 Feb 2—Passenger ferry *Rabaul Queen* sank in a storm off Papua New Guinea; 162 known dead, possibly as many as 500 lost

2013 Jan 9—Commuter ferry *Seastreak Wall Street* struck Manhattan pier; eighty injured

2014 Apr 16—Korean ferry *Sewol* capsizes and sinks off Jindo, Korea; 304 dead

Bibliography

Books

Allen, Craig. *Farwell's Rules of the Road*. Annapolis: Naval Institute Press, 2004.

Bailey, Thomas A. *The* Lusitania *Disaster: An Episode in Modern Warfare and Diplomacy*. New York: Free Press, 1975.

Ballard, Robert D. *Exploring the* Lusitania*: Probing the Mysteries of the Sinking That Changed History*. New York: Warner Books, 1995.

Brown, David G. *White Hurricane: A Great Lakes November Gale and America's Deadliest Maritime Disaster*. New York: International Marine/McGraw-Hill, 2002.

Burton, Hal. *The* Morro Castle. New York: Viking Press, 1973.

Cahill, Capt. Richard A. *Collisions and Their Causes*, 3rd ed. London: The Nautical Institute, 2002.

———. *Disasters at Sea:* Titanic *to* Exxon Valdez. San Antonio, TX: Burke Publishing, 1990.

———. *Strandings and Their Causes*. London: Fairplay Publications, Ltd., 2002.

Carroll, Jonathan. *The Sinking of the* Lancastria*: The Twentieth Century's Deadliest Naval Disaster and How Churchill Made It Disappear*. New York: Graf Publishers, 2005.

Coyle, Gretchen and Deborah Whitcraft. *Inferno at Sea: Stories of Death and Survival Aboard the* Morro Castle. West Creek, NJ: Down the Shore Publishing, 2012.

Crabb, Brian. *The Forgotten Tragedy: The Story of the Sinking of the HMT* Lancastria. Donington, U.K.: Shaun Tyas, 2002.

DeSombre, Elizabeth R. *Flagging Standards: Globalization and Environmental, Safety, and Labor Regulations at Sea*. Cambridge, MA: MIT Press, 2006.

Dobson, Christopher et al. *The Cruelest Night*. Boston: Little, Brown, 1979.

Donn, Clifford B. *Flag of Convenience Registry and Industrial Relations; The Internationalization of National Flag Fleets*. Syracuse: Le Moyne College, Institute of Industrial Relations, 1988.

Farnie, D. A. *East and West of Suez: The Suez Canal in History 1854–1956*. Oxford: Clarendon Press, 1969.

Ferby, Jonathan. *The Sinking of the* Lancastria*: Britain's Greatest Maritime Disaster and Churchill's Cover-Up*. New York: Simon and Schuster, 2005.

Frump, Robert. *Until the Sea Shall Free Them: Life, Death, and Survival in the Merchant Marine*. Annapolis, MD: Naval Institute Press, 2007.

Gallagher, Thomas. *Fire at Sea: The Mysterious Tragedy of the* Morro Castle. Guilford, CT: Lyons Press, 2003.

Goldstein, Richard. *Desperate Hours: The Epic Rescue of the* Andrea Doria. New York: John Wiley and Sons, 2003.

Gordan, Thomas and Max Morgan Witts. *Shipwreck: The Strange Fate of the* Morro Castle. New York: Stein and Day Publishers, 1972.

Hemming, Robert J. *Ships Gone Missing: The Great Lakes Storm of 1913*. Chicago: Contemporary Books, Inc., 1992.

Hilton, George. Eastland: *Legacy of the* Titanic. Stanford, CA: Stanford University Press, 1995.

Hooke, Norman. *Maritime Casualties: 1963–1996, 2nd ed*. London: Lloyd's Maritime Information Services, 1997.

Huber, Mark. *Tanker Operations: A Handbook for the Person-in-Charge (PIC)*. Centreville, MD: Cornell Maritime Press, 2001.

Jones, Nicolette. *The Plimsoll Sensation*. London: Little Brown, 2006.

Kinross, Patrick B. *Between Two Seas: The Creation of the Suez Canal*. New York: Morrow, 1969.

The Manila Amendments to the STCW Convention: A Quick Guide for Seafarers. London: International Shipping Federation and International Chamber of Shipping, 2011.

Meurn, Capt. Robert J. *Watchstanding Guide for the Merchant Officer*. Centreville, MD: Cornell Maritime Press,

1990.

———. *Anatomy of a Collision: Are the Passengers Safe?* Mustang, Oklahoma: Tate Publishing, 2013.

Mostert, Noel. *Supership*. New York: Warner Books, 1975.

O'Sullivan, Patrick. *The* Lusitania: *Unraveling the Mysteries*. Cork, Ireland: Collins Press, 1998.

Peillard, Leonce. *The Laconia Affair*. New York: Putnam, 1963.

Petrow, Richard. *Black Tide: In the Wake of the* Torrey Canyon. London: Hodder and Stoughton, 1968.

Preston, Diana. Lusitania: *An Epic Tragedy*. New York: Walker and Co., 2002.

Plimsoll, Samuel. *Our Seaman: An Appeal*. London: Virtue and Co., 1873. Repr. Hampshire, UK: Kenneth Mason, 1979.

Ratigan, William. *Great Lakes Shipwrecks and Survivals*. Grand Rapids, MI: William B. Eerdmans Publishing Co., 1987.

Sebag-Montiefiore, Hugh. *Dunkirk: Fight to the Last Man*. London: Viking Press, 2006.

Shipley, Robert and Fred Addis. *Wrecks and Disasters: Great Lakes Album Series*. St. Catharines, Ontario: Vanwell Publishing Limited, 1992.

Snow, Edward Rowe. *Sea Disasters and Inland Catastrophes*. New York: Dodd, Mead and Co., 1980.

Sobel, Dava. *Longitude*. New York: Walker, 1998.

Tan, Alan Khee-Jin. *Vessel-Source Marine Pollution: The Law and Politics of International Regulation*. New York: Cambridge University Press, 2006.

Thomas, David. *The Fatal Flaw: Collision at Sea and the Failure of the Rules*. Carmarthenshire, Wales: Phaiacia, 2001.

Venable, Baetjer, Howard, and Civiletti, LLP. *Environmental Criminal Liability in the United States: A Handbook for the Marine Industry*. Washington, D.C.: The Chamber of Shipping of America, 2000.

Wiley, Pat. *The Sinking of the MV* Le Joola: *Africa's* Titanic. irst Steps Publishing, 2012. E-book.

Winslow, Ron. *Hard Aground*. New York: Norton and Company, 1978.

Other Published Sources

Bloodworth, Susan. *Death on the High Seas: The Demise of TOVALOP and CRISTAL. Journal of Land Use and Environmental Law* (Tallahassee, FL: Florida State Univ. College of Law, 1998).

Brodie, Donald. *The* Kirki *Incident,* International Oil Spill Conference (March 1993) proceedings at http://ioscproceedings.org/doi/pdf/10.7901/2169-3358-1993-1-201.

DeGroff, Eric A. "The Application of Strict Criminal Liability to Maritime Oil Pollution Incidents: Is There OPA for the Accidental Spiller?" *Loyola Law Review* 50 (2004): 827–868.

Devanney, Jack. *The Strange History of Tank Inerting*. Tavernier, FL: Center for Tankship Excellence.

Gillis, Carly. *Amoco Cadiz: A Brief History. Counterspill* (April 10, 2011), http://www.counterspill.org.

Horn, Stuart A. and Capt. Phillip Neal. "The *Atlantic Empress* Sinking—A Large Spill Without Environmental Disaster." Abstract of paper in International Oil Spill Conference Proceedings, Mobil Oil Corp., New York, Vol. 1981, Issue 1 (March 1981). http://ioscproceedings.org/doi/pdf/10.7901/2169-3358-1981-1-429.

Kappes, Irwin J. Wilhelm Gustloff. "The Greatest Marine Disaster in History...and Why You Probably Never Heard of It." MilitaryHistoryOnline.com, A Webzine of Community-Submitted Articles. 2003.

McFee, William. "The Peculiar Fate of the *Morro Castle,*" in *The Aspirin Age, 1919–1941,* Samuel Hopkins Adams and Isabel Leighton, eds. (New York: Penguin, 1949), 320.

Moerschel, David C. "Flags of Convenience: The Mercenary Merchant Marine." Master's thesis, American University, 1966. Reproduced by University Microfilms International, Ann Arbor, MI: 1982.

Peterson, Roger A. *Maritime Oil Tanker Casualties 1964–1977: An Analysis of Safety and Policy Issues*. PhD diss., University of Tennessee, 1980.

Rothblum, Dr. Anita M. *Human Error and Marine Safety*. U.S. Coast Guard Research and Development Center. Available at: http://www.bowles-langley.com/wp-content/files_mf/humanerrorandmarinesafety26.pdf.

Index